Improving Operating Leverage Using Hyperautomation

Unlock Strategic Advantages
Across Banking and
Non-Banking Financial
Institutions

Kannan Subramanian R

Apress®

Improving Operating Leverage Using Hyperautomation: Unlock Strategic Advantages Across Banking and Non-Banking Financial Institutions

Kannan Subramanian R
Chennai, Tamil Nadu, India

ISBN-13 (pbk): 979-8-8688-0895-1   ISBN-13 (electronic): 979-8-8688-0896-8
https://doi.org/10.1007/979-8-8688-0896-8

Copyright © 2024 by Kannan Subramanian R

This work is subject to copyright. All rights are reserved by the Publisher, whether the whole or part of the material is concerned, specifically the rights of translation, reprinting, reuse of illustrations, recitation, broadcasting, reproduction on microfilms or in any other physical way, and transmission or information storage and retrieval, electronic adaptation, computer software, or by similar or dissimilar methodology now known or hereafter developed.

Trademarked names, logos, and images may appear in this book. Rather than use a trademark symbol with every occurrence of a trademarked name, logo, or image we use the names, logos, and images only in an editorial fashion and to the benefit of the trademark owner, with no intention of infringement of the trademark.

The use in this publication of trade names, trademarks, service marks, and similar terms, even if they are not identified as such, is not to be taken as an expression of opinion as to whether or not they are subject to proprietary rights.

While the advice and information in this book are believed to be true and accurate at the date of publication, neither the authors nor the editors nor the publisher can accept any legal responsibility for any errors or omissions that may be made. The publisher makes no warranty, express or implied, with respect to the material contained herein.

> Managing Director, Apress Media LLC: Welmoed Spahr
> Acquisitions Editor: Malini Rajendran
> Development Editor: James Markham
> Editorial Assistant: Gryffin Winkler

Cover designed by eStudioCalamar

Distributed to the book trade worldwide by Springer Science+Business Media New York, 1 New York Plaza, Suite 4600, New York, NY 10004-1562, USA. Phone 1-800-SPRINGER, fax (201) 348-4505, e-mail orders-ny@springer-sbm.com, or visit www.springeronline.com. Apress Media, LLC is a California LLC and the sole member (owner) is Springer Science + Business Media Finance Inc (SSBM Finance Inc). SSBM Finance Inc is a **Delaware** corporation.

For information on translations, please e-mail booktranslations@springernature.com; for reprint, paperback, or audio rights, please e-mail bookpermissions@springernature.com.

Apress titles may be purchased in bulk for academic, corporate, or promotional use. eBook versions and licenses are also available for most titles. For more information, reference our Print and eBook Bulk Sales web page at http://www.apress.com/bulk-sales.

Any source code or other supplementary material referenced by the author in this book is available to readers on GitHub. For more detailed information, please visit https://www.apress.com/gp/services/source-code.

If disposing of this product, please recycle the paper

Table of Contents

About the Author ix

About the Technical Reviewer xi

Acknowledgments xiii

Preface xvii

Chapter 1: Enterprise Operating Model 1

    1.1 Overview of a Commercial Bank 2

        1.1.1 Lines of Business 2

    1.2 The "Production Model" of a Bank 12

    1.3 Ullman Triangle 13

    1.4 Enterprise Operating Model 15

        1.4.1 Design of an Enterprise Operating model 16

        1.4.2 Build the Enterprise Operating Model 22

        1.4.3 Operate 28

    1.5 What Is Activity-Based Costing? 32

        1.5.1 Definition – Push Cost Modeling 32

        1.5.2 Objectives and Concept 33

        1.5.3 The ABC Methodology and ENICM 35

    1.6 What Is Time-Driven Activity-Based Costing? 40

        1.6.1 Definition – Pull Cost Modeling 40

        1.6.2 Concept 40

TABLE OF CONTENTS

- 1.6.3 Objective 41
- 1.6.4 Methodology 42
- 1.6.5 TABC Benefits 46
- 1.7 Activity-Based Enterprise Noninterest Cost Management (AENICM) 47
  - 1.7.1 Definition 47
  - 1.7.2 Concept and Objectives 49
  - 1.7.3 Example: Applying AENICM for Payments 49
- 1.8 Siloed and Complex As-Is Environment 53
  - 1.8.1 Banking Applications 53
  - 1.8.2 Complex Banking Operating Environment 57
  - 1.8.3 Enterprise Noninterest Cost Accounting 63

Chapter 2: As-Is Environment – Noninterest Cost Management 67
- 2.1 Financial Accounting and Costing – Chart of Accounts 68
  - 2.1.1 Chart of Accounts – Financial Books 68
  - 2.1.2 Chart of Accounts – ENICM 70
- 2.2 ENICMS in As-Is Environment 85
  - 2.2.1 As-Is Cost Data Capture and Maintenance 86
  - 2.2.2 Example: Allocation 94
  - 2.2.3 Noninterest Cost of Products 126
  - 2.2.4 Costs of Customer/Customer Segment 128
  - 2.2.5 Branch 130
  - 2.2.6 Product Noninterest Revenue 132
- 2.3 Siloed Consequences 133
- 2.4 To-Be Enterprise Operating Model 137
  - 2.4.1 Risk Culture, Focus on Profitability, and Preventive Controls 138
  - 2.4.2 Process-Based Enterprise Operating Model 139
  - 2.4.3 Performance, Risk, Control, and Cost – Policies and Procedures 139

2.4.4 Organization Structure and Human Capital 141

2.4.5 Enterprise IT Governance, Enterprise Process Automation 142

2.4.6 To-Be ENICM System 145

Chapter 3: Using Hyperautomation for implementing Time-Driven ABC 149

3.1 Services- and Process-Based Enterprise Operating Model 150

3.2 Enterprise Architecture 151

3.3 Enterprise Data Management 154

    3.3.1 Noninterest Cost – Customer Master Data 161

    3.3.2 Cost – Metadata 164

    3.3.3 Treasury Operations – Reference Data 166

    3.3.4 Transaction Data 167

3.4 Enterprise Process Automation 167

    3.4.1 Business Goal 167

    3.4.2 Process-Based Enterprise Operating Model 171

    3.4.3 BPMS (Business Process Management Suite) 178

    3.4.4 Bill of Resources (BOR) 186

    3.4.5 Process Automation Examples 190

    3.4.6 Templates: Cost Data Capture and Update 239

    3.4.7 Granular Data Collection 243

    3.4.8 BPMS Case Studies 244

    3.4.9 Enterprise Data Management – Case Study 250

3.5 Process Automation and Time-Driven ABC 251

    3.5.1 Process Mining Based on Event and Process Logs and Simulation 251

    3.5.2 Process-Automated, TDABC Examples 251

3.6 Operational Efficiency and Operating Leverage 265

TABLE OF CONTENTS

Chapter 4: Monitoring Operating Leverage 271

4.1 Operating Leverage Concept 272
  4.1.1 As-Is Cost-Income Ratio 273
  4.1.2 Need to Have Metrics for Operational Efficiency, Effectiveness, and Operating Leverage 277

4.2 Performance, Risk, Control, and Costs 281
  4.2.1 Performance 281
  4.2.2 Enterprise Risk 282
  4.2.3 Risk Appetite 300
  4.2.4 Costs: Fixed and Variable and Reduction and Control 303

4.3 Monitor Operating Leverage 308
  4.3.1 Risk-Based Approach 308
  4.3.2 Monitoring Template 310
  4.3.3 Thirty-Five Examples – Monitoring OL 318

4.4 Critical Business Functions – Operational Efficiency and Operating Leverage 392
  4.4.1 Enterprise Liquidity Management 392
  4.4.2 Branch Network – Right Sizing 397
  4.4.3 Outsourcing 401
  4.4.4 Central Procurement 404
  4.4.5 Carbon Footprint 404

4.5 Economy of Scale 407

4.6 Capabilities and Capacity 409

Chapter 5: Improving Operating Leverage 411

5.1 Continuous Operating Leverage Improvement Program 411

5.2 Theoretical Base for Operating Leverage 419
  5.2.1 Efficiency Structure Theory 419
  5.2.2 Resource-Based Theory 420

5.3 Methods: Improving Operating Leverage 422
    5.3.1 Total Quality Management (TQM)..423
    5.3.2 Sarbanes–Oxley Act (SOX) – Sec 404 and Sec 302 423
    5.3.3 Six Sigma 426
    5.3.4 ITIL and ITSM...428
    Case Studies – Six Sigma, ITIL ISIM 430
    5.3.5 Causal Analysis of Enterprise Risk 432
    5.3.6 Improved Operational Risk Management 441
    5.3.7 Different Types of Cost Reduction Techniques................................442
    5.3.8 Pricing 444
5.4 Tools: Improving OL...445
    5.4.1 Ontology-Driven Knowledge Management (KM) 445
    5.4.2 Enterprise Data Management..449
    5.4.3 Machine Learning and Operating Leverage.....................................452
    5.4.4 Timed Colored Petri Net Model 462
5.5 Implementing Improvements to OE and OL..463
    5.5.1 Standardized Enterprise Operating Model.......................................463
    5.5.2 Risk-Adjusted Return Analytics 469
    5.5.3 Continuous Process Improvement (CPI) 481
    5.5.4 Budgeting 495
5.6 Process and Enterprise Operating Model Efficiency and Maturity.............502

Chapter 6: Conclusion..507
6.1 Bank of the Future Business Delivery 507
6.2 Risk-Adjusted Operating Leverage 512
6.3 Bank of the Future – ERRM Knowledge Management 512

Abbreviations 517

Index..533

About the Author

Kannan Subramanian R is a chartered accountant with 35+ years of experience in the banking and financial services industry and has a good exposure to the financial markets in North America, Europe, and Asia. He has worked for Standard Chartered Bank and for leading banking software solution companies, including the leading global risk management solution provider, Algorithmics, now part of IBM Risk Management & Analytics.

He advises System Design Consulting Prospero AG on strategic matters and in the design of risk management and analytical solutions. He has successfully leveraged his academic knowledge and work experience to provide value to his customers. His passion for the subject motivates him to prioritize his time to write books on automation and risk-reward management in banks. His websites `www.BankERRM.org` and `www.PBORM.org` are knowledge portals on banking.

About the Technical Reviewer

Chartered Accountant **R. Bupathy** is the founder partner of the firm R Bupathy & Co. and is also the chairman of Geojit Financial Services Ltd., India. He is the former president of the Institute of Chartered Accountants of India and is a very senior professional with an excellent track record. He is held in high esteem by the financial industry in India and abroad.

He has been a member of several Indian and international committees including the group constituted by the World Bank for undertaking a study of the System of Corporate Governance in India; National Advisory Committee on Accounting Standards constituted by the Department of Company Affairs, Union Ministry of Finance & Company Affairs, India; and Board Member of Insurance Regulatory Development Authority of India for the year 2003.

He has authored books on taxation and is a recipient of the Certification Award given by the Confederation of Asia Pacific Accountants for his contributions to the accounting profession.

Acknowledgments

I have been in the banking industry for 37 years, and this book, my fifth, is focused on banking operations.

When I wrote my earlier book on enterprise risk-adjusted return management, I could not delve deep into enterprise noninterest cost management as I feared that the book will become unwieldly.

The feedback I got from a cross section of the readers motivated me to take up the unfinished subject of operating cost management. Operating leverage refers to the efficiency and effectiveness with which a bank manages its capabilities to deliver its products and services. As I wrote this book, I expanded the scope to include improvements to performance, risk, control, and cost monitoring.

Activity-based enterprise noninterest cost management (ENICM) is a core component of enterprise risk-adjusted return management (ERRM). **Hyperautomation** uses enterprise process automation technology and advanced analytics (e.g., machine learning) to provide a layer of intelligence for enterprise process automation. The book explains how hyperautomation facilitates the implementation of time-driven activity-based cost allocation, activity-based enterprise noninterest cost management, and operating leverage can be improved.

ACKNOWLEDGMENTS

Basel's recent changes to enterprise risk-adjusted return management requirements[1] make it imperative to take an enterprise approach and transform the bank's operations into an interoperable set of components and processes. Basel's changes to liquidity management require significant changes to enterprise architecture, data management, and processes.

Noninterest cost allocation and funds transfer pricing are two primary drivers that help a bank determine profitability. The book introduces funds transfer pricing, but it does not take a deep dive into the vast subject, as I wish to keep the focus on operating leverage.

Banks should focus on data flows rather than on storage. The data flows should be aligned with process flows. Activity-based costing (ABC) and time-driven activity-based costing (TDABC) are established methodologies for managing noninterest costs. TDABC is one of the building blocks for improving operating leverage.

The variables used to measure operating leverage are risks, controls, costs (fixed and variable), and performance. The book delves deep into these metrics and recommends improvements. I request you to understand the content in the context of maximizing enterprise risk-adjusted returns.

---

[1] Basel III, the net stable funding ratio – https://www.bis.org/bcbs/publ/d295.pdf

Basel III, the liquidity coverage ratio and liquidity risk monitoring tools – https://www.bis.org/publ/bcbs238.pdf

Liquidity risk management and supervision - https://www.bis.org/publ/bcbs248.pdf

Intraday liquidity - https://www.bis.org/publ/bcbs248.pdf

Interest rate risk in the banking book – https://www.bis.org/bcbs/publ/d368.pdf

Interest rate risk in the banking book, April 21, 2016 – https://www.bis.org/bcbs/publ/d368.pdf

FRTB minimum capital requirements for market risk January 2016 – https://www.bis.org/bcbs/publ/d352.pdf and http://www.bis.org/bcbs/publ/d457.htm

ACKNOWLEDGMENTS

Springer Apress is playing an important role in my evolution as an author of books on banking and I thank the Apress team for the professional interactions.

I am grateful to Mr. R. Bupathy for his guidance and expert comments.

It would not have been possible for me to meet the exacting standards of my publishers but for the encouragement from my daughter Radhika and wife Geetanjali.

I am most happy to receive a feedback on the book and engage in a discussion on any banking topic.

Kannan Subramanian R
KannanSubramanianR@BankERRM.org
www.BankERRM.org
www.PBORM.org

Preface

Large banks have become unwieldy and are deferring their decision to transform from a complex, siloed environment into a bank of the future that is event driven and data centric and has an enterprise services-based architecture that is interoperable, scalable, and secure and enhances customer experience.

The non-bank competitors are demonstrating better capabilities in the areas of mobile and peer-to-peer payments. The new players are using the open banking concept to their advantage by leveraging the "API ecosystem" and are managing their operations efficiently. These entities are technically more agile and measure up to retail customer expectations for payments and retail loans. Cost to the customer and service time are key factors for customer acquisition and retention. The non-bank entrants in the financing business are ushering in an "unbundling of retail services," and the quadrant one players are moving toward acquiring customers in the small and medium enterprise segment.

Customers expect a cohesive seamless digital experience across all service channels and require personalized services for high-risk products and grievance management.

Project financing, consortium lending, and trade financing have increased the corporate banking loan book size. Currency trading has become more complex and fragmented. For a long time, the FX market has been characterized by a banker-dealer structure, with intradealer and dealer-counterparty segments. In the last decade, many electronic trading venues have emerged and counterparties have a variety of platforms for executing trades. The emergence of liquidity aggregators, a trading tool, has made it imperative for banks to improve the single-bank platforms.

PREFACE

In many banks, the trading desks manage the collateral in a siloed manner. This has made liquidity and balance sheet management less than optimal.

Operating leverage is about operational resilience, structural operational effectiveness, and sustainable revenue growth. Operating leverage improves the going concern assessment, albeit from an operations perspective.

Complex banking operating environment is characterized by hardwired architecture, siloed processing, and fragmented data. These environments are "application or function centric" where data is a "by-product." Operational resilience continues to be a challenge for many banks.

The enterprise architecture transformation should change the shop floor from a mix of disparate systems and multiple data repositories into an intelligent, end-to-end process-automated, event- and services-driven, architectural environment.

Most banks do not have accurate data on fixed costs, variable costs, and break-even revenue of each product. Banks should provide stakeholders, information on their enterprise noninterest cost management framework, fixed cost base, resource utilization, noninterest cost budget, and the variances in their risk appetite.

This book uses operating leverage as a *forward-looking performance measure*. Operating leverage is driven by a bank's capabilities and its capacity to deliver its products and services. The variables used in measuring operating leverage are performance, risks, controls, and operating costs. Operating leverage is measured by the change in noninterest operating expense in relation to the change in net interest income and noninterest income.

The book introduces the **bill of resources (BOR)**, similar to the bill of materials of the manufacturing industry, as a method for improving enterprise noninterest cost management and as a tool for improving operating leverage. Further, it incorporates the characteristics of financial

PREFACE

product life cycle into process modeling and uses it for analyzing noninterest cost behavior.

Bankers are familiar with the nuances of activity-based costing and time-driven activity-based costing. Risks are inherent in all decisions. The cost of doing business has two dimensions, the cost of business delivery and the cost of risk management.

The noninterest cost management model is an important component of the enterprise risk-adjusted return management model. Banks should factor the causal relationships between market, credit, and liquidity risk with operational risk.

Cost allocation and funds transfer pricing are two primary mechanisms that help a bank determine profitability. This book focuses on the former subject and provides guidance for implementing relevant technology and methodologies that can improve operating leverage.

Chapter 1 provides an overview of a commercial bank, the business functions, the processing environment, and the "as-is" operating model. The growth in transactional volumes has increased the complexity of the processing environment. Several technical processes are not aligned with business processes. Banking software solutions have improved with the evolution of technology. However, the "product-based approach to computerization" has made the processing environment inefficient and risk prone. Further, banks are constrained by their vendor solutions. Vendor-imposed "workarounds" increase the overhead costs and operational risks and are a constraint for process optimization.

Complex processing environments do not have a **true** straight through processing capability, and banks are grappling with the challenges of integrating data across different processing environments.

From an enterprise noninterest cost management (ENICM) perspective, a bank can be viewed either as a financial intermediary or an entity with a "production" model.

PREFACE

In the former case, banks are treated as financial intermediaries that borrow from depositors and lend to borrowers. In the production model, banks use resources as input for providing 24/7 banking service. The output is the portfolio of products and services availed by their customers.

This book uses the production model to explain activity-based enterprise noninterest cost management. Activity-based costing is an enterprise methodology for allocating costs to objects through cost drivers. Activities consume resources, and in the time-driven activity-based costing approach, indirect costs are allocated on basis of unit time taken by resources for completing business activities and accomplishing business goals.

Chapter 2 introduces the current as-is cost management environment in banks. Many banks still have rudimentary or inaccurate systems for cost classification, collection, and allocation. Existing systems are weak in the accurate allocation of support department costs, particularly enterprise information technology and governance, risk, and compliance.

Very few banks have internal service level agreements (SLAs) between support departments and the lines of business. SLAs enable banks to have more accurate metrics for cost allocation.

The chapter illustrates the "as-is allocation procedure" with a complete example. In the as-is scenario, *the profit and loss as per books of account is fully charged out to lines of business, products, customers, and branches.*

An enterprise noninterest cost management system should (a) have a chart of cost accounts; (b) capture at source, wholesome noninterest cost, and noninterest revenue data with sufficient granularity; (c) have a proven methodology for allocating costs; and (d) support the determination of profitability by various dimensions such as line of business, product, customer, and branch. The last phase has a funds transfer pricing dependency.

Chapter 3 provides an introduction into a bank of the future environment and explains the business process management suite (BPMS) technology. Hyperautomation uses enterprise process automation technology and advanced analytics such as machine learning, to provide a layer of intelligence in process orchestration. A banking process has a set of business activities, a deliverable, and starting and ending points. An activity can be either manual or automatic and can be classified as belonging to a front, middle, or back office function.

This book uses the bill of resources (BOR) concept for explaining the process automation in the context of activity-based ENICM. In the manufacturing industry, the master data contained in the bill of materials is the list of the raw materials and assembled components of a product. In a bank, the raw material and the finished product are cash. The bill provides the details of resources required to execute a banking process, and this chapter explains how BOR can be used for implementing an enterprise time-driven ABC system.

Process-based activity analysis provides granular data on front, middle, and back office functions. The cost of doing business is known after the support department's costs are allocated. The details of the process costs are part of the knowledge management database and is used for continuous process improvement. Incorporating the bill of resources in enterprise data management improves the measurement of the usage of resources and improves operational efficiency. *Hyperautomation uses a low-code application platform to facilitate the implementation of ABC or TDABC. Business activity configuration, process modeling, and intelligent processing are its strengths.*

The recent banking regulations on intraday liquidity management, fundamental review of the trading book and interest rate risk in banking book, make it imperative for a bank to take an enterprise approach and transform into a knowledge-based bank.

Enterprise process automation is a critical success factor for a bank of the future. If the cost of hyperautomation is part of the transformation cost, then the cost of the ENICM system is limited to the incremental implementation cost of configuring BPMS for time-driven ABC and cost allocation. There is no extra hardware or software license costs. Hence, the recommendation made in the book will improve a bank's return on investment from a process-automated, activity-based ENICM system.

PREFACE

Process flows should be aligned with the flow of data. The master data of a bank includes the details of its processes. The enterprise process taxonomy is created by decomposing the goals of the bank, to the lines of business, to product and then rolled down as key performance indicators at the business process level. Similarly, the risk appetite statement is rolled down to the process level and specified as key risk indicators.

The ENICM mechanism relies on the quality of cost data capture at the time of occurrence. In the BPMS environment, every transaction updating the P&L has the relevant cost data, for updating the ENICM system simultaneously. Further, the logs provide the time taken by the resource for completing the activities.

Sixteen process automation examples are provided in this chapter, and the narrative explains process modeling and configuration from the perspective of implementing ABC or TDABC. The intelligent business process management suite features include process modeling, rules-based orchestration, document management, process monitoring, and robotic process automation.

A bank's enterprise operating model defines the delivery mechanism to accomplish its business goals. It comprises products and services, staff, systems, policies, and procedures. There are risks, controls, and costs associated with the performance of staff and systems.

Chapter 4 explains the monitoring of operating leverage by focusing on performance, risk, control, and cost. It provides *34 examples* for monitoring these factors at the process level. The examples analyze different business situations from the perspective of performance, risk, control and cost.

Charles Babbage, the pioneer in operations management, process improvement, and analytics, is the author of the Babbage Principle. The principle recommends the reassignment of human capital to business activities by ensuring high-cost workers get to do only high skill tasks. Digitalization of banks has improved the ability to implement the principle. He emphasized the need for knowledge management.

PREFACE

A bank has a knowledge culture when the work environment enables and motivates employees to create, share, and apply knowledge for the enduring success of the institution.

The ENICM system should be designed to work within a forward-looking enterprise risk-adjusted return model. The lean manufacturing principles are value, the value stream, flow, pull, and perfection. Enterprise process automation is consistent with these principles, and time-driven ABC is a form of pull cost modeling. Value stream refers to the focus on eliminating nonvalue adding activities in business processes.

Chapter 5 is on improving operating leverage, and it explains relevant methods for improving a process-based enterprise operating model. The efficiency structure and resource based theories are explained from a banking perspective. The chapter explains the tools available for improving the operations and provides examples for the implementation of the methods and usage of tools. A data-centric, services-based, process-automated enterprise noninterest cost management system, driven by analytics and powered by knowledge management, offers the best of both theories. The ability of a bank to have an optimized cost-efficient enterprise operating model depends on the maturity of the banking processes. Hence, one of the most important responsibilities for a bank's management is to usher in a culture of continuous process and service improvement.

The efficiency and maturity of the model determine the bank's ability to create value for its customers and retain them. This is critical for banks to accomplish their market share objectives.

Many banks report the cost-to-income (CI) ratio. The CI ratio is calculated as total operating costs (excluding bad and doubtful debt charges) to total income (the sum of net interest and noninterest income). The ratio is also referred to as the "efficiency" ratio and is a "point of time ratio" that does not reflect operational resilience or structural efficiency or performance sustainability. *There is an imperative need for banks to develop operational metrics that truly reflect operational efficiency and effectiveness.* Banks that have an enterprise operating model that is efficient and effective, are more resilient.

Chapter 6 concludes the narration by providing an insight into a business delivery framework that allows for improving capabilities, incorporates enterprise knowledge management and facilitates the effective utilization of human capital and technology.

In his speech at the City & Financial 9th Annual Operational Resilience for Financial Institutions Summit 2022, Bank of England's Duncan Mackinnon emphasized the need for banks to rearchitect their business delivery infrastructure.

In their report "Complexity and Riskiness of Banking Organizations: Evidence from the International Banking Research Network," Federal Reserve Bank of New York Staff Reports no. 966 dated May 2021, Claudia M. Buch and Linda Goldberg stress upon the need for *enterprise data* to analyze balance sheet opacity, organization complexity, business complexity, and geographic complexity.

Complexity, in any of these forms, has an adverse impact on operational efficiency and operating leverage.

Structural efficiency and sustainable profitability are strategic growth objectives. Structural analysis of banks' performance requires the capability to decompose profitability of the bank by lines of business, products, and branch. Persistent inefficiency is caused by structural problems in the bank's business model, balance sheet, and enterprise operating model. The root causes could include risk culture, managerial incompetence, and enterprise architectural bottlenecks. Time-varying efficiency factors include volume of business, noninterest costs, productivity, and time.

A bank's competitive position depends on the quality of its value proposition and differentiators. Leveraging human capital and relevant technologies is core to improving operating leverage. Banks should move away from an incremental approach to a customer-centric enterprise transformation for accomplishing business goals. Enterprise process automation, powered by intelligence, creates knowledge-based assembly lines for delivering value to the customers. Hyperautomation is an important capability that a bank should have for an effective enterprise activity-based noninterest cost management and for improving resource capacity utilization. Operating leverage, a forward-looking metric, is about creating and delivering financial value in the form of products and services of a desired quality, efficiently and effectively, to accomplish risk-adjusted return goals.

CHAPTER 1

Enterprise Operating Model

This chapter explains the banking business model with the objective of providing the contextual reference for understanding the as-is (current) enterprise noninterest cost management (**ENICM**) explained in Chapter 2 and the recommendation for a more efficient and accurate activity-based ENICM in Chapter 3.

Section 1.1 provides a summary of a commercial bank's portfolio of products, and in Section 1.2, the production model approach that this book recommends for ENICM, is explained. The production model "*is the conceptual building block*" for implementing an ENICM system using the business process management suite.

Section 1.3 explains the Ullman triangle, the method used in this book to explain concepts.

The enterprise operating model of a bank is explained in Section 1.4 from the perspective of all three lines of business, retail, treasury, and corporate banking. Operating efficiency and ENICM should be understood in the context of how well a bank manages its enterprise operating model. Operating Leverage is a critical sub-component of enterprise risk-adjusted return management (**ERRM**).

Sections 1.5 and 1.6 explain activity-based costing (ABC) and time-driven ABC. When a bank has implemented ABC/TDABC, it has the ability to use an activity based enterprise noninterest cost management model. This is explained in Section 1.7.

Finally, Section 1.8 explains the present siloed and complex banking operating environment in banks.

1.1 Overview of a Commercial Bank

The three lines of business (LOB) of a commercial bank are the treasury, corporate banking, and retail banking divisions. The lines of business are supported by the finance; enterprise information technology; human capital; governance, risk, and compliance (GRC); legal and operations departments. The operations department includes premises management and procurement. Section 1.1.1 provides an overview of the lines of business (LOB) and its products.

1.1.1 Lines of Business
1.1.1.1 Treasury – The Hub of the Bank

Treasury manages the treasury's portfolio of products and enterprise liquidity. The product categories are foreign exchange, money market, commodity, and equity. The treasury portfolio includes the derivative and nonderivative business.

1.1.1.1.1 Treasury Products
1.1.1.1.1.1 Foreign Exchange

FX Spot

A spot deal is a transaction executed at a price agreed today, where one currency is used to buy another currency and settlement is after two business days. The rate is the spot rate. The value date is also the maturity date of the contract and is set two working days forward.

CHAPTER 1 ENTERPRISE OPERATING MODEL

FX Forward

The forward contract is a transaction to buy a currency for another currency, at a rate agreed on the day of the transaction, with a settlement date being an agreed future date.

Outright forward rate = spot rate +/- forward points.

A forward contract is mostly available for all major trading currencies and is transacted on an OTC basis. The maturities vary and are categorized as straight and broken dates. The former are contracts that are quoted for settlement in 1 or 3 or 6 or 12 months. These are widely quoted. Other maturity periods can be negotiated with a bank and are referred to as broken dates.

Currency Option

The buyer (holder) has the right to buy the agreed quantity of currency, at an agreed rate on or before the specified date. Most OTC currency options are European in which the option can be exercised only on expiry date.

Currency Swap

The cash flows in one currency are exchanged for cash flows in another currency. The rate of exchange is settled upfront between the bank and the customer. The principal amounts are also exchanged between the bank and the customer.

Currency Futures

The key difference between the currency futures and FX forward contract is that the futures do not use the line of credit and are well suited for dynamic hedging. The exchange traded currency futures have standard clauses that include (i) contract size and (ii) delivery dates. Currency futures are quoted in sterling, yen, and euro against the US dollar.

CHAPTER 1   ENTERPRISE OPERATING MODEL

1.1.1.1.1.2 Money Market

Bonds

There are different categories of bonds, and the popular ones are (i) coupon bonds and (ii) zero coupon bonds. (i) Coupon bonds have an interest rate for a defined maturity period. The price of the bond is determined based on present value of the future cash flows. The bonds are traded at yield to maturity, and the prevailing rates of interest have a direct impact on the price of the bond. (ii) Zero coupon bonds do not carry an interest rate. They are issued at a discount and repaid at face value on maturity date.

Forward rate agreement is an OTC instrument and is an off-balance sheet instrument. If the rate moved against the bank then it pays the customer the difference between reference rate and the FRA rate based on a notional principal. If the rate moves against the customer, then customer pays the bank. The rates are quoted in terms of the time to start and the time to end of the notional loan period.

A three-month loan starting in three months' time is referred to as 3-on-6.

These are available in major trading currencies and are generally up to two years. Banks prescribe minimum notional principal and are generally available in three-month intervals.

Interest Rate (IR) Caps and Floors

The cap contract sets the maximum interest rate, and the writer of the cap agrees to compensate the buyer if the interest rate rises higher than the strike level. There is no exchange of principal. The floor provides a guaranteed minimum rate for lenders or investors.

Interest Rate (IR) Collar

This involves a simultaneous purchase of a cap agreement and the sale of a floor. It is also possible to sell a cap and buy a floor. In the former case, the key factor is the premium paid by the buyer, the rates the interest rate moves, and the benefits that would accrue because of the interest rate movement.

An interest rate option can be an (i) option in IR futures or (ii) option on FRAs or (iii) options on IRS, i.e., swaptions.

Interest rate swap (IRS) is an exchange of cash flows over a period and is used extensively in asset liability management. The most common IRS is the one party agrees to pay fixed rate interest payments for receiving floating rate payments from the other. Basis swaps have a floating-floating structure. IRS does not involve any exchange of principal, and the settlement is usually on a net difference basis.

Interest rate futures are traded in long-term debt instruments such as three-month Eurodollar short-term deposit rate and long-term debt instruments. Short-term interest rate futures are used for hedging deposits and loans that are exposed to short-term interest rate movements or for speculation. The delivery could be cash or could consist of short-dated securities like treasury bills.

Bond futures are used for hedging or speculating on long-term interest rate movements, e.g., US treasury bond with a maturity period of 15 years or more and UK gilt with a deliverable maturity period between 15 and 25 years.

Other Products

Treasury Bills – These are short-term instruments issued by the government, normally up to 90 days, and are bearer instruments.

Certificate of Deposits (CDs) – These are short-term instruments in the money market.

Repos – Repurchase agreements are borrowings from the money market.

Commercial Papers – These are debt issued by corporates for a short-term period.

CHAPTER 1   ENTERPRISE OPERATING MODEL

1.1.1.1.1.3 Equity

Equity Swap

Equity swap is an agreement based on a notional principal between the bank and its customer where one party pays the other a rate of return based on the equity stock index. The payments are based on an agreed percentage of the notional principal.

Equity Options and Futures

There are two categories of equity options: (i) options on individual equities or (ii) options on stock index. Similar to the options, the futures could be on an individual stock or on the index.

1.1.1.1.1.4 Commodity

Commodity Swap

In a commodity swap between a bank and the customer in which one set of payments is set by the price of a commodity or the commodity index, the other set of payments could be based on fixed or floating rate or a commodity price/index.

Commodity Options and Futures

These could be either (i) options on physicals or (ii) options in commodity futures. One party in the commodity futures contract agrees to sell a specific quantity of a stated commodity, for an agreed price, on a future date and at a specified delivery location. The contract can be settled by delivery or by cash.

1.1.1.2 Corporate Banking

Lending is a core business activity for commercial banks, and the loan book is a major source of revenue and risk. Effective credit risk management is one of most important aspects of a bank's effort to improve its risk-adjusted returns in this line of business.

CHAPTER 1 ENTERPRISE OPERATING MODEL

ENICM requirements are driven by the support required for acquiring, servicing, and managing these large exposures.

1.1.1.2.1 Corporate Banking Products

The profiles of corporate banking products and customers are different from retail. For instance, corporate loan exposures have a higher probability of default than the retail banking customers.

1.1.1.2.1.1 Trade Finance

The portfolio can be categorized as

- A. Funded
- B. Nonfunded products
- A. Funded
  - Packing Credit Advance – This is a type of preshipment credit. Packing credit provides an exporter with finance after goods have been manufactured but before they are shipped.
  - Postshipment Finance – The exporter is paid for the shipment even before the importer pays for the goods.
  - Bills Discounting – The bank buys the bill before it is due for payment and credits the customer's account with a certain percentage of value of the bill. It is an advance against the security of the bill, and the discount represents the interest on the advance from the date of purchase of the bill until it is due for payment.

CHAPTER 1 ENTERPRISE OPERATING MODEL

- Export Credit Refinancing (ECR) – ECR facilities are available for both preshipment and postshipment financing. It is generally available for a select list of commercial products that could vary by country.
- Banker's acceptance is a usance bill of exchange drawn by a customer to his order and accepted by his banker payable on a specified future date.

B. Nonfunded

Letter of Credit (LC)

Different trade financing practices have necessitated LC variants. The different types of LCs include the following:

- Import – The bank substitutes its credit standing for that of its client, the buyer.
- Export – This is from a seller's point of view and availed when the seller is unsure of the creditworthiness of the buyer.
- Revocable, Irrevocable – In a revocable credit, the buyer has the right to amend or cancel the credit at any moment without prior notice to the beneficiary. This is rarely used. In irrevocable credit, the issuing bank guarantees payment to the beneficiary against specified documents drawn in accordance with the terms of the credit.
- Confirmed, Unconfirmed – In a confirmed LC, the exporter receives guarantee of payment from the bank after sight of documents proving shipment of goods.

- Standby letter of credit is under bank guarantee and is paid against presentation of specified documents.

- Revolving – This is a special type of credit wherein (i) the amount of credit "revolves" and the amount is reinstated to its original amount upon utilization subject to validity period and terms and conditions. (ii) The amount of credit varies with time, e.g., a limit of USD50,000 a month within a validity period of six months means that a credit of up to USD50,000 is available each month, for six months.

- Sight – The exporter is paid at sight using proceeds from bill drawn by the importer on his bank.

- Shipping guarantee is a letter of performance and an indemnity issued by a bank on behalf of the buyer or importer.

1.1.1.2.1.2 Corporate Loans

Partnership Act, Trust Act, Society Act, and Companies Act are examples of laws that govern the borrowing entities. Examples of corporate banking products are

- Overdraft and Current Accounts – Corporate current accounts can momentarily be in credit. Overdraft account is a borrowing, and unlike a current account, it is in debit.

- Term loans comprise one of the largest exposures in the corporate lending portfolio, and the term of the loan is typically five years or more.

- Syndicated Loans – These are provided by a consortium of banks. One of the banks plays the role of the lead manager, and the rest are called participant banks. In a process-based scenario, all the banks in the consortium should have a single view of the exposure.

- Overdrafts can be secured or unsecured. Interest is payable only on the money used for the period of withdrawal compounded daily.

- Working capital loans have a short tenor, i.e., less than one year.

1.1.1.3 Retail Banking

This division provides financial products and services to the mass market. It is a competitive and dynamic market. In the last few years, this line of business has been facing a lot of competition from non-banking companies. It is a high volume business with a relatively lower margin. Internet banking, mobile banking, electronic cards, and ATMs are the most commonly used front-office channels.

ENICM is driven by the support required for acquiring and servicing customers in a mass market that has different customer segments with varied financial needs.

1.1.1.3.1 Retail Banking Products

- Savings account opening process typically includes the KYC (middle office) and the dispatch of a welcome kit that could include an e-card. Other important operational activities are (i) domestic clearing service, (ii) customer bill payments to service providers or direct debits, and (iii) international payments.

- Credit card account could be linked to savings or overdraft accounts.

- Term deposits are for fixed periods. An existing customer can use the ATM, mobile, or Internet banking to open a deposit by transferring the surplus from savings or current account. In the event there is a loan against the deposit, a lien is marked on the deposit and the bank takes possession of the deposit receipt.

- Locker rentals.

- Retail Loans – This is a very generic term, and banks offer a variety of loans to the mass market. The nature of the loan could vary depending on various aspects including the customer type, the interest computation method (fixed/floating/hybrid/rule of 78), the collateral (secured, fully/partly, unsecured), the drawdown schedule, and the repayment schedule.

  - Home loans constitute an important source of revenue for most retail banks. The loan is secured by taking a mortgage on the home and would remain in effect until the loan is fully repaid.

  - Other retail loans include (a) home improvement loans, (b) vehicle loan, (c) student loans, and (d) consumer durable (personal) loan.

Risk-adjusted return management in lending requires a holistic, process-based approach for loan appraisal, disbursement, credit and risk monitoring, collateral valuation, and document management.

CHAPTER 1   ENTERPRISE OPERATING MODEL

Siloed and complex operations has resulted in a significant increase in indirect costs and in the decrease of operational efficiency. The failure to allocate costs accurately has resulted in the misrepresentation of the real consumption of resources. The error margins in allocating indirect costs is adversely impacting business decisions such as pricing of retail loans.

1.2 The "Production Model" of a Bank

From an ENICM perspective, a bank can be viewed either as (a) a financial intermediary or (b) an entity with a production model.

The production model is an important concept for ENICM. Unlike a manufacturing entity, the "raw material" that is consumed by the bank and the "finished goods" are money. Table 1-1 and Figure 1-1 illustrate the different features of the two models. Figure 1-1 highlights the core differences between the models. Asset and liability products are categorized as "cost objects" for allocating direct and indirect noninterest costs.

Table 1-1. ENICM models

	Production Model	Intermediary Model
	This book uses the production model concept to explain enterprise non-interest cost management **(ENICM)**	More relevant for Enterprise Risk Adjusted Return Management
Inputs	Employees and their usage of time **(Bill of Resources)**	Liabilities
	Fixed Assets	Equity Capital and Borrowings
	Systems and its usage **(Bill of Resources)**	Retained Earnings
	Premises and its occupancy	Customer Deposits
Output	Loans (assets)	Assets
	Deposits (liabilities)	Loans
	Investments (assets)	Investments
	Risk adjusted Revenue	

Production model, illustrated in the top part of Figure 1-1, is for noninterest cost allocation and the intermediary model. It uses resources such as human capital and technology for delivering products and services.

CHAPTER 1 ENTERPRISE OPERATING MODEL

The lower part of the figure is for enterprise risk-adjusted return management. Banks are financial intermediaries that borrow from retail depositors and lend to creditworthy borrowers. The sources of funds include debt and equity. The applications are loans, investments, non-IT fixed assets, and technology infrastructure.

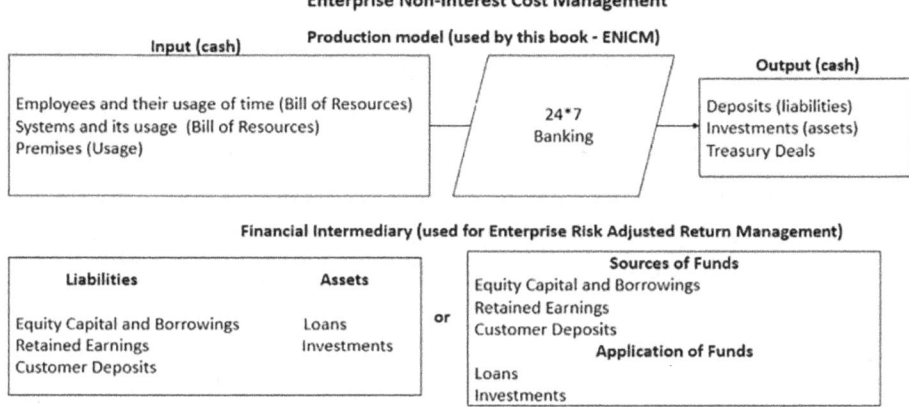

Figure 1-1. ENICM models

As discussed in Section 1.1, the treasury is the hub of the bank; it is the "bank" within a bank. The retail and corporate bank divisions use the treasury to manage its liquidity.

1.3 Ullman Triangle

This method uses concept, symbol, and thing, as vertices of a triangle to **explain the meaning** of a term, a representation, or a theorem.

- The concept is a submission made by a theorist. It is represented by a symbol and is abstracted by a real life object.

CHAPTER 1   ENTERPRISE OPERATING MODEL

- A symbolic version of a thought-process can be expressed in words and/or diagrams. It is denoted as a symbol (e.g., a process).

- The thing itself is the real-world object. This is the core of the theorist's submission (e.g., the cost of a banking process or noninterest cost of a product).

A triangle is chosen as the representation for the method, since it has three coordinates. Interestingly, coordination is referred to by decision-makers as the "**meshing of actions.**" The action could be risk event, an opportunity or activities that follow the risk or opportunity identification. Concept can also be described using properties, relations, and axioms.

Conceptual analysis is relevant for stating the hypotheses or constructing theories, but it is not focused on testing. It is about clarifying the meaning of a given submission.

Felix E. Oppenheim, an author, has provided the following framework for a concept, and it is relevant for ENICM and enterprise risk-adjusted return management. He submits that a **concept** should be

- Operational in the broadest sense.

- Able to establish definitional connections with other terms (symbol and thing) and draw attention to the theoretically important aspects of the subject matter that might easily be overlooked as desirable.

- Able to open to empirical inquiry; the concept should not be a definition that does not permit an empirical investigation.

- Defined in such a way that it can be converted into a set of rules.

CHAPTER 1   ENTERPRISE OPERATING MODEL

In modeling parlance, "the thing" is the desired output, and the symbols are the processes/calculations that create the output from a statement of intent or input.

This book uses the Ullman triangle to explain various concepts.

1.4 Enterprise Operating Model

Figure 1-2 uses the Ullman triangle to explain a bank's enterprise operating model. The design and implementation of the operating model has an impact on the quality of an activity-based enterprise noninterest cost management program.

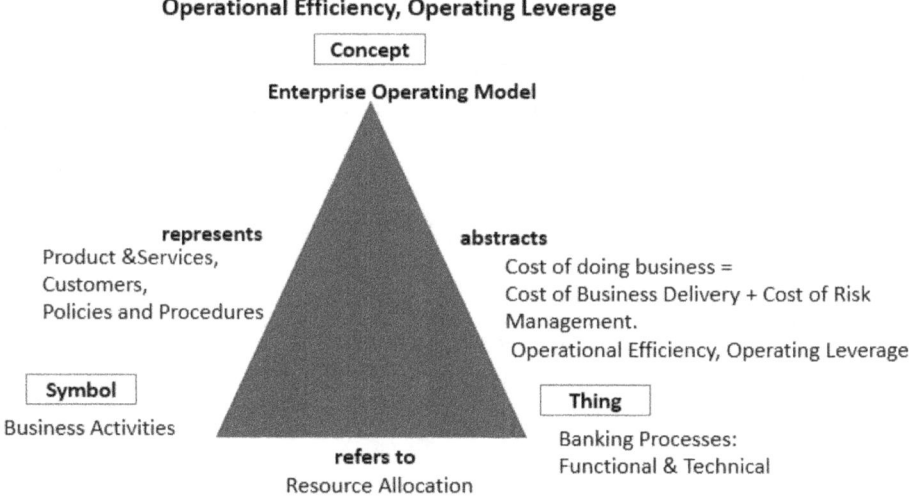

Figure 1-2. *Enterprise operating model – concept*

CHAPTER 1   ENTERPRISE OPERATING MODEL

A good enterprise operating model provides an effective framework for accomplishing corporate goals:

- It is holistic.
- It establishes ownership for processes and/or activities.
- It aligns technical processes with business processes.
- It assigns and integrates systems and staff for the execution of policy and procedures.
- It is scalable to meet organization's growth targets.
- It has the right mix of preventive and detective controls.

1.4.1 Design of an Enterprise Operating model

Figure 1-3 provides an overview of the key elements that go into the design of a bank's operating model. The inputs to this phase include

- Business goals
- The approved master list of products and services
- Organization structure
- Target market and delivery channels

CHAPTER 1   ENTERPRISE OPERATING MODEL

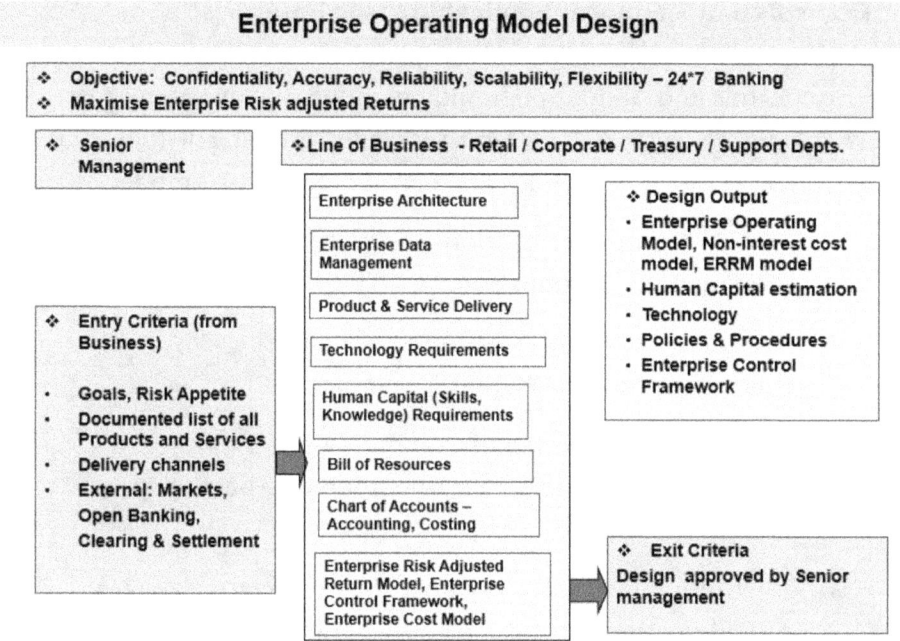

Figure 1-3. Enterprise operating model design

An overview of the lines of business and products is provided in Section 1.1. The efficiency of the business delivery depends on the enterprise architecture and use of relevant technologies.

The approved design will include

- Enterprise architecture design
- Approved technologies
- Policy and procedures
- Enterprise goals and business processes inventory

CHAPTER 1   ENTERPRISE OPERATING MODEL

Controls and Standards applicable to the Enterprise Operating Model

The controls and standards should be understood in the context of a *risks, controls, costs, and performance* of the model. The following frameworks/methods/guidelines are relevant for a bank's model:

   I. COSO – Committee of Sponsoring Organizations of the Treadway Commission.

  II. Sarbanes–Oxley Act (SOX) – Sec 302 and Sec 404; this is explained in Chapter 5, Section 5.3.2.

 III. International Chamber of Commerce – ICC's guidelines on trade finance operations are best practices.

  IV. *International Swaps and Derivatives Association* (ISDA)[1] provides guidelines for the netting and collateralization of treasury transactions and includes approaches for netting of transactions between counterparties. The characteristics of derivative transactions create an operational need for having standards in the areas of credit, documentation, transaction valuation, collateral valuation, and collateral management.

   V. Financial Action Task Force (FATF) – The FATF issued a list of 40 recommendations for curbing money laundering and the financing of terrorism.

  VI. Information System Audit and Control Association's COBIT.

 VII. Six Sigma is explained in Chapter 5, Section 5.3.3.

---

[1] https://www.isda.org/book/2005-isda-collateral-guidelines/
https://www.isda.org/2019/09/04/isda-taxonomy-2-0-finalized/

CHAPTER 1 ENTERPRISE OPERATING MODEL

An important aspect of the above frameworks/methods/guidelines is **the emphasis on *processes*** for improving efficiency.

ICC and ISDA are specific to the specified products, and FATF applies to all types of financial transfer/payments. A brief narrative is provided below for *COSO and COBIT*.[2]

Figure 1-4 illustrates a customized version of the COSO model. The three dimensions of the model are relevant for ENICM.

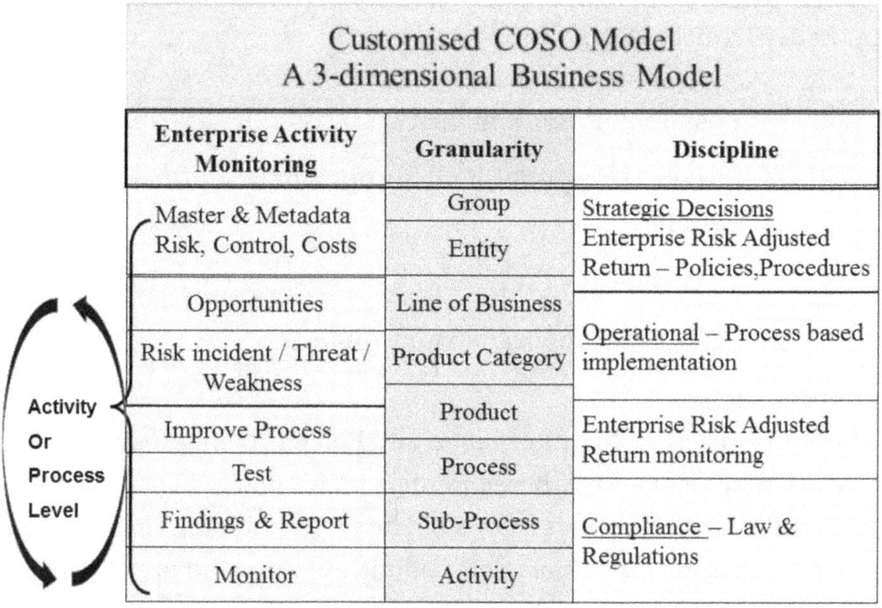

Customised COSO Model
A 3-dimensional Business Model

Enterprise Activity Monitoring	Granularity	Discipline
Master & Metadata Risk, Control, Costs	Group	Strategic Decisions
	Entity	Enterprise Risk Adjusted Return – Policies, Procedures
Opportunities	Line of Business	Operational – Process based implementation
Risk incident / Threat / Weakness	Product Category	
Improve Process	Product	Enterprise Risk Adjusted Return monitoring
Test	Process	
Findings & Report	Sub-Process	Compliance – Law & Regulations
Monitor	Activity	

(Activity Or Process Level)

Figure 1-4. Customized COSO model

Performance, risk, control, and cost (PRCC) monitoring is explained in Chapter 4. The strategic, operations, reporting, and compliance dimension of the COSO cube could be referred to as the PRCC discipline.

---

[2] https://www.coso.org/

CHAPTER 1   ENTERPRISE OPERATING MODEL

This facilitates the implementation of the enterprise risk-adjusted return model and that includes monitoring operational efficiency and operating leverage.

The dimensions for enterprise process monitoring are (a) internal environment, (b) objective setting, (c) event identification, (d) cost of doing business, (e) risk assessment, (f) risk response, (g) control activities, (h) control's cost-benefit analysis, (i) information and communication, and (j) monitoring.

Granularity – This refers to data capture from the process level and the accuracy with which it can be rolled up to the entity, lines of business, and support department levels.

A COSO application example is as follows:

Activity – Loan monitoring and the COSO coordinates could be

- Operations – Corporate banking operations and credit appraisal
- Line of Business – Corporate
- Process – Loan application and appraisal

COBIT

Control Objectives for Information and Related Technology (COBIT) provides a process- and risk-based framework for managing enterprise IT risks, and the latest version is COBIT 5. The COBIT domains are planning, acquiring and implementation, delivery and support, and monitoring. Table 1-2 provides an overview of COBIT.

The following are critical success factors for implementing a *COBIT-*based[3] enterprise control framework:

- KRI and KPI owners could be at various levels of the bank.

---

[3] https://www.isaca.org/resources/cobit

CHAPTER 1 ENTERPRISE OPERATING MODEL

- Risk owners and control owners should work together. The former has the primary responsibility for risk identification.

- Control owners have primary responsibility for maintaining control effectiveness. Together, with risk owners, they should ensure that residual risk is within acceptable limits.

- Cost owners have to work with the risk and control owners and ensure that budgeted costs are not exceeded.

Table 1-2. COBIT IT framework

COBIT	Bank's technical processes
COBIT's Enterprise IT Control Framework	
COBIT takes an enterprise approach.	Banks should transform from a 'siloed architecture' to a loosely coupled enterprise architecture design
The framework promotes process focus and process ownership	For an effective enterprise risk adjusted return management, a bank should take a process-based approach to building the operating model.
Divides a Bank's IT into 34 processes belonging to 4 domains	The 4 domains are relevant for banks.
The control framework provides guidance on fiduciary, quality and security requirements. It provides seven information criteria that can be used to generically define what the business needs from enterprise IT.	A data centric enterprise architecture improves ROI.
Several banks across the world use COBIT (i)as a control framework (ii) for IT Risk management and (iii) IT Governance. These areas overlap.	

COBIT is aligned with SOX and COSO. A bank can derive a control framework by aligning the enterprise IT and functional control frameworks, with the business goals.

CHAPTER 1   ENTERPRISE OPERATING MODEL

The following are also relevant for building the enterprise operating model:

- Data Protection Acts have been promulgated in several countries to safeguard the privacy of individuals and confidentiality of the records.
- Computer Misuse Act seeks to deter the use of technology for illegal or harmful purposes.

A bank could derive the controls for its model from frameworks discussed in the design phase. There are three broad areas for consideration:

- Production environment
- Nonproduction (noncustomer service/purely internal) environment
- Business continuity planning including disaster recovery

Figure 3-12 in Section 3.4.2 of Chapter 3 illustrates a customized COSO, COBIT, and SOX enterprise control framework that is built within a process-based enterprise operating model.

Section 4.3 in Chapter 4 explains performance, risk, control, and cost monitoring and the recommended approach is compliant with the frameworks explained above in this section.

1.4.2 Build the Enterprise Operating Model

Figure 1-5 illustrates the elements that go into building the operating model. The inputs to this phase include

CHAPTER 1 ENTERPRISE OPERATING MODEL

- The approved master list of products and services
- Infrastructure design
- Approved technology
- Chart of accounts
- Policy and procedures
- Business processes inventory, KPIs, and KRIs

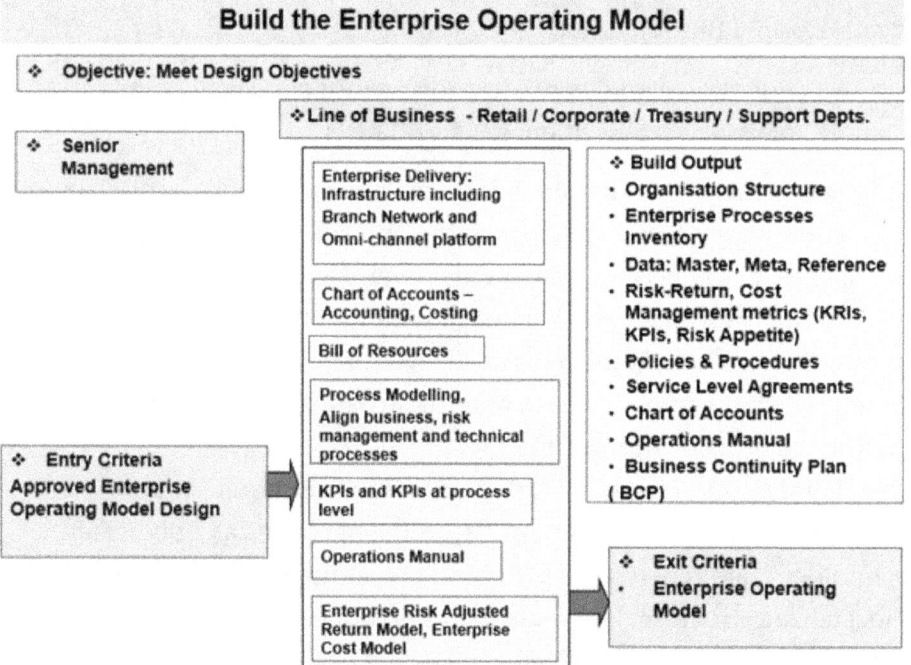

Figure 1-5. Build the operating model

The following are the steps to complete the build of the model:

- Organization structure and staff assignment
- Configuring the enterprise risk-adjusted return and enterprise cost management models

- Embedding policies and procedures with the banking processes
- Enterprise data model
- Technology infrastructure readiness
- Operationalizing the service level agreements
- Optimizing premises utilization
- Chart of accounts
- Operations manual
- Functional and technical process modeling with details of resource allocation, KPIs, and KRIs.

The organization structure reflects the risk culture of a bank. The independence given to audit, inspection, internal control, and risk management groups is reflected in the organization structure.

The empowerment of risk management functions is critical for accomplishing risk-reward goals at all levels. Similarly, the structure should reflect the importance of enterprise data management and continuous process improvement.

Several multinational banks have provided a separate support function for each line of business, e.g., retail banking has a dedicated technology team. Their scale of operation justifies the staff assignment for a specialized structure. Domestic banks do not have support functions dedicated to each line of business.

CHAPTER 1   ENTERPRISE OPERATING MODEL

The key operational aspects that are covered by policy and procedures are

- Promotion of ethical and professional standards of business.

- Organization structure, role clarity, decision-making, responsibility, and accountability. The Know Your Employee program is managed by human capital department but owned by respective lines of business/support department.

- The Know Your Employee and Know Your Customer programs require good enterprise data management for providing a single view of the employee and customer. The processes include due diligence and enhanced due diligence.

- Usage of technology.

- Key risk indicators and key performance indicator setting and monitoring.

- Proactive management of early warning signals.

Figure 1-6 provides a business view of a commercial bank. The enterprise operating model should not be *a "band-aided" siloed structure.* The figures depicts (i) the e-channels and branch network, (ii) the lines of business, (iii) marketing and sales as a function that supports the three lines of business, (iv) the middle-office risk management groups, and the (v) the back office.

The support departments service (i) each other and (ii) the lines of business. The operations department functions include premises, travel desk, non-IT repairs and maintenance, and procurement of office supplies.

CHAPTER 1   ENTERPRISE OPERATING MODEL

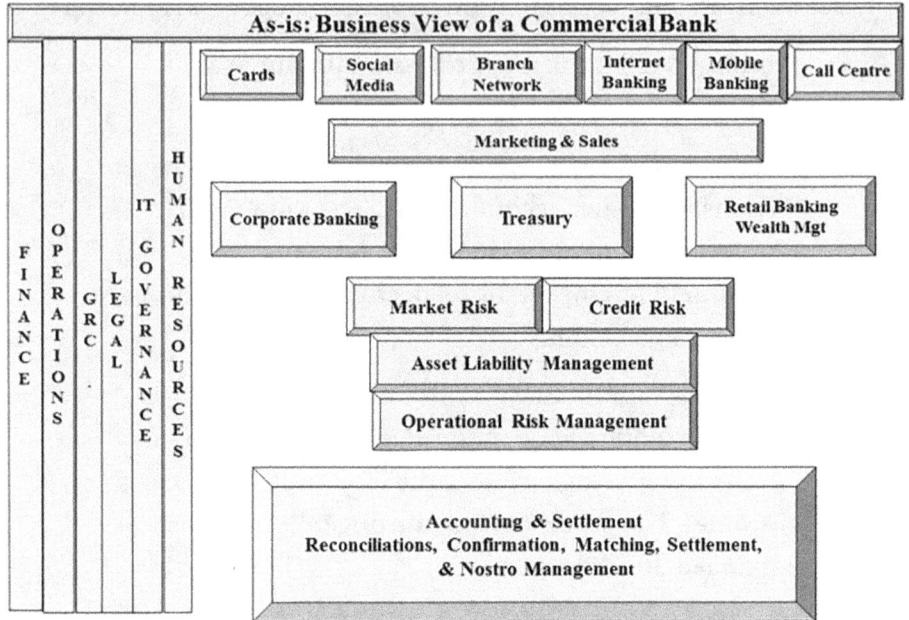

Figure 1-6. As-Is Business View

Process-Based Enterprise Operating Model

The ENICM model is a subcomponent of the ERRM model. The cost of managing operational risk should factor *Basel's operational risk events*[4]. The following are the seven Basel operational risk incident categories:

- Internal fraud.

- External Fraud – Could be caused (i) with the connivance of staff, (ii) by a former employee, (ii) by an independent act of an external party, and (iv) a former external party.

---

[4] https://www.bis.org/basel_framework/chapter/OPE/10.htm?inforce=20191215

- Employment Practice and Workmen Safety – These events could include fire, building weakness, and staff safety during late shifts.

- Clients, Products, and Business Practices – These cover aspects related to selling of financial products, means adopted by bank to get business, and customer relationship issues.

- Damage to Physical Assets – This includes IT and non-IT assets.

- Business disruption and system failure are low frequency, high severity incident.

- Execution, delivery, and process management covers banking operational incidents that could be traced to a staff, system, policy, organization, or an external source.

Operational risk management is further explained in Chapter 4, Section 4.2.2.4.

While designing and building the operating model, the following standards should be considered:

- ISO 8583 is a financial standard for payment card messages.

- ISO 11568 specifies the principles to manage keys used in cryptosystems in the retail banking.

- ISO 20000 is the first international standard for information technology service management and is fully compatible and supportive of the ITIL (IT Infrastructure Library) framework.

- ISO 20022 standard is financial industry's message scheme for (i) payments, (ii) securities, (iii) trade services, (iv) cards, and (v) FX.

- ISO/IEC 15504 is an international standard for process assessment and process improvement. Process capability is measured by analyzing process performance or capability indicators collected during the process assessment. It enables to determine the process maturity using a six-level capability scale.

- BS 25999-2 is a British standard for business continuity management. ISO 22301 is not specific to banking and is a generic requirement for business continuity management.

- ISO/IEC 27001 is the best-known standard for information security management system (ISMS).

- ISO 27002 outlines hundreds of potential controls and control mechanisms as per guidance provided within ISO 27001. It has evolved from BS7799 and ISO17799.

- BS ISO 38500 is an enterprise IT governance standard.

1.4.3 Operate

The inputs to the "operations" phase are

- Delivery infrastructure
- Human capital, role definitions, and staff KPIs
- Policies, procedures, and operations manual
- Functional and technical process
- Business continuity plan

CHAPTER 1   ENTERPRISE OPERATING MODEL

The following are important aspects of operations:

- Staff skill improvement and productivity
- System performance including business continuity Plan (BCP)
- Risk and performance monitoring
- Risk mitigation
- Customer education on products and services
- Continuous process improvement

Figure 1-7 illustrates the 24/7 enterprise operating model of a bank.

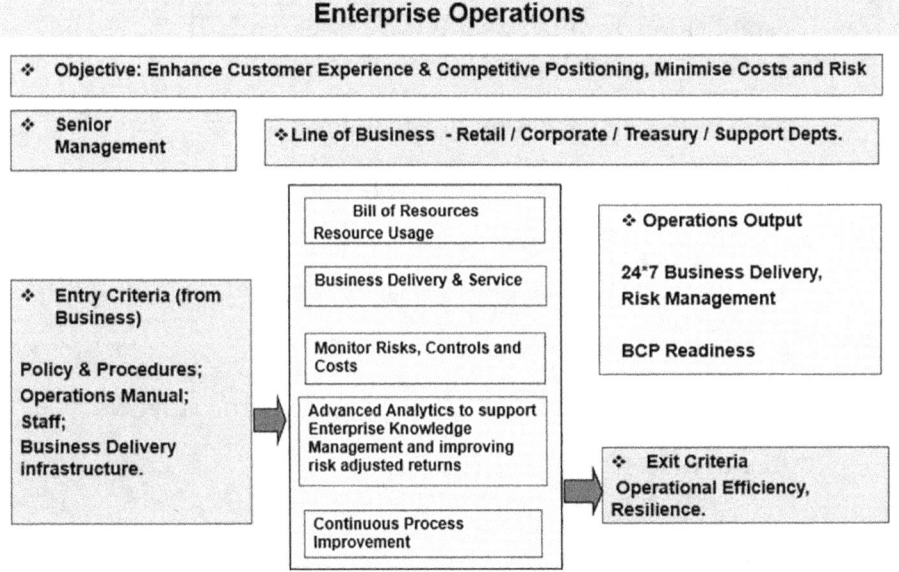

Figure 1-7. Operations

1.4.3.1 Design of Enterprise Operating Model: Case Studies

- Banco Supervielle S.A. (Argentina) – COBIT implementation

   Case Introduction

   The bank planned to improve its enterprise governance to attain its business goals.

   Statement of Work

   The key tasks were (a) aligning technology with business, (b) improving internal controls, (c) establishing ownership for IT processes, and (d) ensuring better compliance.

   The bank used COBIT in the following areas:

   - Training on control framework and best practices for all IT areas
   - Aligning IT processes with COBIT guidelines
   - Redefining roles and responsibilities
   - Development of COBIT-based performance metrics

   Key Benefits

   ✓ The bank was able to reach the target process maturity level.

CHAPTER 1   ENTERPRISE OPERATING MODEL

- Bancolombia – COSO and COBIT

  Case Introduction

  Bancolombia had a weak IT governance, and the problems include broken processes, weak governance, weak audit, poor documentation, and a reactive management approach.

  Statement of Work

  The bank decides to implement COSO and COBIT for attaining its goal.

  Key Benefits

  - ✓ Enterprise-wide alignment of technology with business processes
  - ✓ Better compliance
  - ✓ Staff productivity improvement with better role definition and ownership
  - ✓ Improved risk identification and mitigation

- Bank of Nova Scotia COBIT

  Case Introduction

  BNS had to comply with the regulations set by *SUGEF, the regulator in Costa Rica*. This included implementing SUGEF specified processes.

  Statement of Work

  The bank decided to implement COBIT for complying with the SUGEF directive and trained its staff on a process-based approach to managing operations.

Enterprise IT Governance

In its first phase, the bank analyzed 17 processes that required reaching maturity level 3. In the second phase, 17 processes were identified and analyzed. The objective was to gradually optimize the enterprise operating model maturity level within three years.

Key Benefits

✓ Enterprise-wide alignment of technology with business processes

✓ Auditable and measurable processes

✓ Improved control

✓ Better enterprise IT governance

1.5 What Is Activity-Based Costing?[5]
1.5.1 Definition – Push Cost Modeling

The costs that appear as debits in the bank's P&L need to be understood and monitored from the perspective of its financial products and customers.

Activity-based costing methodology identifies business activities and assigns the cost of each activity to the products/services. The operating costs are charged to lines of business and products.

---

[5] http://dl.groovygecko.net/anon.groovy/clients/kaplan/DL/Demo_2016/Accounting_equation/Assets/CIMATerminology.html

1.5.2 Objectives and Concept

The objectives of the methodology are to

- Allocate overheads on the basis of consumption of resources
- Support cost causation analysis
- Improve the accuracy of noninterest financial product costs
- Use this information to improve product mix and pricing decisions
- Identify and if possible eliminate nonvalue-added activities
- Identify and monitor the high-cost activities and processes
- Identify opportunities for cost reduction
- Support performance, risk, control, and cost monitoring
- Support continuous process improvement
- Achieve operational efficiency

Concept

Figure 1-8 illustrates the concept of ABC. It is a form of "*push cost modeling*" that uses static cost drivers. The costs are pushed down from cost centers to lines of business, product, and branch.

Activities consume resources, have a cost, and have a business function. There are dependencies between front-, middle-, and back-office functions. Some activities spread across the line of business. When a bank has documented its business processes and activities, getting consensus on cost allocation methodology and profitability metrics is easier.

CHAPTER 1   ENTERPRISE OPERATING MODEL

ABC has two phases. In the first phase, activities are linked to resources that consume costs, and in the second phase, the cost of the activities is linked to cost objects, namely, products, customers, and branches.

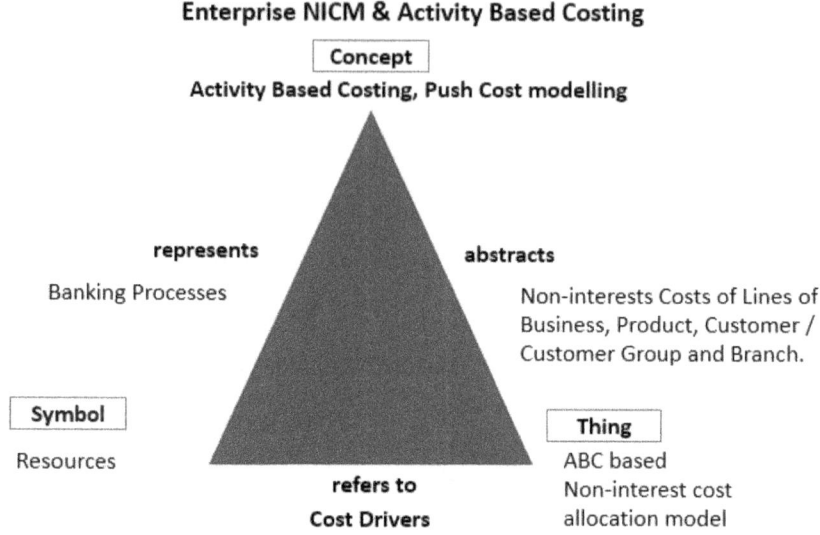

Figure 1-8. *Activity-based costing – concept*

Activity-based costing is a scientific approach to ENICM. By taking this approach, the bank can identify inefficient activities and implement corrective action to improve operational efficiency.

As illustrated in Figure 1-9, delivery of products consume activities and activities consume resources.

i. Direct costs can be traced directly to one output, e.g., the advertising cost of a new product.

ii. Indirect costs result from sharing of resources.

CHAPTER 1   ENTERPRISE OPERATING MODEL

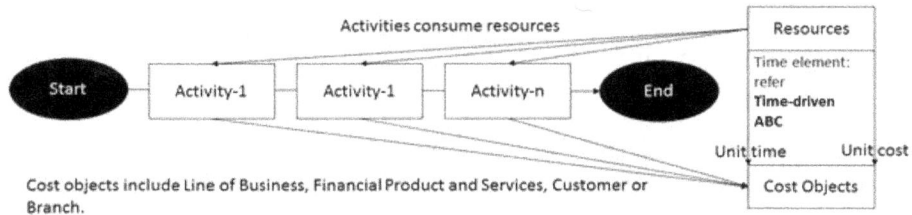

Figure 1-9. *Resource consumption by business activities*

The method requires the rolling down of business objectives and delivery mechanism into business activities and processes, selecting suitable cost drivers, creating cost pools, calculating the overhead application rate, and allocating the costs based on the applicable rate. Cost pools (coded as cost centers) are created for an activity or activity group, and cost drivers provide the metrics for allocating the costs to financial products, customers, lines of business, and branches.

1.5.3 The ABC Methodology and ENICM

The following two examples provide *the nuances of banking processes and activities* in the context of activity-based enterprise noninterest cost management.

(i)   FX Forward Contract – Input

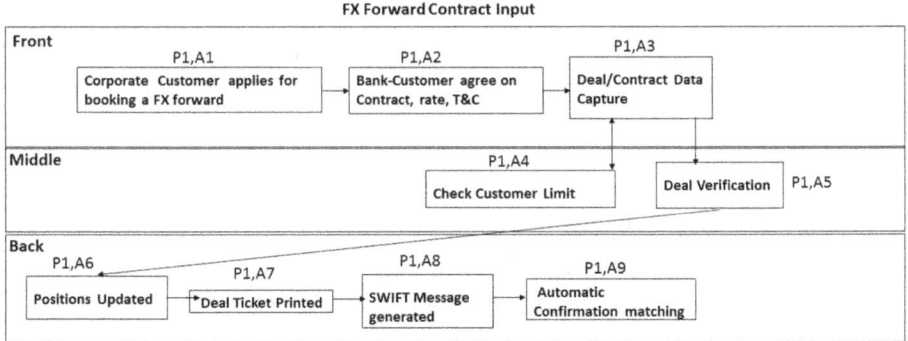

Figure 1-10. *Activities – FX forward contract input*

35

CHAPTER 1   ENTERPRISE OPERATING MODEL

Figure 1-10 and Table 1-3 illustrate the flow of activities in a FX forward contract deal input process. The figure groups the activities in three distinct business delivery lanes, front, middle, and back. The front office refers to customer-facing functions, risk management roles perform the middle-office functions, and back office relates to accounting and settlement functions. Each activity consumes resources. The main resource categories are staff and system. For staff, the time spent by the staff for completing the activity is expressed in time units. For system activities, the system logs provide data for ENICM.

Table 1-3. *FX Forward Contract input – Activity dimensions*

	F X Forward Contract: Deal Input				
Activity Id	**Description**		**Resources**		**Cost of Activity**
		Staff	**System**	**Others**	
P1A1	A prospect interacts directly with the bank using an omni-channel platform or interacts with an official at a branch				
P1A2	Customer is educated on Terms and Conditions				
P1A3	The deal / contract is input in the system				
P1A4	Middle office – risk management				
P1A5	Deal is verified by a different bank official				
P1A6	Position Updated				

(continued)

CHAPTER 1   ENTERPRISE OPERATING MODEL

Table 1-3. (*continued*)

F X Forward Contract: Deal Input					
Activity Id	Description	Resources			Cost of Activity
		Staff	System	Others	
P1A7	Deal Ticket				
P1A8	SWIFT Message				
P1A9	Confirmation Matching				
Cost of Process		=			$\sum$ **of activity cost**

Figure 1-11 and Table 1-4 illustrate the flow of activities in an interest rate swap deal input process.

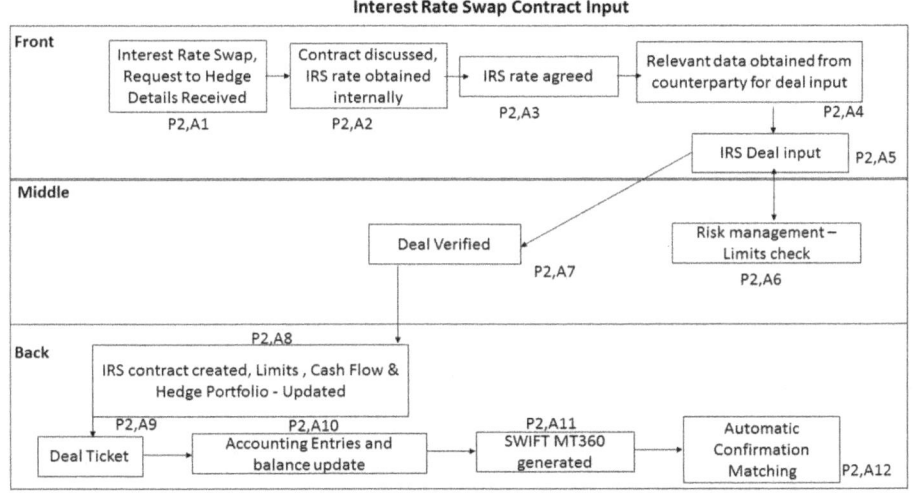

Figure 1-11. Activities – interest rate swap deal input

37

CHAPTER 1   ENTERPRISE OPERATING MODEL

Table 1-4. *Interest rate swap deal input – Activity dimensions*

Activity Id	Description	Interest Rate Swap: Deal Input			Cost of Activity
		Resources			
		Staff	System	Others	
P2A1	A prospect interacts directly with the bank using an omni-channel platform or interacts with an official at a branch				
P2A2	Customer educated on risks and a contract is finalised				
P2A3	Interest rate swap rate is agreed				
P2A4	Bank gets relevant contract data				
P2A5	Deal Input				
P2A6	Risk management				
P2A7	Verification				
P2A8	Positions Update				
P2A9	Deal Ticket				
P2A10	G.L. Accounting				
P2A11	SWIFT				
P2A12	Confirmation matching				
Cost of Process		=			Σ of activity cost

CHAPTER 1   ENTERPRISE OPERATING MODEL

ABC identifies the most appropriate way of tracing and assigning indirect and shared expenses (commonly referred to as overhead) to final cost objects by (a) identifying work activities performed to produce outputs, (b) assigning or mapping consumed resource utilized by activities, (c) identifying outputs for which the activities are performed, and (d) assigning activity costs to the outputs.

Table 1-5 illustrates the information that can be produced by an ENICM system using activity-based costing.

Table 1-5. *Output of an enterprise noninterest cost management system*

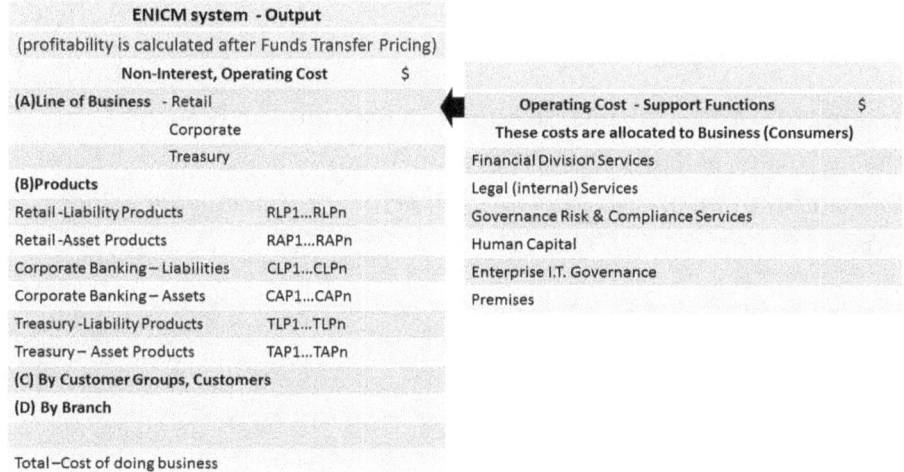

Activity-based costing (ABC) is a bottom-up, data-driven approach for enterprise noninterest cost management. ABC methodology paved the way for developing the time-driven activity-based costing methodology.

The key difference between ABC and TDABC explained below is that ABC has many cost drivers, whereas TDABC uses time as the cost driver.

CHAPTER 1   ENTERPRISE OPERATING MODEL

1.6 What Is Time-Driven Activity-Based Costing?[6]

1.6.1 Definition – Pull Cost Modeling

What is time-driven activity-based costing (TDABC)?

As illustrated in Figure 1-12, TDABC is a time-driven variant of the traditional activity-based costing method. It is a form of **pull cost modeling** that uses the time taken by a resource assigned to an activity, for calculating the noninterest cost of product or service.

1.6.2 Concept

This noninterest cost calculation approach uses the unit time for performing each activity. The cost per unit time of resource and the cost of the consumption of resources for each activity are calculated using this data.

---

[6] https://hbswk.hbs.edu/item/time-driven-activity-based-costing
http://dl.groovygecko.net/anon.groovy/clients/kaplan/DL/Demo_2016/Accounting_equation/Assets/CIMATerminology.html

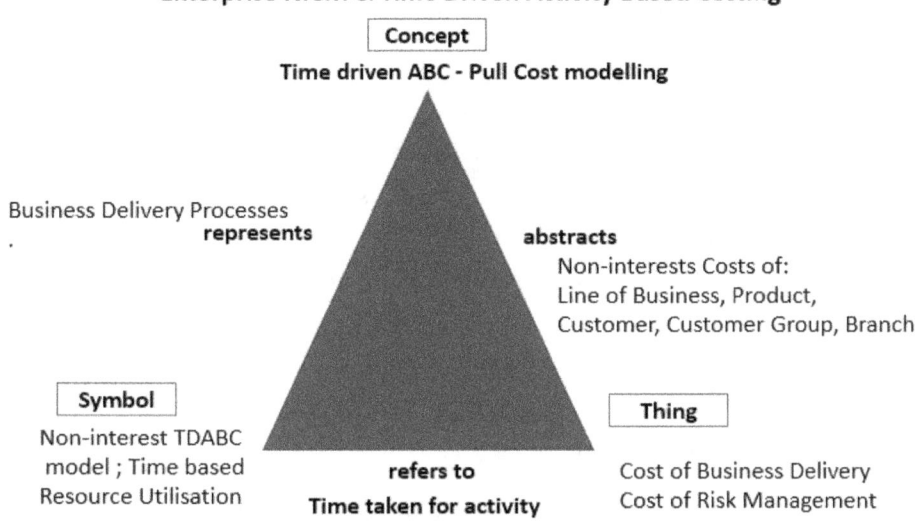

Figure 1-12. *Time-driven ABC – concept*

TDAMC model enables a bank to assess its capacity utilization. The units of time consumed by staff and systems for completing business activities form the basis for calculating the cost of business processes.

1.6.3 Objective

TDABC model helps to identify and measure unutilized capacity using time as a dynamic cost driver. This paves the way for optimizing resource allocation and utilization. As a bank improves process maturity, it attains operational efficiency and can move to a higher level of business operation.

The management accountant (or cost accountant) uses ABC to focus on resource usage, not spending.

CHAPTER 1   ENTERPRISE OPERATING MODEL

1.6.4 Methodology

TDABC is based on an equivalence method that uses time as cost allocation driver. A bank could review system logs, human capital self-assessment details, and banking activity levels to "measure" the utilization of staff and system. The bank's management should specify the acceptable "appetite for an error in estimation," and the middle-level managers could estimate the resource utilization in terms of time spent on activities.

Table 1-6. TDABC – template for a FX forward contract input process

		FX forward contract: deal input				
Activity Id	Description	Resources				Cost of Activity
		Staff	System	Time	Others	
P1A1	A prospect interacts directly with the bank using an omnichannel platform or interacts with an official at a branch	Activity time (estimation – bank's policy specifies acceptable error margin)	Estimation using system logs	Time taken by each resource for each activity		
P1A2	Customer is educated on terms and conditions					

(*continued*)

CHAPTER 1 ENTERPRISE OPERATING MODEL

Table 1-6. (*continued*)

	FX forward contract: deal input					
Activity Id	Description	Resources				Cost of Activity
		Staff	System	Time	Others	
P1A3	The deal/ contract is input in the system					
P1A4	Middle office – risk management					
P1A5	Deal is verified by a different bank official					
P1A6	Position updated					
P1A7	Deal ticket				This could be digital	
P1A8	SWIFT message					
P1A9	Confirmation matching					
	Process rate					**$\sum$ of activity cost**

CHAPTER 1   ENTERPRISE OPERATING MODEL

Bank managers can estimate the utilization rate of the resources as a percentage of the theoretical capacity.

Table 1-7. *TDABC – Template for an interest rate swap deal input process*

Activity Id	Description	Interest Rate Swap: Deal Input				Cost of Activity
		Staff	System	Time	Others	
		Resources				
P2A1	A prospect interacts directly with the bank using an omni-channel platform or interacts with an official at a branch					
P2A2	Customer educated on risks and a contract is finalised	Activity time (estimation – bank's policy specifies acceptable error margin	Estimation using System Logs	Time taken by each resource for each activity		
P2A3	Interest rate swap rate is agreed					
P2A4	Bank gets relevant contract data					
P2A5	Deal Input					

(*continued*)

Table 1-7. (continued)

	Interest Rate Swap: Deal Input				
Activity Id	Description	Resources			Cost of Activity
		Staff	System	Time	Others
P2A6	Risk management				
P2A7	Verification				
P2A8	Positions Update				
P2A9	Ticket				
P2A10	G.L. Accounting				
P2A11	SWIFT				
P2A12	Confirmation matching				
	Process rate	=			Σ of activity cost

By having data on the unit time to perform each instance of the activity, the bank is able to quantify the cost of each activity. It can also measure the unused capacity of its resources.

The following are the TDABC steps:

- Identify resource groups and the activities for which they are used
- Estimate the capacity of each group
- Calculate the cost per time unit
- Determine the required time units for each activity
- Calculate the cost per transaction or banking process

CHAPTER 1   ENTERPRISE OPERATING MODEL

- Calculate the cost of products, customers, and branches
- Measure the unutilized capacity of resources and take corrective action (Chapters 4 and 5)

1.6.5 TABC Benefits

- It is dynamic because it adapts to the volume produced.
- Ability to scale to enterprise-wide model.
- Provides an insight into process maturity and capacity utilization.
- By adding volume to the cost model, TDABC makes scenario analysis possible.

The following are common benefits that can accrue from an ABC or TDABC implementation:

- Ability to identify staff reliability and measure productivity
- Measure system usage and return on investments in technology
- Identify the main causes of operational inefficiency
- Monitor cost of operations
- Identify the most and least profitable customers, products, and branches
- Accurately determine costs, revenues, and resource requirements
- Accomplish their operational efficiency and operating leverage objectives

1.7 Activity-Based Enterprise Noninterest Cost Management (AENICM)

1.7.1 Definition

AENICM is an approach to *managing* noninterest costs, and it focuses on business activities to improve operational efficiency.

1.7.1.1 Measure

Cost is a monetary measure of the amount of resources consumed for operating a bank and delivering products and services.

1.7.1.2 Noninterest Cost Classification

Classification of cost is the grouping of costs based on its nature (subjective classification) and purpose (objective classification).

The classification of *noninterest costs*[7] is as follows.

1.7.1.2.1 Nature

The major noninterest costs are system, staff, and premises.

1.7.1.2.2 Direct and Indirect

Traceability of the cost drives this classification. Direct costs are those that can be identified fully with a cost determines center. Indirect costs need to be allocated to cost centers using cost drivers. Cost centers can be lines of business, products, or a support department.

---

[7] https://www.icmai.in/upload/CASB/Glossary-Feb2015-Revised.pdf

1.7.1.2.3 Fixed, Variable, and Semivariable

Figure 1-13 illustrates the characteristics of fixed, variable, and semivariable expenses. Variable expenses move in relation to the change in the level of operation, and semivariable expenses vary with level of operation, but it is not linear.

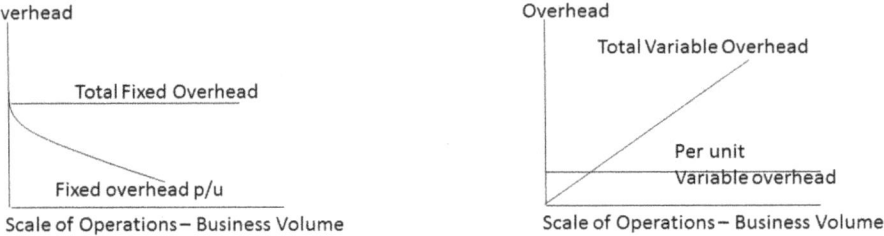

Figure 1-13. Fixed and variable costs

1.7.1.2.4 Function

Costs can be classified under front-, middle-, or back-office functions.

1.7.1.2.5 Other Classifications

- Controllability
- Optionality (discretionary or mandatory)
- Materiality (significance of impact on business)

1.7.1.3 Disclosure

The bank's cost management policy should provide guidance on changes in classification of cost. In most situations, a change is made only if it is required by law or for complying with a Cost Accounting Standard or for improving the noninterest cost management disclosures.

CHAPTER 1 ENTERPRISE OPERATING MODEL

1.7.2 Concept and Objectives

AENICM uses an activity-based costing approach, ABC or TDABC, for monitoring and managing noninterest, operational costs. The objectives are (i) to minimize, if not eliminate, nonvalue adding business activities and (ii) simplify or improve value-added services. This is illustrated in Figure 1-14.

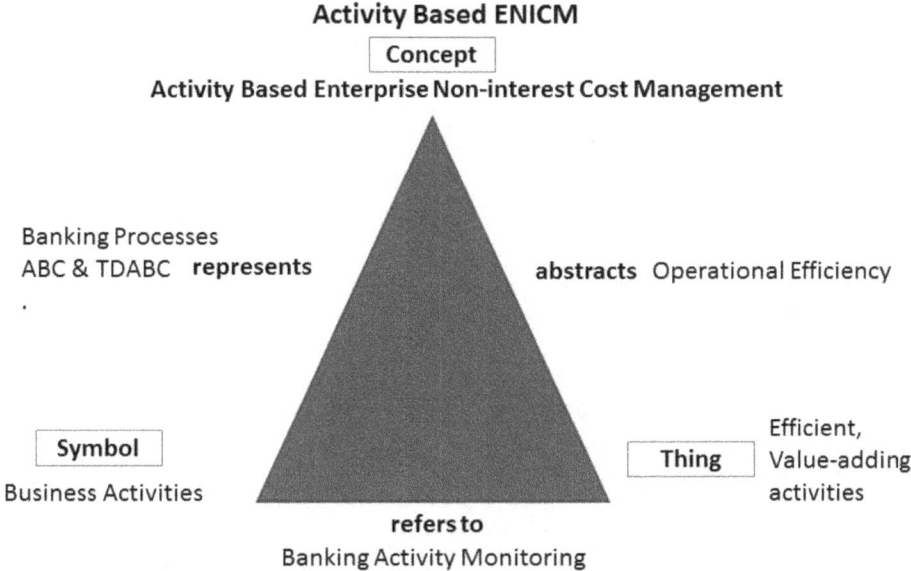

Figure 1-14. Activity-based enterprise noninterest cost management concept

1.7.3 Example: Applying AENICM for Payments

Applying Activity-Based Enterprise Noninterest Cost Management for Payment Activities

Payment transactions includes front-, middle-, and back-office activities. The transactions can be triggered by retail, corporate, or treasury customers. Additionally, there can be internal bank transfers or intrabank transfers.

CHAPTER 1   ENTERPRISE OPERATING MODEL

> This demonstrates the link between operational risk and other risk types, e.g., liquidity risk.

Basel's Committee on Payment and Settlement Systems (**CPSS**) and the technical committee of the International Organization of Securities Commissions (**IOSCO**) have published the Principles for Financial Market Infrastructure (**FMI**). The FMI refers to the entity that is set up to carry out centralized, multilateral payment, clearing, settlement, or recording activities. The ecosystem includes the participants that use the system, and the Central Bank will be one of the stakeholders. The principles apply to one or more of the following systems:

- Payment system
- Central securities depository
- Securities settlement system
- Central counterparty
- Trade repository

Banks should review their enterprise architecture and data management capabilities and ensure that it is consistent with the FMI requirements.

Central Bank real-time gross settlement initiatives have introduced several important changes to domestic clearing processes. In most countries, the Central Bank or an entity controlled by it owns and operates a real-time gross settlement system. Some are multilateral settlement service for clearing houses and financial exchanges.

CHAPTER 1 ENTERPRISE OPERATING MODEL

There are two types of RTGS: (i) the collateral-based system, e.g., CHAPS (UK), TARGET 2 (Europe), and SIC (Swiss National Bank). In this type, the banks can obtain intraday liquidity at no fee against collateral; and (ii) in a fee-based system (e.g., Fedwire, United States), the banks can obtain intraday liquidity without collateral by paying the requisite amount.

Society for Worldwide Interbank Financial Telecommunications (SWIFT) provides a secure delivery of payment and confirmation infrastructure for treasury and correspondent banking areas.

Figure 1-15 illustrates the payment activities across the lines of business and functions. *The operating leverage perspective of the enterprise liquidity hub and enterprise liquidity management is discussed in Chapter 4, Section 4.2.2.3 and 4.4.1, and Chapter 5, Section 5.3.5.3 and 5.3.5.4.*

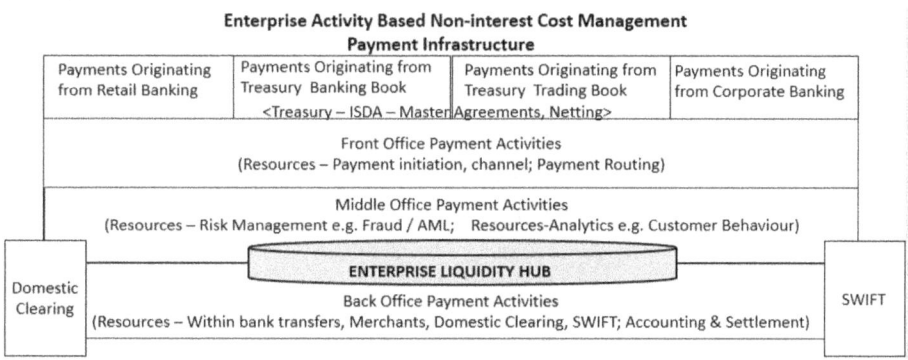

Figure 1-15. *Bank's payment processing overview*

The Basel Committee of Banking Supervision defines funding liquidity as the ability of banks to meet their liabilities and unwind or settle their positions as they become due. The IMF defines funding liquidity as the ability of solvent institutions to make payments in a timely fashion.

Over the years, volatility has increased in the financial markets, customer behavior has changed, and derivatives have added to the complexity of treasury operations. These factors have influenced asset liability management (ALM) methods, tools, and techniques. ALM has

CHAPTER 1 ENTERPRISE OPERATING MODEL

emerged as a science where both sides of the balance sheet have to be holistically and dynamically managed to mitigate interest rate, market, and liquidity risks.

An efficient enterprise risk-adjusted return management (ERRM) framework can provide a capability to manage risks on an intraday basis. Banks may need to restructure their organization so that enterprise liquidity management (ELM) becomes a core competency area within treasury.

Intraday liquidity is necessary for the smooth functioning of the international payment and settlement system. The banking ecosystem includes the global payment and settlement network, and the payment market infrastructures include the clearing houses and central counterparties. The large banks also provide correspondence banking services.

The components of the ecosystem work in a dynamic, interdependent environment that makes the banking industry more vulnerable to systemic risks. A bank should assess the impact of its dependency on the external payment infrastructure and its architectural model should support the smooth functioning of the network.

A bank's payment infrastructure should be user friendly and secure. Time is a critical aspect of payments.

Intense competition, tech-savvy customers, and increasing sophistication of the financial markets mandate the bank to manage its payment infrastructure as a "Mission Critical Application."

The term efficiency can be used as a technical measure of production. In this case, the number of payments that can be processed in a minute or an hour. It can also be used in a holistic manner as in the cost of a payment process.

1.8 Siloed and Complex As-Is Environment

The banking industry has always been an early adopter of new technology. However, it has been using a product-centric approach to automation. By taking an incremental approach for automating their business requirements, many banks are increasing the complexity of their operations. They are not resolving the known risks and limitations. The weakness is predominantly in their enterprise architecture and data governance.

Many banks still extract, transform, and load their fragmented data from disparate systems for noninterest cost management.

1.8.1 Banking Applications

1.8.1.1 Core Banking Solution

The scope of a core banking system includes

- Savings and current accounts.
- Retail loans and deposits.
- Domestic clearing.
- Corporate loans and trade finance.
- Collateral management support corporate and retail loans. It includes mark to market and insurance features.
- SWIFT – International payments.
- Treasury module covers front-office deal capture, basic risk management, and back-office settlement including nostro reconciliation.

CHAPTER 1   ENTERPRISE OPERATING MODEL

- Interfaces:
  - ATM interfaces should be ISO8583 compliant and support "on-us" and "off-us" transactions.
  - The cards interfaces should also be ISO 8583 complaint and support a full range of POS transactions originating at various outlets. Banks' card payment infrastructure should be compliant with Payment Card Industry–Data Security Standard (PCI-DSS) and ISO 20022.
  - IVR/call center interface supports account-related information and service management.
  - Integration with external payment, clearing, and settlement systems.

1.8.1.2 General Ledger

Medium-sized and small banks use the GL module of the core banking solution. The GL of a large bank could be a standalone system. Most banks have a chart of accounts. Policies and procedures guide its maintenance.

Some of the key features of the GL are as follows:

- Users have the flexibility to define the chart of accounts.
- Centralized definition and accounts (i.e., one GL).
- The GL is integrated with the transaction/deal capture systems and is an accounting system that comes with period-end processing.
- It comprises customer accounts and internal accounts (house accounts).

1.8.1.3 Lending

Many banks use a lending software solution for their retail and corporate loan books. The scope includes collateral management and basic credit risk management features. Collateral management for corporate banking is wider in scope.

The main features of a lending solution includes

- Loan origination, workflow management, credit rating, and collections.

- For corporate loans, the solution supports covenant monitoring and credit risk monitoring.

1.8.1.4 Trade Finance

Trade finance is an important business segment of corporate banking. Although some core banking solutions have a trade finance module, many banks use a specialized standalone trade finance solution that is integrated with their core banking and the treasury management systems.

The solution coverage would include letter of credit, guarantees, packing credit advance, bills discounting, export credit refinancing, and banker's acceptance/usance bill of exchange.

Most vendor-supplied solutions are SWIFT certified and have an interface to the back-end core banking system.

1.8.1.5 Treasury Management System

The main features of a multicurrency treasury management system are as follows:

- A broad coverage of instruments including foreign exchange spot and forwards, deposits, loans, repos, zero and fixed coupon bonds, floaters, forward rate agreements, futures, options, exotics, index linked derivatives, and funds.

- Interface to Reuters, Bloomberg, and other data providers for rate feeds. This data covers the full range of asset classes and instruments.

- Blotters, deal/trade capture, and automatic generation of deal tickets.

- Nostro account reconciliation, settlement by asset classes, partial settlement and carry forward of unsettled portion possible, autogeneration of settlement instructions.

- Banking book and trading book, final statement of accounts, and interface to GL.

1.8.1.6 Customer Relationship Management Solution

The key features of a customer relationship management solution are as follows:

- Prospect and Customer Management – This would include (a) managing the information contained in the financial accounts and service request of customers and (b) providing different views on the customer profile that includes static information and financial activities.

- Opportunity Management – Supports collaboration across multiples sales channels, sales pipeline visibility, and forecasting.

- Campaign management.

1.8.1.7 Support Functions

- Human capital

    As per the mandate given by management, the human capital group drives and facilitates the identification of top performers, identifies training needs, and executes recruitment programs.

    Many medium- and small-sized banks have rudimentary human capital systems, with some having only a payroll system.

- Legal

    From an automation perspective, this is *another neglected support department.* An enterprise process-automated approach for the legal department functions will improve operational efficiency.

1.8.2 Complex Banking Operating Environment

The global financial crisis of 2007–2008 had many lessons for bankers and banking regulators. Lawmakers realized the need to prevent and mitigate the risks of leveraging and other factors that caused the crisis. The United States and other countries improved their legal framework to prevent another similar financial crisis. Risk management experts emphasized the need for an enterprise approach to risk management. One of the important challenges facing the global banking industry is the siloed and complex operating environment in most banks.

CHAPTER 1   ENTERPRISE OPERATING MODEL

David Levy's Work on Complexity

Medium- and large-sized banks are facing the challenge of a complex banking operating environment. They are finding it difficult to reduce operating costs, minimize risks, and improve their market share.

Both, the complexity and chaos theories, attempt to reconcile the unpredictability of nonlinear dynamic systems using the metrics of order and structure. This is a finding from David Levy's treatment of complexity in his work titled "Applications and Limitations of Complexity Theory in Organizational Theory and Strategy."

Joel Moses' Work on Complexity and Flexibility

Joel Moses in "Complexity and Flexibility" classifies a system as complex when it is composed of many parts that interconnect in intricate ways. This would apply to many banks that have several computer servers, with different banking applications, in some cases with different versions of the same application in different locations and band-aided datasets. The theory states that the metric for intricateness is the amount of information contained in the system.

Joseph Sussman's Work on Complexity

Joseph Sussman, in "The New Transportation Faculty," defines complexity as an environment where the **degree and nature of the relationships is imperfectly known** between groups of related subsystems. The theory also provides the reason on why correlations among different risk factors are either unknown or estimated wrongly. It applies to all risk types, operational, market, credit, and liquidity. This applies to all banks, irrespective of their size.

This makes the risk outcomes difficult to predict. These environments are prone to risk, and banks with such an environment carry a large operational risk exposure.

CHAPTER 1   ENTERPRISE OPERATING MODEL

CBOE is characterized by one or more of the following:

- A fragmented enterprise architecture with "band-aided" data repositories. Weakness in architecture is a source of high severity risks.
- A weak enterprise operating model.
- A nonstandardized business delivery model.
- Weak alignment of technical processes with business processes.
- Lack a pan-bank data model and weak data quality.
- Violation of principle such as onetime data capture, multifactor authentication, single point of storage, and assigning ownership over data.
- No true straight through processing (STP) capability.
- Lack of continuous process improvement culture.
- Operational inefficiency with low staff productivity.
- Unable to achieve the desired return on investment in technology.
- Unsatisfactory customer retention.
- Weak enterprise IT governance.
- Weakening competitive position.
- Limited ability to improve enterprise risk-adjusted returns.

Banks are aware that the workflow of the software applications need not necessarily match the business processes of the bank. In many implementations, nonvalue adding changes are made to processes and procedures in order to make the software solution pass user acceptance testing. These "workarounds" pose significant risks to the bank.

CHAPTER 1   ENTERPRISE OPERATING MODEL

An important consequence is that the bank is locked into the workflow imposed by the vendor's application, and the ability to reengineer/improve the processes is limited. Risks introduced by workarounds are rarely quantified and monitored.

Figure 1-16 provides a "simple" view of a CBOE. A multinational American bank with its processing headquarters in Asia has 126 systems in an Asian country and supports eight countries in the region. In a CBOE, within each line of business, there are plethora of systems and many data repositories.

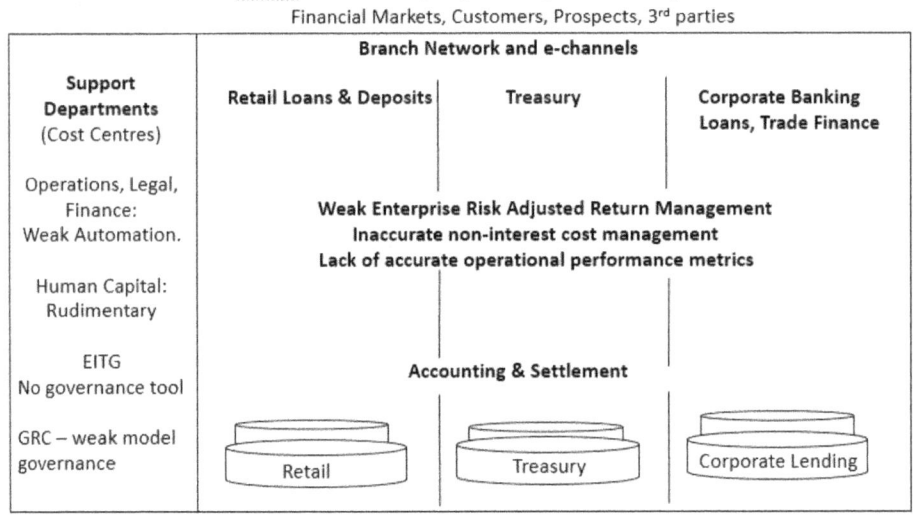

Figure 1-16. Siloed complex banking operating environment

The Different Operating Environment Scenarios

Figure 1-17 illustrates three scenarios. Scenario 3 depicts a complex transaction processing scenario. The bank does not have a process inventory, and it struggles to survive in a competitive landscape. In scenario 2, the bank has recognized the importance of processes, but workflow automation is driven by the underlying software solutions. There is limited ability to improve operational efficiency.

CHAPTER 1 ENTERPRISE OPERATING MODEL

In the first scenario, the bank is using a business process management suite (**BPMS**) for enterprise process automation. In this scenario, risks, controls, cost, and performance are monitored, and there is proactive risk-return management. The bank has the ability to maximize enterprise risk-adjusted returns.

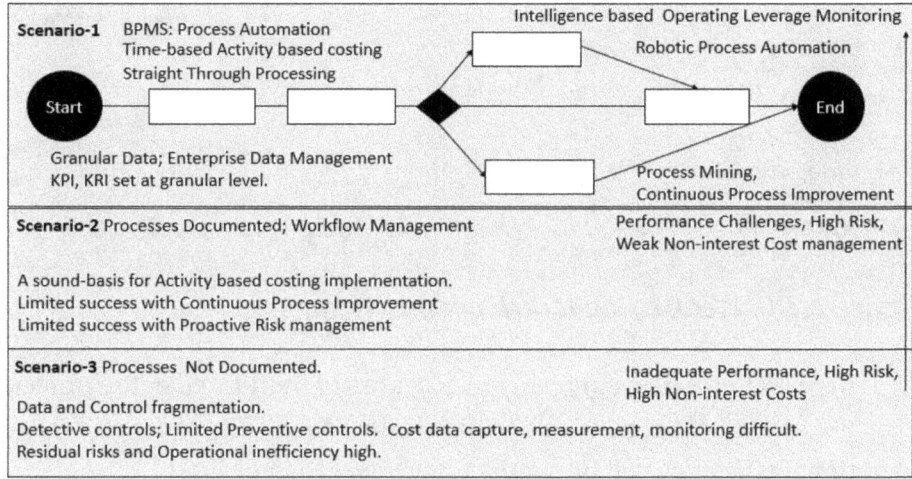

Figure 1-17. Operating model scenarios

Straight Through Processing (STP)

Straight through processing is crucial for the effectiveness of managing operations. The existence of a number of functions in business delivery, across the front, middle, and back office, makes STP a critical success factor for managing operations.

Weak STP that is prevalent in scenarios 2 and 3 of Figure 1-17 is illustrated in Figure 1-18.

CHAPTER 1   ENTERPRISE OPERATING MODEL

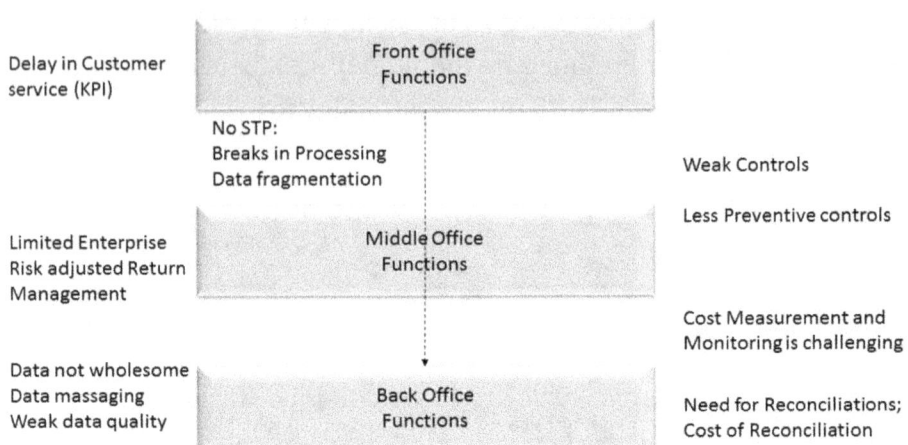

Figure 1-18. *Weak straight through processing*

If performance, risk, control, and cost are not monitored at the process level, then the residual risks will be higher than the risk appetite and operational efficiency will be significantly lower than desired.

Complex banking operating environment will always be a constraint for the growth strategies of any bank. The environment is a constraint for

- Activity-based enterprise noninterest cost management
- Taking informed decisions on pricing of products and services
- Using and monitoring service level agreements
- Monitoring and proactively managing KRIs and KPIs at granular level
- Implementing a continuous process improvement culture
- Maximizing risk-adjusted returns

CHAPTER 1   ENTERPRISE OPERATING MODEL

Why are banks continuing in a CBOE? The answer lies in the cliché philosophy, "If it ain't broken, why fix it."

- Bank's CTO and CISO may not have made a business case for transformation. The bank management may not have seen any report that quantifies the risks from the existing environment and the rewards from using relevant technologies.

- There are technical solutions like using middleware for integrating disparate systems. This is a short-term survival approach.

- Some would argue that transforming the bank is both risky and costly. The task requires a relatively big, skilled team to deliver. Some senior managers take what they consider as the middle path, modernization of a siloed environment rather than transforming the institution as a bank of the future.

1.8.3 Enterprise Noninterest Cost Accounting

Table 1-8 illustrates how the financial accounting books and costing books complement each other. Funds transfer pricing is an important component of profitability determination. Many banks use cost reduction as a tool to help accomplish their profit targets.

The building blocks of an enterprise overhead management system include wholesome cost data capture, measurements of consumed resources, and allocation methodology. Knowledge management supports the monitoring of operational efficiency, supporting zero-based activity-based budgeting, and providing actionable intelligence for decision-making.

CHAPTER 1   ENTERPRISE OPERATING MODEL

Table 1-8. *Financial and costing books*

	Financial Accounting & Cost Accounting in a Bank	
	Accounting Books	Cost Accounting Books
Objective	Financial Status as at a given date	Determine non-interest costs and profitability of different business dimensions
Usage	Both require a Chart of Accounts. The content is different and the finance department needs to ensure consistency. They have different methodologies, standards and practices.	
	Used for financial reporting and compliance	Used for cost & profitability monitoring, management
Monitoring focus	How much money was spent?	How efficiently were the resources used?

1.8.3.1 Profitability and Enterprise Risk-Adjusted Return Management

All the three lines of business have sources and application of funds. The treasury is a centralized funding and liquidity management center. Its responsibility includes liquidity pricing and managing maturity mismatches, among other control functions.

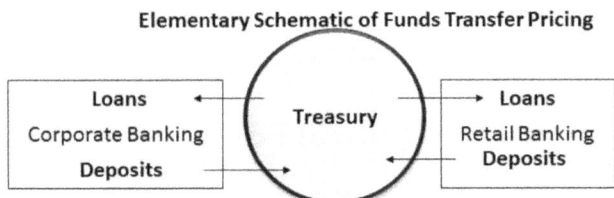

Figure 1-19. *Funds transfer pricing – simple view*

1.8.3.2 Funds Transfer Pricing (FTP)

Funds transfer pricing (FTP)[8] is a treasury-driven function that is managed by the Asset Liability Committee (ALCO). The deposits mobilized by retail and corporate banking are placed with treasury. The funding for the

---

[8] Funds transfer pricing https://www.cafral.org.in/sfControl/content/LearningTakeaWays/827201455252PMPaper_Funds_Transfer_Pricing_in_Banks.pdf

CHAPTER 1 ENTERPRISE OPERATING MODEL

loan books of corporate and retail banking is provided by treasury. The objectives of FTP are to improve the quantitative aspect of efficient product pricing and profitability management. Funds transfer pricing is linked to liquidity and balance sheet management. A bank manages the profitability of its lines of business and products by implementing measures to improve the **risk-adjusted net interest margin.** A key function of the treasury, with support from ALCO, is to manage the cost of funding. Banks try to manage the uncertainties of interest-based income by diversifying its products and services to include fee-based income.

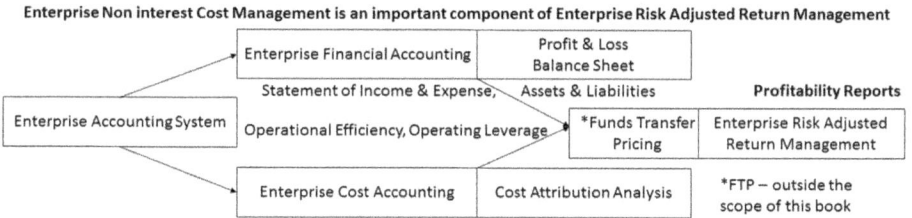

Figure 1-20. ENICM is a subcomponent of ERRM

Table 1-9. Funds transfer pricing components

Funds Transfer Pricing components	Coverage in this book
Effective borrowing rate for a specific currency, value and tenor	
Operational costs related to time deposits and non-maturing deposits	Yes
Expected Loss Charge is to cover the potential loss on account of a borrower default	
High Quality Liquid Assets-buffer costs	
Spreads	
Operational Costs related to Lending activities	Yes
Other Costs linked directly to specific product or customer	Yes
Effective Lending rate for a specific currency, value and tenor	

Most banks do not have accurate noninterest cost data and that adversely impacts the accuracy of the data used for funds transfer pricing.

65

CHAPTER 1　ENTERPRISE OPERATING MODEL

Figure 1-21 illustrates risk-adjusted economic value-added pricing of financial products. Enterprise noninterest cost management is critical for accurate pricing of products.

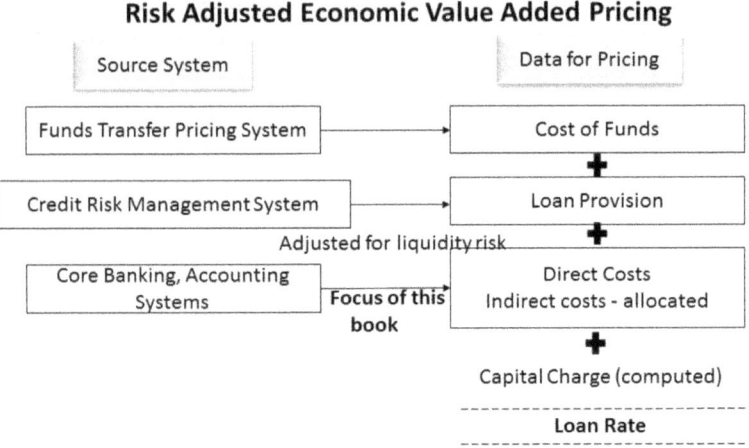

Figure 1-21. Risk-adjusted economic value-added pricing

In some banks, treasury prices the liquidity and market risk of the loan, while the credit risk department prices the credit cost. The liquidity management team of the treasury manages the maturity mismatch between cash outflows and inflows. Corporate banking decides on the commercial margin that is appropriate for a customer after getting the input on the credit risk of the borrower.

Funds transfer pricing and liquidity transfer pricing are out of the scope of this book, and the focus is on using enterprise process automation for enterprise noninterest cost management.

The next chapter explains ENICM in the as-is environment, defines the target environment for ENICM, and identifies the gaps that should be resolved for a successful implementation of an ENICM system.

CHAPTER 2

As-Is Environment – Noninterest Cost Management

This chapter explains the chart of accounts and the enterprise noninterest cost management system in the as-is environment. Section 2.1 provides examples of the chart of accounts, and Section 2.2 explains the cost allocation approach with an example.

In the as-is scenario, the profit and loss (P&L) as per books of account *is fully charged out* to the lines of business, products, customers, and branches as per the allocation rules approved by the senior management. In the next chapter, under the section of using process automation for activity-based noninterest cost management, the significant risk in the "fully charge out" approach is explained. Section 2.3 explains the consequences of a siloed approach to enterprise risk-adjusted return management.

Section 2.4 provides a summarized view of the target enterprise operating model and an overview of the gaps that a bank needs to resolve for accomplishing operating leverage objectives.

To maintain continuity, the P&L example used in this chapter is used in the next chapter for explaining time-driven ABC in a process-automated environment.

CHAPTER 2   AS-IS ENVIRONMENT – NONINTEREST COST MANAGEMENT

2.1 Financial Accounting and Costing – Chart of Accounts

2.1.1 Chart of Accounts – Financial Books

Table 2-1a is a simple illustration of a bank's chart of accounts for financial reporting. There is no standard structure for the codification.

Table 2-1a. *Chart of accounts – accounting books*

General Ledger: Charts of Accounts for Financial Statements			
01	Domestic Currency	015	Savings Accounts
011	Fixed & Current Assets	01501	Savings Accounts – Staff
01101	Fixed Assets	01502	Savings Accounts – Non-Staff
01102	Current Assets	016	Fixed Deposits
01103	Investments	01601	Fixed Deposits – 1 Year
012	Capital & Long Term Borrowing	01602	Fixed Deposits – 3 Year
012-01	Equity Share Capital	01603	Recurring Deposits
012-02	Other Long Term Borrowing	017	Contingent
012-03	Current Liabilities	01701	Contingent Assets
013	Corporate Loans	01702	Contingent Liabilities
013-01	10 year Loan	018	P&L Debits
013-02	Packing Credit Advance	018-01	P&L Debit category-1
013-04	Corporate Overdraft	018-02	P&L Debit category-2
014	Retail Loans	019	P&L Credits
01401	Current Account - Individuals	019-01	P&L Credit category-1
01402	Current Account – Proprietary firms	019-02	P&L Credit category-2
01403	Current Account – Small & Medium Enterprises	*The products will roll-up as balance sheet items.*	

In this example, a 12-digit account number would look like

Curr	Curr	A/c Head	Sub H	Sub H	C1	C2	C3	C4	C5	Ref	Ref

- First Two – Currency.
- First Three – A balance sheet or a P&L section heading.
- First Five – A product or for nonproduct. Nonproduct is internal and could refer to a balance sheet or P&L section subheading.

CHAPTER 2   AS-IS ENVIRONMENT – NONINTEREST COST MANAGEMENT

- 6th to 10th – External customer number or an internal code for house (internal) account.
- First Ten Put Together – A customer or an internal account.
- Last Two – Subreferences for multiple accounts of the same kind.

016/01/12345 is a one-year fixed deposit account: customer Id:12345. If multiple one-year deposits are held, then the subreference is used to create a new account number, e.g., 016/01/12345/*01* and 016/01/12345/*02*.

As the treasury business model and functions are different from retail and corporate banking, the treasury's chart of accounts could have the same account code, but the product, heading, subheading, and internal numbers will reflect the business transactions.

The following are the distinctive features:

(i) Domestic and foreign currency management is an integral part of a treasury management system.

(ii) Treasury has a banking book (**BB**) and a trading book (**TB**).

(iii) There are four major product categories – currency market, money market, commodity market, and equity market.

(iv) Derivatives accounting is different from the accounting treatment for nonderivatives. There are some unique costs linked to the derivative business.

(v) The risk management needs are different from retail and corporate banking (middle-office functions).

(vi) The back-office functions such as nostro reconciliation and settlement are different.

CHAPTER 2   AS-IS ENVIRONMENT – NONINTEREST COST MANAGEMENT

(vii)   The management of off-balance sheet items has a material impact on operating leverage.

Table 2-1b. *Treasury – chart of accounts*

Treasury Balance Sheet is shown separately as it comprises the Banking Book & the Trading Book
The Chart of Accounts should build this into the structure
From an ENICM perspective, costs of supporting BB & TB activities are gathered under separate cost centres

	Treasury Banking Book (BB)		
01	Domestic Currency		
01104	Domestic Certificate of Deposits		**Treasury Trading Book (TB)**
01105	Domestic Government Bonds	02200	JPY Position
01106	Domestic Corporate Bonds	03200	DEM Position
01107	Currency Swap	04200	GBP Position
01108	Interest Rate Swap		
02	JPY	01104	Bond Trading
02104	JPY Certificate of Deposits	01105	Commercial Paper
02105	JPY Government Bonds	01106	Treasury Bills Trading
03	DEM		
04	GBP		

In many banks, the chart of accounts is **structured** on the basis of the lines of business. This improves the accuracy of the accounting book and facilitates compliance.

The P&L and balance sheet item codification is for the entire bank. It includes internal accounts and customer accounts of treasury, retail banking, and corporate banking.

2.1.2   Chart of Accounts – ENICM

This classification and codification **of noninterest costs** in this section are illustrative.

CHAPTER 2   AS-IS ENVIRONMENT – NONINTEREST COST MANAGEMENT

The data items mentioned in this section are required for ENICM, and the objective of the section is to support the narrative on cost allocation. For each ENICM data repository, the entity and currency identifier are unique.

- Profit center codes include
    - Line of business
    - Corporate customer code or retail mass market code
    - Line of business + product
    - Branch
- Cost center codes of support departments should reveal the (i) support function, (ii) service, and (iii) activity group or activity. The branch can be included or derived from customer code.

The P&L section of the financial accounting chart of accounts is mapped to this ENICM chart of accounts. The mapping table will be part of the master data of the bank.

- Lines of Business – Retail (RET), corporate (COR), and treasury (TRY).

    Support Departments – Enterprise IT (EIT); human capital (HCD); operations (OPS); governance, risk, and compliance (GRC); legal (LEG); and finance (FIN).

- Customer – Retail has only groups/segment. Corporate and treasury will have customer group and customer codes. The latter is for tracking profitability at the customer level.

- Product – The offering to the customer.

CHAPTER 2   AS-IS ENVIRONMENT – NONINTEREST COST MANAGEMENT

- Activity Group – For lines of business, this refers to the four phases of the product life cycle – sales, onboarding, operations, and closure (SL, OB, OP, and CL). *The activity group can be a process.*

- Activity Subgroup – For lines of business, this refers to the function: front or middle or back office. This could be a subprocess.

- Branch – BRH.

2.1.2.1 Line of Business: Product-Customer codification

Section 2.1.2.1 illustrates the customer-product codification for the lines of business, Section 2.1.2.2 illustrates the codification of cost centres for a line of business and Section 2.1.2.3 illustrates the codification for the support departments.

Tables 2-2a and 2-2b provide the customer-product codification structure for the three lines of business.

Table 2-2a. *Corporate and Retailing Banking – Product-Customer codification*

Corporate			Retail		
Line of Business	Product	Customer	Line of Business	Product	Customer Segment Code
COR	L10	CG1 (Group)	RET	HLS	R01
COR	L10	CG2 (Group)	RET	COD	R02
COR	L10	CG3 (Group)	RET	VHL	R03
COR	L10	CC1	RET	FD1	R01
COR	L10	CC2	RET	SAV	R02
COR	L10	CC3	RET	LOC	R03

CHAPTER 2   AS-IS ENVIRONMENT – NONINTEREST COST MANAGEMENT

Table 2-2b. *Treasury – Product-Customer codification*

Treasury		
Line of Business	Product	Customer
TRY	IRS	TG1 (Group)
TRY	CBD	TG2 (Group)
TRY	COD	TG3 (Group)
TRY	FXF	TC1
TRY	FRA	TC2
TRY	BIL	TC3

This book recommends having codes to represent (a) Product Life Cycle for Retail and Corporate Banking and (b) Front, Middle and Back office activities for all lines of business. This is illustrated in Figure 2-1. The codification supports the implementation of the Bill of Resources approach.

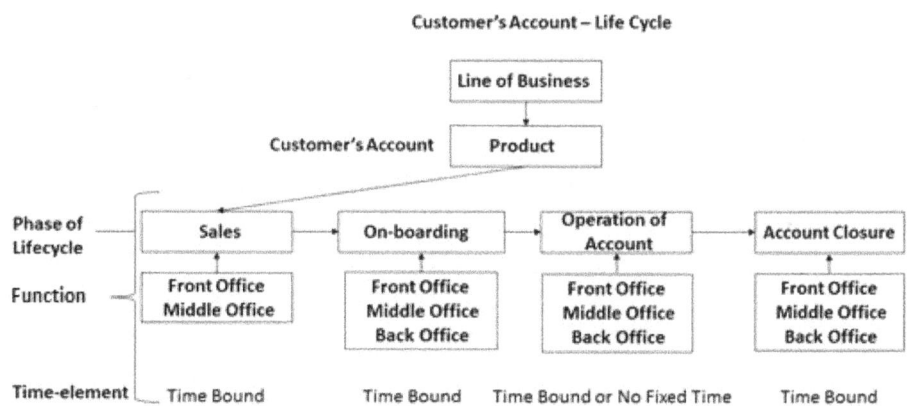

Figure 2-1. *Customer account operational phases*

CHAPTER 2 AS-IS ENVIRONMENT – NONINTEREST COST MANAGEMENT

Tables 2-3 and 2-4 provide a set of codes for customer-product linked activities using the product life cycle approach. It supports the monitoring of customer acquisition & retention costs.

Table 2-3. *Corporate Banking: Product-Customer-Activity-Branch codification*

Corporate Customer: Chart of Accounts

Line of Business	Product	Customer Code	Activity Group	Activity Sub Group	Branch
COR	L10		Sales / Negotiations	FO	Every customer has a home branch.
COR	L10		On boarding	FO	
COR	L10	CC1	Operations	MO (Collateral Management)	
COR	L10		Operations	MO (Site Visits)	
COR	L10		Operations	MO (Credit Rating)	
COR	L10		Closure	BO	

Table 2-4. *Retail Banking: Product-Customer-Activity-Branch codification*

Retail Customer Segment: Chart of Accounts

Line of Business	Product	Customer Segment Code	Activity Group	Activity Sub Group	Branch
RET	RETHLS		Sales / Negotiations	FO	Although retail customer will have a home branch, since it is a mass market, there is no branch link for a customer segment.
RET	RETHLS	R01	On boarding	FO	
RET	RETHLS		Operations	MO (Collateral Management)	
RET	RETHLS		Operations	MO (Credit Rating)	
RET	RETHLS		Closure	BO	

Tables 2-5 and 2-6 extend the above structure to provide the profit centre codes for the lines of business.

CHAPTER 2 AS-IS ENVIRONMENT – NONINTEREST COST MANAGEMENT

Table 2-5. *Retail and Corporate Banking Profit Centre codes*

Chart of Accounts – Enterprise Non Interest Cost Management

Line of Business	Product	Customer	Activity Group	Activity Sub-group	Branch Id	Profit Centre Code
RET	HLS	R01	OB	FO	BRH	RET/HLS/R01/OB/FO/BRH
RET	HLS	R02	OP	MO	BRH	RET/HLS/R02/OP/MO/BRH
RET	VHL	R01	CL	BO	BRH	RET/VHL/R01/CL/BO/BRH
RET	COD	R01	SL	FO	BRH	RET/COD/R01/SL/CO/BRH
RET	SAV	R01	OP	BO	BRH	RET/SAV/R01/OP/BO/BRH
RET	FD1	R03	CL	BO	BRH	RET/FD1/R03/CL/BO/BRH
RET	LOC	R01	OP	FO	BRH	RET/LOC/R01/OP/FO/BRH
COR	LCI	CG1	OP	MO	BRH	COR/LCI/CG1/OP/MO/BRH
COR	L05	CC1	OP	FO	BRH	COR/L05/CC1/OP/FO/BRH
COR	L10	CC2	SL	MO	BRH	COR/L10/CC2/SL/MO/BRH
COR	COA	CG1	OP	MO	BRH	COR/COA/CG1/OP/MO/BRH
COR	LCI	CC1	OP	BO	BRH	COR/LCI/CC1/OP/BO/BRH
COR	WCL	CG2	OB	MO	BRH	COR/WCL/CG2//OB/MO/BRH
COR	SDL	CC2	SL	BO	BRH	COR/SDL/CC2/SL/BO/BRH

Table 2-6. *Treasury Profit Centre codes*

Chart of Accounts – Enterprise Non Interest Cost Management

Line of Business	Product	Customer	Activity Group	Activity Sub-group	Branch Id	Profit Centre Code
TRB (Banking Book)	FXF	TG1	OP	MO		TRB/FXF/TG1/OP/MO/BRH
TRB	FRA	TG2	OP	BO		TRB/FRA/TG2/OP/BO/BRH
TRB	IRS	TC1	CL	BO	Not Mandatory	TRB/IRS/TC1/CL/BO/BRH
TRB	COD	TG3	OP	FO		TRB/COD/TG3/OP/FO/BRH
TRB	BIL	TC2	OP	MO		TRB/BIL/TC2/OP/MO/BRH
TRT (Trading Book)	CBD	TG2	OP	MO		TRT/CBD/TG2/OP/MO/BRH

Treasury Deals have the following four activity groups: (i) Pre-Deal (ii) Trade (iii) Operations – this group will include accounting, confirmations, collateral management, reconciliation activities and (iv) Closure – this group will include settlement and accounting activities.

CHAPTER 2   AS-IS ENVIRONMENT – NONINTEREST COST MANAGEMENT

2.1.2.2 Line of Business – Cost Centre Codes

Table 2-7 illustrates the cost centres for the Retail Banking division. Internal customer codes for a line of business could be the cost classification codes such as EMP for employee cost or EIT for enterprise IT.

Table 2-7. Retail Banking – Cost Centre codes

Retail Banking Similar for Corporate Banking & Treasury	Code
Employee Cost (e.g. payroll update)	RET/EMP/ZZZ/ZZ/ZZ/ZZZ
Enterprise I.T. (this SLA based charge for Retail)	RET/EIT/ZZZ/ZZ/ZZ/ZZZ
Rent (fully occupied by retail)	RET/RNT/ZZZ/ZZ/ZZ/BRH
Legal (SLA based charge)	RET/LEG/ZZZ/ZZ/ZZ/ZZZ
Governance, Risk & Compliance (SLA)	RET/GRC/ZZZ/ZZ/ZZ/ZZZ
Depreciation (assets owned by Retail Banking)	RET/DEP/ZZZ/ZZ/ZZ/ZZZ
Insurance (insurance taken on retail banking assets)	RET/INS/ZZZ/ZZ/ZZ/ZZZ
Travel (employee's id)	RET/TRV/ZZZ/ZZ/ZZ/ZZZ

The codes for Corporate Banking and Treasury is similar to the Retail Banking codification. For instance employee cost centre for Treasury will be TRY/EMP/ZZ/ZZ/ZZZ and for Corporate Banking, it will be COR/EMP/ZZ/ZZ/ZZZ. Generally, banks do not use branch code for analysis of treasury data.

2.1.2.3 Support Departments

Human Capital activities include:

- Recruitment, Appraisal, Transfer, Training and Skill Upgradation,
- Promotion, Compensation,
- Enforcement of Code of Conduct,

- Workplace interaction, Harassment, Grievance Management, Mandatory leave and
- Termination of staff and external staff.

Enterprise Information Technology (I.T) Governance

The governance model will

- Allow the evaluation of the use of technology to improve business processes.
- Align technology with business
- Prioritise resource deployment.

Figure 2-2 shows the Enterprise Information Technology Governance components.

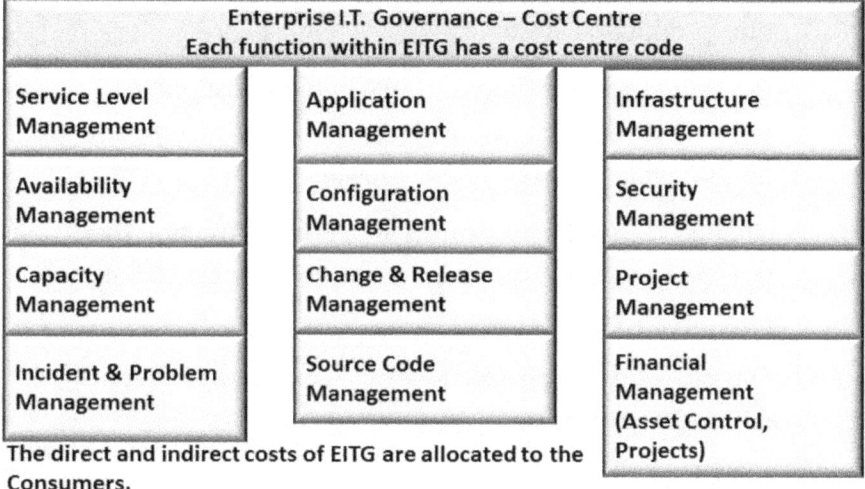

Figure 2-2. EITG components

Enterprise Information Technology Governance (EITG) knowledge comprises objectives, strategy, policies, procedures and best practices. The other is the Enterprise I.T. Governance tool, a software asset owned by the department for managing the operations.

CHAPTER 2 AS-IS ENVIRONMENT – NONINTEREST COST MANAGEMENT

A brief description of the EITG functions are as follows:

- Service Level Management- includes both internal (with bank) and external (vendors) service level agreements. The latter falls within vendor management;

- Availability Management-This refers to infrastructure support for a 24*7 business. It would include the servers, routers, messaging, bridges, operating systems, system software, firewalls, load balancing and internet management;

- Incident Management – this covers support issues and risk events reported to the EITG helpdesk;

- Application Management – includes production and non-production systems;

- Programme Management – large banks constitute a project office to drive critical projects. This is a function that is invoked by a business decision;

- Change Management – this is very critical function that is a weakness in several banks. The consequences are operational risk events;

- Source Code management includes escrow agreements with software vendors;

- Capacity Management - Business growth figures are inputs for this forward-looking exercise. Based on projected growth, the Infrastructure team ensures that the risks of having capacity constraints are minimised;

- Enterprise Security - A data centric approach is mandatory. This would include both Preventive and Detective controls. A critical success factor is the optimised number of security layers. In the present generation of banking applications, internet and mobile security are two risk areas;
- Site Management - This primarily refers to all aspects of the Production, Backup and Disaster Recovery activities.

Business Continuity Planning (BCP)

BCP is recovery of all business functions affected by a disruptive event. This is planned enterprise-wide. A risk assessment and impact analysis is the basis of BCP.

EITG's primary objectives are:

- Ensure a data centric enterprise security. The confidentiality, reliability and accuracy of data is a critical success factor;
- Service quality includes service availability for a 24*7 operation and includes customer experience KPIs. Capacity planning to ensure that the technology infrastructure keeps up with the business growth.

Finance Department

Finance Department:

- Owns the chart of accounts - financial and costing;
- Owns the general ledger and the financial statements;
- Ensures accurate mapping of the chart of accounts (G.L.) to cost management and risk management systems;
- Supports the data lineage efforts in the bank.

CHAPTER 2   AS-IS ENVIRONMENT – NONINTEREST COST MANAGEMENT

Legal

Bank's legal department (a) initiates legal action to protect the bank's interests and (b) defends the bank in legal cases.

Governance, Risk & Compliance

Enterprise risk adjusted return governance is about how a bank defines and enforces its risk adjusted return business culture. Figure 2-3 illustrates the scope of the governance from the board room to the trading desk.

The four risk types on the right are market risk, credit risk, asset liability management (liquidity risk) and operational risk. The treasury's four product groups are Foreign Exchange (FX) / Currency, Money Market (MM), Equity (EQ) and Commodity (Comm).

Enterprise Risk Adjusted Return Governance

Enterprise, Strategic Level
Business Goals
Risk **Capacity** to attain business goals; Bank's Balance Sheet Management
Enterprise Risk Oversight

Lines of Business
Policy Finalisation and implementing
Risk Appetite Framework and Risk Appetite Statements defined for all RISK TYPES.
Risk Tolerances defined.
Key Risk Indicators, Key Performance Indicators at banking processes level, product and customer or customer segment levels.

	M.R.	C.R.	ALM	O.R.
Treasury				
Corporate				
Retail				

Within LOB, Operational Level
Risk Limits operational at various levels: Department / Product / Industry / Counterparty / Customer / Trader / Relationship Manager levels

E.g. Treasury

F.X	MM	EQ	Comm
Risk Types			
Trading Desks			

Figure 2-3. *Enterprise Risk Adjusted Return Governance*

Note   MR stands for Market risk, CR for Credit Risk, ALM for Asset Liability Management (this includes Liquidity Risk); OR for Operational risk.

CHAPTER 2   AS-IS ENVIRONMENT – NONINTEREST COST MANAGEMENT

The following are some important enterprise risk adjusted return governance functions:

- Implementing the desired risk culture throughout the bank;
- Increasing the engagement between the board, senior management and external stakeholders on risk governance issues;
- Implementing an enterprise risk ontology that is part of the enterprise data ontology to ensure that there is a common understanding of concepts, models and data-items;
- Developing a common understanding of risk, its appetite, tolerance and capacity across the bank;
- Ensuring that the enterprise risk management infrastructure is available and operational;
- Aligning business strategy with risk governance;
- Quantifying, monitoring and reporting risks internally to ensure that they are consistent with the risk appetite framework;
- Stating and monitoring the deliverables of the risk committees;
- Strengthening the risk management function, including the stature of the CRO. The CRO is responsible for enterprise risk management and ensures that the risk profile is consistent within the risk appetite framework (RAF) and statement (RAS). With, the support of the

CHAPTER 2   AS-IS ENVIRONMENT – NONINTEREST COST MANAGEMENT

risk committees, the CRO is responsible for monitoring and recommending strategies to prevent, mitigate or transfer risks;

- Empowering the roles of the EA, CTO and CDO.

Operations

The operations department includes several functions and the cost types are illustrated in Table 2-8.

Table 2-8. Operations Department

Operations Department	
Costs	As with the case of all other support departments, operations will have its share of direct & indirect expenses. The total cost of the department is allocated to other support departments, LOBs, products, customers, branches.
Rent, Utilities	
Office Supplies	
Repairs & Maintenance	
Travel Desk – this should have a cost owner identified at the time of approval	

Tables 2-9 and 2-10 are examples for Support Department codes. Code '**US'** refers **to internal user** i.e. line of business availing the service of the support department.

CHAPTER 2 AS-IS ENVIRONMENT – NONINTEREST COST MANAGEMENT

Table 2-9. *Support Department codes*

Support Department	\multicolumn{4}{c}{Chart of Accounts Enterprise Non Interest Cost Management}			
Support Department		Function	Activity Group	Sub-group	Code
Enterprise I.T. Governance	EIT	SLM	NW	OP	EIT/SLM/NW/OP/BRH
	EIT	SLM	SV	OP	EIT/SLM/SV/OP/BRH
	EIT	INM	HP	TK	EIT/INM/HP/TK/BRH
Human Capital	HCD	REC	G1	IV	HCD/REC/G1/IV/BRH
(Activity Grouped by Skills)	HCD	OBD	G2	ID	HCD/OBD/G2/ID/BRH
	HCD	TER	G6	DA	HCD/TER/G6/DA/BRH
Operations - Premises	OPS	PRE	RN	US	OPS/PRE/RN/US/BRH
	OPS	OFS	TY	PR	OPS/OFS/TY/PR/BRH
	OPS	RAM	TY	US	OPS/RAM/TY/US/BRH
Finance	FIN	BOK	US	ZZ	FIN/BOK/US/ZZ/ZZZ
	FIN	BUD	US	ZZ	FIN/BUD/US/ZZ/ZZZ
Legal	LEG	Initiation: DEF (sued) or Plaintiff (PTF)	US	ZZ	LEG/DEF/US/ZZ/ZZZ
					LEG/PTF/US/ZZ/ZZZ

The following are explanatory points for Table 2-9:

EITG

The Enterprise I.T. Governance scope could vary by bank;

- SLM, NW stands for Service level management, Network Usage;

- SV Service level management;

- INM/HP/TK Incident Management, Helpdesk, Ticket raised;

Human Capital

This book recommends grouping staff by skills. This could be implemented by including the staff skill grade in the cost centre code.

REC, OBD, TER stand for Recruitment, staff on-boarding and termination;

CHAPTER 2 AS-IS ENVIRONMENT – NONINTEREST COST MANAGEMENT

G1,G2,G6 – refers to staff skill grade and
IV,ID,DA – refer to interview, induction and disable access.

- REC/G1/IV Recruit Grade-1 Interview;
- OB2/G2/ID On-boarding G2 induction;
- TER/G6/DA Terminate G6 disable user access.

Operations

- PRE/RN/US Premises, Rent, line of business;
- OFS/TY/PR Office Supply, category / type, procurement;
- RAM/TY/US Repairs & Maintenance, Type/Category/ line of business, BOK/US/OP/ZZZ Book keeping, line of business;

Finance

- BUD/US/OP Budgeting, line of business;

Legal

- DEF/US/ Defendant, line of business; PTF/US/ Plaintiff, line of business.

The branch code could be used where appropriate e.g. repairs and maintenance (non IT) of the branch.

GRC

The cost of the GRC department is becoming more expensive for banks, as enterprise risk adjusted return management is a mandatory capability. Risk management skills are expensive. Table 2-10 provides a sample GRC cost centre codification. A branch code may be required.

CHAPTER 2 AS-IS ENVIRONMENT – NONINTEREST COST MANAGEMENT

Table 2-10. GRC Department codes

Chart of Accounts – Enterprise Non Interest Cost Management

Support Department	Code	Function	Activity Group	Activity Sub-group	Cost Centre Code
Governance Risk & Compliance	GRC	Governance	Enterprise Risk Adjusted Return Management	Stress Testing	GRC/GOV/ER/ST/BRH
		Risk Management	Market Risk	Pre-deal Analytics	GRC/RIM/MR/AI/BRH
		Risk Management	Credit Risk	Concentration Risk	GRC/RIM/CR/CT/BRH
		Risk Management	Operational Risk	Staff	GRC/RIM/OR/HC/BRH
		Risk Management	Liquidity Management	Liquidity Coverage	GRC/RIM/LM/LC/BRH
		Compliance	Anti Money Laundering	Reporting	GRC/COM/ML/RP/BRH

The Financial Chart of Accounts and the Enterprise Non-Interest Cost Chart of Accounts should be consistent at all times. Enterprise Data Governance facilitates establishing data lineage.

2.2 ENICMS in As-Is Environment

The three main phases in enterprise noninterest cost allocation are

(i) Defining business activities.

(ii) Identification of *direct costs* and allocating it to relevant cost centers. When there is process automation, the ENICM and the accounting systems can be updated simultaneously.

(iii) Allocating the *indirect costs* as per approved methodology.

CHAPTER 2   AS-IS ENVIRONMENT – NONINTEREST COST MANAGEMENT

The next chapter provides more clarity on "HOW" to implement ABC/TDABC and accomplish enterprise noninterest cost management objectives.

2.2.1 As-Is Cost Data Capture and Maintenance

Many banks do not have an accurate enterprise ABC system because of the weak enterprise data management in the as-is architecture. Figure 2-4 provides a view of the as-is environment.

Cost data capture in the transaction capture systems is not wholesome and the weakness is further aggravated by fragmented datasets. At the transaction level, banks should be able to capture cost data at the time of occurrence. In the as-is environment, the source data is warehoused periodically, i.e., collected and aggregated, and the ENICM system is used to plug the data gap as a "data maintenance activity."

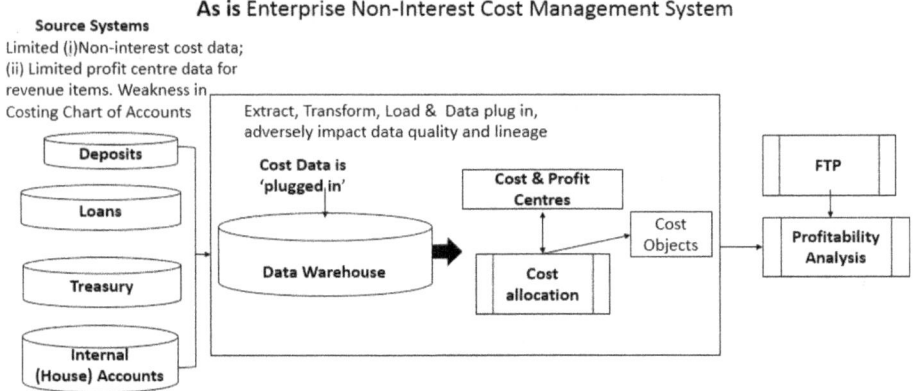

Figure 2-4. *As-is ENICMS*

Direct costs can update the cost objects (e.g., LOB, products, customers) directly. Indirect costs update cost pools, i.e., cost center, and using cost drivers, the costs in each pool are allocated to consumers of the service. The nature of the cost pools are different. The consumers of the services are charged on the basis of drivers such as staff full-time equivalent or system usage.

CHAPTER 2   AS-IS ENVIRONMENT – NONINTEREST COST MANAGEMENT

Table 2-11 provides an overview of cost items in a bank's profit and loss account. It excludes interest expense and loan write-off. In the as-is environment, the cost data captured in P&L transactions is limited in scope.

Table 2-11. *Sample bank P&L account heads*

Bank's P&L (Non-interest, Non – Loan_write-off) Expenses	
Cost-item (staff)	Cost-item (non-staff)
Salaries;	IT related expenses;
Pension costs and other staff-related benefit costs;	Office expenses;
	Advertising and public relations;
Social security costs;	Travel and accommodation expenses;
Share-based compensation arrangements;	External advisory fees;
External employees;	Audit and non-audit services;
Education.	Postal charges;
	Depreciation of property and equipment;
	Amortisation of intangible assets;
	Impairments and reversals on property and equipment and intangibles;
	Regulatory costs;
	Contributions and subscriptions.

A weak cost management mechanism does not allow a bank to accurately measure the profitability by various dimensions, e.g., customer, product, and branch.

2.2.1.1 As-Is ENICM Scenarios

Table 2-12 provides an overview of the three different as-is ENICM environments. The "inaccurate ENICM" system is the "best situation" in the siloed environment, the "weak ENICM" applies to banks that lack the management commitment to improve their operations, and the "unsatisfactory ENICM" category is rudimentary and unreliable for decision-making.

Most small banks would fall under the weak ENICM category. International banks have inaccurate ENICM system, although their IT spending is high. Many regional (operations in more than one country) and medium-sized banks have an unsatisfactory ENICM system.

CHAPTER 2   AS-IS ENVIRONMENT – NONINTEREST COST MANAGEMENT

In the as-is environment, the best case business situation is one which has an inaccurate ENICM.

Table 2-12. *As-is ENICM environments*

The As Is Enterprise Non-interest Cost Management Environment			
	Inaccurate System	Unsatisfactory ENICM	Weak ENICM
Enterprise Risk Adjusted Return Management- Policies and Procedures	Yes but as is environment is siloed	Limited ERRM capability; Siloed as is environment	No ERRM capability
Enterprise Non Interest Management – Policies and Procedures	Yes but as is environment is siloed	Limited scope; Siloed as is environment	No ENICM capability
Implementation of a Cost Management methodology	Yes	Inaccurate	No
Costing Chart of Accounts	Yes	Yes	No
Cost Allocation Accuracy	Violates error threshold	Inaccurate – rudimentary system	
Process documentation	Limited process improvement	No process improvement	Limited
Process Automation	Limited	Not used	Not Used
Cost Data Capture	Limited	Not available – use a data warehouse for cost data plug-in	Limited data for cost management
Cost of Banking Processes	No accurate data	Not possible to accurately measure	
Profitability Reports	Violates error threshold	Inaccurate for decision making	Not possible

Accuracy-bank's policy should document the acceptable error margin in cost allocation to keep ENICM simple.

Banks should transform their business and enterprise operating model in order to move toward an accurate ENICM. The "gaps" in the present environment are explained in Section 2.4 after an explanation on the present allocation procedures.

It is important for bank managements to remember that the enterprise noninterest cost management model is a sub-set of the enterprise risk-adjusted return model.

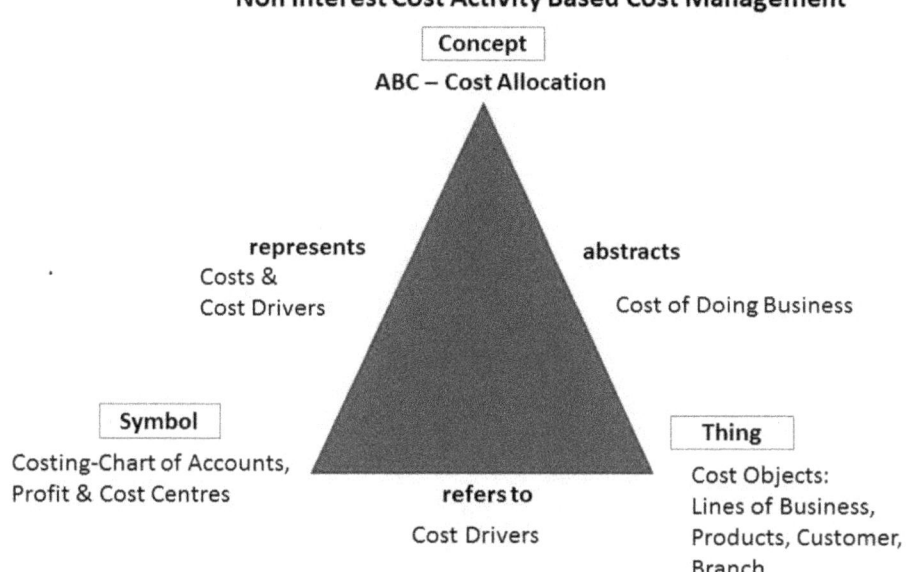

Figure 2-5a. Cost allocation concept

Figure 2-5a illustrates the concept of noninterest cost allocation. **Cost of doing business** is the sum of its two dimensions: **the cost of business delivery and the cost of risk management**.

Figure 2-5b illustrates treasury's cost of doing business by showing the business delivery.

CHAPTER 2   AS-IS ENVIRONMENT – NONINTEREST COST MANAGEMENT

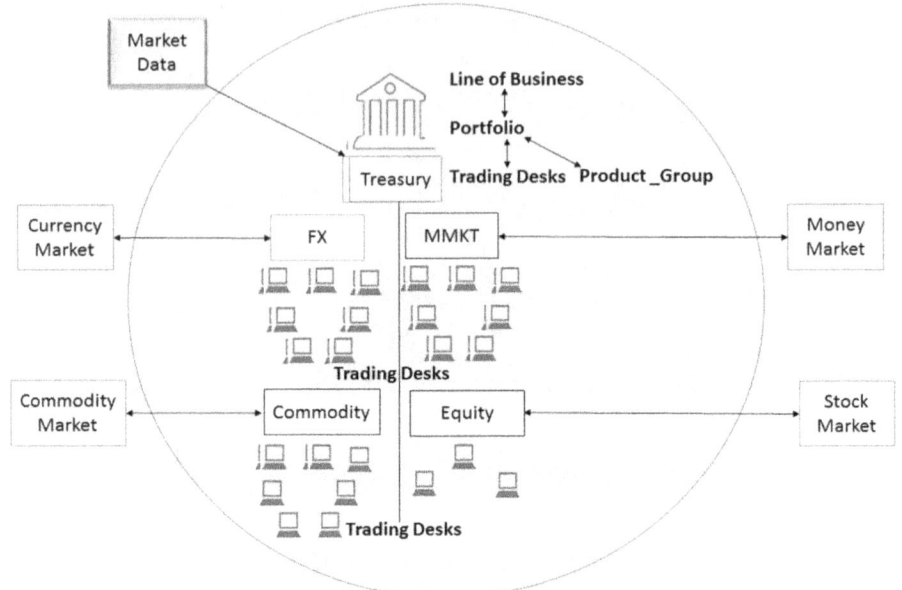

Figure 2-5b. *Treasury business delivery environment*

Treasury's cost of risk management will include staff, system, and other tangible assets for

  i. Predeal analytics
 ii. Mark to market
iii. Sensitivities
- Scenario based
- Analytical

 iv. Value at risk
- Risk metrics
- Monte Carlo simulation
- Historical simulation

  v. Stress testing

CHAPTER 2   AS-IS ENVIRONMENT – NONINTEREST COST MANAGEMENT

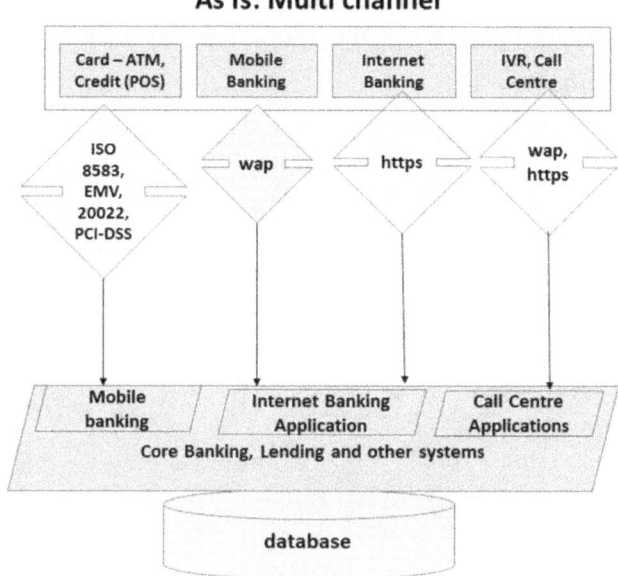

Figure 2-5c. Banks without omnichannel

Banks without an omni-channel platform may be exposed to higher operating costs and risks. Their efficiency levels will be lower. Retail banking is the largest internal consumer of a bank's omni channel platform's service.

Lending and credit risk management are the focus areas of Retail and Corporate banking. Retail banking deposits are an importance source of funding for a commercial bank.

The cost items in a cost pool are allocated to the cost objects through cost drivers, e.g., premises cost is allocated on the basis of the square feet occupied.

The cost allocation methodology documents a list of cost centers (pools) and the basis for the allocation for each pool. The pool comprises a homogenous set of cost items. The cost allocation methodology is reviewed annually prior to the preparation of the operating budget.

The lines of business use the services of the support functions to deliver business. It is the treasury, retail banking, and corporate banking divisions that drive the growth and profitability of a commercial bank.

CHAPTER 2   AS-IS ENVIRONMENT – NONINTEREST COST MANAGEMENT

Hence, the three LOBs take ownership for the costs as illustrated in Figure 2-6 and are tagged as profit centers. The support departments are tagged as cost centers.

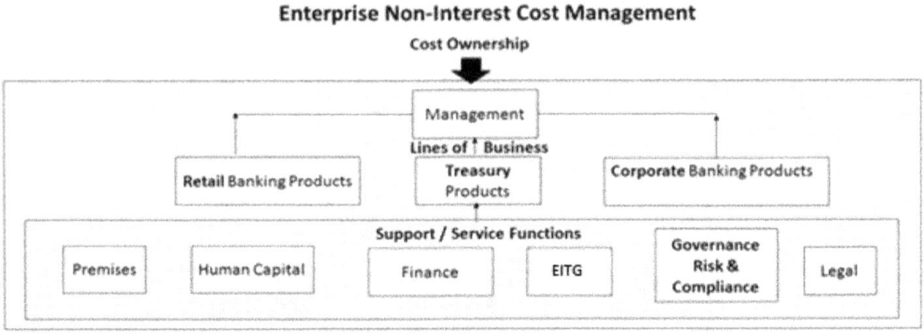

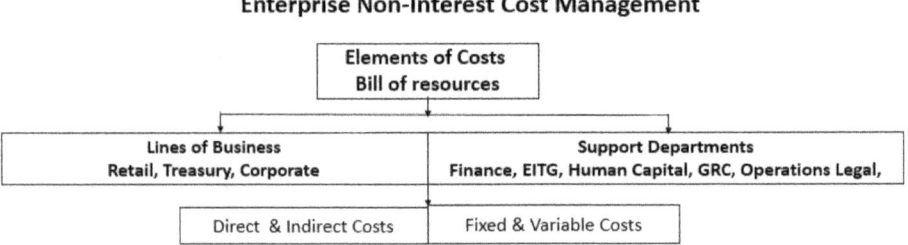

Figure 2-6.   *Ownership of costs*

Figure 2-7 emphasizes on the need to focus on staff and technology costs as they are two primary drivers for optimizing risk-adjusted returns. Other significant costs could include GRC and premises.

This book introduces the bill of resources, an adaptation of the bill of materials used in the manufacturing industry, as a tool for activity-based enterprise noninterest cost management. This is explained in Chapters 3 and 4.

Figure 2-7.   *Elements of costs*

92

Tables 2-13a and 2-13b provide an insight into cost drivers.

Table 2-13a. *Cost drivers*

Banking function/ department	Cost drivers	Comments
HR – staff (across functions; across lines of business)	Full-time equivalence of work done	Employees with 100% FTE, the cost can be taken as a direct cost
Operations: Shared premises – rent paid Repairs and maintenance of shared premises Office supplies, consumables Utilities	Floor area Indents Floor area	Premises maintenance cost is a linked cost. Insurance cost Common area – unlinked cost allocated based on an agreed basis (policy)
Depreciation	Direct – asset ownership Joint ownership – resource drivers	Joint asset ownership cost allocation is a policy line item
Marketing and advertisement	Direct or allocated on agreed basis	Policy guideline for allocation basis prior to approval for joint campaigns

Table 2-13b. Cost drivers

Enterprise architecture, technology, software, and data	Cost drivers
Hardware and network – own	Annual maintenance contract, system usage
Software – own	Own systems (direct), application usage
Services – own	Service level agreement, tickets raised
Hardware and network – vendor provided	Contract, service level agreement
Software – vendor provided	Contract, service level agreement
Vendor services	Contract, service level agreement

2.2.2 Example: Allocation

A sample bank's profit and loss account is illustrated in Table 2-14a. The P&L figure is then split as direct and indirect costs.

In Table 2-14a

  i) The split of the P&L costs as direct and indirect is based on observations made in as-is environments.

  ii) Depreciation, insurance, sales and marketing, director fees, auditor fees, legal fees, consultant charges, and travel are taken as direct cost, and the cost objects are known at the time of data capture.

  iii) All support department costs incur indirect costs.

  iv) Premises, office supplies, and travel costs are grouped under operations department. Operations department will have its share of direct and indirect costs.

CHAPTER 2   AS-IS ENVIRONMENT – NONINTEREST COST MANAGEMENT

Direct costs do not update a cost pool, they update the cost objects (e.g., line of business, product). Indirect costs update a cost center (cost pool) and are then allocated to cost objects based on the allocation rules.

Table 2-14a. *P&L accounting books (direct and indirect breakup is an assumption)*

Operating Cost - Books of Account $ - in millions	P&L	ENICM	
		Direct Cost	Indirect Cost
			Allocation – a ENICM process
Depreciation	20	20	
Insurance on Assets	5	5	
Employee cost	300	210	90
Enterprise I.T. Governance cost	200	50	150
Operations: Premises Rent & Utilities	150	15	135
Operations: Office supplies	100	10	90
Sales & Marketing	80	80	
Director's fees	2	2	
Audit fees	3	3	
Legal fees	4	4	
Consultant Charges	6	6	
Operations: Repairs & Maintenance (non-I.T.)	25	10	15
Operations: Travel	10	10	
Total	905	425	480

Depreciation, insurance, and audit fees are managed by the finance department. However, depreciation and insurance charge are borne by the relevant lines of business and support departments. Indirect employee cost is allocated to lines of business (and products, customers) based on full-time equivalent (FTE) data.

IT repairs and maintenance is part of enterprise ITG cost.

CHAPTER 2   AS-IS ENVIRONMENT – NONINTEREST COST MANAGEMENT

Table 2-14b. Operations

Operations department – costs in this example	Comment
Premises rent and utilities	Includes space occupied by premises department
Office supplies (mostly centralized)	It is assumed that procurement and internal distribution is managed by operations
Repairs and maintenance	This is not IT related
Travel	It is assumed that operations manages the travel desk

In the financial books of account, there is no separate cost classification for governance, risk, and compliance, legal, or finance departments. The ENICM's chart of accounts should be designed to manage these cost centers (example in Section 2.1.2.3).

The following are the steps in allocation as illustrated in Section 2.2.2.

Tables 2-14c and 2-14d provide the section-wise details on the enterprise noninterest cost allocation examples.

CHAPTER 2   AS-IS ENVIRONMENT – NONINTEREST COST MANAGEMENT

Table 2-14c. *Cost allocation – lines of business*

Section	Brief description
2.2.2.1	Direct cost compilation of lines of business and support departments
2.2.2.2	Indirect cost allocation
2.2.2.3	Support department cost allocation to lines of business; please note the data in the table below
2.2.2.4	Ensuring the P&L figures in the books of account and ENICM system are in balance (this is an important milestone in the allocation process)

The ENICM system allocation result (refer Table 2-31) explained in **2.2.2.4** is shown here for a better appreciation of the **expected output** at this stage.

	Total Cost (Direct+ Indirect Cost)	Allocation of Support Department Cost	Total
Retail Banking	383,200,000	43,800,000	427,000,000
Corporate Banking	223,150,000	45,000,000	268,150,000
Treasury	163,500,000	46,350,000	209,850,000
Total	769,850,000	135,150,000	905,000,000

The following are important enterprise noninterest cost management verification procedures:

- The total costs as reflected in the ENICM system must tally with the books of account cost (general ledger).
- Management costs are allocated to the lines of business.
- Total operating costs = $\sum$ treasury costs + $\sum$ corporate banking costs + $\sum$ retail banking costs.

The allocation example then illustrates the calculation of cost of products, customers, and branches.

Table 2-14d. *Cost allocation – products and branch*

Section	Brief description
2.2.3	Calculation of the cost of products by lines of business
2.2.4	Calculation of the cost of servicing customers/customer segments (or groups)
2.2.5	Branch cost
2.2.6	Noninterest revenue of products

This narrative explains the "high level as-is" approach that is being adopted by many banks.

2.2.2.1 Direct Cost – ENICM Update

Direct costs are those for which cost ownership is established for the full amount. The principles of measurement are as per bookkeeping principles, and standards and the full amount are allocated to the cost object, i.e., cost center or profit center.

This section illustrates the allocation of the direct costs to the relevant cost owner. This is based on factors such as

- Asset ownership
- One hundred percent full-time equivalent, i.e., dedicated staff for the activity
- SLAs between enterprise IT and users
- SLAs between GRC and the users
- Occupied area in the case of premises
- Indents for office supplies

All support departments (a) have staff, (b) use systems and IT services, and (c) need premises. Further, the human capital will have its share of direct employee cost, enterprise IT will have its assets, and the operations department also needs premises. This will be their direct costs.

Tables 2-15a, 2-15b, 2-15c, 2-15d, and 2-15e show the direct cost allocation to lines of business and support departments. The data is from Table 2-14a, P&L. The source data capture should facilitate the capture of cost data. In the *as-is environment*, much of this data are "plug-ins" in the data warehouse.

2.2.2.1.1 Depreciation

- Allocation of Costs – Depreciation shall be traced to the cost object using the asset register.

Shared asset costs can be categorized under the following:

- In the case of exclusive use of an asset by a single service, depreciation and other costs (e.g., repairs and maintenance) associated with the asset are a direct cost that is charged to the asset owning profit or cost center.

- Nonexclusive asset costs are treated as an indirect overhead allocation. The identified cost driver will drive the allocation.

If depreciation cannot be directly traced to a specific cost object, it can be assigned based on either of the following principles:

- Cause and Effect – Cause is the business activity, and effect is the incurrence of cost.

- Benefits Accrued – Depreciation can be allocated on the basis of benefits realized by cost objects.

CHAPTER 2   AS-IS ENVIRONMENT – NONINTEREST COST MANAGEMENT

Left-hand side of Table 2-15a provides an example for depreciation. It is assumed that the full depreciation amount can be traced to the cost object.

2.2.2.1.2 Direct Staff Cost

Presently, in many banks having an ENICM system, the FTE data is collected from the staff and is approved by the employee's supervisor.

On the right-hand side of Table 2-15a, direct staff cost is shown. Important points to observe for direct staff cost compilation are as follows:

- Direct costs are those for which staff FTE is 100%, i.e., full-time staff for a product, or a support function, i.e., *it is not shareable*.

- Principles of measurement are as per policies and standards.

- Allocation of Costs – The full amount is allocated to the cost object, i.e., cost center or profit center.

Table 2-15a. Direct cost allocation

Depreciation - Direct allocation based on Fixed Assets ownership by LOBs & Support Depts.		Allocation of Direct staff cost with 100% FTE	
Depreciation	20,000,000	Direct Cost	210,000,000
Allocations		100% FTE based allocation	
Retail	8,500,000	Retail	60,000,000
Treasury	6,000,000	Treasury	50,000,000
Corporate	4,000,000	Corporate	40,000,000
Management	100,000	Management	30,000,000
Operations	150,000	Operations	2,500,000
Enterprise I.T. Governance	600,000	Enterprise I.T. Governance	5,000,000
Finance	150,000	Finance	5,000,000
Legal	50,000	Legal	2,500,000
GRC	250,000	GRC	10,000,000
Human Capital	200,000	Human Capital – HC Staff	5,000,000
Total allocated	20,000,000	Total allocated	210,000,000

Table 2-15b illustrates the allocation of EITG and premises costs.

2.2.2.1.3 Enterprise IT Governance

- Direct costs are those for which the EITG department can identify the cost as consumed by a specific profit or cost center. This may or may not be governed by a service level agreement.

- Principles of measurement are as per policies and standards.

- Allocation of Costs – The full amount is allocated to the cost object, i.e., cost center or profit center.

2.2.2.1.4 Premises

- Direct costs are those that are attributable in full to the occupation of the premises by the "user" profit or cost center.

- Principles of Measurement – As per policies and standards.

- Allocation of Costs – The full amount is allocated to the cost object, i.e., cost center or profit center.

- EITG department has its shares of IT assets. The AMC, repairs, and maintenance costs are shown in Table 2-15b as $1,000,000.

- Operations department occupies space, and the cost of it is shown as $300,000 in Table 2-15b.

CHAPTER 2 AS-IS ENVIRONMENT – NONINTEREST COST MANAGEMENT

Table 2-15b. *Direct cost allocation*

Enterprise I.T. Governance – Direct Cost allocation (e.g. Annual Maintenance Contract Charges or Service Level Agreement Charges – that can be charged directly)	
Direct Cost	50,000,000
Retail	25,000,000
Treasury	15,000,000
Corporate	5,000,000
Management	1,000,000
Enterprise I.T. Governance (for their Assets)	1,000,000
Operations	300,000
Finance	500,000
Legal	200,000
GRC	1,750,000
Human Capital	250,000
Total allocated	**50,000,000**

Premises: Rent & Utilities Direct Cost allocation	
Direct Cost	15,000,000
Retail	7,000,000
Treasury	1,000,000
Corporate	4,000,000
Management	500,000
Enterprise I.T. Governance	500,000
Operations – own cost	300,000
Finance	500,000
Legal	200,000
GRC	500,000
Human Capital	500,000
Total allocated	**15,000,000**

The operations department also occupies premises. Hence, as shown earlier in Table 2-15b right-hand side, of the total direct premises cost of $15,000,000, $300,000 is shown as the premises cost debited to operations; the rest is allocated to LOBs and other support departments.

2.2.2.1.5 Office Supplies

Table 2-15c illustrates office supply, sales and marketing, and insurance costs.

Office supplies, part of the operations department, include (i) consumables and (ii) assets that can be fully depreciated in the year of purchase. In some banks, procurement is a centralized function.

- Direct costs are those that can be fully identified with a line of business or a support department.
- Principles of measurement are as per policies and standards.
- Allocation – The costs directly traceable shall be assigned to the relevant product sold or services rendered.

2.2.2.1.6 Sales and Marketing

Banks are facing intense competition from within the industry and from non-banking players. Banks are attempting to increase their customer base using data analytics and marketing campaigns.

- Direct costs of sales and marketing are the expenses related to the sale of products and services. It includes all indirect expenses incurred in promoting the banks and its portfolio of offerings. It includes salaries, travelling expenses of sales personnel, commission to sales agents, brand promotion, advertisement, publicity, sponsorships, and endorsements.

- Principles of Measurement – The aggregate of the cost of resources consumed in the selling and distribution activities of the products and services.

- Allocation – The costs directly traceable shall be assigned to the relevant product sold or services rendered.

2.2.2.1.7 Insurance

- Insurance cost shall be traced to the cost object using the asset register or employee master record (e.g., key employee insurance). *It is not necessary that the asset should be owned by the bank (e.g., lease agreement).*

- If insurance cannot be directly traced to a specific cost object, it can be assigned based on either of the following principles:

    i. Cause and Effect – Cause is the business activity, and effect is the incurrence of cost.

ii. Benefits Accrued – Insurance can be allocated on the basis of benefits realized by cost objects.

- Shared Assets – Similar to the allocation of depreciation costs.

Table 2-15c. Direct cost allocation

Office Supplies Direct Cost Allocation - Who owns the indent?	
Direct Cost	10,000,000
Retail	4,000,000
Treasury	800,000
Corporate	2,000,000
Management	200,000
Enterprise I.T. Governance	2,000,000
Operations	200,000
Finance (own consumption)	200,000
Legal	50,000
GRC	400,000
Human Capital	150,000
Total allocated	10,000,000

Sales and Marketing: Direct Cost Allocation	
Direct Cost	80,000,000
Retail	50,000,000
Treasury	1,000,000
Corporate	14,000,000
Management	15,000,000
Total allocated	80,000,000

Insurance on Assets: Direct Cost Allocation Asset Ownership	
Direct Cost	5,000,000
Retail	3,000,000
Treasury	1,000,000
Corporate	1,000,000
(for the example- taken only LOBs; Insurance should cover all assets – Management & Support Department)	
Total allocated	5,000,000

Table 2-15d illustrates repairs and maintenance (non-IT) and travel costs.

2.2.2.1.8 Repairs and Maintenance

- This should be consistent with depreciation and insurance. The cost shall be traced to the cost object using the asset.

- Principles of measurement are as per policies and standards.

- If repairs and maintenance cannot be directly traced to a specific cost object, it can be assigned based on either of the following principles:

    i. Cause and Effect – Cause is the business activity, and effect is the incurrence of cost.

    ii. Benefits Accrued – Insurance can be allocated on the basis of benefits realized by cost objects.

2.2.2.1.9 Travel

- Travel expenses include all modes of transport, domestic and international travel.

- Principles of measurement are as per policies and standards.

- Direct costs are those for which the business need is fully identified with a cost object.

Table 2-15d. *Direct cost allocation*

Repairs & Maintenance allocation Who owns / uses the asset?	
Repairs & Maintenance	10,000,000
Retail	4,000,000
Treasury	1,500,000
Corporate	1,500,000
Management	500,000
Operations	800,000
Enterprise I.T. Governance	1,000,000
Finance	100,000
Legal	50,000
GRC	500,000
Human Capital	50,000
Total allocated	**10,000,000**

Travel Allocation Purpose of Travel determines cost centre	
Travel	10,000,000
Retail	1,500,000
Treasury	1,000,000
Corporate	1,250,000
Management	1,500,000
Operations	500,000
Enterprise I.T. Governance	1,500,000
Finance	250,000
Legal	500,000
GRC	1,000,000
Human Capital	1,000,000
Total allocated	**10,000,000**

CHAPTER 2   AS-IS ENVIRONMENT – NONINTEREST COST MANAGEMENT

2.2.2.1.10 Director, Auditor Fees, and External Professional Services

- The bank's director fees and auditor fees are charged directly to management and rolled down the cost structure.

- Costs of external professional services of banking consultants or lawyers will depend on the business need. If it is directly traceable to a line of business or to product or function (e.g., IT audit by an independent entity), it will be directly allocated to the relevant profit or cost center.

    i. Principles of measurement are as per policies and standards.

    ii. Allocation of Costs – Where fully traceable, the full amount is allocated to the cost object. If it is shared cost, then it is allocated on the basis of an agreed ratio.

Table 2-15e. Direct cost allocation

Direct Cost Director Fees, Auditor fees, External Consultant & Legal Charges				
		Charged to	Management	Line of Business
Director's fees, allowances	2,000,000	Management	2,000,000	
Auditor	3,000,000	Management	3,000,000	
Consultant Fees	6,000,000	Management or Line of Business	1,000,000	Treasury 2,000,000; Corporate Banking 3,000,000
Lawyer	4,000,000			Corporate Banking 4,000,000
	15,000,000		6,000,000	9,000,000
				Treasury: 2,000,000 Corporate: 7,000,000

CHAPTER 2   AS-IS ENVIRONMENT – NONINTEREST COST MANAGEMENT

2.2.2.1.11 Compilation of Direct LOB Cost

The section illustrates the compilation of the direct costs of the lines of business. The roll down of LOB's cost to the products could be based on the total asset/liability value (e.g., home loans to salaried people; three-year time deposits from retired individuals).

Using the data from the tables above, Tables 2-16a and 2-16b illustrate the direct costs of LOBs and the management.

When the P&L transaction is posted, these direct costs update the lines of business profit center code. It is then allocated within the LOB to products and customers.

Table 2-16a. *Line of business – direct cost allocation*

Retail Banking – Direct Cost		Corporate Banking – Direct Cost	
Employee Cost	60,000,000	Employee cost	40,000,000
Enterprise I.T. Governance cost	25,000,000	Enterprise I.T. Governance cost	5,000,000
Premises: Rent & Utilities	7,000,000	Premises: Rent & Utilities	4,000,000
Office supplies	4,000,000	Office supplies	2,000,000
Sales & Marketing	50,000,000	Sales & Marketing	14,000,000
Depreciation on own assets	8,500,000	Depreciation on own assets	4,000,000
Insurance	3,000,000	Insurance	1,000,000
Repairs & Maintenance (non-I.T.)	4,000,000	Repairs & Maintenance (non-I.T.)	1,500,000
Travel	1,500,000	Consultant Fees	3,000,000
Total	163,000,000	Lawyer	4,000,000
		Travel	1,250,000
		Total	79,750,000

The bank's cost management policy should provide guidance on the allocation of management's costs to LOBs.

CHAPTER 2   AS-IS ENVIRONMENT – NONINTEREST COST MANAGEMENT

Table 2-16b. *Line of business – direct cost allocation and management's direct cost*

Treasury – Direct Cost		Management – Direct Cost	
Employee cost	50,000,000	Employee cost	30,000,000
Enterprise I.T. Governance cost	15,000,000	Enterprise I.T. Governance cost	1,000,000
Premises: Rent & Utilities	1,000,000	Premises: Rent & Utilities	500,000
Office supplies	800,000	Office supplies	200,000
Sales & Marketing	1,000,000	Sales & Marketing	15,000,000
Depreciation on own assets	6,000,000	Depreciation on own assets	100,000
Insurance	1,000,000	Repairs & Maintenance (non-I.T.)	500,000
Repairs & Maintenance (non-I.T.)	1,500,000	Director's fees, allowances	2,000,000
Consultant Fees	2,000,000	Auditor	3,000,000
Travel	1,000,000	Consultant	1,000,000
		Travel	1,500,000
Total	**79,300,000**	**Total**	**54,800,000**

Table 2-17 illustrates the allocation of costs gathered under management and rolled down to the lines of business, based on bank policy.

Table 2-17. *Management cost allocation*

Management Cost – Allocated to Lines of Business		
Opening Balance	54,800,000	
	Allocation:	
	Retail	18,200,000
	Corporate	18,400,000
	Treasury	18,200,000

Table 2-18 shows the direct costs of the lines of business *after allocation of management cost.*

CHAPTER 2   AS-IS ENVIRONMENT – NONINTEREST COST MANAGEMENT

Table 2-18. *Total direct cost of lines of business*

Lines of Business Direct Cost after allocation of Management Cost

		Allocation	Total
Retail Banking	163,000,000	18,200,000	181,200,000
Corporate Banking	79,750,000	18,400,000	98,150,000
Treasury	79,300,000	18,200,000	97,500,000
LOB Total			376,850,000
Direct Cost of Support Departments			48,150,000
Total Direct Cost			425,000,000

2.2.2.1.12 Direct LOB Costs – LOB to Products

Each line of business has to define a policy for allocating its direct costs to its product portfolio. Costs that can be fully identified with a specific product are fully charged to it directly.

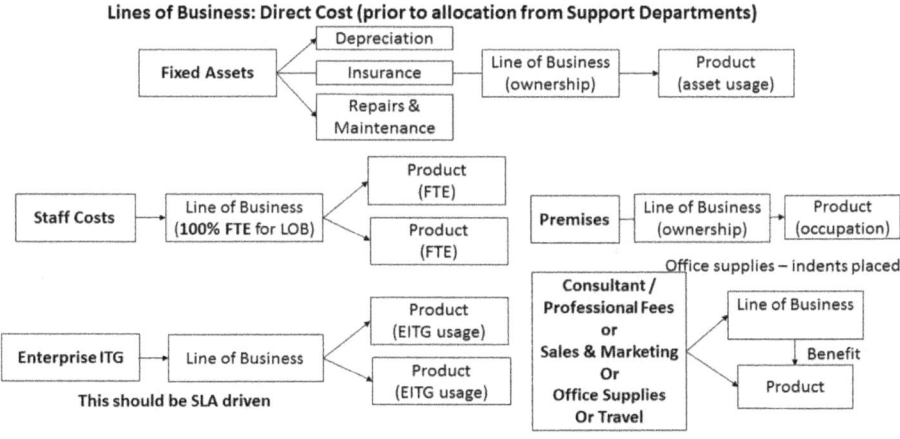

Figure 2-8. *Line of business – cost allocation roll down*

109

CHAPTER 2   AS-IS ENVIRONMENT – NONINTEREST COST MANAGEMENT

Tables 2-18a, 2-18b, and 2-18c show the direct cost of each LOB allocated to its portfolio of products.

An optional measure for allocating line of business costs to products is based on the asset or liability value.

Table 2-18a. *Direct costs of treasury products*

Treasury Products – Direct Cost

	TRBFXF	TRBCRS	TRBIRS	TRICDS	Prodt-5 MM	Prodt-6 Commodity	Prodt-7 Equity	Total
Depreciation	1,000,000	1,000,000	900,000	800,000	800,000	750,000	750,000	6,000,000
Insurance	200,000	200,000	150,000	150,000	100,000	100,000	100,000	1,000,000
Employee cost	7,500,000	7,500,000	9,000,000	8,000,000	8,000,000	5,000,000	5,000,000	50,000,000
Enterprise I.T.G.	3,000,000	3,000,000	2,000,000	2,000,000	2,000,000	1,500,000	1,500,000	15,000,000
Premises	200,000	200,000	150,000	150,000	100,000	100,000	100,000	1,000,000
Office Supplies	150,000	150,000	100,000	100,000	100,000	100,000	100,000	800,000
Sales & Marketing	200,000	200,000	150,000	150,000	100,000	100,000	100,000	1,000,000
Consultant Charges	1,000,000		1,000,000					2,000,000
Repairs & Maint.	300,000	300,000	200,000	200,000	200,000	150,000	150,000	1,500,000
Travel	200,000	200,000	150,000	150,000	100,000	100,000	100,000	1,000,000
Management's Cost	2,600,000	2,600,000	2,600,000	2,600,000	2,600,000	2,600,000	2,600,000	18,200,000
Product Total	16,350,000	15,350,000	16,400,000	14,300,000	14,100,000	10,500,000	10,500,000	97,500,000

Direct staff costs at LOB level can be allocated to products on the basis of the time sheets of the staff. Depreciation, insurance, and repairs and maintenance can be charged on asset usage of products.

Table 2-18b. *Direct costs of retail products*

Retail Products – Direct Cost

	RETSAV	RETFD1	RETHLS	RETCOD	RETCCD	RETLOC	Prodt-7	Total
Depreciation	4,000,000	2,000,000	500,000	500,000	500,000	500,000	500,000	8,500,000
Insurance	1,200,000	800,000	200,000	200,000	200,000	200,000	200,000	3,000,000
Employee cost	15,000,000	12,500,000	12,500,000	5,000,000	5,000,000	5,000,000	5,000,000	60,000,000
Enterprise I.T.G.	7,000,000	3,000,000	5,000,000	2,500,000	2,500,000	2,500,000	2,500,000	25,000,000
Premises	2,000,000	1,500,000	1,500,000	500,000	500,000	500,000	500,000	7,000,000
Office Supplies	1,000,000	1,000,000	1,000,000	250,000	250,000	250,000	250,000	4,000,000
Sales & Marketing	20,000,000	8,000,000	5,000,000	5,000,000	4,000,000	4,000,000	4,000,000	50,000,000
Repairs & Maint.	1,500,000	250,000	250,000	500,000	500,000	500,000	500,000	4,000,000
Travel	300,000	200,000	200,000	200,000	200,000	200,000	200,000	1,500,000
Management's Cost	2,600,000	2,600,000	2,600,000	2,600,000	2,600,000	2,600,000	2,600,000	18,200,000
Product Total	54,600,000	31,850,000	28,750,000	17,250,000	16,250,000	16,250,000	16,250,000	181,200,000

CHAPTER 2 AS-IS ENVIRONMENT – NONINTEREST COST MANAGEMENT

Table 2-18c. *Direct costs of corporate banking products*

Corporate Products – Direct Cost

	CORLCI	CORCOA	CORL10	CORSDL	Prodt-5	Prodt-6	Prodt-7	Total
Depreciation	500,000	500,000	600,000	600,000	600,000	600,000	600,000	4,000,000
Insurance	200,000	200,000	150,000	100,000	150,000	100,000	100,000	1,000,000
Employee	5,000,000	5,000,000	6,000,000	6,000,000	6,000,000	6,000,000	6,000,000	40,000,000
Enterprise I.T.G.	1,000,000	1,000,000	600,000	600,000	600,000	600,000	600,000	5,000,000
Premises	500,000	500,000	600,000	600,000	600,000	600,000	600,000	4,000,000
Office Supplies	250,000	250,000	300,000	300,000	300,000	300,000	300,000	2,000,000
Sales & Marketing	1,000,000	1,000,000	2,400,000	2,400,000	2,400,000	2,400,000	2,400,000	14,000,000
Lawyer's fees				2,000,000			2,000,000	4,000,000
Consultant Charges	1,500,000	1,500,000						3,000,000
Repairs & Maint.	300,000	200,000	200,000	200,000	200,000	200,000	200,000	1,500,000
Travel	125,000	125,000	200,000	200,000	200,000	200,000	200,000	1,250,000
Management's Cost	2,628,000	2,628,000	2,628,000	2,628,000	2,628,000	2,628,000	2,632,000	18,400,000
Product Total	13,003,000	12,903,000	13,678,000	15,628,000	13,678,000	13,628,000	15,632,000	98,150,000

2.2.2.1.13 Support Department's Direct Cost

Tables 2-19a, 2-19b, and 2-19c illustrate the compilation of direct costs of each of the six support department. This data is obtained from Tables 2-15a, 2-15b, 2-15c, and 2-15d.

Table 2-19a. *Direct cost of support departments*

Operations Department's Direct Cost	
Employee cost	2,500,000
Enterprise I.T. Governance cost	300,000
Premises: Rent & Utilities	300,000
Office supplies	200,000
Depreciation on own assets	150,000
Repairs & Maintenance (non-I.T.)	800,000
Travel	500,000
Total	4,750,000

Enterprise I.T. Governance Department's Direct Cost	
Employee cost	5,000,000
Enterprise I.T. Governance cost	1,000,000
Premises: Rent & Utilities	500,000
Office supplies	2,000,000
Depreciation on own assets	600,000
Repairs & Maintenance (non-I.T.)	1,000,000
Travel	1,500,000
Total	11,600,000

The operations department manages the non-IT assets of the bank. It includes owned assets and leased and rental assets.

CHAPTER 2 AS-IS ENVIRONMENT – NONINTEREST COST MANAGEMENT

Table 2-19b. Direct cost of support department

Finance Department's Direct Cost		Legal Department's Direct Cost	
Employee cost	5,000,000	Employee cost	2,500,000
Enterprise I.T. Governance cost	500,000	Enterprise I.T. Governance cost	200,000
Premises: Rent & Utilities	500,000	Premises: Rent & Utilities	200,000
Office supplies	200,000	Office supplies	50,000
Depreciation on own assets	150,000	Depreciation on own assets	50,000
Repairs & Maintenance (non-I.T.)	100,000	Repairs & Maintenance (non-I.T.)	50,000
Travel	250,000	Travel	500,000
Total	**6,700,000**	**Total**	**3,550,000**

Table 2-19c. Direct cost of support departments

GRC Department's Direct Cost		Human Capital Department's Direct Cost	
Employee cost	10,000,000	Employee cost	5,000,000
Enterprise I.T. Governance cost	1,750,000	Enterprise I.T. Governance cost	250,000
Premises: Rent & Utilities	500,000	Premises: Rent & Utilities	500,000
Office supplies	400,000	Office supplies	150,000
Depreciation on own assets	250,000	Depreciation on own assets	200,000
Repairs & Maintenance (non-I.T.)	500,000	Repairs & Maintenance (non-I.T.)	50,000
Travel	1,000,000	Travel	1,000,000
Total	**14,400,000**	**Total**	**7,150,000**

In the as-is environment, banks treat the cost of governance, risk, and compliance in a siloed way. It is important to identify the direct and indirect costs of the GRC function. For example, the cost of risk models owned by a line of business is a direct charge to the line of business. Similarly, the costs of specialized staff risk management functions such as treasury's risk management of derivatives can be allocated directly to the line of business, whereas shared risk management services such as the cost of anti-money laundering functions would need to be allocated based on staff full-time equivalent and transaction/customer volumes.

CHAPTER 2   AS-IS ENVIRONMENT – NONINTEREST COST MANAGEMENT

The improvements to GRC cost management is explained in Section 4.3.3.6 example xxii and Section 4.3.3.8 of Chapter 4.

Table 2-20 is the compilation of the support department's direct costs.

Table 2-20. *Summarized direct cost of support department*

Direct Cost of Lines of Support Departments	
Operations	4,750,000
Enterprise I.T. Governance	11,600,000
Finance	6,700,000
Legal	3,550,000
GRC	14,400,000
Human Capital	7,150,000
Total	48,150,000

The next section is on indirect cost.

2.2.2.2 Indirect Cost

Table 2-21 serves as a "checkpoint" for this example and provides a reference to costs shown in the books of account and the allocation of the costs in the ENICM system.

CHAPTER 2   AS-IS ENVIRONMENT – NONINTEREST COST MANAGEMENT

Table 2-21. *Reference table for this cost allocation example*

Operating Cost - Books of Account	P&L	\multicolumn{4}{c}{ENICM}			
$ - in millions		Direct Cost	Table Refer	Indirect Cost	Table Refer
Depreciation	20	20	2-15a	0	N.A.
Insurance on Assets	5	5	2-15c	0	N.A.
Employee cost	300	210	2-15a	90	2-23
Enterprise I.T. Governance cost	200	50	2-15b	150	2-24
Operations: Premises Rent & Utilities	150	15	2-15b	135	2-25
Operations: Office supplies	100	10	2-15c	90	2-26
Sales & Marketing	80	80	2-15c	0	N.A.
Director's fees	2	2	2-15e	0	N.A.
Audit fees	3	3	2-15e	0	N.A.
Legal fees	4	4	2-15e	0	N.A.
Consultant Charges	6	6	2-15e	0	N.A.
Operations: Repairs & Maint (non-I.T.)	25	10	2-15d	15	2-27
Operations: Travel	10	10	2-15d	0	N.A.
Total	**905**	**425**		**480**	

Indirect costs are allocated to lines of business using the bank's cost management methodology. It is recommended that the methodology is simple, ensures that there is no breach to the bank's allocation error appetite, and maintains data lineage.

Table 2-22a. *Indirect cost – basis for allocation*

		Indirect Cost - Basis for Allocation
Employee cost	90	Staff cost of the Lines of Business are allocated (i)using the Full Time Equivalent & Product Code; (ii) Full Time Equivalence & Customer code. This is based on staff submission. It is approved by the supervisor.
Enterprise I.T. Governance cost	150	Usage of Enterprise I.T. Governance;
Operations: Premises Rent & Utilities	135	Shared Office; Square Feet Occupied
Operations: Office supplies	90	Central Purchasing; Indents placed
Operations: Repairs & Maintenance (non-I.T.)	15	Shared Office - Square Feet Occupied
Total	**480**	

CHAPTER 2   AS-IS ENVIRONMENT – NONINTEREST COST MANAGEMENT

The indirect cost allocation is illustrated in the following sections.

Table 2-22b. *Indirect cost – basis for allocation*

Section	Cost
2.2.2.2.1	Indirect employee cost (where the work has been shared across business products or support functions)
2.2.2.2.2	Indirect EITG cost
2.2.2.2.3	Indirect premises cost
2.2.2.2.4	Indirect office supply cost
2.2.2.2.5	Indirect repairs and maintenance cost

2.2.2.2.1 Indirect Employee Cost

Tables 2-23a, 2-23b, and 2-23c are examples of indirect employee cost on the basis of FTE (staff-product). Table 2-23d is on the basis of FTE (account manager-customer).

Table 2-23a. *Basis of allocating indirect staff costs*

\	\	ENICM System maintains the FTE for all Employees						
Staff Id	Line of Business	Product-Id	Product-Id	Product-Id	Product-Id	Product-Id	Product-Id	Product-Id
Id1	Retail	50%		50%				
Id6	Retail		50%					
Id7	Retail				60%	30%	10%	
Id8	Retail						50%	50%
Id10	Retail		40%	60%				
Staff Id	Line of Business	Product-Id	Product-Id	Product-Id	Product-Id	Product-Id	Product-Id	Product-Id
Id2	Corporate	75%	25%					
Id5	Corporate						75%	25%
Id9	Corporate				60%	40%		
Staff Id	Line of Business	Product-Id	Product-Id	Product-Id	Product-Id	Product-Id	Product-Id	Product-Id
Id3	Treasury				60%	40%		
Id4	Treasury			60%	30%	10%		

115

CHAPTER 2   AS-IS ENVIRONMENT – NONINTEREST COST MANAGEMENT

Extending from Section 2.2.2.1.2 direct staff cost, Table 2-23b shows the indirect staff costs of lines of business. To restate the point on FTE data, this data is prepared by each employee, approved by their supervisor, and captured in the human capital system. The cost is allocated to products based on FTE.

Table 2-23b. *Indirect employee cost on the basis of FTE*

	Human capital indirect cost (pool)
Retail	40,000,000
Treasury	15,000,000
Corporate	35,000,000
Total	**90,000,000**

Table 2-23c. *Indirect employee cost on the basis of FTE*

Retail Products – Employee Indirect Cost
Based on FTE of Retail Banking Employees

	RETSAV	RETFD1	RETHLS	RETCOD	RETCCD	RETLOC	Prodt-7	Total
Employee Indirect Cost	11,000,000	8,500,000	8,500,000	3,000,000	3,000,000	3,000,000	3,000,000	40,000,000

Treasury Products – Employee Indirect Cost
Based on FTE of Treasury Employees

	TRBFXF	TRBCRS	TRBIRS	TRICDS	Prodt-5 MM	Prodt-6 Commodity	Prodt-7 Equity	Total
Employee Indirect Cost	2,250,000	2,250,000	3,000,000	2,500,000	2,500,000	1,000,000	1,000,000	15,000,000

Corporate Products – Employee Indirect Cost
Based on FTE of Corporate Banking Employees

	CORLCI	CORCOA	CORL10	CORSDL	Prodt-5	Prodt-6	Prodt-7	Total
Employee Indirect Cost	8,000,000	7,000,000	4,000,000	4,000,000	4,000,000	4,000,000	4,000,000	35,000,000

The granular level for capturing cost data for lines of business is the customer-product or customer group-product level. From the lowest level, the data can be rolled up as per the requirements of cost management. Table 2-23d gives the template for indirect cost allocation by customer

CHAPTER 2   AS-IS ENVIRONMENT – NONINTEREST COST MANAGEMENT

or customer group. The allocation is done on the basis FTE of account manager. For retail banking, noninterest cost management is at a customer-segment level.

Table 2-23d. *Indirect employee cost on the basis of FTE*

Retail Customer Segments – Employee Indirect Cost
Based on FTE of Retail Banking Employees

	R01	R02	R03	Total
Employee Indirect Cost				40,000,000

Treasury Customers / Customer Groups – Employee Indirect Cost
Based on FTE of Treasury Employees

	TG1	TG2	TC1	TC2	TC3	Total
Employee Indirect Cost						15,000,000

Corporate Customers / Customer Groups – Employee Indirect Cost
Based on FTE of Corporate Banking Employees

	CG1	CG2	CC1	CC2	CC3	Total
Employee Indirect Cost						35,000,000

2.2.2.2.2 Indirect Enterprise IT Governance Cost

Table 2-24a shows the EITG indirect costs allocated to lines of business and support departments. This is based on the costs incurred by EITG (150 million) and the SLAs with each user group.

Table 2-24a. *EITG indirect cost allocation to LOB*

	EITG Indirect Costs
Retail	72,000,000
Treasury	18,000,000
Corporate	30,000,000
	120,000,000
Support departments	30,000,000
Total	150,000,000

Enterprise I.T. Governance Indirect Cost - Allocation	
Retail Banking	72,000,000
Treasury	18,000,000
Corporate Banking	30,000,000
Finance	5,000,000
Legal	1,000,000
GRC	15,000,000
Operations: Premises	1,000,000
Human Capital	8,000,000
Total	150,000,000

CHAPTER 2   AS-IS ENVIRONMENT – NONINTEREST COST MANAGEMENT

Tables 2-24b, 2-24c, and 2-24d provide an overview of cost allocation of EITG cost to products. This is based on usage and tickets raised by helpdesk.

Table 2-24b. *EITG indirect cost allocation to treasury products*

Treasury Products – Enterprise I.T. Governance Service Cost

EITG	TRBFXF	TRBCRS	TRBIRS	TRICDS	Prodt-5 MM	Prodt-6 Commodity	Prodt-7 Equity	Total
Network Usage	2,000,000	2,000,000	2,000,000	2,000,000	1,000,000	500,000	500,000	10,000,000
Helpdesk Management	1,150,000	1,150,000	1,150,000	1,150,000	1,150,000	1,150,000	1,100,000	8,000,000
Total	3,150,000	3,150,000	3,150,000	3,150,000	2,150,000	1,650,000	1,600,000	18,000,000

Table 2-24c. *EITG indirect cost allocation to retail products*

Retail Products – Enterprise I.T. Governance Cost

EITG	RETSAV	RETFD1	RETHLS	RETCOD	RETCCD	RETLOC	Prodt-7	Total
Network Usage	8,000,000	8,000,000	8,000,000	8,000,000	4,000,000	2,000,000	2,000,000	40,000,000
Shared Servers	800,000	700,000	700,000	700,000	700,000	700,000	700,000	5,000,000
Helpdesk Management	9,000,000	6,500,000	3,500,000	2,000,000	2,000,000	2,000,000	2,000,000	27,000,000
Total	17,800,000	15,200,000	12,200,000	10,700,000	6,700,000	4,700,000	4,700,000	72,000,000

Table 2-24d. *EITG indirect cost allocation to corporate banking products*

Corporate Banking Products – Enterprise I.T. Governance Cost

EITG	CORLCI	CORCOA	CORL10	CORSDL	Prodt-5	Prodt-6	Prodt-7	Total
Network Usage	3,500,000	3,500,000	1,500,000	1,500,000	1,500,000	1,500,000	1,000,000	14,000,000
Server Usage	1,000,000	1,000,000	600,000	600,000	600,000	600,000	600,000	5,000,000
Helpdesk	1,800,000	1,800,000	1,500,000	1,500,000	1,500,000	1,500,000	1,400,000	11,000,000
Total	6,300,000	6,300,000	3,600,000	3,600,000	3,600,000	3,600,000	3,000,000	30,000,000

CHAPTER 2   AS-IS ENVIRONMENT – NONINTEREST COST MANAGEMENT

Since almost all software applications are associated to one or more banking product, the usage data is available from system logs and EITG records.

The EITG costs are allocated to customer and customer segments on the basis of transaction volumes.

Technology is used by all departments. Hence, as shown on Table 2-24e, the EITG costs are also allocated to other support departments.

Table 2-24e. *EITG indirect cost allocation to other support departments*

Enterprise I.T. Governance: Indirect cost – Allocated to other Support Departments

EITG	Total Cost	Finance	Legal	GRC	Operations	Human Capital
Helpdesk	18,400,000	4,000,000	700,000	10,000,000	700,000	3,000,000
Network Usage	6,900,000	500,000	200,000	3,000,000	200,000	3,000,000
Server Usage	4,700,000	500,000	100,000	2,000,000	100,000	2,000,000
Total	30,000,000	5,000,000	1,000,000	15,000,000	1,000,000	8,000,000

2.2.2.2.3 Indirect Premises – Rent and Utilities

As shown in Table 2-22a, indirect cost of premises is 135,000,000. Table 2-25a shows this indirect cost, allocated to LOBs and support departments.

CHAPTER 2   AS-IS ENVIRONMENT – NONINTEREST COST MANAGEMENT

Table 2-25a

Operations: Premises Indirect Cost Allocation	
Retail Banking	60,000,000
Treasury	18,000,000
Corporate Banking	30,000,000
Finance	5,000,000
Legal	1,000,000
GRC	7,000,000
Enterprise I.T. Governance	10,000,000
Human Capital	4,000,000
Total	135,000,000

Premises costs are allocated on the basis of the square feet of occupation.

Table 2-25b Premises indirect cost allocation to products

The space occupied by product teams is used as the basis for allocation.

Table 2-25b

Premises Indirect Cost - allocated to Treasury Products
Based on Square Feet Occupied

TRBFXF FX	TRBCRS FX	TRBIRS MM	TRICDS	Prodt-5 MM	Prodt-6 Commodity	Prodt-7 Equity	Total
3,000,000	2,000,000	4,000,000	4,000,000	3,000,000	1,000,000	1,000,000	18,000,000

Premises Indirect Cost - allocated to Retail Products
Based on Square Feet Occupied

RETSAV	RETFD1	RETHLS	RETCOD	RETCCD	RETLOC	Prodt-7	Total
20,000,000	10,000,000	10,000,000	5,000,0000	5,000,0000	5,000,0000	5,000,0000	60,000,000

Premises Indirect Cost - allocated to Corporate Products
Based on Square Feet Occupied

CORLCI	CORCOA	CORL10	CORSDL	Prodt-5	Prodt-6	Prodt-7	Total
7,500,000	7,500,000	3,000,000	3,000,000	3,000,000	3,000,000	3,000,000	30,000,000

2.2.2.2.4 Office Supplies – Indirect Cost

Lines of business and departments place an indent for consumables. Procurement is part of the operations department. It is assumed that the bank has a centralized procurement function. Hence, 90% of the total office supply cost is indirect.

Table 2-26a. *Office supplies – indirect cost allocation*

Operations: Office Supplies Indirect Cost Allocation	
Retail Banking	20,000,000
Treasury	15,000,000
Corporate Banking	25,000,000
Finance	5000,000
Legal	5000,000
GRC	5000,000
Operations	5000,000
Human Capital	10,000,000
Total	90,000,000

The allocation is based on the details of the indent placed. The loans department has a lot of document management activities. Trade financing is inherently a document processing business.

CHAPTER 2 AS-IS ENVIRONMENT – NONINTEREST COST MANAGEMENT

Table 2-26b. *Office supplies – indirect cost allocation*

Office Supplies Indirect Cost - allocated to Treasury Products
Based on Indents

TRBFXF FX	TRBCRS FX	TRBIRS MM	TRICDS	Prodt-5 MM	Prodt-6 Commodity	Prodt-7 Equity	Total
2,500,000	2,500,000	2,000,000	2,000,000	2,000,000	2,500,000	2,50,000	15,000,000

Office Supplies Indirect Cost - allocated to Retail Products
Based on Indents

RETSAV	RETFD1	RETHLS	RETCOD	RETCCD	RETLOC	Prodt-7	Total
9,000,000	6,000,000	1,000,000	1,000,000	1,000,000	1,000,000	1,000,000	20,000,000

Office Supplies- Indirect Cost - allocated to Corporate Products
Based on Indents

CORLCI	CORCOA	CORL10	CORSDL	Prodt-5	Prodt-6	Prodt-7	Total
8,000,000	7,000,000	2,000,000	2,000,000	2,000,000	2,000,000	2,000,000	25,000,000

2.2.2.2.5 Indirect Repairs and Maintenance Cost

The non-IT repairs and maintenance costs are allocated based on the details of the job requests.

Table 2-27a. *Non-IT repairs and maintenance costs*

Operations: Repairs & Maintenance (non-I.T.) Indirect Cost Allocation Branch Repairs & Maintenance	
Retail Banking	10,000,000
Corporate Banking	5,000,000
Total	15,000,000

Repairs to premises is allocated on the basis of the occupation (square feet) by the product groups. Other non-IT repairs could be based on asset ownership.

CHAPTER 2   AS-IS ENVIRONMENT – NONINTEREST COST MANAGEMENT

Table 2-27b. Non-IT repairs and maintenance costs

Repairs & Maintenance (non-I.T.) Indirect Cost - allocated to Retail Products
Branch – Repair & Maintenance

RETSAV	RETFD1	RETHLS	RETCOD	RETCCD	Prodt-6	Prodt-7	Total
2,000,000	2,000,000	3,000,000	750,000	750,000	750,000	750,000	10,000,000

Repairs & Maintenance (non-I.T.) Indirect Cost - allocated to Corporate Banking Products
Branch – Repair & Maintenance

CORLCI	CORCOA	CORL10	CORSDL	Prodt-5	Prodt-6	Prodt-7	Total
1,000,000	1,000,000	600,000	600,000	600,000	600,000	600,000	5,000,000

2.2.2.2.6 Summary of Indirect Cost Allocation

Table 2-28 is a summarization of the allocation of 480 million indirect cost.

Table 2-28. Indirect cost collation and summarization

Indirect Cost	Retail	Treasury	Corporate	Support Departments	Total
Employee	40,000,000	15,000,000	35,000,000		90,000,000
Enterprise I.T. Governance	72,000,000	18,000,000	30,000,000	30,000,000	150,000,000
Operations: Premises	60,000,000	18,000,000	30,000,000,	27,000,000	135,000,000
Operations: Office Supplies	20,000,000	15,000,000	25,000,000	30,000,000	90,000,000
Operations: Repairs & Maintenance	10,000,000	0	5,000,000	0	15,000,000
	202,000,000	66,000,000	125,000,000	87,000,000	480,000,000

Table 2-29 provides a view of the allocation of all indirect costs to lines of business and support departments.

Table 2-29. *Direct and indirect costs by LOBs and support departments*

Direct & Indirect Cost – Lines of Business & Support Departments

	Direct Cost		Indirect Cost		Total
Retail Banking	181,200,000		202,000,000		
Corporate Banking	98,150,000		125,000,000		
Treasury	97,500,000		66,000,000		
		376,850,000		393,000,000	769,850,000
Support					
Operations	4,750,000		5,000,000		9,750,000
Enterprise I.T. Governance	11,600,000		20,000,000		31,600,000
Finance	6,700,000		15,000,000		21,700,000
Legal	3,550,000		3,000,000		6,550,000
GRC	14,400,000		27,000,000		41,400,000
Human Capital	7,150,000		17,000,000		24,150,000
		48,150,000		87,000,000	
Total		425,000,000		480,000,000	905,000,000

2.2.2.3 Allocate Support Department Costs

This section illustrated the allocation of support department costs, after charge in, to lines of business.

Table 2-30a. *Support department costs allocated to LOBs*

Department	Department Cost	Basis for allocating to Lines of Business	Retail	Corporate	Treasury
Legal	6,550,000	Average legal cases over last 5 years	1,550,000	4,000,000	1,000,000
Operations: Premises	9,750,000	Square Feet Occupied	5,000,000	3,000,000	1,750,000
Enterprise I.T. Governance	31,600,000	SLAs with LOBs	12,000,000	10,000,000	9,600,000
Finance	21,700,000	Time - Finance Staff FTE	4,700,000	9,000,000	8,000,000
GRC	41,400,000	Time – GRC Staff FTE	7,400,000	12,000,000	22,000,000
Human Capital	24,150,000	Time – H.R. Staff FTE	13,150,000	7,000,000	4,000,000
Total	135,150,000		43,800,000	45,000,000	46,350,000

CHAPTER 2   AS-IS ENVIRONMENT – NONINTEREST COST MANAGEMENT

The breakdown of the costs shown in Table 2-30a is illustrated in Tables 2-30b, 2-30c, and 2-30d.

A Recap – Please refer to Tables 2-19a, 2-19b, and 2-19c for the opening balances.

Table 2-30b. *Support department costs allocated to LOBs*

Legal Department Cost - Allocation to LOBs			
Opening Balance	3,550,000		
Indirect cost Charge In:		Allocation	
Premises	1,000,000	Retail	1,550,000
Enterprise I.T. Governance	1,000,000	Treasury	1,000,000
Office Supplies	1,000,000	Corporate	4,000,000
Total	6,550,000		6,550,000

Operations Department Cost - Allocation to LOBs			
Opening Balance	4,750,000		
Indirect cost Charge In:		Allocation	
Enterprise I.T. Governance	1,000,000	Retail	5,000,000
Office Supplies	4,000,000	Treasury	1,750,000
		Corporate	3,000,000
Total	9,750,000		9,750,000

Table 2-30c. *Support department costs allocated to LOBs*

Enterprise I.T. Governance Department Cost Allocation to LOBs			
Opening Balance	11,600,000		
Indirect cost Charge In:		Allocation	
Premises	10,000,000	Retail	12,000,000
Office Supplies	10,000,000	Treasury	9,600,000
		Corporate	10,000,000
Total	31,600,000		31,600,000

Finance Department - Cost allocation to LOBs			
Opening Balance	6,700,000		
Indirect cost Charge In:		Allocation	
Premises	5,000,000	Retail	4,700,000
Enterprise I.T. Governance	5,000,000	Treasury	8,000,000
Office Supplies	5,000,000	Corporate	9,000,000
Total	21,700,000		21,700,000

Table 2-30d. *Support department costs allocated to LOBs*

GRC Department - Cost allocation to LOBs			
Opening Balance	14,400,000		
Indirect cost Charge In:		Allocation	
Premises	7,000,000	Retail	7,4000,000
Enterprise I.T. Governance	15,000,000	Treasury	22,000,000
Office Supplies	5,000,000	Corporate	12,000,000
Total	41,400,000		41,400,000

Human Capital Department		Cost allocation to LOBs	
Opening Balance	7,150,000		
Indirect cost Charge In:		Allocation	
Premises	4,000,000	Retail	13,150,000
Enterprise I.T. Governance	8,000,000	Treasury	4,000,000
Office Supplies	5,000,000	Corporate	7,000,000
Total	24,150,000		24,150,000

The book recommends that banks have internal SLAs between lines of business and GRC. The SLAs could form the basis for indirect GRC cost allocation.

2.2.2.4 Lines of Business – Direct and Indirect Cost

This table shows that after cost allocation, the source accounting book and the target cost accounts in the ENICM system *are in balance.*

Table 2-31. Financial and costing books are in balance

	Total Cost (Direct+ Indirect Cost)	Allocation of Support Department Cost	Total
Retail Banking	383,200,000	43,800,000	427,000,000
Corporate Banking	223,150,000	45,000,000	268,150,000
Treasury	163,500,000	46,350,000	209,850,000
Total	769,850,000	135,150,000	905,000,000

2.2.3 Noninterest Cost of Products

This section provides an overview of the cost of products. The direct cost of the products are from the tables.

CHAPTER 2   AS-IS ENVIRONMENT – NONINTEREST COST MANAGEMENT

2.2.3.1 Noninterest Cost of Treasury Products

Table 2-32a. *Noninterest cost of treasury products*

Cost of Treasury Products

	TRBFXF	TRBCRS	TRBIRS	TRICDS	Prodt-5 MM	Prodt-6 Commodity	Prodt-7 Equity	Total
Direct Cost	16,350,000	15,350,000	16,400,000	14,300,000	14,100,000	10,500,000	10,500,000	**97,500,000**
Indirect Cost								
Employee	2,250,000	2,250,000	3,000,000	2,500,000	2,500,000	1,250,000	1,250,000	**15,000,000**
Enterprise I.T. Governance	3,150,000	3,150,000	3,150,000	3,150,000	2,150,000	1,650,000	1,600,000	**18,000,000**
Premises	3,000,000	2,000,000	4,000,000	4,000,000	3,000,000	1,000,000	1,000,000	**18,000,000**
Office Supplies	2,500,000	2,500,000	2,500,000	2,500,000	2,000,000	1,500,000	1,500,000	**15,000,000**
Support Services	6,630,000	6,630,000	6,630,000	6,630,000	6,630,000	6,630,000	6,570,000	**46,350,000**
Total	33,880,000	31,880,000	35,680,000	33,080,000	30,380,000	22,530,000	22,40,000	**209,850,000**

2.2.3.2 Noninterest Cost of Retail Products

Table 2-32b. *Noninterest cost of retail products*

Cost of Retail Products

	RETSAV	RETFD1	RETHLS	RETCOD	RETCCD	RETLOC	Prodt-7	Total
Direct Cost	54,600,000	31,850,000	28,750,000	17,250,000	16,250,000	16,250,000	16,250,000	**181,200,000**
Indirect Cost								
Employee	11,000,000	8,500,000	8,500,000	3,000,000	3,000,000	3,000,000	3,000,000	**40,000,000**
Enterprise I.T. Governance	17,800,000	15,200,000	12,200,000	10,700,000	6,700,000	4,700,000	4,700,000	**72,000,000**
Premises	20,000,000	10,000,000	10,000,000	5,000,000	5,000,000	5,000,000	5,000,000	**60,000,000**
Office Supplies	9,000,000	6,000,000	1,000,000	1,000,000	1,000,000	1,000,000	1,000,000	**20,000,000**
Repairs&Maint.	1,250,000	1,250,000	2,500,000	1,250,000	1,250,000	1,250,000	1,250,000	**10,000,000**
Support Services	6,258,000	6,257,000	6,257,000	6,257,000	6,257,000	6,257,000	6,257,000	**43,800,000**
Total	119,908,000	79,057,000	69,207,000	44,457,000	39,457,000	37,457,000	37,457,000	**427,000,000**

2.2.3.3 Noninterest Cost of Corporate Banking Products

Table 2-32c. *Noninterest cost of corporate banking products*

Cost of Corporate Banking Products

	CORLCI	CORCOA	CORL10	CORSDL	Prodt-5	Prodt-6	Prodt-7	Total
Direct Cost	13,003,000	12,903,000	13,678,000	15,628,000	13,678,000	13,628,000	15,632,000	**98,150,000**
Indirect Cost								
Employee	8,000,000	7,000,000	4,000,000	4,000,000	4,000,000	4,000,000	4,000,000	**35,000,000**
Enterprise I.T. Governance	6,300,000	6,300,000	3,600,000	3,600,000	3,600,000	3,600,000	3,000,000	**30,000,000**
Premises	7,500,000	7,500,000	3,000,000	3,000,000	3,000,000	3,000,000	3,000,000	**30,000,000**
Office Supplies	8,000,000	7,000,000	2,000,000	2,000,000	2,000,000	2,000,000	2,000,000	**25,000,000**
Repairs&Maint.	1,250,000	1,250,000	500,000	500,000	500,000	500,000	500,000	**5,000,000**
Support Services	12,500,000	12,500,000	4,000,000	4,000,000	4,000,000	4,000,000	4,000,000	**45,000,000**
Total	56,553,000	54,453,000	30,778,000	32,728,000	30,778,000	30,728,000	32,132,000	**268,150,000**

2.2.4 Costs of Customer/Customer Segment

This section provides an overview of the cost of customers and customer groups/segments. In the as-is environment, the approach to allocating noninterest costs to customers is as follows:

Direct Cost to Customer – This could be legal expenses.

Indirect costs:

- Employee – The account or relationship manager (FTE).

- System – This could be allocated (i) using system usage, e.g., volumes of transactions to the account/ATM transactions/credit card transactions/from the allocation to the products, or (ii) allocated from the products (Section 2.2.3).

All other costs, associated with line of business or support department, have limited direct connection to the customer. Hence, the product costs are charged to the customers to balance the costing books.

CHAPTER 2   AS-IS ENVIRONMENT – NONINTEREST COST MANAGEMENT

2.2.4.1 Retail Customer Cost

Table 2-33a. *Noninterest customer-product – retail banking*

Retail Banking: Customer Segment-Product Cost

Mass Market ↓	RETSAV	RETFD1	RETHLS	RETCOD	Prodt-5	Prodt-6	Prodt-7	Total
R01: High Net Worth								
R02: Salaried Employees	\multicolumn{7}{The metrics for allocating the total products costs could be (i) balance of the account (ii) account activity (iii) time spent by staff and (iv) special technology service deployment. Iii & iv are relevant for High Net Worth segment.}	
R03 - Self-Employed Individuals								
Total	119,908,000	79,057,000	69,207,000	44,457,000	39,457,000	37,457,000	37,457,000	**427,000,000**

Direct cost could include premises. Some banks have dedicated technology enabled premises for high-net-worth customers.

The indexing of data should facilitate customer-product views. Customer segment is a rolled-up value of underlying customer records.

Table 2-33b. *Noninterest cost – retail customer group*

Retail Customer Segment cost

Mass Market →	R01 High Net Worth	R02 Salaried Employees	R03 Self-Employed Individuals	Total
Direct Cost				
Indirect Cost				
Employee				
Enterprise I.T. Governance				
Premises				
Office Supplies				
Repairs & Maint				
Management				
Support Services				
				427,000,000

The indirect costs are allocated from cost pools using **customer_segment and product combination**. The ENICM database should be designed to support data processing using the combined data-item

or

the retail product costs shown in Table 2-32b are allocated to the customer segments using average balance or account activity volume.

CHAPTER 2   AS-IS ENVIRONMENT – NONINTEREST COST MANAGEMENT

2.2.4.2 Corporate Customer Cost

Table 2-33c. *Noninterest cost – corporate banking customer or customer group*

Corporate Customer Cost

	CG1	CG2	CC1	CC2	CC3	Total
Direct Cost						79,750,000
Indirect Cost						
Employee						35,000,000
Enterprise I.T. Governance						30,000,000
Premises						30,000,000
Office Supplies						25,000,000
Repairs & Maint.						5,000,000
Management						18,400,000
Support Services						45,000,000
Total						268,150,000

> In corporate banking, customer profitability could be tracked using the 80-20 principle. Customers that bring in 80% of the revenue, are tracked individually.
> Others are categorised by industrial segment. In the former case, the ENICM database design should support the combined data-item, customer_product.

Table 2-33d. *Noninterest customer-product – corporate banking*

Corporate Banking Customer Group-Product Cost

	CORLCI	CORCOA	CORL10	CORSDL	Prodt-5	Prodt-6	Prodt-7	Total
CG1								
CG2								
CC1								
CC2								
CC3								
Total	56,725,000	54,425,000	30,750,000	30,750,000	32,700,000	30,700,000	32,100,000	268,150,000

> the corporate banking product costs shown in Table 2-32c are allocated to the customer or customer segments using average balance or account activity volume.

2.2.5 Branch

This section provides an overview of the cost of each branch, and the approach to allocating noninterest costs to customers is as follows:

- Direct Cost to Branch – These are mostly Operations related.

- Systems like ATM or customer service kiosks are part of bank's premises. If it is located in a branch, then the cost can be directly allocated to the branch.

CHAPTER 2   AS-IS ENVIRONMENT – NONINTEREST COST MANAGEMENT

Indirect Costs

Employee and Systems – This is allocated from the products.

As customers have a home branch, it is important to have that as part of master data in ENICM system.

All other costs will be allocated from LOBs or products, and the books are balanced.

The total retail banking cost is 427,000,000, and for corporate banking, total cost is 268,150,000. The total cost of 695,150,000 is assumed as total branch costs.

Table 2-34a. *Branch cost*

	Branch Cost					
	Branch-1	Branch-2	Branch-3	Branch-4	Branch-'nnnn'	Total
Direct Cost						242,750,000
Indirect Cost						
Employee						75,000,000
Enterprise I.T. Governance						102,000,000
Premises						90,000,000
Office Supplies						45,000,000
Repairs & Maint.						15,000,000
Management						36,600,000
Support Services						88,800,000
Total						695,150,000

Table 2-34b. *Branch cost by lines of business*

Branch Cost

	Retail Banking	Corporate Banking	Total
Direct Cost	163,000,000	79,750,000	242,750,000
Indirect Cost			
Employee	40,000,000	35,000,000	75,000,000
Enterprise I.T. Governance	72,000,000	30,000,000	102,000,000
Premises	60,000,000	30,000,000	90,000,000
Office Supplies	20,000,000	25,000,000	45,000,000
Repairs & Maint.	10,000,000	5,000,000	15,000,000
Management	18,200,000	18,400,000	36,600,000
Support Services	43,800,000	45,000,000	88,800,000
Total	427,000,000	268,150,000	695,150,000

2.2.6 Product Noninterest Revenue

Source-System Generated Entries

Software solutions, like the core banking or trade finance, automatically debit the customer for fee, commission, and charges, as per application configuration. There could also be entries. In all cases, the relevant profit center codes should be captured for processing in the ENICM system.

Table 2-35. *Product noninterest revenue*

Treasury Products – Non-interest Direct Revenue							
	TRBFXF	TRBCRS	TRBIRS	TRICDS	Prodt-5 MM	Prodt-6 Commodity	Prodt-7 Equity	Total
Fees								
Commission								
Charges								

Retail Banking Products – Non-interest Direct Revenue							
	RETSAV	RETFD1	RETHLS	RETCOD	RETCCD	RETLOC	Prodt-7	Total
Fees								
Commission								
Charges								

Corporate Banking Products – Non-interest Direct Revenue							
	CORLCI	CORCOA	CORL10	CORSDL	Prodt-5	Prodt-6	Prodt-7	Total
Fees								
Commission								
Charges								

2.3 Siloed Consequences

From the above, we can infer that what is happening in the as-is environment is a "regrouping" of the P&L accounts under cost centers and a full charge out to products and customers.

While this gives a cost accountant a template to view the costs, the siloed environment does not support accurate cost measurement and makes it challenging to monitor and manage noninterest costs.

In the as-is environment, the processing components are less harmonious. The enterprise architecture is not the sum total of the underlying simple components. Therefore, it is necessary to decompose and construct the enterprise into logical parts such as services and data elements.

CHAPTER 2 AS-IS ENVIRONMENT – NONINTEREST COST MANAGEMENT

A bank could choose a service-oriented architecture or a microservice architecture approach and then build a loosely coupled, *interoperable set of components*[1] that are consistent with enterprise architecture principles.

Time-driven ABC uses time and unit cost of activity, derived from resources used, to measure the utilized capacity.

Table 2-36a. *As-is environment – total resource supplied = total used*

Retail Banking		Total Cost Allocated
Total Supplied	As is: Cost of resources supplied is 'assumed' as fully utilised	427,000,000
Total Used		427,000,000
Unused Capacity	In the 'as is' environment, this is not measured by most banks.	

Corporate Banking		Total Cost Allocated
Total Supplied	As is: Cost of resources supplied is 'assumed' as fully utilised	268,150,000
Total Used		268,150,000
Unused Capacity	In the 'as is' environment, this is not measured by most banks	

Treasury		Total Cost Allocated
Total Supplied	As is: Cost of resources supplied is 'assumed' as fully utilised	209,850,000
Total Used		209,850,000
Unused Capacity	In the 'as is' environment, this is not measured by most banks	

Table 2-36b illustrates the breakup of bank staff costs by lines of business, direct (dedicated), shared indirect staff costs and support staff cost allocations.

---

[1] Interoperability – http://eitbokwiki.org/Interoperability

Table 2-36b. *Staff cost of lines of business*

Staff costs of lines of business				
	Retail banking	Corporate banking	Treasury	Total
Direct staff costs – 100% FTE	60,000,000	40,000,000	50,000,000	150,000,000
Allocation				
Management staff cost	10,000,000	10,000,000	10,000,000	120,000,000
Indirect staff costs of LOBs using FTE	40,000,000	35,000,000	15,000,000	
Total LOB staff cost	110,000,000	85,000,000	75,000,000	270,000,000
Support department Staff cost				30,000,000
Total staff cost				300,000,000

Support department costs are allocated to lines of business on the basis of internal service level agreements, policies, and procedures.

Some banks build surplus capacity to manage growth in the short term. Banks also build redundancy for being resilient. The redundancy cost is a business continuity management cost and the bank's ENICM policy will determine the allocation of it to the lines of business, products and branches.

Please compare Table 2-36 with Table 3-9 in Section 3.6, Chapter 3.

CHAPTER 2 AS-IS ENVIRONMENT – NONINTEREST COST MANAGEMENT

The following are the consequences of a siloed and legacy environment:

i. The senior management has limited information on profitability. Even in banks that invest in technology, senior managers have data on profits but not accurate data on profitability. They do not have wholesome data on profit margins, cost of risk management, and customer-related expenses such as selling, marketing, and customer support. Banks need to have data and a methodology to accurately determine customer and product profitability.

ii. Bank is unable to build an enterprise risk-adjusted return model.

iii. There is no actionable intelligence for minimizing unutilized capacity. Staff productivity, return on investment in technology, and resource utilization cannot be measured accurately.

iv. Pricing of loans could be erroneous.

v. The bank management is unable to get a grip over the behavior of costs.

vi. There are frequent internal disputes at the senior management level over the issues of cost allocation and funds transfer pricing.

vii. Service level management is inadequate.

viii. The bank is unable to implement a process improvement culture.

CHAPTER 2   AS-IS ENVIRONMENT – NONINTEREST COST MANAGEMENT

ix. It is a challenge to identify nonvalue adding activities.

x. Unable to monitor the cost of controls.

xi. Difficulty in setting and monitoring key performance indicators and key risk indicators.

xii. Limited success with quality improvement programs and unable to quantify the cost of quality.

xiii. Customer experience goals are not accomplished.

2.4 To-Be Enterprise Operating Model

Section 1.8.2 in Chapter 1 provides an introduction into a complex operating environment. The complexity is a consequence of a business function-centric computerization of a bank. The focus has not been on the delivery of (a) timely, consistent, and clean data to internal consumers and (b) actionable intelligence to decision-makers. Until now, in a bank's computerization projects, data was a "by-product."

Most banks do not have an ENICM system. Even those who have a system find the as-is architecture a constraint to efficiently manage cost data. At the source, banks should be able to capture noninterest cost transaction data related to product, customer, cost, or profit center. The update of financial and costing books should be done in the same instance. Enterprise data management should facilitate establishing the data lineage from data capture to the final noninterest cost data allocation process.

CHAPTER 2   AS-IS ENVIRONMENT – NONINTEREST COST MANAGEMENT

Target Enterprise Operating Model – Gaps

Sections 2.4.1, 2.4.2, 2.4.3, 2.4.4, 2.4.5, and 2.4.6 highlight the limitations or weaknesses that prevent a bank from having an activity-based ENICM and ERRM **capabilities.** Banks should resolve these gaps in order to improve operational efficiency and operating leverage.

2.4.1 Risk Culture, Focus on Profitability, and Preventive Controls[2]

It is important that the bank management treats activity-based enterprise noninterest cost management (AENICM) as a component of enterprise risk-adjusted return management (ERRM). The risk culture manifests itself in the business approach. Examples include a "Too Big to fail" business approach, unfair practices, indifference toward regulatory compliance, complex product offering, and aggressive selling of products and services.

A weak risk culture is reflected in

- Corrupt business ethics and unacceptable business practices
- Aggressive business targets
- Inadequate business capabilities such as enterprise risk-adjusted return management and activity based enterprise cost management
- Failure in improving profitability
- Lack of independence for audit and governance, risk, and compliance functions

---

[2] Corporate governance principles for banks- https://www.bis.org/bcbs/publ/d328.pdf

2.4.2 Process-Based Enterprise Operating Model

A bank's enterprise operating model defines the delivery mechanism to accomplish its business goals. It comprises products and services, staff, systems, policies, and procedures. In executing the model, the bank is able to deliver business to the markets. There is an associated cost and risk. The efficiency and maturity of the model determines the bank's ability to create value for its customers at optimized cost and minimal risk. The process approach to managing operations has found acceptance in many banks. A significant number of banks in advanced countries and in emerging markets have documented their banking processes. Banking processes drive the flow of business delivery. A continuous process improvement culture significantly improves the efficiency of the model.

2.4.3 Performance, Risk, Control, and Cost – Policies and Procedures

It is not possible for a bank to implement an effective enterprise risk-adjusted return model without a stable activity-based enterprise noninterest cost management system.

To implement an ABC or TDABC cost model, banks must identify the activities that comprise a banking process, assign resources, and identify cost drivers for allocating the overhead. The allocation rules should ensure that a cost is not allocated more than once.

Figure 2-9 illustrates the relationship between the two models.

CHAPTER 2 AS-IS ENVIRONMENT – NONINTEREST COST MANAGEMENT

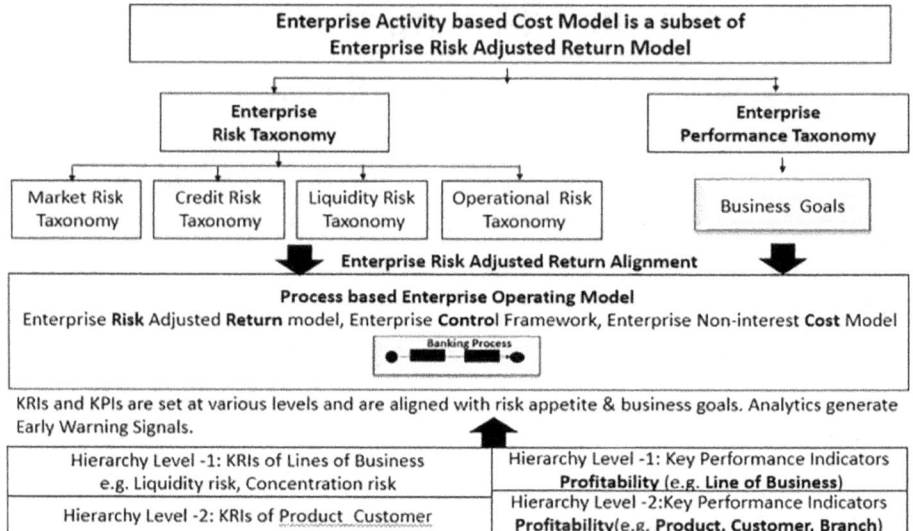

Figure 2-9. *Taxonomy – ERRM and AENICM models are intertwined.*

Policies are decision-making guidelines. Risk management process is the transformation of business goals into outputs based on procedures that define the sequence of business tasks. Risk management processes use risk models with in-built intelligence. Lack of best practices or a weak implementation of policies and procedures has been the root cause for poor performance of banks.

Risk Appetite Statement (RAS) and Alignment with Controls and Cost

The RAS is an important component of an ERRM program, and implementation requirements depend on the size and complexity of the bank's operations. Risk appetite represents the levels of risk a bank is willing to take in pursuit of its objectives. A high-risk appetite indicates an aggressive approach to business and has a direct impact on its capital and resources.

CHAPTER 2   AS-IS ENVIRONMENT – NONINTEREST COST MANAGEMENT

A RAS offers a systematic and holistic approach to managing risk exposures and concentration. The guidance provided in the RAS factors the (i) severity of the risk as assessed by appropriate formulas or models and (ii) the direction of risk. This refers to the movement of the residual risk over the previous period (e.g., 12 months) and projected over the next 12 months.

Operationalizing the RAS requires the definition of the risk limits and configuring the risk management processes with the values. A risk limit has three components: (i) a metric, (ii) a risk mitigation procedure, and (iii) a bound — a value that should not be breached.

2.4.4 Organization Structure and Human Capital

Organization structure is closely linked to corporate governance and risk culture. This is the responsibility of the management, and it cannot be "treated" like a technical or business functional gap.

Figure 2-10. To-be – bank's organization structure

Most medium and small banks merge technology and operations divisions under one department. Given the digitalization of the banking business, this is *not recommended* and it is important that even small-sized banks have a *separate enterprise IT governance department*.

The cost management function could fold under the chief financial officer (finance department). The work will involve active interaction with the lines of business and the GRC department.

2.4.5 Enterprise IT Governance, Enterprise Process Automation

An agile bank of the future should build new capabilities and improve existing ones. It is widely acknowledged that the lack of data is a major constraint for improving enterprise risk-adjusted returns and accurate enterprise noninterest cost management.

Data Challenges (A Recap)

- Chart of accounts.

Section 2.1 gives an appreciation of the chart of accounts. Some banks do not have an enterprise cost chart of accounts function, and some of those who have a costing chart of accounts have not synchronized the financial and costing charts.

- Cost data capture at source.
- Lack of an enterprise IT governance tool.
- The human capital management system is rudimentary, and it is not possible to have wholesome data on the employees.

Figure 2-11a and Table 2-37 provide an overview of the core capabilities required for improving operational efficiency and operating leverage.

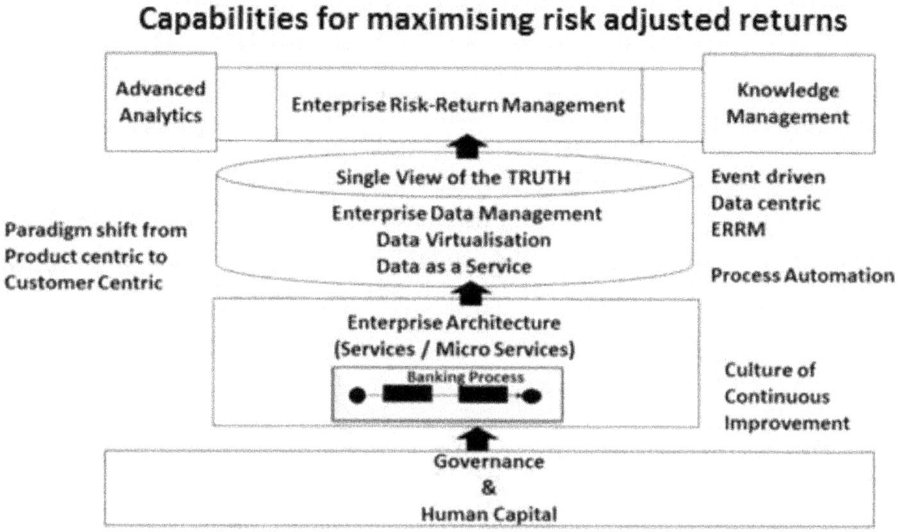

CHAPTER 2 AS-IS ENVIRONMENT – NONINTEREST COST MANAGEMENT

Capabilities for maximising risk adjusted returns

```
                    ┌──────────────────────────────┐
[Advanced          │ Enterprise Risk-Return       │         [Knowledge
 Analytics]        │ Management                   │          Management]
                    └──────────────────────────────┘
                              ▲
                    ╭─────────────────────────╮
                    │  Single View of the TRUTH│   Event driven
                    │  Enterprise Data Management│  Data centric
Paradigm shift from │  Data Virtualisation     │   ERRM
Product centric to  │  Data as a Service       │
Customer Centric    ╰─────────────────────────╯   Process Automation
                              ▲
                    ┌──────────────────────────────┐
                    │ Enterprise Architecture      │
                    │ (Services / Micro Services)  │   Culture of
                    │   ●■━━■●  Banking Process    │   Continuous
                    └──────────────────────────────┘   Improvement
                              ▲
                    ┌──────────────────────────────┐
                    │         Governance           │
                    │             &                │
                    │       Human Capital          │
                    └──────────────────────────────┘
```

Figure 2-11a. *Capability structure for maximizing enterprise risk-adjusted return*

Gap resolution for attaining the target ERRM and AENICM models should be done in a holistic way. The nuances of the business requirements, business targets, risk management capabilities, and risk appetite *vary by bank*.

Table 2-37. *Capabilities required for AENICM and ERRM*

Capability	Basis
Enterprise risk adjusted return model – methodology.	Methods, Models, Techniques – Data Science
Enterprise Architecture - Services Oriented Architecture / Micro-Services Architecture; Event driven	Architecture
Enterprise Banking Processes – Automation, Robotic Process automation	Architecture, Technology, Process Improvement, Data Science
Enterprise Data Management; Data is an Asset (as custodian, data is a liability that needs to secured and protected)	Data Science
Date Lake & Data Warehouse, Data Virtualisation, Data as a Service, Data Streaming, Graph Database, In-memory management.	
Knowledge Management	Architecture & Technology
Enterprise Liquidity Hub	Data Science
Real Time, Simultaneous checking of all risk types	
Human Capital Management	Knowledge Culture; Data Science
Optimise Risk adjusted return	Risk Culture
Improved Risk Measures	Methods, Models, Techniques Data Science

CHAPTER 2   AS-IS ENVIRONMENT – NONINTEREST COST MANAGEMENT

In the as-is environment, the fragmented datasets appear like "spaghetti boxes" and operations are complex. As banks delay their decision to transform, they continue to invest in technology in an incremental way. For instance, many banks implemented the blockchain technology in areas such as trade finance and payments. The usage of the technology in these areas has its merits. However, what the banks have added is one more layer of complexity to their enterprise architecture. This is an example of product or technology-centric approach, as the new "layer" is *expected to work* seamlessly with other disparate systems and fragmented data repositories.

Knowledge management and advanced analytics are explained in the next chapter under improving operating leverage.

Figure 2-11b provides a high level view of a process-based business architecture. It is an enriched version of Figure 1-17 in Chapter 1 as it introduces the elements of enterprise process automation and activity-based enterprise noninterest cost management.

Figure 2-11b. *To-be – business architecture*

As a banking process is orchestrated, the order of update is the accounting books and then the ENICM system. While the GL is indexed on the account code and is governed by the chart of accounts, the enterprise cost database is indexed on the cost/profit center code and is governed by a costing chart of accounts. *Sections 3.4.3, 3.4.4, 3.4.5, 3.4.6, 3.4.7, 3.4.8, 3.4.9, and 3.4.10 in Chapter 3 further explain services-based enterprise architecture, process automation, and data management.*

Activity-based enterprise noninterest cost management **(AENICM)** is a critical capability required for decision-making and is a core component of ERRM. Without timely and updated information on costs, companies end up making highly subjective and ad hoc decisions. Sometimes, these decisions are simply based on "what has worked in the past."

A bank that has implemented cost management will have the ability to know the actual cost of doing business from different perspectives. The costs can be rolled up or down in various levels including process and product levels. This provides sufficient data to senior management for pricing the products and to manage their noninterest cost budgets.

When "cost of maintaining customer accounts" is known, the bank can take a decisions on what can be levied as charges for account operations and take steps to reduce the cost of the enterprise operating model. The cost of a process is a metric for process improvement. A good design for the AENICM system will establish data lineage and eliminate the need for reconciliation with the general ledger.

2.4.6 To-Be ENICM System

ENICM System

A weak enterprise cost management model does not allow a bank to accurately measure the net profitability at various levels such as corporate customer, product, branch, or geography.

CHAPTER 2   AS-IS ENVIRONMENT – NONINTEREST COST MANAGEMENT

Figure 2-12 illustrates the three main objectives of an ENICM system. The system should (a) capture costs **at origination**, (b) update the ENICM system with direct costs as the financial transaction is posted, (c) allocate indirect costs as per policy and procedure, (d) determine profitability by various dimensions (e.g., line of business, product, customer, branch), and (e) ensure data consistency between the ENICM system and the books of account.

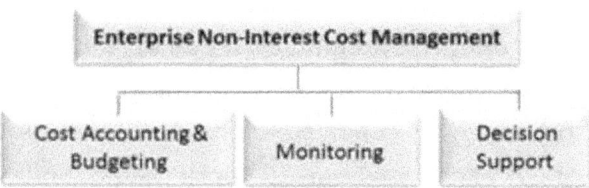

Figure 2-12. *Three main objectives of an ENICM system*

A process-based, bottom-up, activity-based enterprise cost model is built by analyzing banking processes and activities across lines of business and front-office, middle-office (risk management), and back-office functions.

With this level of granularity, banks can implement an effective continuous process improvement program and accomplish their operational efficiency objectives. This is illustrated in Figure 2-13.

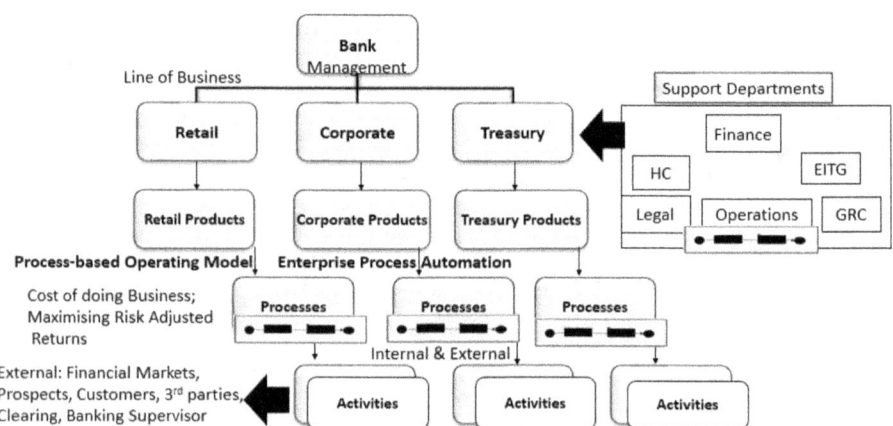

Figure 2-13. *To-be – cost allocation using process automation*

146

CHAPTER 2   AS-IS ENVIRONMENT – NONINTEREST COST MANAGEMENT

ENICM System Components

In a process-automated environment, all business activities are identified and modeled. It is possible to capture cost data at origination and measure the cost of a business process accurately.

ABC and TDABC minimize subjectivity in accounting for costs by tracing costs through activities. The methodology guides on (a) what activities are really needed (value-added activities) in order to accomplish a mission, deliver a service, or meet customer demand; (b) how activities can be modified to achieve cost savings or product, function, and process improvements; and (c) what are the nonvalue adding activities.

Figure 2-14 illustrates the to-be activity-based enterprise noninterest cost management system components. The cost is captured at source, and the accounting and costing books are updated simultaneously.

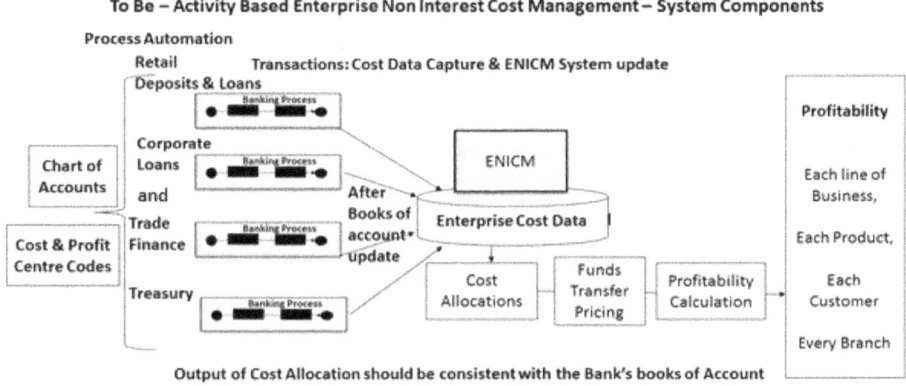

Figure 2-14. *To-be AENICM components*

The next chapter explains the business process management suite (BPMS) technology and hyperautomation, with automation examples.

147

CHAPTER 3

Using Hyperautomation for implementing Time-Driven ABC

This chapter focuses on using the business process management suite technology for enterprise process automation. Sections 3.1, 3.2, and 3.3 provide an introduction into services- and process-based enterprise operating model, enterprise architecture, and enterprise data management. These are **capabilities** that a bank should build or improve on.

The quality of data determines the accuracy of the noninterest cost allocation and profitability calculations. This book recommends that a bank pays attention to what data it has prior to selecting a method or a model to manage risks, controls, and costs. Many ABC and TDABC implementations have been ineffective because of data quality issues. Mature enterprise data governance ensures that the enterprise noninterest cost model is "fit for purpose."

CHAPTER 3   USING HYPERAUTOMATION FOR IMPLEMENTING TIME-DRIVEN ABC

By choosing a process-based approach, a bank is better placed, to align data with processes and establish data lineage. An event and loosely coupled, services-based, data as a service enterprise architecture improves the accuracy of ENICM and ERRM systems. Figure 3-1 provides an overview of this approach.

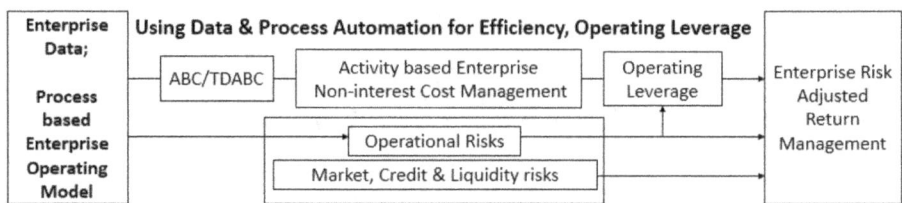

Figure 3-1. *Data-centric, process-automated operations*

Section 3.4 explains enterprise process automation using hyperautomation. Using a bill of resources is a unique feature of this book, and this is explained using the examples on enterprise process automation and the examples on monitoring operating leverage in Chapter 4.

Section 3.5 uses the previous Chapter 2 cost allocation example to explain how time-driven ABC can easily be implemented using hyperautomation. Finally, Section 3.6 provides dashboards that summarizes granular performance, risk, control, and cost management.

3.1 Services- and Process-Based Enterprise Operating Model

In the as-is environment, several technical processes are not aligned with the business processes. Banks are restrained by vendor-provided workarounds, and in some functional areas, the software solutions are entangled with business processes and procedures. These are complex environments that do not have a *"true"* straight through processing environment. There are "store and forward mechanisms" that are not visible to the user. The growth in transactional volumes has increased the complexity of the processing environment.

The enterprise operating model of a bank comprises of production and nonproduction environments. The nonproduction environment refers to activities in the noncustomer service offices and the "testing environments" of GRC and enterprise IT.

The nonproduction environment has its share of direct and indirect costs and risk.

The agile bank of the future will be able to create more value for its customers by adopting the frameworks and technologies recommended in this book. It is important to implement a governance framework that manages operations within a *single enterprise framework.*

3.2 Enterprise Architecture

An end-to-end automation of a bank using relevant technologies is a challenge for most banks. This requires a multidisciplinary team with experience in managing change and executing a large business transformation program. New banks will need to ensure that their approach and methodologies are in keeping with international best practices and implement frameworks that give them the capabilities and competencies to derive the advantage of economies of scale and compete with established banks.

Banking operations can change from a complex, siloed, hardwired environment into a set of coherent, loosely coupled, business activities that are intelligent, services based, *event driven*,[1] process automated and have a data-centric model.

The transformed bank will have customer-oriented business model that is powered by knowledge and managed on an exception basis, by a skilled workforce.

The benefits of the transformation can be seen at the bank's shop floor level. There is more automation and less people. Improved process efficiency leads to better customer experience.

Service-Oriented Architecture (SOA)

SOA is a model that comprises services, service providers, service consumers, and the service registry. Financial institutions have increasingly adopted SOA in the last few years, as it offers benefits that are relevant to the business needs of a bank of the future.

In the distributed software model, larger applications are broken into smaller components. The services can be integrated in a consistent manner, and a component-based architecture would allow the existence of components in different locations. A good example is the integration of Internet banking with the back-end accounting system.

---

[1] Event driven
https://developer.ibm.com/technologies/messaging/articles/advantages-of-an-event-driven-architecture/
https://docs.microsoft.com/en-us/azure/architecture/guide/architecture-styles/event-driven
Events in treasury credit risk management – https://www.isda.org/a/cKwEE/TheCreditEventProcess.pdf

CHAPTER 3   USING HYPERAUTOMATION FOR IMPLEMENTING TIME-DRIVEN ABC

SOA embraces both *vertical and horizontal silos* through interoperable services.[2] SOA can be user-driven, integration-driven, process-driven, data-driven, or enterprise SOA. In the last few years, microservices have gained traction in the user industries. Table 3-1 provides a comparison of SOA and microservices architecture.

Table 3-1. *Service-oriented architecture and microservices*

SOA	Microservices
It is based on the concept of business functionality reuse and uses the service sharing principle	It uses the bounded context concept. Each service is a single entity that can do only one thing using a single data unit
It uses the entire subsystem as a service and focused on coupling for reusing the service.	It is focused on service decoupling and logic separation.
Communication takes place using an enterprise service bus or message queuing.	Communication takes place using the REST/SOAP API layer.
Used in enterprise projects.	The projects are smaller in scope
SOA supports the propagation of the heterogeneous protocol used in multiple subsystems.	It reduces the choice for integrating the subsystem/services, it supports integration for the service which uses common communication protocol.
DevOps and CICD are yet to get popular with SOA based architecture.	It is focused on DevOps, cloud-based, container-based deployment with the CICD pipeline.
Support Multithreaded with multiple parallel IO operations.	Most of the application is single-threaded and in comparison, has less IO operations.
SOA is based on model programming.	Microservices is based on component-based programming.
It can be developed by using MuleESB, MS BizTalk as a middleware component.	It can be developed by using the NETTY or Spring cloud library.

Risk incidents and opportunities are events and could happen simultaneously. Event-driven architecture fits very well with enterprise risk-adjusted return management requirements. Further, concepts, such as early warning signals, cause-effect consequence, state transition, time-to-cause, impact, and recover, are part of the "enterprise event ontology." When this architecture is used with analytics and data as a service, it is a powerful tool for the bank to effectively manage the enterprise risk-adjusted return and activity-based enterprise noninterest cost management models. Enterprise architecture should be aligned with enterprise data architecture.

---

[2] Interoperability – http://eitbokwiki.org/Interoperability

CHAPTER 3   USING HYPERAUTOMATION FOR IMPLEMENTING TIME-DRIVEN ABC

Figure 3-2 provides an overview of the enterprise architecture approach.

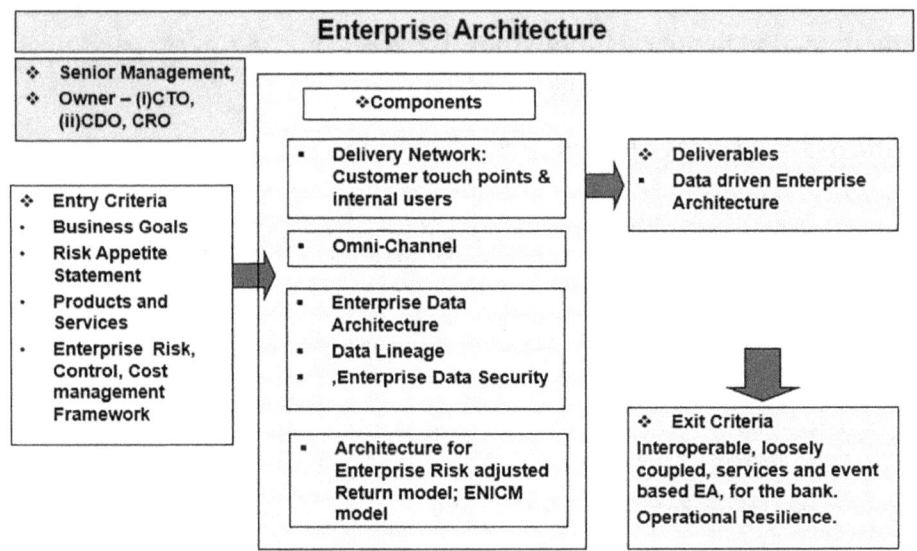

Figure 3-2. Enterprise architecture

It is important for banks to evaluate technologies in terms of relevance for its business requirements operational risk and return on investment.

3.3 Enterprise Data Management

Taxonomy

A *taxonomy*[3] is a high-level business structure that groups related business components and defines their relationship. Taxonomies provide a vocabulary that facilitates the usage of information assets. A user of the taxonomy can grasp the business meaning of the structure with some basic domain knowledge. One of the best practices in defining a taxonomy is

---

[3] https://www.isda.org/2019/09/04/isda-taxonomy-2-0-finalized/

that it should be holistic, simple, and easy to navigate. Taxonomy is meant to be simple illustrations of data dimensions.

Ontology[4] is wider in scope and application.

Ontology

- Facilitates communication by creating a common understanding of the terms across lines of business, systems, policies, procedures, and processes

- Supports interoperability between services, a core requirement for enterprise risk return optimization

- Provides reliability by ensuring there is consistency in the usage of the terms

- Supports **reusability**, as the terms can be used in the same intended manner across systems

---

Reusability is an important BPMS cost-saving feature.

Financial institutions are moving toward ontology-driven systems. Several global initiatives have published taxonomies and ontologies for specific areas of banking. The ontology-driven system design is consistent with the nature of AENICM and ERRM models. Figure 3-2a is the taxonomy of a commercial bank. The treasury is the hub of the bank.

---

[4] https://spec.edmcouncil.org/fibo/ontology_tools.html

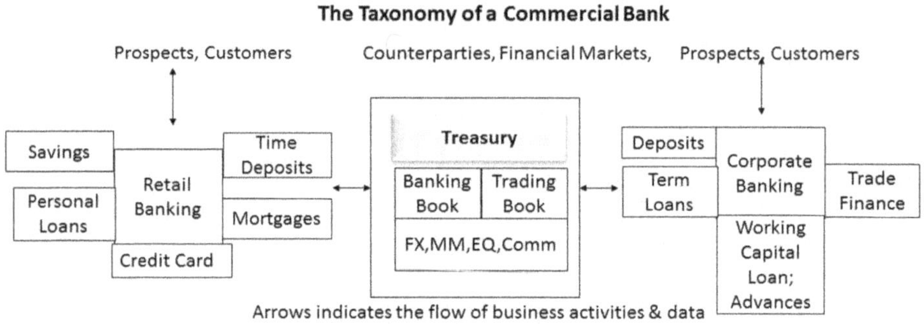

CHAPTER 3   USING HYPERAUTOMATION FOR IMPLEMENTING TIME-DRIVEN ABC

The Taxonomy of a Commercial Bank

Figure 3-2a. *Taxonomy of a commercial bank*

Figures 3-2b, 3-2c, 3-2d, and 3-2e provide a perspective of enterprise activity-based noninterest cost management.

Figure 3-2b. *Activity based enterprise non-interest cost management*

Figure 3-2c illustrates the deployment of human capital across front-, middle-, and back-office functions for each line of business. The support departments provide services to the management and the three lines of business.

CHAPTER 3   USING HYPERAUTOMATION FOR IMPLEMENTING TIME-DRIVEN ABC

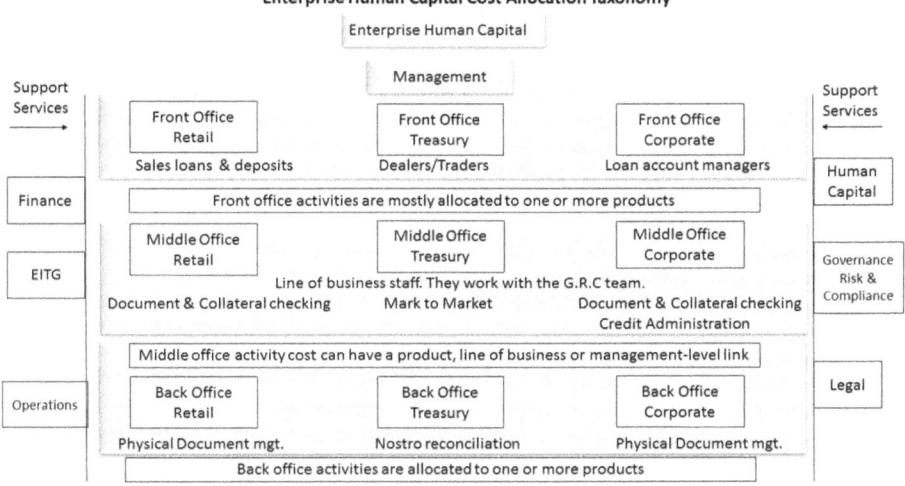

Figure 3-2c. Human capital – noninterest cost allocation taxonomy

Enterprise data architecture should be aligned with the business architecture. The architecture should provide a stable platform for the execution of the ERRM and activity-based ENICM models.

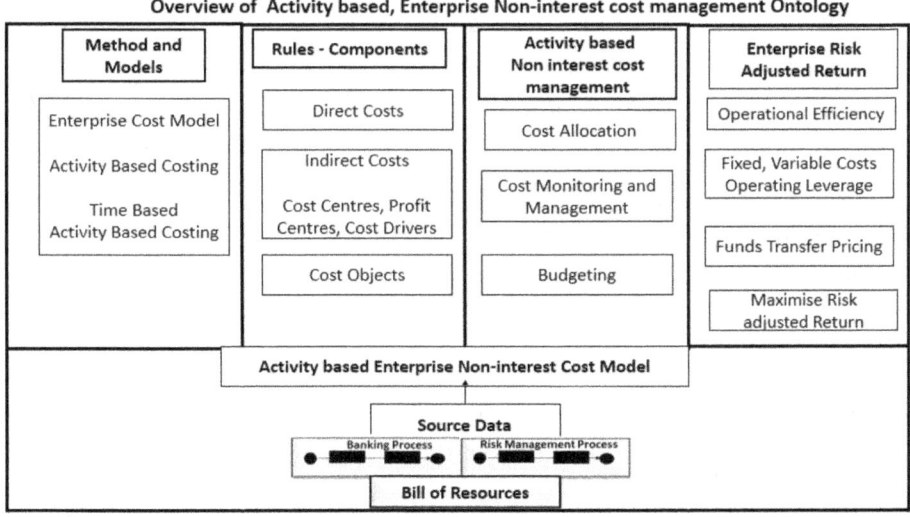

Figure 3-2d. Activity-based, enterprise noninterest cost management (AENICM) ontology

CHAPTER 3   USING HYPERAUTOMATION FOR IMPLEMENTING TIME-DRIVEN ABC

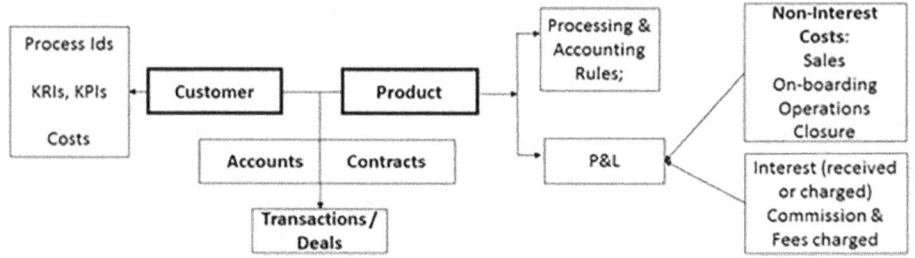

Figure 3-2e. *Customer-account level taxonomy*

A popular measure of banking efficiency is the net interest margin (NIM). NIM is the spread between interest revenues and interest costs. It reveals how effective a bank has been in managing its earning assets with least costly, sources of funding. This book recommends that banks to adopt risk-adjusted NIM**.**

As mentioned earlier, funds transfer pricing is beyond the scope of this book.

A bank's profitability and growth depends on how it manages its enterprise liquidity. This requires a real-time payment processing capability, enterprise liquidity hub, and enterprise data governance.

Cost Data Owners (ENICM System)

Banks should define and identify data owners who are responsible and accountable for one or more cost data categories and subcategories (line of business data, treasury/corporate/retail data, or at product level). They should have the authority to define the classification, security, and consumption of all data items.

Most banks have a problem with their data quality. Big domestic banks and the international banks have a significant operational risk exposure arising from fragmented data. Figure 3-3 provides an overview of the approach to building an enterprise data model.

CHAPTER 3   USING HYPERAUTOMATION FOR IMPLEMENTING TIME-DRIVEN ABC

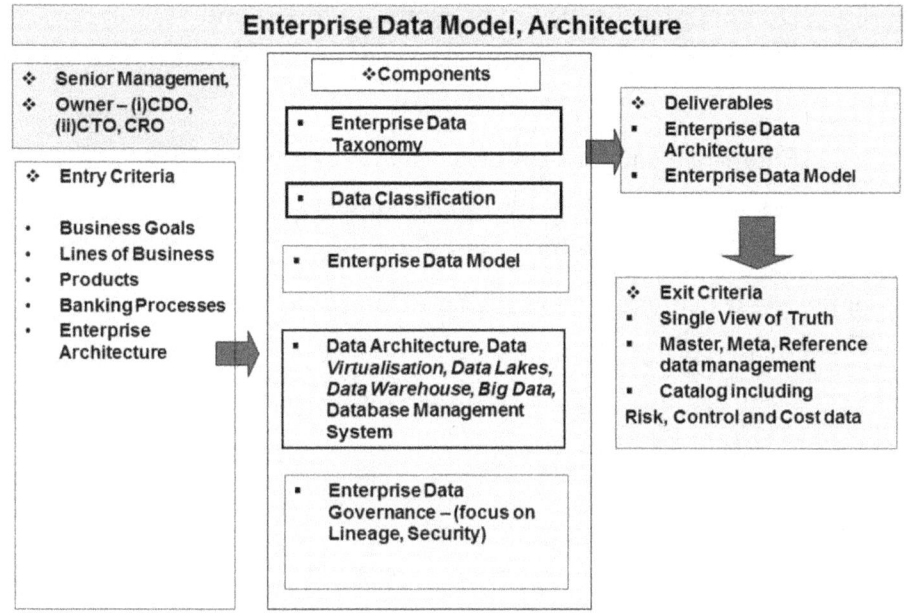

Figure 3-3. *Enterprise data architecture and management*

Core principles of enterprise data architecture and management are as follows:

- Focus on data flow not on storage.

- Data lineage is critical for activity-based enterprise cost management.

- Leverage data with appropriate data management systems (e.g., graph database).

- The enterprise data management should facilitate machine learning.

- Embrace open source technologies.

- Think of the EITG team as data service providers not as a technology support team.

159

CHAPTER 3   USING HYPERAUTOMATION FOR IMPLEMENTING TIME-DRIVEN ABC

- Democratize the data management process and empower users to consume data for accomplishing their work objectives.

- Enterprise data privacy and protection is mandatory and should be embedded in all aspects of hardware and software architecture design.

Figure 3-4 provides a view of the core data structure of the ENICM system.

Overview of an ENICM data structure

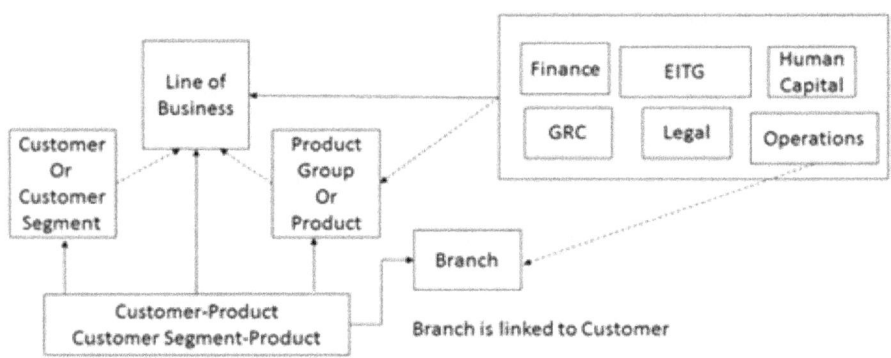

Figure 3-4. Overview of ENICM data structure

Dotted lines are derived relationships. Customers are linked to products offered by a bank, and the products belong to a line of business. The account is a combination of a customer and a product. It is at this granular level, costs, risks, and returns are collected, analyzed, and managed.

The following sections delve into master, meta, and reference data aspects of enterprise data management.

160

CHAPTER 3   USING HYPERAUTOMATION FOR IMPLEMENTING TIME-DRIVEN ABC

3.3.1 Noninterest Cost – Customer Master Data

Master data represents the business objects that are shared across the enterprise and creates a single version of the truth about the objects. Figure 3-5 provides an example of the master customer data for a bank. The table (inset) showing customer profitability after funds transfer pricing provides a reference for the collection of data to determine customer profitability.

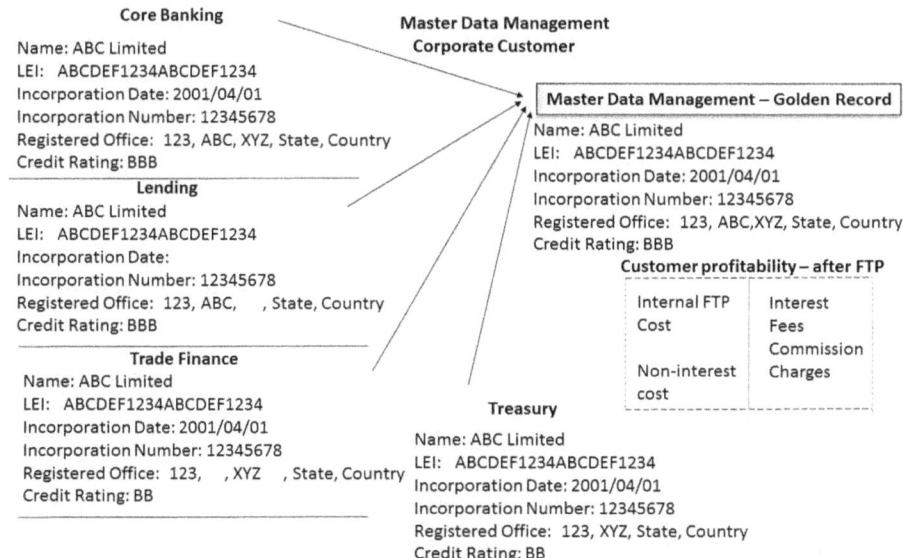

Figure 3-5. Master customer data

Figure 3-6 provides an overview of the master, meta, and transaction data for a line of business.

CHAPTER 3   USING HYPERAUTOMATION FOR IMPLEMENTING TIME-DRIVEN ABC

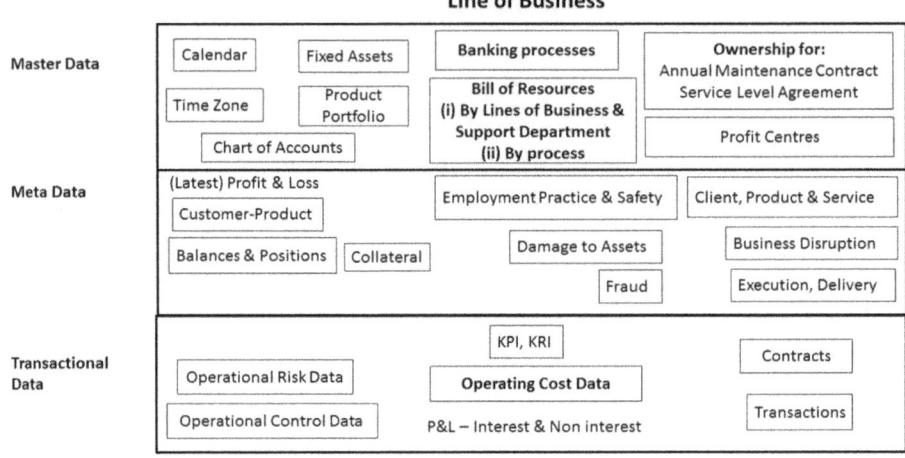

Figure 3-6. *Master, meta, and transaction data for a line of business*

Master data management helps data consumers have one common understanding of all data items and makes its usage consistent across the bank. It includes the financial product, the bank's customer, an employee, or a branch. The master data and the chart of account structure should be consistent.

It facilitates process automation and is called the "**Golden Source**," as all lines of business use the same dataset.

Financial Products and Enterprise Costs

Banks offer multiple asset and liability products. The noninterest cost are rolled up from processes to individual products, to product group, to the line of business, and then to the bank level.

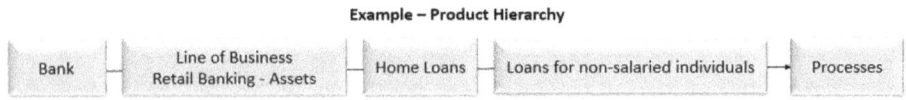

Figure 3-7. *Product hierarchy*

For example, *there may be a variety of residential-mortgage loan products*. They will differ in the terms and conditions. This would include type of interest rate (floating, fixed), the actual rate, term, interest computation method, processing fees, collateral, customer profile, and in some cases location of asset and/or customer. The following are examples:

- The purpose of a regular home loan could include the purchase of newly built unit or under construction property, purchase of preowned homes, and renovation.
- "Switch" home loan refers to a facility to transfer from another bank provided the borrower satisfies the eligibility criteria that would include a good credit history and stipulated documentation.
- A home loan for citizens living overseas.
- A FlexiPay home loan for young salaried borrowers that tweaks the amount and method of equal monthly instalments. Most banks do this by defining a moratorium period.
- Home loan designed especially for government employees.
- Home loan for people serving in the army.
- Loan to the customer for purchasing a plot for construction of a dwelling unit.
- Home loans designed for nonsalaried individuals.
- Reverse mortgage loan for senior citizens provides an additional source of income against mortgage of the borrower's residential house property.

CHAPTER 3   USING HYPERAUTOMATION FOR IMPLEMENTING TIME-DRIVEN ABC

3.3.2 Cost – Metadata

Business metadata includes business terms, definitions, business rules, policies, and constraints. It defines the semantics of a business concept and its realization in physical data assets. Business metadata is *primarily descriptive in nature*, and it makes it possible for business users to know what data they have, the permissions, and how to access it.

Tables 3-2a, 3-2b, and 3-2c provide a view of the FTE data of staff by product customer. This is a very critical input for enterprise noninterest cost allocation.

Table 3-2a. *Corporate banking staff FTE – metadata*

	Corporate Banking Employee F.T.E.						
Emp Id: 12345	CORLCI	CORCOA	CORL10	CORSDL	Prodt-5	Prodt-6	Prodt-7
CG1							
CG2							
CC1							
CC2							
CC3							

Table 3-2b. *Treasury staff FTE – metadata*

	Treasury Employee F.T.E.						
Emp Id: 54321	TRBFXF	TRBCRS	TRBIRS	TRICDS	Prodt-5 MM	Prodt-6 Commodity	Prodt-7 Equity
CG1							
CG2							
CC1							
CC2							
CC3							

Table 3-2c. *Retail banking staff FTE – metadata*

	Retail Banking Employee F.T.E.						
Emp Id: 11223	RETSAV	RETFD1	RETHLS	RETCOD	RETCCD	RETLOC	Prodt-7
R01							
R02							
R03							

CHAPTER 3   USING HYPERAUTOMATION FOR IMPLEMENTING TIME-DRIVEN ABC

By building the enterprise metadata layer, a bank can remove inconsistencies across the data architecture and ensure that the data relationships and hierarchies are accurate.

Figures 3-8 and 3-9 are very important from the perspective of enterprise noninterest cost allocation management. The quality of human capital and EITG data has a direct impact on the quality of noninterest cost management and risk-adjusted returns.

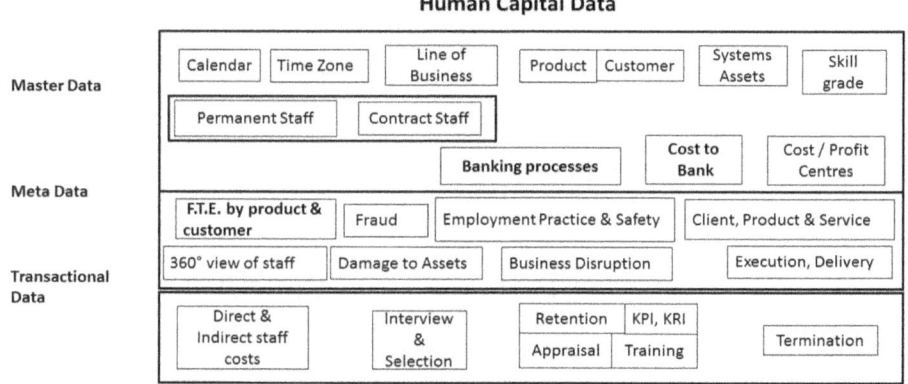

Figure 3-8. *Human capital master, meta, and transaction data*

A data catalog organizes the bank's data items across many systems. It contains critical information about each data element and supports establishing lineage. The catalog facilitates data democratization. An authorized user can discover, understand, and consume data sources.

A **cost data catalog** has resource usage data and can significantly improve time-driven activity-based enterprise noninterest cost management. The Bill of Resources can be linked to the Data Catalog to facilitate the monitoring of performance, risk, control and cost.

CHAPTER 3   USING HYPERAUTOMATION FOR IMPLEMENTING TIME-DRIVEN ABC

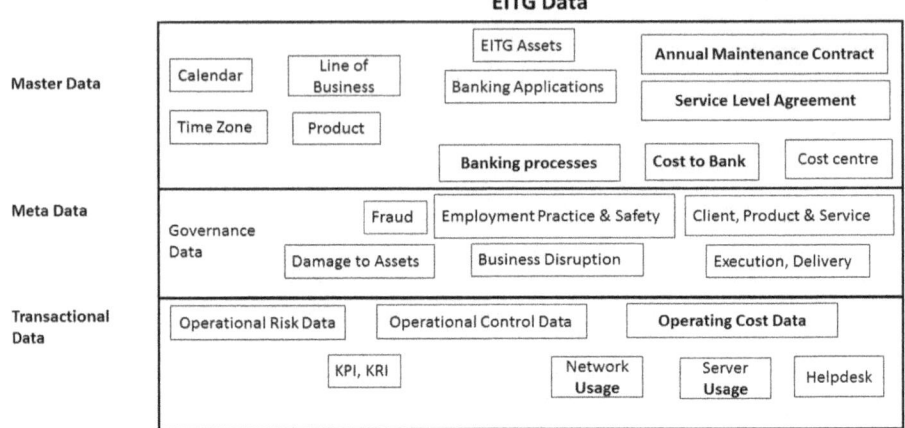

Figure 3-9. EITG master, meta, and transaction data

3.3.3 Treasury Operations – Reference Data

Reference data refers to the list of common codes or values used by different applications across a bank. It provides the context for business transaction details. The following are relevant for a bank[5]:

- Bloomberg's instrument reference data

- CUSIP Global Services' CUSIP (Committee on Uniform Security Identification Procedures)

- International Swaps and Derivatives Association's financial products markup language

- IHS Markit's reference data

- Standard Industrial Classification (SIC)

---

[5] https://www.isda.org/category/infrastructure/fpml/
https://ihsmarkit.com/products/pricing-and-reference-data.html
https://www.naics.com/sic-codes-industry-drilldown/

Although the Internet and mobile technologies have provided banks with a capability to move toward a customer-centric business delivery, most banks have been unable to leverage relevant technologies for maximizing business returns. They will need to focus on unlocking the value in their data, albeit, in compliance with relevant laws and regulations. A customer-centric business model that is powered by enterprise architecture, data management, and security will help them to stay relevant and competitive.

3.3.4 Transaction Data

This is explained in Section 3.4.6, after process automation examples.

3.4 Enterprise Process Automation

Sections 3.4.1 and 3.4.2 extend the narrative in Chapter 1, Section 1.4, on building an operating model.

3.4.1 Business Goal

Top-Down Approach

Business process modeling is a top-down approach, but it also requires an upward pass, to ensure consistency and alignment between *business goals and banking process objectives*. Shareholders set the goals for a bank. Goal breakdown to the process level helps in defining key performance indicators at the operational level. The SMART standard for goal setting is defined below:

- Specific – It should be a business task and an area of performance.

- Measurable – Capable of having metrics defined in measuring and monitoring the performance.

CHAPTER 3   USING HYPERAUTOMATION FOR IMPLEMENTING TIME-DRIVEN ABC

- Attainable – This should take a risk-adjusted return basis.

- Realistic – The economy, competition, and customer behavior.

- Time – The time horizon for accomplishing the goals.

The "ART" part of the standard is closely linked to the risk culture of the bank.

It is recommended that the goal of a bank be mapped to the organization structure in a manner that role clarity (KPIs) and accountability can be established and rolled down the organization.

Figure 3-10a illustrates the goal breakdown mechanism from the bank level to the line of business, to the products and finally to the processes, and Figure 3-10b highlights the human capital aspect.

Figures 3-10a and 3-10b focus on performance, resources, and processes.

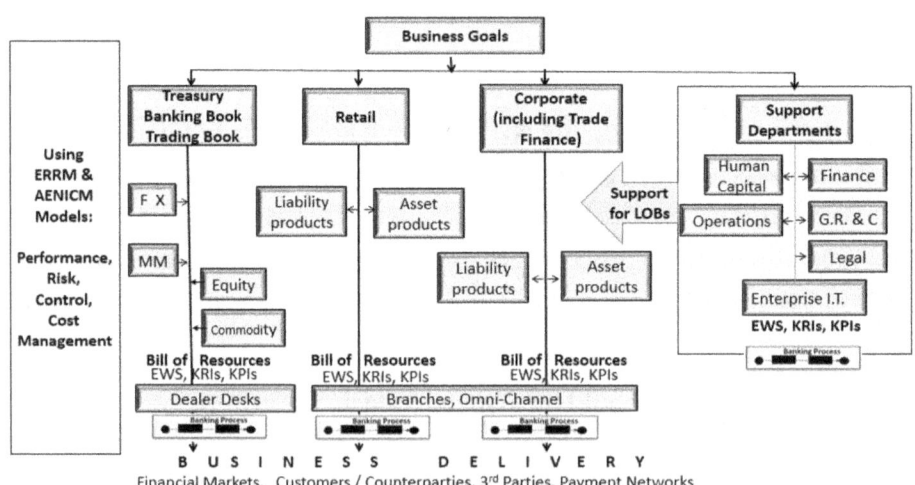

Figure 3-10a. *Goal breakdown*

168

CHAPTER 3   USING HYPERAUTOMATION FOR IMPLEMENTING TIME-DRIVEN ABC

Goal breakdown, as illustrated in Figure 3-10a, could involve the following:

(a) Lines of business goal roll down

The line of business and geographical breakdown of the goals are important, as the position in the hierarchy is linked to decision-making authority.

(b) Goal roll down for support functions.

The senior management should align their service and delivery support structure with the business delivery structure. In some banks, support functions have service level agreements (SLA) with the business units. The SLAs determine what would be the most effective model for the alignment of support functions with business functions.

Operational efficiency and operating leverage are influenced by

(i) Alignment of goals of lines of business with support departments

(ii) The independence of functions such as GRC, internal control, and audit

(iii) SLA management between service provider and user

The following are the *inputs* for building a **process-based enterprise operating model**:

- The goals of the bank

- The organization structure for accomplishing the goals, staff-roles-KPIs. Figure 3-10b illustrates the specification of skill grades at various levels of the bank. The goal roll down should be aligned with staff skills.

CHAPTER 3   USING HYPERAUTOMATION FOR IMPLEMENTING TIME-DRIVEN ABC

- Product portfolio and the delivery of banking products to customers across channels, including physical branches.

- E-channel platform details.

- Branch network.

- Service standards defined for providing a differentiation in the market.

- Internal and external service level agreements.

- KPIs and KRIs at the process level.

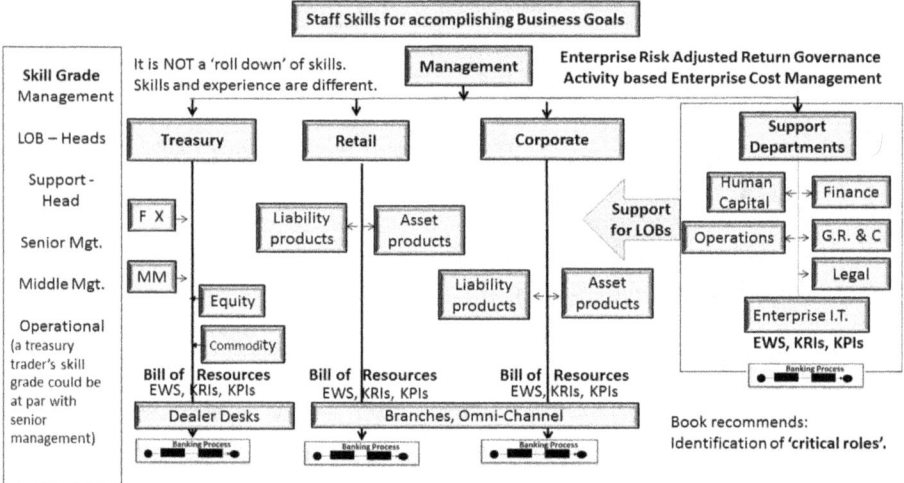

Figure 3-10b. *Goal breakdown – KPIs – staff skills, system, and accountability*

The **bill of resources management** should be consistent with the goal breakdown. The bill of resources for each line of business and support department should be gradually broken down to the process level.

3.4.2 Process-Based Enterprise Operating Model

The bank's process inventory is a core component of the digital transformation, and it provides the capability to orchestrate banking activities across lines of business, staff, and systems. In a services-based enterprise architecture, it can be integrated with enterprise data management. The architecture recommended in this book provides a bank with enduring information technology asset that can be leveraged fully for minimizing risks and maximizing returns.

This would include both business and technical processes. The documentation of the processes is possible only after the business delivery specification is available.

Tables 3-3a, 3-3b, 3-3c, and 3-3d are process inventory examples.

Table 3-3a. *Process inventory*

Savings Account Processes	Sub Processes — Activities common to Savings & Current Account
Account Opening	Change in Name of an Account
Domestic Clearing	Change in Signature
International Payments	Change in Operating Instructions
Closure of an Account	Intimation of Loss of Debit or Credit Card
	Change in Nomination in an Account
	Change of Address in an Account
	Creation of Standing Instruction
	Withdrawal of Standing Instruction
	Issue of Tax deduction on interest certificate
	Balance Confirmation
	Processing of a Death Claim

The inventory includes both *business and technical processes*. The documentation of the processes is possible only after the master list of business products and services is available. The product/service delivery process requires the definition of the following:

- What is the purpose of the process? Who owns the product/service? Who owns the process?
- Who performs the process? Where is it performed?
- What are inputs to the process? What are the outputs of the process?
- *Does it have a bill of resources?*
- *What is the resource consumption of an activity?*
- When does the process begin (event, date)?
- What activities are automated?
- What is the entry criterion? Policy and procedures will determine this.
- When does the process end? Operating procedure manual will have the details.
- What is the exit criterion? Operating procedure manual/operating manual provides guidance on procedures to deliver business.
- What are the set of the activities between the beginning and the end of the process?

The process owner will be responsible for defining its orchestration and estimating (initially) the cost and residual risks. Processes can be purely internal and those that require integration with external systems. Examples of "purely" internal processes could be back-office accounting activities. External processes would include integration with external RTGS and SWIFT infrastructure.

CHAPTER 3   USING HYPERAUTOMATION FOR IMPLEMENTING TIME-DRIVEN ABC

Table 3-3b. *Process inventory*

Trade Financing	(Continued) Trade Financing
Advising an Export LC with or without Confirmation	Negotiation of an Export Bill
Advising Amendment of an Export LC	Discounting of an Export Bill
Re-instatement of a Revolving Export LC	Import Bills under collection
Closure of an Export LC	Processing of Overdue Export Bills
Establishment of an Import LC	Bank Guarantee issuance
Amendment of an Import LC	Invocation of a Bank Guarantee
Closure of an Import LC	Closure of a Bank Guarantee

Table 3-3c. *Process inventory*

	Treasury Deal Input
	FX Spot
Loans	FX Forward
Credit Appraisal	Currency Swap
Origination	Purchase / Sale of Treasury Bill
Collateral – acceptance, valuation, substitution, expiry, return	Purchase / Sale of Bond
Disbursal	Purchase / Sale of Certificate of Deposits
Repayment	Interest Rate Swap
Internal Rating	Forward Rate Contract
Overdue Processing	Option Contract
	Futures Contract
Additional – Syndicate Loan	**Sub Processes – common to all LOBs**
Request for Participation from other banks	Customer Identification Check
Distribution of Repayment / Interest Income to other bank	Anti Money Laundering Checks
Request for Funds from participant banks	Know Your Customer Program - Analytics
	Due Diligence Procedures - Analytics

Table 3-3d. *Process inventory*

Support Department: EITG	Support Department: Human Capital
Incident Management	Staff Recruitment
Release Management	Staff Retention
Change Management	Staff Termination
Configuration Management	
Capacity Planning	
Service Level Management	

173

CHAPTER 3   USING HYPERAUTOMATION FOR IMPLEMENTING TIME-DRIVEN ABC

Figure 3-11a depicts enterprise process taxonomy, and Figure 3-11b depicts a high-level credit risk management process.

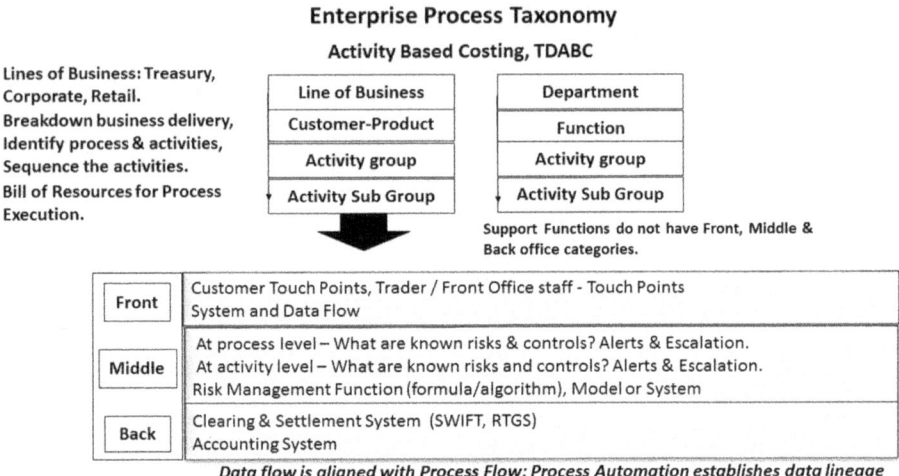

Figure 3-11a. *Enterprise process taxonomy*

Goal Roll Down to Process Level

The line of business goals are decomposed to product goals and then rolled down as KPIs and KRI (inputs from risk appetite statement) at the business process level. The process is decomposed into a set of activities.

Process ownership should be synchronized with product, service, and support ownership. The process owner will be responsible for its orchestration, cost, and residual risks.

Processes can be internal or external. The latter are processes with customer involvement. Examples of internal processes are intrabranch asset movement, movement of cash from vault to tellers or ATMs.

In building the process inventory, several subprocesses (e.g., KYC) that can be **reused** in other processes are identified.

CHAPTER 3   USING HYPERAUTOMATION FOR IMPLEMENTING TIME-DRIVEN ABC

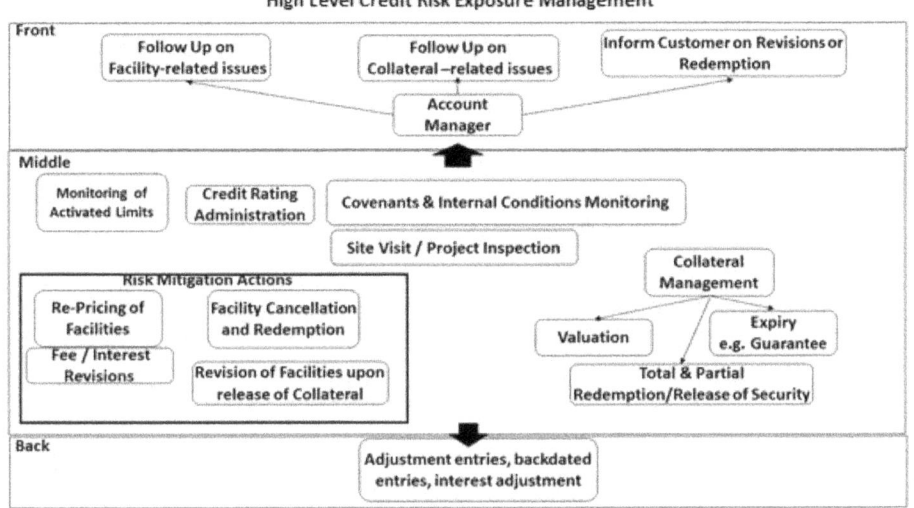

Figure 3-11b. *Process taxonomy*

Figure 3-11b provides an example of front, middle, and back-office functions:

- Front-office functions refer to customer facing activities.

- Middle-Office Functions – The risk management and compliance functions fall into this category. It is still early years for banks in the implementation of an ERR model. Banks are increasing their focus on preventive controls, and hence, risk management is also a front-office function.

- Back-Office Functions – The back-office includes accounting, settlement, reconciliations, budgeting, procurement (reporting to finance division in some banks), premises management, and reporting. Risk management is also a critical function for this layer. In many banks, settlement risk needs more attention from risk managers.

CHAPTER 3 USING HYPERAUTOMATION FOR IMPLEMENTING TIME-DRIVEN ABC

Figure 3-12 illustrates a **customized process-based enterprise control framework** that is aligned with the COSO and COBIT frameworks. It also adheres to the core principles of Sarbanes–Oxley Act (SOX).

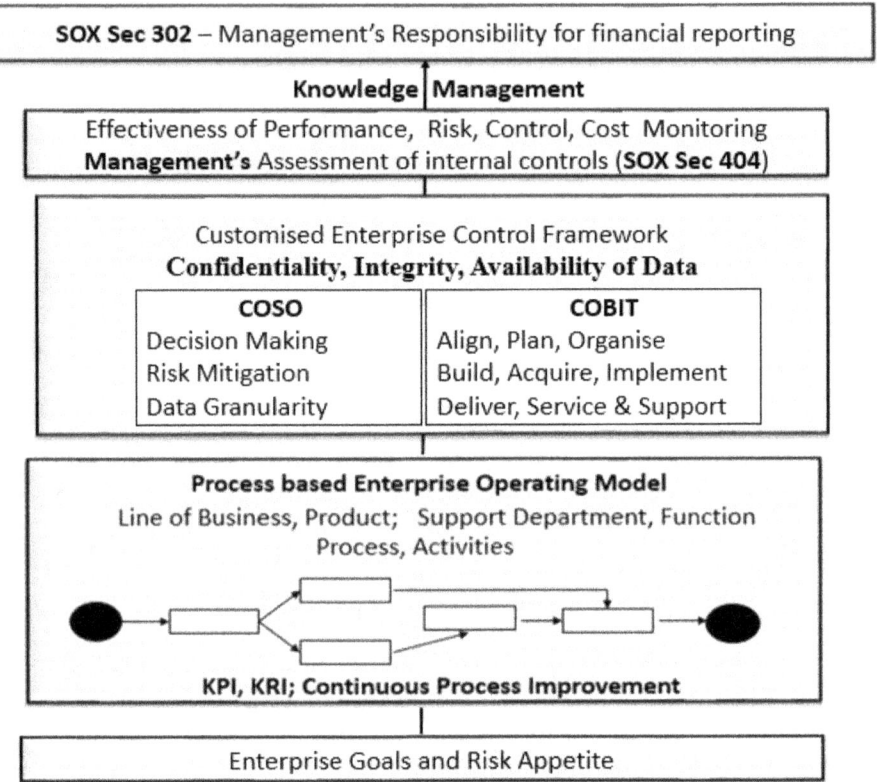

Figure 3-12. Process-based customized enterprise control framework

Figure 3-13a provides a template for a banking process definition.

CHAPTER 3   USING HYPERAUTOMATION FOR IMPLEMENTING TIME-DRIVEN ABC

The process definitions are the bedrock of an enterprise process taxonomy and an *event-driven architecture.*[6]

Defining the activity of each end-to-end process with the associated rules (policies and procedures) is an important task in process modeling. The following are important aspects of modeling:

- KRIs and KPIs
- Defining customer touch points
- Defining the activities and the navigation path
- Controls (e.g., limit)
- The alert mechanism for exception management

---

[6] Event driven
https://developer.ibm.com/technologies/messaging/articles/advantages-of-an-event-driven-architecture/
https://docs.microsoft.com/en-us/azure/architecture/guide/architecture-styles/event-driven
Events in Treasury Credit risk management https://www.isda.org/a/cKwEE/TheCreditEventProcess.pdf

CHAPTER 3   USING HYPERAUTOMATION FOR IMPLEMENTING TIME-DRIVEN ABC

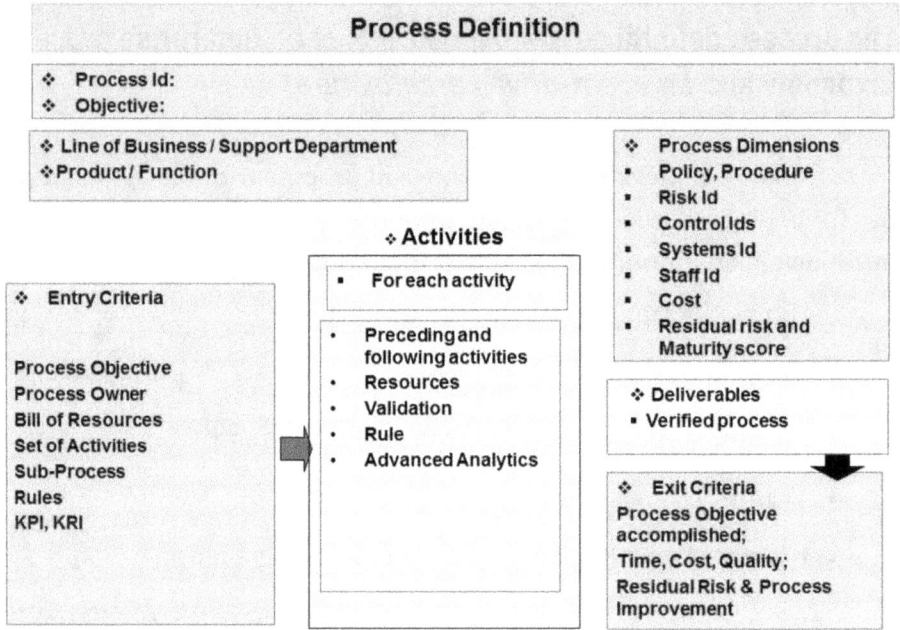

Figure 3-13a. *Process definition*

In order to manage the operational costs and risks, the bank should have an end-to-end view of the process and have data on

- Resource consumption
- Data lineage
- Cost of the process
- Residual risk, i.e., post mitigation

3.4.3 BPMS (Business Process Management Suite)

The following are the components of the BPM suite:

i. Business processes modeling notation (BPMN)

ii. BPM engine

iii. Intelligence and rules engine

iv. Enterprise document management

v. Enterprise case management

vi. Business and process activity monitoring

vii. Middleware – Enterprise application integration

3.4.3.1 Business Process Modeling

The business delivery of a product or service cuts across the front-, middle-, and back-office functions of a bank. Business process modeling is a core component of BPMS, and a bank can use it for analyzing and designing business processes.

Business Process Execution Language (BPEL)[7] is an XML-based language that defines enterprise business processes within Web services. BPEL and BPMN are open standards, and the notations are used for describing and executing business processes. The key objective of BPEL is to standardize the format of process flow definition so that banking activities can be seamlessly executed using web services.

BPEL supports two different types of business processes:

- Executable processes model follows the orchestration paradigm.

- Abstract processes use process descriptions that specify the mutually visible message exchange behavior of each of the parties involved in the protocol, without revealing their internal behavior.

---

[7] https://www.oracle.com/technical-resources/articles/matjaz-bpel.html (BPEL)

CHAPTER 3 USING HYPERAUTOMATION FOR IMPLEMENTING TIME-DRIVEN ABC

The **B**usiness **P**rocess **M**odeling **N**otation (BPMN)[8] is a graphical notation that defines the tasks in process modeling. It is a standard set of conventions that describe business processes.

This book has not used the BPM modeling conventions for the figures and processes. The objective is to *improve the narrative by using illustrations that do not appear too technical.*

A sample treasury process model is shown in Figure 3-13b.

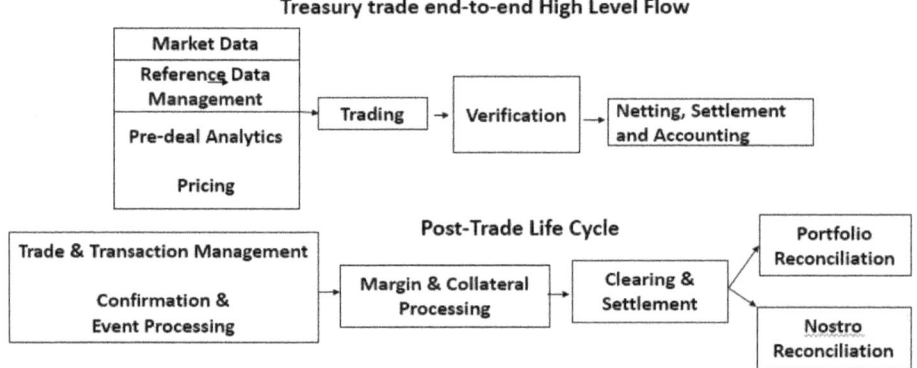

Figure 3-13b. *High-level treasury process model*

Subprocesses

When designing a BPM-based solution, it is important to identify the subprocesses that can be reused in several other business areas. In a banking environment, customer identification activity (part of KYC) is a subprocess that can reused in any new account opening process.

---

[8] https://docs.oracle.com/cd/E23943_01///user.1111/e15177/model_bus_procs_bpmcu.htm (BPMN)

> Reusable processes, in terms of total processes, are almost 25–30% for retail banking and about 20% for corporate banking and treasury.

An example of a core set of activities that are reused are customer identification process (**CIP**) and know your customer (**KYC**) process. A CIP or a KYC (due diligence) could vary by product and customer; however, the core set of activities remains the same and is reused. Across lines of business, many of the underlying activities are common and can be regrouped/redefined/remodeled as a different process.

"Called/Invoked Process"

Some risk management process are invoked during banking process orchestration. These are *risk mitigation processes for known risks* and referred in this section as called or invoked process. The management of unknown risks requires event-driven architecture and knowledge management capabilities.

3.4.3.2 BPM Engine and Process Orchestration

The BPM engine executes, controls, and monitors business processes. It can orchestrate a defined end-to-end process or multiple processes. As it executes the defined process, it collaborates with systems and data service requests, supports manual intervention, and provides the ability to have an intelligent and rule-based process execution. Web services have become a preferred way to manage a solution deployment.

Controls at the process level can be preventive and detective.

CHAPTER 3   USING HYPERAUTOMATION FOR IMPLEMENTING TIME-DRIVEN ABC

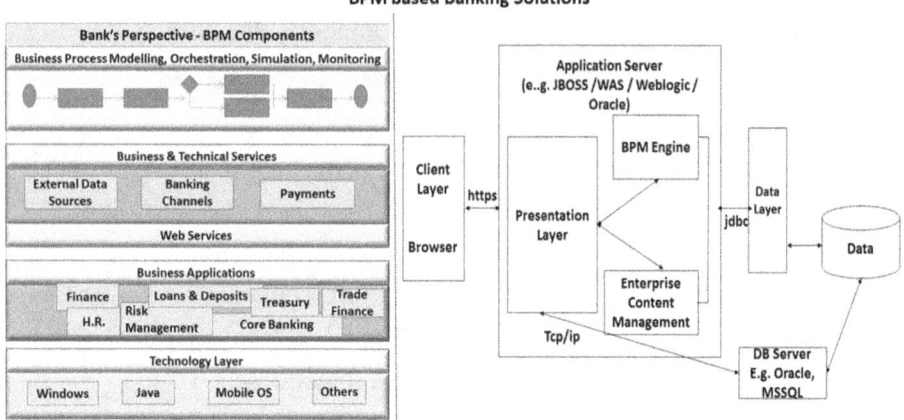

Figure 3-14. Business process management suite – overview of components

3.4.3.3 Intelligence and Rules Engine

The design of the BPMS stack has evolved from having a rules engine to "intelligence-powered" processing platform. The following are the standard features of this component:

- Rules can be configured in a BPMS solution. However, this book recommends a real-time integration with an advanced analytics and enterprise knowledge management systems. Machine learning algorithms will provide a "layer of intelligence."

- Preventive controls are enabled.

- Dynamic routing of messages is enabled.

- Real-time alerts are generated.

3.4.3.4 Enterprise Document/Content Management

A very important component from a banking perspective is the ability to have document management capabilities at the process level. Trade finance and lending are two document intensive banking business functions that can benefit immensely when process orchestration is coupled with document management capabilities.

3.4.3.5 Case Management

This significantly improves business activity monitoring and supports the collaboration of internal control, audit, legal, and GRC teams.

3.4.3.6 Business Activity Monitoring (BAM)

BAM provides a real-time monitoring of processes. This provides an ability to proactively manage atypical behavior. It can also be used to improve customer experience in functions such as customer onboarding, retail loan approval, and complaint management. BAM improves the monitoring of internal service level agreements.

3.4.3.7 Middleware – Enterprise Application Integration (EAI)

Some BPMS vendors offer an integration engine within the BPMS stack. Some banks have used it as a "quick fix" solution to resolve operational problems are caused by a siloed environment. However, the bank will not have the ability to (a) implement an activity-based ENICM model, (b) implement a process-based enterprise risk-adjusted return model, (c) implement a continuous process improvement culture, and (d) improve risk-adjusted, operational efficiency and leverage.

It is imperative for a bank to improve enterprise architecture by using a services-based approach, i.e., SOA and microservice.

3.4.3.8 Robotic Process Automation (RPA)

RPA software automates repetitive, rules-based banking activities. It can be used for banking and risk management processes. The method used for selecting the processes determines the quality of the automation. The following points have to be considered prior to implementing RPA:

- RPA is not recommended for a complex environment.
- Processes must not have a history of changes.
- Banks must have a continuous process improvement culture.

The following are key benefits of RPA:

- Decreased cycle times and improved throughput
- Improved service levels, i.e., SLAs are met
- Improved accuracy
- Operational efficiency at minimum cost

References for technical aspects of Enterprise Architecture Overview and Business Process Management Tools are provided in the links below.[9]

3.4.3.9 Hyperautomation

Hyperautomation uses enterprise process automation technology and advanced analytics such as machine learning to provide a layer of intelligence in process orchestration.

---

[9] https://docs.appian.com/suite/help/22.4/Enterprise_Architecture_Overview.html
https://appian.com/blog/acp/business-process-management/business-process-management-tools.html

BPMS and Service-Oriented (Enterprise) Architecture[10]

BPMS can be implemented without a service-oriented architecture. However, the full benefits of process automation can be realized only in an SOA environment, as there is a convergence in the implementations. When BPMS is implemented in a SOA environment, alignment of business with technology is easier, operational efficiency improves significantly, and operational risks are minimized.

Risk Management and Robotic Process Automation

Several risk management processes can be brought under robotic process automation, e.g., certain types of hedging, retail credit scoring, and collateral valuation.

Business process automation's **inherent capability** is the facilitation of activity-based costing and time-driven ABC. **The additional cost for a bank is the "delta implementation effort."**

3.4.3.10 SOA-BPMS Convergence

The full benefits of process automation can be realized only in an SOA environment, as there is a convergence in the implementations. When BPMS is implemented in a SOA environment, alignment of business with technology is easier, operational efficiency improves significantly, and operational risks are minimized.

---

[10] https://www.oracle.com/technical-resources/articles/enterprise-architecture/soa-integration.html
https://www.redbooks.ibm.com/redpapers/pdfs/redp4495.pdf

Table 3-4. *SOA-BPMS convergence*

Business Process Management Suite	Service Oriented Architecture
It is driven by the bank's Lines-of-business.	This is driven by the technology group of the bank. It paves the way for an Enterprise Architecture approach to managing a bank's automation needs
It is a top-down approach	It is a bottom–up approach
The business processes are owned by the respected Line of Business or support function (e.g. HR). Staff can be assigned ownership for processes.	Processes are owned by respective group of I.T.Service Management e.g. Release Management, Configuration Management.
Key Performance Indicators can be set. Activity based costing of business delivery can be accomplished.	Key Performance indicators can be set.

Banking services are automated from an end-to-end business perspective that cuts across the lines of business, front-, middle-, and back-office functions, and geographies.

Process automation works well in a SOA environment. Reusability of processes and subprocesses helps the banks reap the benefits of a lean and efficient architecture. This allows a bank to seize business opportunities, e.g., the "go to market" is quicker.

3.4.4 Bill of Resources (BOR)

Bill of materials (BOM), used in the manufacturing industry, has a hierarchical structure. It is a list of assemblies, subassemblies, components, and materials that are required to make a product. It also contains instructions on assembling the product.

BOM provides clarity on what goes into manufacturing a product. Process and quality improvement initiatives examine the bill of materials with the objective of improving the cost of production and the quality of the product. The BOM could be treated like an end-to-end process that is influenced by standards, units of measure, and scale of operation.

CHAPTER 3   USING HYPERAUTOMATION FOR IMPLEMENTING TIME-DRIVEN ABC

This book recommends using the **bill of resources concept for activity-based, enterprise noninterest cost management in banks**. It is similar to the BOM but is tweaked for an industry that has cash as the raw material and finished good.

Figures 3-15a, 3-15b, and 3-15c illustrate the usage of a bill of resources in a commercial bank. Figure 3-15a illustrates the process-based approach to managing operational efficiency and operating leverage.

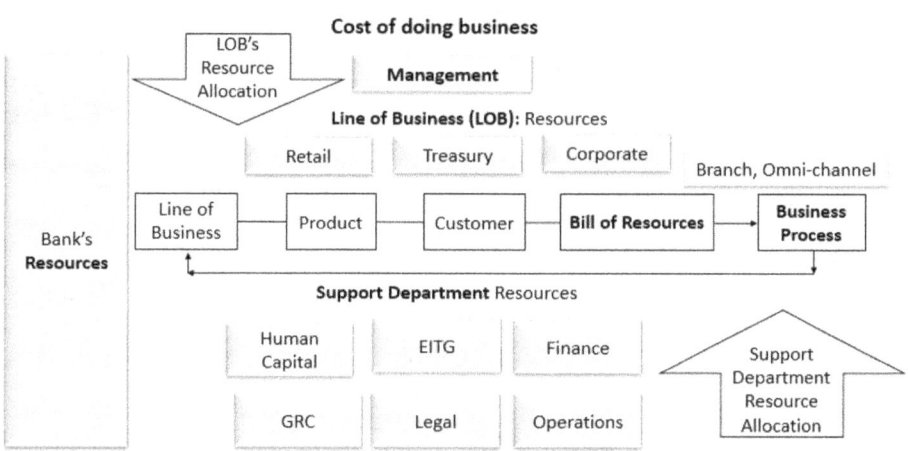

Figure 3-15a. *Bill of Resources - Lines of Business, Product-Customer process link*

Figure 3-15b provides a view of cost allocation in a process-automated environment that uses the bill of resources for monitoring and managing operational efficiency.

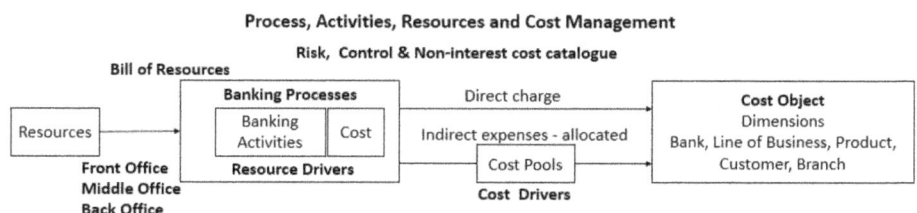

Figure 3-15b. *Bill of Resources facilitates AENICM*

CHAPTER 3   USING HYPERAUTOMATION FOR IMPLEMENTING TIME-DRIVEN ABC

In the manufacturing industry, the key element driving *Total Quality Management* and *Just in Time* programs is information on customer and product. The bill of materials provides the information of the product.

Similarly, BOR facilitates operational efficiency improvement initiatives in banks. The details in this chapter and the next guide the bank on using BOR in a process-automated environment.

Figure 3-15c maps the BOR to the product life cycle. The four phases in Figure 3-15c are

  i) Sales and marketing activities

  ii) Customer onboarding

  iii) Account operation

  iv) Closure of accounts

This is examined further in Tables 3-5a and 3-5b.

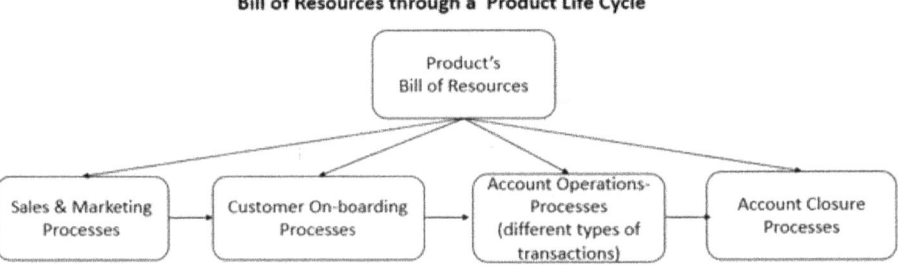

Figure 3-15c. *Bill of Resources management through a product life cycle*

Table 3-5a takes a closer look of the application of the bill of resources at the process level for activity-based enterprise cost management.

188

CHAPTER 3   USING HYPERAUTOMATION FOR IMPLEMENTING TIME-DRIVEN ABC

Table 3-5a. *Using the bill of resources*

Bill of Resources for a Process

Process Id:							
	Direct Staff	Support Staff			System(s)	Other Resources	Activity Cost & Date of Measurement
		Sales	Finance Legal	GRC			
A1							
A2							
A3							
A4							
A5							
A6							

Section 3.5 of this chapter provides examples of using bill of resources for time-driven ABC.

The following are important tasks for implementing activity-based ENICM in a process-automated environment:

- Document all the business processes of the banks. Processes are modeled using BPMS technology.

- Have a comprehensive set of BORs and align them with the processes.

- The CFO should develop and own the costing chart of accounts.

- Cost and profit center data should be captured at source, i.e., at origination.

- Process orchestration should update cost data in accounting and cost accounting (ENICM) system simultaneously.

- Determine estimated volume for each process.

- Using bill of resources, determine the resources for each activity.
- Using cost of resources, determine the unit cost of each activity; initially, this will be an estimate and will get more accurate using log data.
- Data lineage between the books of account and the enterprise cost database must be maintained.

Process Automation and Data Lineage

In a data-driven method, the logical data model must be completed before the process modeling design stage. It is important to align data flows with process flows.

Important aspects of constructing a logical process model are

- Identification of the data elements required for completing the activities.
- Decisions that will be made during the execution of the process. These include decisions about which path the process should take (invoking a risk management process or a subprocess) to accomplish the process objective.

Activity-based enterprise noninterest cost management

- The main tasks in monitoring a business process are measuring the time taken by each activity and resources consumed by it.

Bill of resource mentioned in some figures and tables is the Bill of Resources.

3.4.5 Process Automation Examples

This section provides an insight into process automation using BPMS:

CHAPTER 3 USING HYPERAUTOMATION FOR IMPLEMENTING TIME-DRIVEN ABC

Each examples has three sections:

Section i Bill of resources (note: employee assignment is driven by dual control and segregation of duties policy)

Section ii Process model

Section iii Activities and its dimensions

The following are the examples:

Process 1 New term deposit opening – new customer

Process 2 Existing customer's new term deposit

Process 3 Home loan application – salaried individuals

Process 4 Corporate term loan application

Process 5 Credit risk appraisal of corporate loan application

Process 6 Corporate customer onboarding

Process 7 Corporate loan disbursement

Process 8 Corporate loan credit risk monitoring

Process 9 Index-linked CDS deal input

Process 10 Interest rate swap deal input

Process 11 OTC derivative

Process 12 GRC – anti-money laundering and countering the financing of terrorism

CHAPTER 3   USING HYPERAUTOMATION FOR IMPLEMENTING TIME-DRIVEN ABC

Process 13 EITG – incident management

Process 14 Human capital – recruitment

Process 15 Human capital – retention

Process 16 Human capital – termination

In these examples, the allocation of resources using the bill of resources as the underlying concept is demonstrated by providing a template for mapping resources to activities.

In a hyperautomation environment, time consumed by resources is available in the logs data.

The usage of sub-processes, Intelligent process orchestration, case management and robotic process automation are explained in these examples. This is how hyperautomation can be used for improving operating leverage.

All the examples have this structure shown in Figure 3-16. The bill of resources shows the staff, system, and other resources (e.g., documents) that are used by the process. The process flow is the end-to-end flow of business activities to accomplish an objective (goal breakdown), and the activity table is an information table for process modeling and activity-based enterprise cost management.

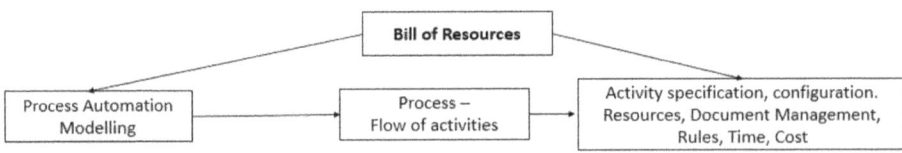

Figure 3-16. *Process modeling dimensions*

CHAPTER 3   USING HYPERAUTOMATION FOR IMPLEMENTING TIME-DRIVEN ABC

Time taken by each activity in a new home loan process is a critical input for Time-Driven ABC. This is explained in Section 3.5.

3.4.5.1 Retail

Table 3-5b. *Generic example –* u*sing the bill of resources for retail banking*

Resources	Sales & Marketing processes	On-Boarding processes	Account Operation Processes	Closure processes
↓ Front Office Staff, System, Other Tangible Resources	Sales process New & Existing customer		Examples: Cash deposit, Withdrawal, Cheque clearing, Internal account transfer, Domestic Funds Transfer, International Wire Transfers, Bill Payments,	Closure request
Middle Office Staff, System, Other Tangible Resources	Credit Appraisal process	Verification of on-boarding	Enterprise Risk Adjusted Return Management; Account behaviour; Dormant account, activation	
Back Office Staff, System, Other Tangible Resources		On-boarding Process (i) New or (ii) existing customer	Accounting & Settlement	

Process 1 New Term Deposit Opening – New Customer

- Goal – Enterprise operating model Effectiveness – market share of deposits
- Section i Bill of resources

Process 1	Performance: End-to-end incident-free execution; KPI time taken							
	P1A1	P1A2	P1A3	P1A4	P1A5	P1A6	P1A7	P1A8
Activity: Front, **m**iddle, **b**ack **office**	F	F	M	M	B	B	F	M

CHAPTER 3   USING HYPERAUTOMATION FOR IMPLEMENTING TIME-DRIVEN ABC

Process 1	Performance: End-to-end incident-free execution; KPI time taken							
	P1A1	P1A2	P1A3	P1A4	P1A5	P1A6	P1A7	P1A8
				Resource				
i) Employee	E1	E2						
ii) System			S1	S2	S2	S2	S2	S2
iii) Other resources							FD receipt	
Cost of activity								

Process cost = sum of the activity costs.

- Section ii Process model

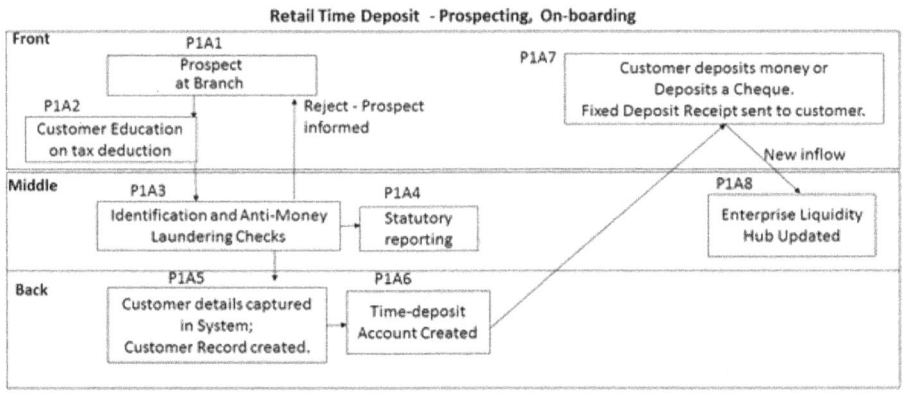

Subprocess	Customer identity checking
	AML checking for retail banking customers
	Customer education for certain retail products, as per GRC directive
Intelligence	AML compliance process

(*continued*)

Robotic process	AML checking for retail deposit accounts
	Customer identity checking of all new customers
Case management	Document management or incident management

- Section iii Activities and its dimensions

Activity Id	Description	Risk/control	Time taken	Cost
P1A1	A **prospect** visits the branch	System and network availability Data security	Units	
P1A2	Customer is educated on taxation aspects. There may be paperwork to complete	Customer experience is improved when the bank educates the customer on the product Customer education is mandatory in the selling of certain financial products	Units	Manual task Customer education on tax implications
P1A3	Customer identity checking and anti-money laundering processes could qualify for robotic process automation	Operational risk Customer identity AML check	Units	Cost of risk management

If checks fail, prospect is informed and process ends

(*continued*)

CHAPTER 3   USING HYPERAUTOMATION FOR IMPLEMENTING TIME-DRIVEN ABC

Activity Id	Description	Risk/control	Time taken	Cost
P1A4	Bank reports suspicious activity to the regulator		Units	Rule and alert management
P1A5	If identity verification and AML checks are cleared, then a customer record is created		Units	Data integration
P1A6	A fixed deposit account is created		Units	Data integration
P1A7	The deposit account is funded by the customer. Fixed deposit receipt is given to customer		Units	Enterprise document management
P1A8	Enterprise liquidity hub is updated		Units	Data integration

Normal end of process

Process 2 Existing Customer's New Term Deposit

- Goal – Market share of deposits
- Section i Bill of resources

CHAPTER 3 USING HYPERAUTOMATION FOR IMPLEMENTING TIME-DRIVEN ABC

Process 2	Performance: End-to-end incident-free execution; KPI time taken						
	P2A1	P1A2	P2A3	P2A4	P2A5	P2A6	P2A7
Activity: Front, middle, back office	F	F	B	B	F	M	M
			Resources				
Employee					E11		
System	S1	S2	S2	S2	S2	S2	S3
Other resources							FD receipt, document mgt
Cost of activity							

Process cost = sum of the activity costs.

- Section ii Process model

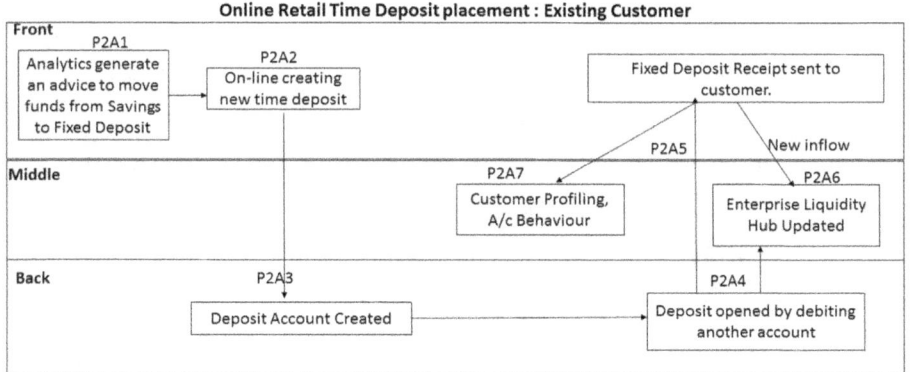

197

CHAPTER 3   USING HYPERAUTOMATION FOR IMPLEMENTING TIME-DRIVEN ABC

Intelligence	360° view of customer; customer profiling; behavioral analysis
Robotic process	With reference to section 3.4.3.8 of this chapter and section 5.5.3.3. of Chapter 5, this process is eligible for robotic process automation

- Section iii Activities and its dimensions

Activity Id	Description	Risk and control	Time taken	Cost
P2A1	An alert from the bank encourages an existing customer to open a time deposit account		Units	Advanced analytics
P2A2	Customer opens a new deposit by transferring money from savings account	System and network availability Data security	Units	User input
P2A3	FD account created		Units	
P2A4	Fixed deposit is opened		Units	
P2A5	Bank issues a fixed deposit receipt		Units	Fixed deposit receipt – cost
P2A6	Enterprise liquidity hub updated		Units	
P2A7	Analytics: customer profile; account behavior. Know Your Customer is enriched		Units	Advanced analytics

Normal end of process

CHAPTER 3   USING HYPERAUTOMATION FOR IMPLEMENTING TIME-DRIVEN ABC

Process 3 Home Loan to Salaried Individuals

- Business Goal – Market share of retail credit
- Section i Bill of resources

Process 3	Performance: End-to-end incident-free execution; time taken						
	P3A1	P3A2	P3A3	P3A4	P3A5	P3A6	P3A7
Activity: Front, middle, back **office**	F	M	M	M	M	M	F
		Resources					
Employee	E1	E2					
System		S2	S1	S1	S1	S1	S1
Other resources	Doc mgt	Doc mgt		Doc mgt		Doc mgt	Doc mgt
Cost of activity							

Process 3 (continued)	P3A8	P3A9	P3A10	P3A11	P3A12
Activity: front, middle, back office	B	B	B	B	M
Employee	E1	E2			
System	S1	S1	S3	S1	S1
Other resources					
Cost of activity					

Process cost = sum of the activity costs.

- Section ii Process model

CHAPTER 3   USING HYPERAUTOMATION FOR IMPLEMENTING TIME-DRIVEN ABC

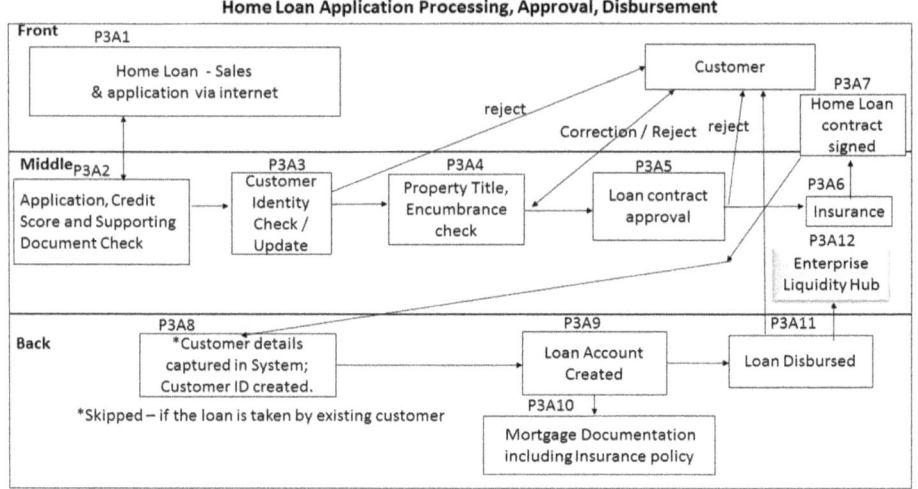

Subprocess	Application checking for retail asset products
	AML checking for retail banking customers (individuals)
Intelligence	Customer need from profile; monitoring of customer experience
	Loan document content management
Robotic process	AML checking for retail banking customers (individuals)
	External credit scoring (API-based data integration)
Case management	Document management (title deeds)

- Section iii Activities and its dimensions

CHAPTER 3   USING HYPERAUTOMATION FOR IMPLEMENTING TIME-DRIVEN ABC

Activity Id	Description	Risk/control	Time taken	Cost
P3A1	A prospect interacts online for a home loan Credit scoring and decision on loan approval This is a reusable automatic process	System and network availability Data security Credit risk – applications with credit score lower than minimum are rejected and the process ends	Units	Cost of risk management
P3A2	Bank receives the documents Customer identity checking is a reusable process Semiautomatic	GRC policy on documents required If the check fails, prospect is informed and process ends	Units	Document checking and management
P3A3	Prospect might need to be contacted for completing the submission Semiautomatic		Units	Retail customer identity checking – manual AML check Subprocess
Identity check failure – process ends				

(*continued*)

CHAPTER 3   USING HYPERAUTOMATION FOR IMPLEMENTING TIME-DRIVEN ABC

Activity Id	Description	Risk/control	Time taken	Cost
P3A4	Property title and encumbrance check	Operational and credit risk	Units	This is a manual task; document management
Property title check fails – process ends				
P3A5	If P3A4 is successful, then officer checks and approves			
P3A6	Customer takes an insurance policy and assigns to the bank		Units	Manual checking Document management
P3A7	Home loan contract is signed		Units	Digital or manual
P3A8	Customer Id is created for a NEW customer. Skipped if it an existing customer	System controls include the following: Data protection Segregation of duties Dual checking	Units	
P3A9	Loan account is created		Units	
P3A10	Loan documents are captured in the enterprise document management system		Units	User input approval Document management

(*continued*)

202

CHAPTER 3   USING HYPERAUTOMATION FOR IMPLEMENTING TIME-DRIVEN ABC

Activity Id	Description	Risk/control	Time taken	Cost
P3A11	Funds disbursed as per home loan contract		Units	Data integration
P3A12	Enterprise liquidity hub updated	Subsequently, for every loan repayment, the enterprise liquidity hub updated	Units	Data integration
Normal end of process				

3.4.5.2 Corporate

Table 3-5c. Using the bill of resources

Bill of Resources Corporate Banking (generic example)
Resources assigned to processes

Resources	Sales & Marketing processes	On-Boarding processes	Account Operation processes	Closure processes
Front Office Staff, System, Other Tangible Resources	Sales process New & Existing Customer		Letter of Credit Issuance Guarantee Account Relationship	Loan Account Closure
Middle Office Staff, System, Other Tangible Resources	Credit Appraisal process	On-boarding approval process	Enterprise Risk Adjusted Return Management; Account behaviour; Customer Profiling	Due Diligence
Back Office Staff, System, Other Tangible Resources		On-boarding Process New customer or existing customer	Loan Disbursement Loan Repayments Accounting & Settlement	

Process 4 Corporate Term Loan Application

- Business Goal – Enterprise risk-adjusted return
- Section i Bill of resources

Process 4	Performance: End-to-end incident-free execution; time taken				
	P4A1	P41A2	P4A3	P4A4	P4A5
Activity: Front, middle, back office	F	F	M	M	M
Employee	E1	E2			
System	S1	S1	S1	S2	S1
Other resources	All activities – document management				
Cost of activity					

Process cost = sum of the activity costs.

- Section ii Process model

Intelligence	Matching against risky profiles
	Search on directors and business entity
Robotic process	AML checking for corporate banking customers
Case management	Inadequate AML program

CHAPTER 3   USING HYPERAUTOMATION FOR IMPLEMENTING TIME-DRIVEN ABC

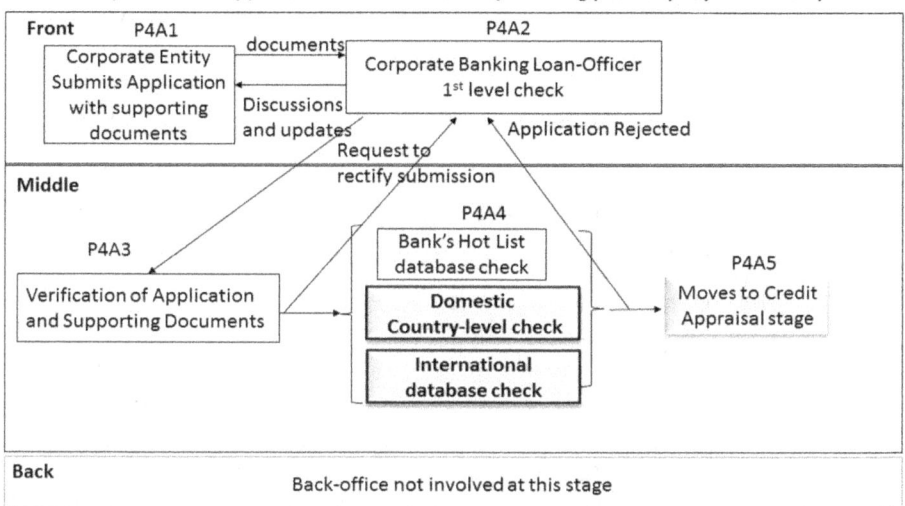

- Section iii Activities and its dimensions

Activity Id	Description	Risk/control	Time taken	Cost
P4A1	Prospect interacts with corporate banking loan manager		Units	Loan manager's business development effort
P4A2	Bank receives the documents	Policies for corporate loans specify the documents required in support of the application	Units	Manual

(*continued*)

205

CHAPTER 3   USING HYPERAUTOMATION FOR IMPLEMENTING TIME-DRIVEN ABC

Activity Id	Description	Risk/control	Time taken	Cost
P4A3	Credit administration checks the documents		Units	Cost of risk management
P4A4	Identity checking is done for the following: The company All the directors and the executive team (people who have the mandate to manage bank accounts)	If the check fails, prospect is informed and process ends Company and director background and anti-money laundering checks	Units	Cost of risk management AML checking could be a robotic process automation
	Identity/anti-money laundering checks fail – process ends			
P4A5	The details are captured in the system		Units	User input Enterprise document management
	Normal end of process			

Process 5 Credit Risk Appraisal of Corporate Loan Application

- Business Goal – Risk-adjusted net interest margin
- Section i Bill of resources

CHAPTER 3 USING HYPERAUTOMATION FOR IMPLEMENTING TIME-DRIVEN ABC

Process 5	Performance: End-to-end incident-free execution; time taken				
	P5A1	P5A2	P5A3	P5A4	P5A5
Activity: Front, middle, back office	M	M	M	M	F
Employee	E11	E12	E13	E14	E15
System	S1	S2	S3	S1	S1
Other resources	All activities – document management				
Cost of activity					

Process cost = sum of the activity costs.

- Section ii Process model

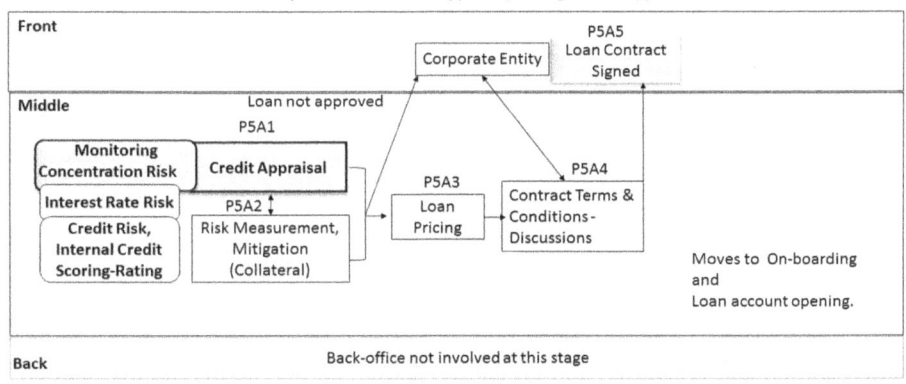

Intelligence	Knowledge management for loan pricing
Robotic process	Internal credit rating
Case management	Credit appraisal not done properly

CHAPTER 3   USING HYPERAUTOMATION FOR IMPLEMENTING TIME-DRIVEN ABC

Activity Id	Description	Risk/control	Time taken	Cost
P5A1	Credit appraisal includes verifying purpose of loan; concentration risks; borrower's credit worthiness; evaluation of project financials Corporate credit scoring is a reusable process	Data: Economic and industry data Credit risk management policies and procedures	Units	Cost of risk management
P5A2	Estimation of credit risk	Risk appetite policy	Units	Subprocess Data integration
P5A3	Assessing collateral requirements Loan pricing	Risk-adjusted net interest margin FX, interest rate, and borrower risks	Units	Semiautomatic
P5A4	Discussions with customers on terms and conditions Decision on loan approval Customer is informed if loan is rejected		Units	Manual
P5A5	Loan contract signed		Units	Enterprise document management

Normal end of process

CHAPTER 3   USING HYPERAUTOMATION FOR IMPLEMENTING TIME-DRIVEN ABC

Process 6 Corporate Customer Onboarding

- Business Goal – Market share of corporate credit
- Section i Bill of resources

Process 6	Performance: End-to-end incident-free execution; time taken					
	P6A1	P6A2	P6A3	P6A4	P6A5	P6A6
Activity: Front, middle, back office	B	B	B	B	B	M
Employee						E12
System	S1	S1	S1	S1	S1	
Other resources				Document mgt		
Cost of activity						

Process cost = sum of the activity costs.

- Section ii Process model

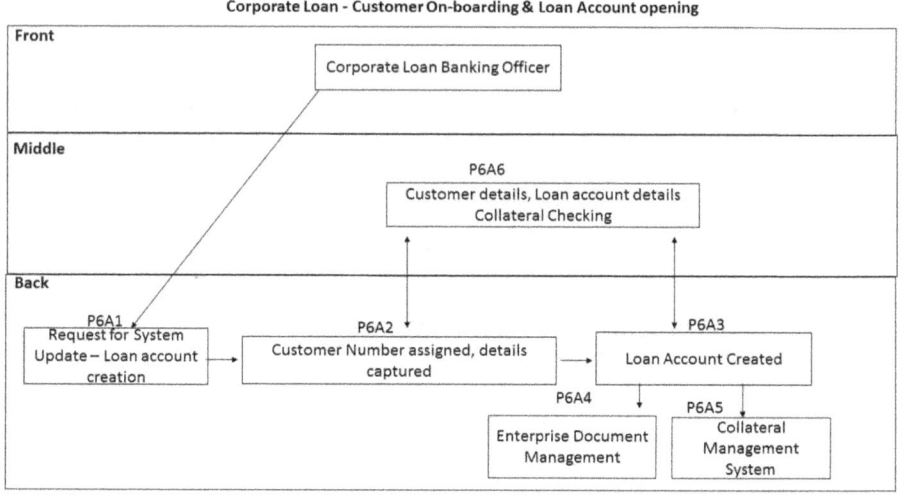

CHAPTER 3   USING HYPERAUTOMATION FOR IMPLEMENTING TIME-DRIVEN ABC

Intelligence	Loan document content management
Case management	Loan documentation incident

- Section iii Activities and its dimensions

Activity Id	Description	Risk/control	Time taken	Cost
P6A1	After loan contract is signed, account manager send documents to back office	Dual control Segregation of duties	Units	Enterprise document management
P6A2	Customer Id is created		Units	User input Data integration
P6A3	Loan account is created		Units	User input Data integration
P6A4	Enterprise document management system update		Units	Enterprise document management
P6A5	Centralized collateral management update		Units	Data integration
P6A6	Middle-office checking of system updates		Units	Rule and alert

Normal end of process

Process 7 Corporate Loan Disbursement

- Business Goal – Enterprise risk-adjusted return management
- Section i Bill of resources

CHAPTER 3 USING HYPERAUTOMATION FOR IMPLEMENTING TIME-DRIVEN ABC

Process 7	Performance: End-to-end incident-free execution; time taken		
	P7A1	P7A2	P7A3
Activity: Front, middle, back office	M	B	M
Employee			
System	S1	S1	S1
Other resources			
Cost of activity			

Process cost = sum of the activity costs.

- Section ii Process model

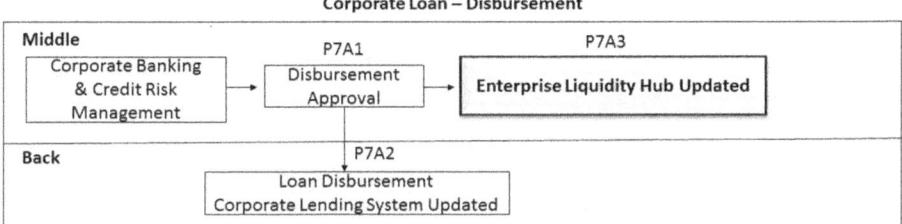

Intelligence	Intraday liquidity management; liquidity risk management

- Section iii Activities and its dimensions

Activity Id	Description	Risk/control	Time taken	Cost
P7A1	Approval for disbursement provided by credit administration	Contract specifications checked	Units	Data integration

(*continued*)

211

CHAPTER 3   USING HYPERAUTOMATION FOR IMPLEMENTING TIME-DRIVEN ABC

Activity Id	Description	Risk/control	Time taken	Cost
P7A2	Funds disbursed and system updated	Dual control and segregation of risks	Units	Cost of risk management
P7A3	Enterprise liquidity hub updated	Enterprise risks, market, credit, and liquidity includes this exposure	Units	Data integration

Normal end of process

Process 8 Corporate Loan Credit Risk Management (Example for Cost of Risk Management)

This is a credit risk monitoring process model that has five components as shown in Section ii of this example. Each component could be taken as a process.

- Business Goal – Enterprise-minimize risk-maximize return

- Section i Bill of resources

Process 8	Performance: End-to-end incident-free execution; time taken							
	P8A1	P8A2	P8A3	P8A4	P8A5	P8A6	P8A7	P8A8
Activity: Front, **m**iddle, **b**ack office	M	M	M	M	M	M	M	B
Employee	E14					E23	E24	E25
System	S1	S2	S2	S2	S2	S2	S2	S3

(*continued*)

Process 8	Performance: End-to-end incident-free execution; time taken							
	P8A1	P8A2	P8A3	P8A4	P8A5	P8A6	P8A7	P8A8
Other resources								Document mgt
Cost of activity								

Process cost = sum of the activity costs.

These examples also illustrate the cost of risk management.

Subprocess	Mark to market
	Internal credit rating
Intelligence	External event tracking; account behavior; staff (relationship manager) behavior; recommendation on collateral quality and coverage of exposure
Robotic process	Mark to market
	Internal credit rating
Case management	Weak credit monitoring

- Section ii Process model

CHAPTER 3   USING HYPERAUTOMATION FOR IMPLEMENTING TIME-DRIVEN ABC

Credit Risk Monitoring at Loan level

```
Middle                  Scheduled Event        P8A1    Site Visit /
                              (A)          ─────────►  Project Inspection
─────────────────────────────────────────────────────────────────────────
Scheduled Event         P8A2
Risk Engine          (B)◄──► Probability of default │ Loss Given Default │ Exposure at Default
Calculations:
─────────────────────────────────────────────────────────────────────────
                              P8A3   Mark to Market
                         (C)◄───P8A4──► Expiry - e.g. Guarantee
                              P8A5
                              ──► Total & Partial Redemption/Release of Security
─────────────────────────────────────────────────────────────────────────
                         (D)   P8A6   Internal Credit Rating
                                      Administration
─────────────────────────────────────────────────────────────────────────
                         (E)   P8A7   Change in External Credit Rating
─────────────────────────────────────────────────────────────────────────
Back        P8A8    Revised Limits, Collateral, Change in Terms & Conditions including Loan Pricing; Documentation
```

- Section iii Activities and its dimensions

Activity Id	Description	Risk/control	Time taken	Cost
A – P8A1 loan terms and conditions monitoring	This is a scheduled event, and the banker checks in person the utilization of the loan and the collateral	Segregation of duties Site inspection data update in the lending system	Units	User input Data integration
B – P8A2 credit risk quantification	Calculation of the following: Probability of default Loss given default Exposure at default	Risk engine using enterprise risk data Bank might ask for more collateral and/or change loan pricing	Units	Cost of risk management Data integration

(*continued*)

CHAPTER 3   USING HYPERAUTOMATION FOR IMPLEMENTING TIME-DRIVEN ABC

Activity Id	Description	Risk/control	Time taken	Cost
C – Internal event for credit risk management	Mark to market is a scheduled event	Bank might ask for more collateral and/or change loan pricing	Units	Event – time Subprocess Data integration
P8A3 collateral management can trigger	Monitoring expiry dates on collateral	This can trigger an internal event seeking more collateral	Units	Alert-based event – time
P8A4 internal event for credit risk management P8A5 internal event for credit risk management	Partial or full release of collateral	Dual control and segregation of duties	Units	User input Cost of risk management Data integration
D – P8A6 internal credit rating	Internal assessment of the company financials and credit rating	Site inspection data, company announcements, media reports, and market factors are key inputs Bank might ask for more collateral and/or change loan pricing	Units	Credit risk management subprocess Data integration

(*continued*)

CHAPTER 3   USING HYPERAUTOMATION FOR IMPLEMENTING TIME-DRIVEN ABC

Activity Id	Description	Risk/control	Time taken	Cost
E – P8A7 change in external rating			Units	Conditional event Credit risk management subprocess
P8A8 back-end systems	Accounting: lending and centralized collateral management system	Lending and centralized collateral management system	Units	Data integration

3.4.5.3 Treasury

Table 3-5d. Using the bill of resources

Resources	Pre-deal processes	Deal Booking processes	Settlement processes
Bill of Resources Treasury (generic example)			
Resources assigned to processes			
Front Office Staff, System, Other Tangible Resources	Negotiations with counterparty	Deal Entry	
Middle Office Staff, System, Other Tangible Resources	Pre-deal analytics	Deal Verification	Due Diligence; Enterprise Risk Adjusted Return Management;
Back Office Staff, System, Other Tangible Resources		Accounting	Nostro Management; Settlement

CHAPTER 3   USING HYPERAUTOMATION FOR IMPLEMENTING TIME-DRIVEN ABC

Process 9 Index-Linked CDS Deal Input

Credit default swaps (CDS) are OTC derivatives that enables the transfer of a particular credit risk exposure from one counterparty to another. It can be compared to a tradable insurance contract that protects against the default of the reference entity. A lot of effort has gone into the standardization of CDS contracts, and they are the building blocks of CDS indices.

- Business Goal – Market share of treasury business, maximize risk-adjusted return from the deal

- Section i Bill of resources

Process 9	Performance: End-to-end incident-free execution; time taken							
	P9A1	P9A2	P9A3	P9A4	P9A5	P9A6	P9A7	P9A8
Activity: Front, middle, back office	M	F	M	F	B	B	B	B
Employee	E1	E2	E3					
System	S2	S1	S1	S1	S1	S1	S1	S1
Other resources					Doc mgt	Content mgt		
Cost of activity								

P9A1 is a middle-office function, and the output is viewed by front officer, treasury trader.

This is a good example for taking risk management to the front office, i.e., trading desks. This is the approach for improving risk-adjusted operating leverage.

CHAPTER 3   USING HYPERAUTOMATION FOR IMPLEMENTING TIME-DRIVEN ABC

Process cost = sum of the activity costs.

- Section ii Process model

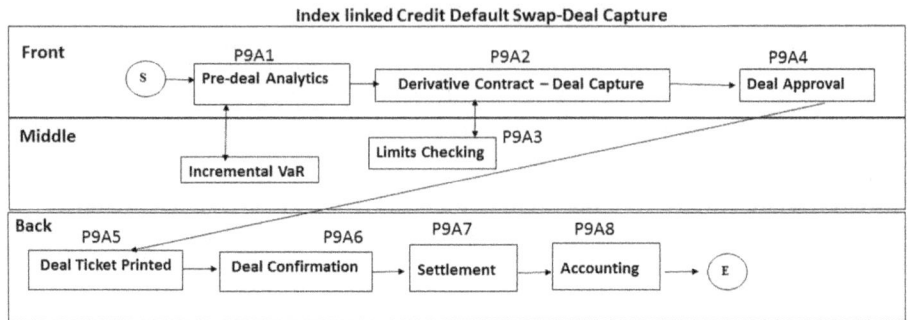

Intelligence	Predeal analytics, recommendation on collateral quality, and coverage of exposure
Robotic process	Predeal analytics
Case management	Atypical deals

- Section iii Activities and its dimensions

Activity Id	Description	Risk/control	Time taken	Cost
P9A1	Predeal analytics capability provides traders a risk assessment prior to trade commitment Processing is a middle-office function. Output is presented to the front office	The deal data is seamlessly integrated in real time with enterprise risk data	Units	User input Predeal analytics subprocess Conditional event, enterprise risk management Subprocess Data integration

(*continued*)

218

CHAPTER 3 USING HYPERAUTOMATION FOR IMPLEMENTING TIME-DRIVEN ABC

Activity Id	Description	Risk/control	Time taken	Cost
P9A 2	The deal details are input in the treasury management system		Units	User input Data integration
P9A3	The risk exposure on account of deal is checked	Limits management supports the management of risk as per defined risk appetite and tolerance	Units	Cost of risk management Data integration
P9A4	The deal is approved if there is no limit violations		Units	User input Data integration

If there is a limit excess situation, the deal is either rejected or goes through an exception escalation approval process

Activity Id	Description	Risk/control	Time taken	Cost
P9A5	Deal ticket is printed		Units	
P9A6	SWIFT confirmation is completed		Units	Data integration
P9A7	The settlement process is initiated		Units	Data integration
P9A8	Accounting is done on the basis of the approved deal ticket		Units	Data integration

Normal end of process

CHAPTER 3   USING HYPERAUTOMATION FOR IMPLEMENTING TIME-DRIVEN ABC

Process 10 Interest Rate Swap Deal Input

- Business Goal– Market share of treasury business, maximize risk-adjusted return from the deal
- Section i Bill of resources

Process 10	Performance: End-to-end incident-free execution; time taken						
	P10A1	P10A2	P10A3	P10A4	P10A5	P10A6	P10A7
Activity: Front, middle, back office	F	M	M	M	F	F	B
Employee	E1				E2	E3	E4
System	S1	S2	S2	S1	S1	S1	S1
Other resources							
Cost of activity							

			P10A8		P10A9		P10A10
			B		B		B
			S1		S1		
Cost of activity							

CHAPTER 3 USING HYPERAUTOMATION FOR IMPLEMENTING TIME-DRIVEN ABC

Process cost = sum of the activity costs.

- Section ii Process model

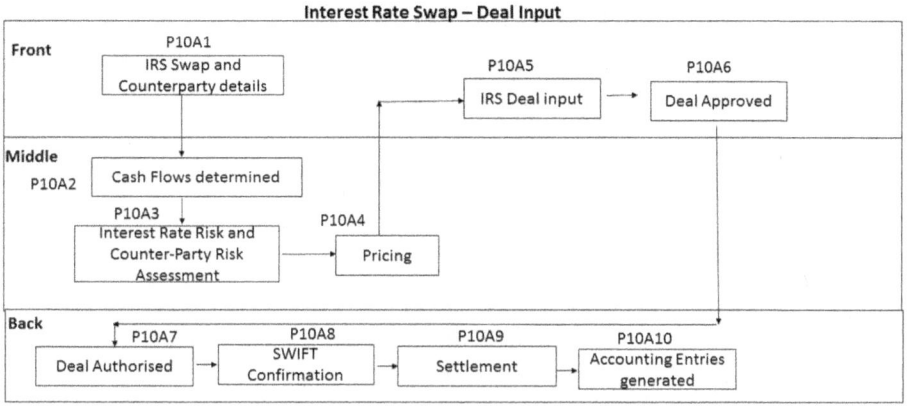

Intelligence	Predeal analytics
Case management	Atypical deals

- Section iii Activities and its dimensions

Activity Id	Description	Risk/control	Time taken	Cost
P10A1	Negotiation on terms and conditions		Units	User input
P10A2	Cash flows are determined		Units	Cost of risk management

(*continued*)

CHAPTER 3   USING HYPERAUTOMATION FOR IMPLEMENTING TIME-DRIVEN ABC

Activity Id	Description	Risk/control	Time taken	Cost
P10A3	Assessment of market, credit, and liquidity risks	Enterprise data management is a critical success factor "Single view of truth" 360° view of customer/counterparty	Units	Cost of risk management Enterprise risk management Subprocess Data integration
P10A4	Risk-adjusted pricing of the deal		Units	Data integration
P10A5	Deal is input into treasury management system	IRS contract created, limits, cash flow, and portfolio – updated Deal slip generated	Units	User input
P10A6	Deal is approved	Dual control	Units	User input
P10A7	Deal is authorized in the back office for settlement and accounting	Segregation of duties	Units	Cost of risk management

(*continued*)

CHAPTER 3   USING HYPERAUTOMATION FOR IMPLEMENTING TIME-DRIVEN ABC

Activity Id	Description	Risk/control	Time taken	Cost
P10A8	SWIFT confirmation is generated		Units	Data integration
P10A9	Settlement		Units	Data integration
P10A10	Accounting for the deal		Units	Data integration
Normal end of process				

Process 11 OTC Derivative

- Business Goal – Market share of treasury business; maximize risk-adjusted return of the deal
- Section i Bill of resources

Process 11	Performance: End-to-end incident-free execution; time taken							
	P11A1	P11A2	P11A3	P11A4	P11A5	P11A6	P11A7	P11A8
Activity: Front, middle, back office	M	F	B	B	F	M	B	F
Employee	E31	E32	E33	E34	E35	E36		
System	S1	S1	S1	S1	S1	S1	S1	S1
Other resources								
Cost of activity								

223

CHAPTER 3   USING HYPERAUTOMATION FOR IMPLEMENTING TIME-DRIVEN ABC

	P11A9	P11A10	P11A11
	M	B	B
	S2	S1	S1
Cost of activity			

Process cost = sum of the activity costs.

- Section ii Process model

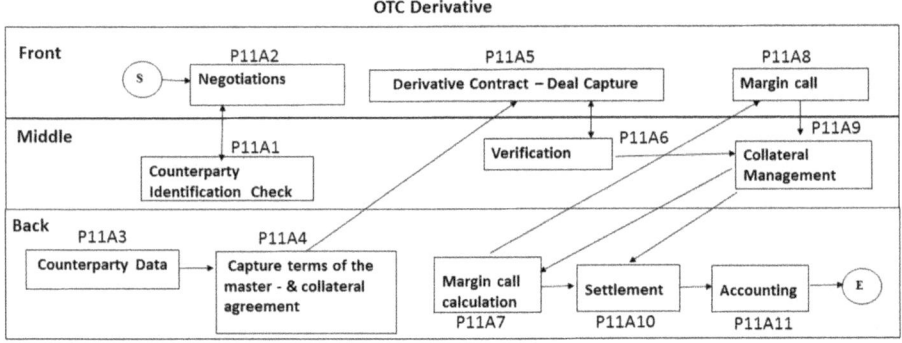

Intelligence	Knowledge management – counterparty; collateral

- Section iii Activities and its dimensions

224

CHAPTER 3   USING HYPERAUTOMATION FOR IMPLEMENTING TIME-DRIVEN ABC

Activity Id	Description	Risk/control	Time taken	Cost
P11A1	Counterparty identification check	Industry standard template for onboarding counterparties	Units	User input
P11A2	Validate counterparty business need, negotiations	Legal documentation standardization (e.g. ISDA Clause Library) • Electronic negotiation of legal framework and digitalization of legal framework into a centrally shared legal documentation repository	Units	User input
P11A3	Capture counterparty data		Units	Conditional event Enterprise risk management Subprocess Data integration
P11A4	Capture terms of the master and collateral agreement		Units	Data integration
P11A5	Trade capture		Units	User input
P11A6	Trade verification	Dual control, segregation of duties	Units	User input
P11A7	Margin call calculation		Units	User input
P11A8	Margin call to counterparty		Units	Data integration

(*continued*)

CHAPTER 3 USING HYPERAUTOMATION FOR IMPLEMENTING TIME-DRIVEN ABC

Activity Id	Description	Risk/control	Time taken	Cost
P11A9	Manage collateral inventory		Units	
P11A10	Settlement		Units	
P11A11	Accounting		Units	
Normal end of process				

Dynamic hedging could be an intelligence powered, robotic set of processes.

3.4.5.4 Support Department – GRC

Process 12 Anti-money Laundering and Countering the Financing of Terrorism

- Business Goal – Governance, compliance
- Section i Bill of resources

Process 12	Performance: End-to-end incident-free execution; time taken								
	P12A1	P12A2	P12A3	P12A4	P12A5	P12A6	P12A7	P12A8	P12A9
Activity: Front, middle, back office	F	M	B	B	M	F	B	B	M
Employee	E51				E52				

(*continued*)

CHAPTER 3 USING HYPERAUTOMATION FOR IMPLEMENTING TIME-DRIVEN ABC

Process 12	Performance: End-to-end incident-free execution; time taken								
	P12A1	P12A2	P12A3	P12A4	P12A5	P12A6	P12A7	P12A8	P12A9
System	S1	S2	S1	S2		S1	S2	S2	S2
Other resources							Reporting		
Activity cost									

Process cost = sum of the activity costs = cost of risk management.

- Section ii Process model

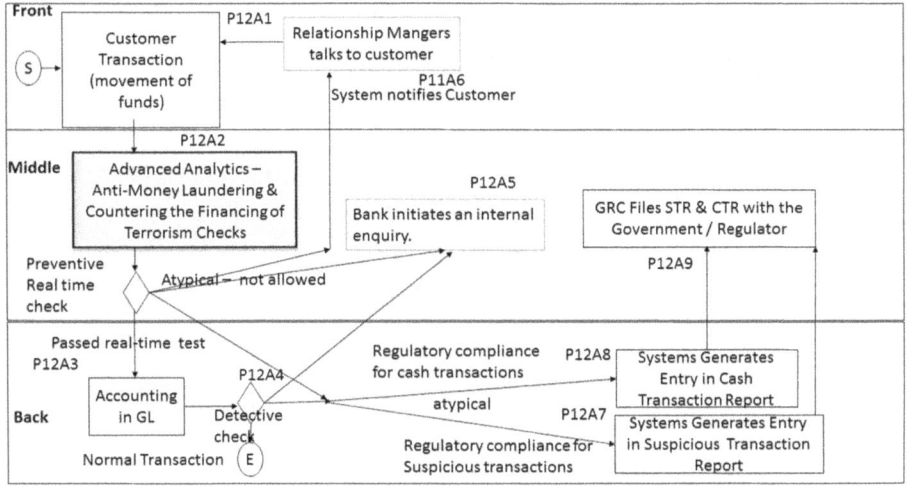

STR, suspicious transaction report; CTR, cash transaction report (compliance reports)

CHAPTER 3   USING HYPERAUTOMATION FOR IMPLEMENTING TIME-DRIVEN ABC

This can be an intelligence powered, robotic automated process.

- Section iii Activities and its dimensions

Process component Id	Description	Risk/control	Time taken	Cost
P12A1	A financial transaction is posted		Units	User input
P12A2	The transaction is routed to the AML-CFT analytics engine	Enterprise data management, single view of customer is important Intelligence and rule-based operational risk management	Units	Data integration
P12A3	If the preventive checks do not flag an alert, then the transaction is allowed to update the system, subject to the clearance of other controls		Units	Data integration

(*continued*)

CHAPTER 3   USING HYPERAUTOMATION FOR IMPLEMENTING TIME-DRIVEN ABC

Process component Id	Description	Risk/control	Time taken	Cost
P12A4	The AML-CFT continues to run in the background and can still detect an atypical activity at a later stage		Units	Conditional event Rules (atypical Y/N) AML-CFT operational risk management
P12A5	GRC conducts a due diligence or enhanced due diligence when there is an alert	AML due diligence subprocess	Units	Subprocess AML due diligence
P12A6	System generates an entry in suspicious activity report		Units	Data integration
P12A7	System generates an entry in cash transactions report		Units	Report generation
P12A8	Bank files the SAR, CTR reports with the regulator		Units	Reporting – data integration
P12A9	Customer management	Customer management in this situation is a regulatory and compliance issue	Units	Case management

CHAPTER 3 USING HYPERAUTOMATION FOR IMPLEMENTING TIME-DRIVEN ABC

3.4.5.5 Support Department – EITG
Process 13 Incident Management

- Business Goal – Enterprise IT governance
- Section i Bill of resources

Process 13 Performance: End-to-end incident-free execution; time taken									
	P13A1	P13A2	P13A3	P13A4	P132A5	P13A6	P13A7	P13A8	P13A9
Activity: Front, middle, back office	F	M	M	M	M	M	M	M	M
Employee	E61		E62	E63	E64	E65			E69
System	S1	S2	S2	S2	S2	S2	S2	S2	S2
Other resources									
Activity cost									

Process cost = sum of the activity costs.

- Section ii Process model

CHAPTER 3   USING HYPERAUTOMATION FOR IMPLEMENTING TIME-DRIVEN ABC

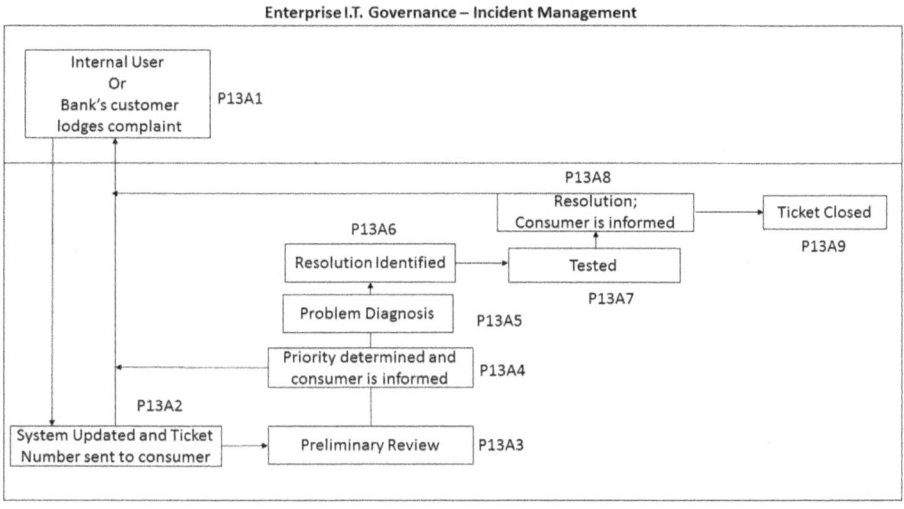

Subprocess	Preliminary diagnosis
	Detailed investigation
	Incident resolution
Intelligence	Knowledge management of external threats
Robotic process	Intrusion detection
Case management	Risk categories include customer complaint, damage to asset, business disruption, business delivery
	This data is available for internal control, audit, and GRC

- Section iii Activities and its dimensions

Process component Id	Description	Risk/control	Time taken	Cost
P13A1	Scrutiny of the complaint	This could an internal or external event	Units	Manual
P13A2	Incident recorded, ticket raised	Service level agreement	Units	

(*continued*)

CHAPTER 3 USING HYPERAUTOMATION FOR IMPLEMENTING TIME-DRIVEN ABC

Process component Id	Description	Risk/control	Time taken	Cost
P13A3	Preliminary review		Units	Manual
P13A4	Priority determined		Units	Manual
P13A5	Problem identification, risk assessment		Units	Manual
P13A6	Correction identified	Segregation of duties	Units	Manual
P13A7	Corrective measures tested and implemented	Actions are based on SLA commitments	Units	Manual
P13A8	Issue resolved		Units	
P13A9	Incident ticket closed		Units	
	Normal end of process			

3.4.5.6 Support Department – Human Capital

The three phases of managing employees are shown in Figure 3-17.

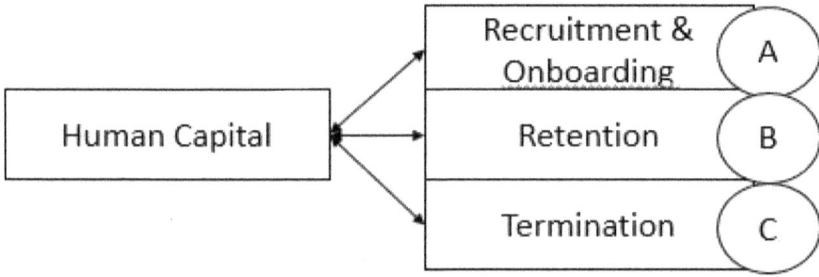

Figure 3-17. Human capital management cycle

CHAPTER 3   USING HYPERAUTOMATION FOR IMPLEMENTING TIME-DRIVEN ABC

Process 14 Human Capital – Recruitment and Employee Onboarding

- Business Goal – Minimize operational risk, maximize business return from investment in human capital
- Section i Bill of resources

Process 14 Performance: End-to-end incident-free execution; time taken									
	P14A1	P14A2	P14A3	P14A4	P14A5	P14A6	P14A7	P14A8	P14A9
Activity: Front, middle, back office	F	M	M	B	B	F	F	M	F
Employee	E81	E81	E81	E81		E82	E82	E82	E82
System	S1	S1	S1	S1	S1	S1	S1	S1	S1
Other resources									
Activity cost									

	P14A10	P14A11
	B	M
	E83	
	S1	S2
	Activity cost	

Process cost = sum of the activity costs.

- Section ii Process model

233

CHAPTER 3 USING HYPERAUTOMATION FOR IMPLEMENTING TIME-DRIVEN ABC

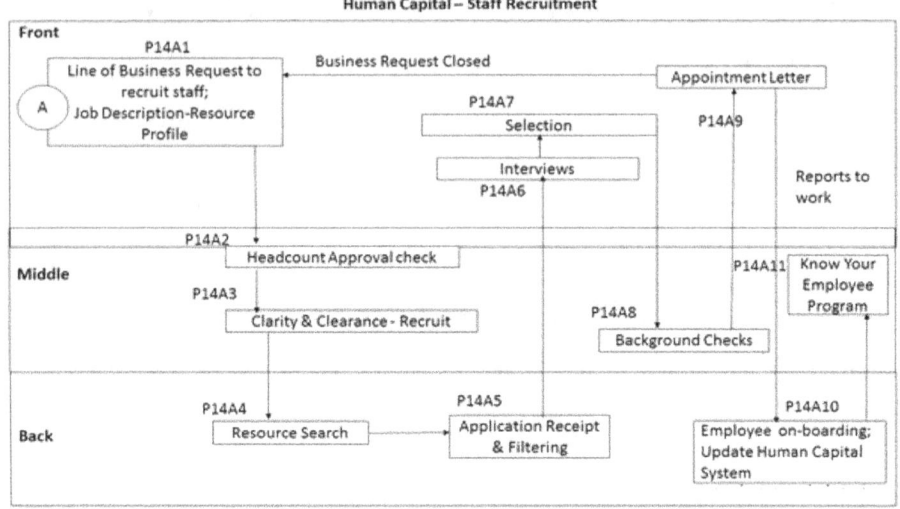

Intelligence	Staff behavioral analysis, staff profile
Robotic process	Financial profile

- Section iii Activities and its dimensions

Activity Id	Description	Risk/control	Time taken	Cost
P14A1	HR receives recruitment request		Units	
P14A2	HR checks for headcount approval		Units	Operational risk management
P14A3	If the request has the approval, then HR discusses the request with the relevant manager		Units	

(*continued*)

CHAPTER 3 USING HYPERAUTOMATION FOR IMPLEMENTING TIME-DRIVEN ABC

Activity Id	Description	Risk/control	Time taken	Cost
P14A4	HR initiates a resources search		Units	
P14A5	HR and recruiting manager prepare long-list candidates		Units	
P14A6	HR organizes the interviews		Units	
P14A7	HR and recruiting manager short-list the candidates		Units	
P14A8	HR does the background checks		Units	
P14A9	HR sends appointment letter to selected candidate		Units	
P14A10	Staff joins the bank and goes through an induction program		Units	
P14A11	From this stage, Know Your Employee program is invoked for the employee	Know Your Employee program needs a 360° view of staff – enterprise data management	Units	Operational risk management
Normal end of process				

CHAPTER 3   USING HYPERAUTOMATION FOR IMPLEMENTING TIME-DRIVEN ABC

Process 15 Human Capital – Retention

- Business Goal – Minimize operational risk, maximize business return from investment in human capital

- Section i Bill of resources

Process 15 P15A3	Activity: Front, middle, back office	P15A1	P15A2
M	Employee	M	M
E87	System	E85	E86
S1	Other resources	S2	S1
	Activity cost		

Process cost = sum of the activity costs.

- Section ii Process model

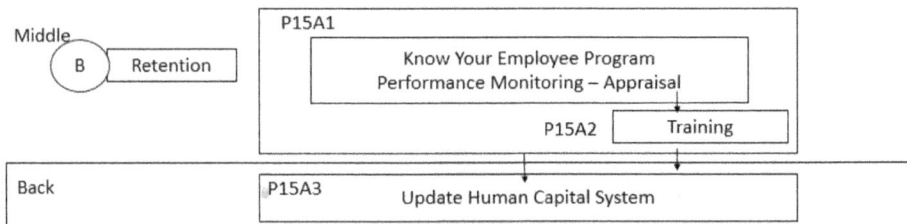

- Section iii Activities and its dimensions

236

CHAPTER 3   USING HYPERAUTOMATION FOR IMPLEMENTING TIME-DRIVEN ABC

Process component Id	Description	Risk/control	Time taken	Cost
P15A1	Know Your Employee program Performance appraisal	Quantified work objectives Approved template Escalation mechanism	Units	Subprocesses Data integration
P15A2	Staff training		Units	Data integration
P15A3	Human capital system updated		Units	Update

Process 16 Human Capital – Termination

- Business Goal – Minimize operational risk
- Section i Bill of resources

P16	Performance: End-to-end incident-free execution; time taken						
	P16A1	P16A2	P16A3	P16A4	P16A5	P16A6	P16A7
Activity: Front, middle, back **office**	M	M	M	M	M	B	M
Employee	E91	E92	E93	E94	E95		
System	S1	S1	S1	S1	S1	S1	S1
Other resources							
Activity cost							

Process cost = sum of the activity costs.

237

CHAPTER 3   USING HYPERAUTOMATION FOR IMPLEMENTING TIME-DRIVEN ABC

- Section ii Process model

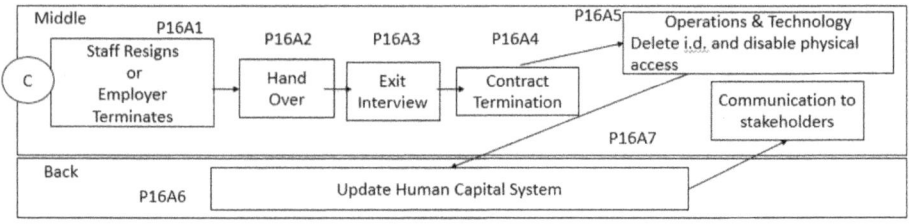

- Section iii Activities and its dimensions

Know Your Employee (KYE) program's staff profile is a useful input for managing the resignation process. It is the same program that could recommend a termination.

Activity Id	Description	Risk/control	Time taken	Cost
P16A1	Staff submits resignation or decision to terminate the service of an employee	KYE program: Staff profile		
P16A2	Handover		Units	
P16A3	Exit interview		Units	Operating risk management
P16A4	Contract terminated and settlement		Units	
P16A5	Communication to stakeholders		Units	

(*continued*)

CHAPTER 3   USING HYPERAUTOMATION FOR IMPLEMENTING TIME-DRIVEN ABC

Activity Id	Description	Risk/control	Time taken	Cost
P16A6	Delete ID, disable physical access		Units	Operational risk management
P16A7	Update human capital system, enterprise risk data, and enterprise knowledge management		Units	Data integration

Process ownership should be synchronized with product, service, and support ownership. The process owner will be responsible for its orchestration, cost, and residual risks.

3.4.6 Templates: Cost Data Capture and Update

Tables 3-6a, 3-6b, 3-6c, and 3-6d illustrate the capture of cost data at source. This is followed by a schematic of the update of books of account and the ENICM system in Tables 3-18a, 3-18b, 3-18c, and 3-18d.

Table 3-6a is an example of a direct cost, advertising, updating the ENICM system with the product code. Profit center code RETHLS is debited with 50,000 on account of advertising, a direct cost.

CHAPTER 3 USING HYPERAUTOMATION FOR IMPLEMENTING TIME-DRIVEN ABC

Table 3-6a. *Capture of cost data at source*

Process Automation: Cost data capture and ENICM System update		
Cost: Advertising; Product: Home Loan-Salaried		
Transaction Type Id	P&L Debit	
Posting date	20240101	
Posted By	ABC	
Debit Account Number	Advertising	
Credit Account Number	Vendor Id.	
Cost Data:	Profit Centre Code	RETHLS
Transaction Amount	500,000	
Narration	Advertising for Home Loans- Individuals with Income from Salary – Cost centre is product code RETHLS	
Reference		
Verified By	XYZ	

Table 3-6b is an example of a direct cost, legal expense, updating the customer in the ENICM system. The relevant product is also known. Profit center code CORCC1L10 is debited with 750,000 on account of legal expenses, a direct cost.

Table 3-6b. *Capture of cost data at source*

Process Automation: Cost data capture and ENICM System update		
Cost: Legal; Product: 10 Year Term Loan; Corporate Customer Id: (borrower)		
Transaction Type Id	P&L Debit	
Posting date	20240101	
Posted By	ABC	
Debit Account Number	Legal Expenses	
Credit Account Number	Law Firm Id.	
Cost Data:	Profit Centre Code	CORCC1L10
Transaction Amount	750,000	
Narration	Lawyer expenses – Loan recovery; **ENICM – debit to customer- product CC1L10**	
Reference	NPA_Cat01	
Verified By	XYZ	

CHAPTER 3 USING HYPERAUTOMATION FOR IMPLEMENTING TIME-DRIVEN ABC

Table 3-6c is an example of a direct cost, repairs, updating the relevant branch in the ENICM system. In this example, the branch with a profit center code of 001 is debited with 750,000. The branch premises cost is allocated to the lines of business based on space occupied. It could also be directly allocated to the lines of business, if the information is made available for data capture.

Table 3-6c. *Capture of cost data at source*

Process Automation: Cost data capture and ENICM System update			
Cost: Repairs (Operations Department, Premises) **Branch Id**			
Transaction Type Id	P&L Debit		
Posting date	20240101		
Posted By	ABC		
Debit Account Number	Repairs		
Credit Account Number	Contractor		
Cost Data:		Profit Centre Code	**001**
Transaction Amount	750,000		
Narration	**ENICM – debit to Branch for premises repairs**		
Reference	BRH Repair		
Verified By	XYZ		

Table 3-6d is an example of a direct cost, insurance expense, updating the LOB in the ENICM system. The asset register should have the ownership details. Profit center code RET is debited with 750,000 on account of insurance on the LOB's assets, a direct cost.

CHAPTER 3   USING HYPERAUTOMATION FOR IMPLEMENTING TIME-DRIVEN ABC

Table 3-6d.   Capture of cost data at source

Process Automation: Cost data capture and ENICM System update			
Cost: Insurance	Lines of Business: Retail		
Transaction Type Id	P&L Debit		
Posting date	20240101		
Posted By	ABC		
Debit Account Number	Insurance		
Credit Account Number	Insurance provider		
Cost Data: Cost Centre Code		Profit Centre Code	RET
Transaction Amount	750,000		
Narration	ENICM – Retail fixed assets insurance		
Reference	RETINS		
Verified By	XYZ		

Figures 3-18a, 3-18b, 3-18c, and 3-18d depict the **update of books of account and the ENICM system in the same process flow.**

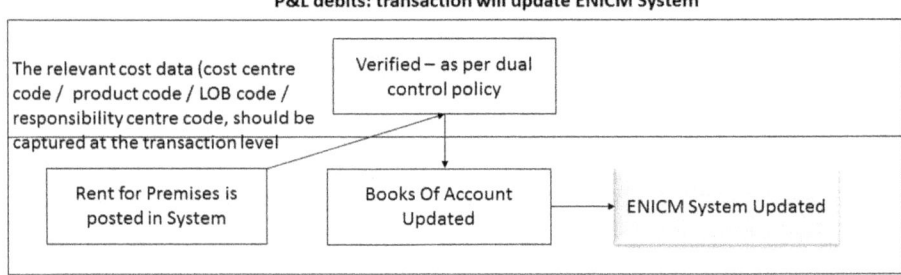

Figure 3-18a.   Update of financial and costing books

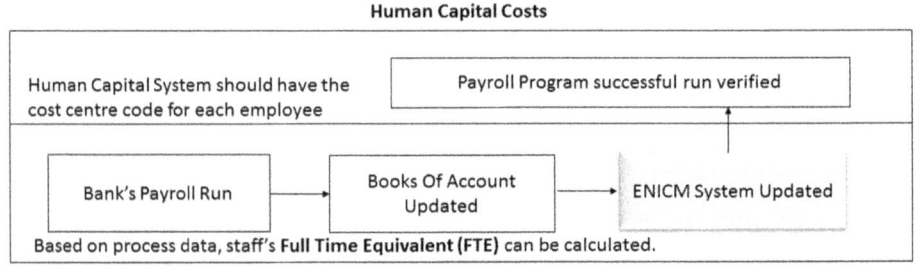

Figure 3-18b.   Update of financial and costing books

242

Figures 3-18c and 3-18d depict the ENICM update for revenue items.

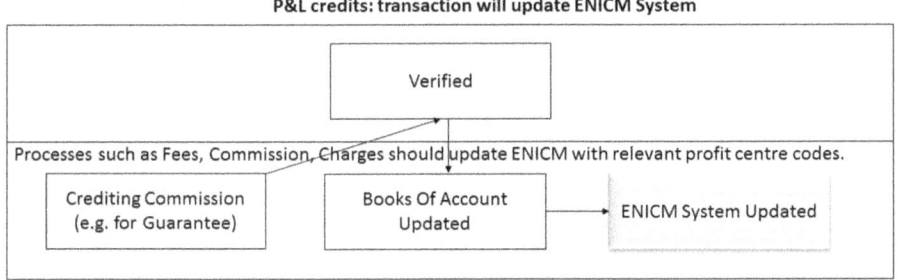

Figure 3-18c. *Update of financial and costing books*

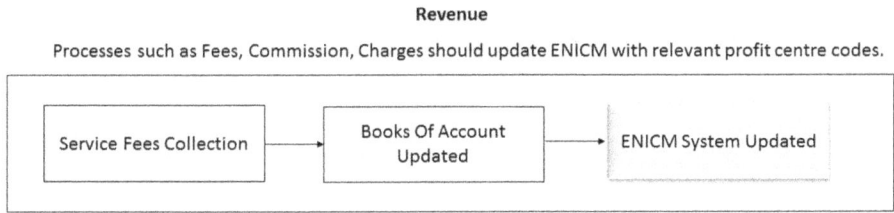

Figure 3-18d. *Auto-generated or manually posted revenue entries i..e. P&L credits*

In case of system generated entries, the metadata will provide the data for mapping to the relevant profit or cost center.

3.4.7 Granular Data Collection

While most transaction processing accounting systems provide sufficient data for bookkeeping, the BPMS provides a bank to make its *source data collection more wholesome.*

Table 3-7 provides an example of the data that can be collected and used for improving operational efficiency and operating leverage. The data that can be collected at the process level include product, customer, and resource usage.

CHAPTER 3   USING HYPERAUTOMATION FOR IMPLEMENTING TIME-DRIVEN ABC

***Table* 3-7.** *Process automation and data for TDABC*

Line Of Business	Process: Customer On-boarding Product	Staff	Resources System	Other Tangible assets	Unit Cost	Activity Time
RET	Home Loan					
COR	5 Year Loan					

Process automation enabled TDABC is explained in Section 3.5.

3.4.8 BPMS Case Studies

A. **Tools for improving operational efficiency – case studies**

- BNY Mellon Wealth Management – BPMS

   Case Introduction[11]

   The project was an extension to earlier initiatives to automate risk and compliance functions.

   Statement of Work

   BNY Mellon Wealth Management automated customer onboarding processes. Management made a commitment to implement continuous process improvement.

   Key Benefits

   - Business activity monitoring.

---

[11] http://www.wallstreetandtech.com/it-infrastructure/bny-mellon-takes-bpm-to-higher-level/240166045?cid=nl_wt_daily&elq=339c52be35e04acb9577dd657da0d4cd

- Continuous process improvements.
- Process automation helped the bank to increase business growth.

- Wells Fargo – BPMS

Case Introduction[12]

Wells Fargo merged its trust operations with Wachovia. The management decided to create a new process-based target enterprise operating model.

Statement of Work

The two teams worked together to model and analyze existing processes in business process modeling and simulation. After mapping, the processes were simulated for projected volumes.

Key Benefits

- Good design increased process reusability.
- Bank made significant savings in cost of operations.
- Operational efficiency improved.

- INDUS Ind Bank – BPMS

Case Introduction[13]

Bank understood the need for a process-based model.

---

[12] http://www.banktech.com/architecture-infrastructure/how-wells-fargo-used-bpm-to-merge-its-tr/226700086?printer_friendly=this-page

[13] http://www.firstbiz.com/biztech/indusind-banks-on-newgen-for-bpm-soln-9223.html

CHAPTER 3   USING HYPERAUTOMATION FOR IMPLEMENTING TIME-DRIVEN ABC

Statement of Work

Bank used BPMS for customer onboarding and service.

Key Benefits

- Customer service performance metrics fully met

- Deutsche Bank – SOA, BPMS[14]

Case Introduction

Bank understood that using BPMS can be "a differentiator" and enhance their competitive position.

Statement of Work

Customer onboarding processes were automated using BPMS in a SOA environment.

Key Benefits

- Staff productivity increased by 20% as process automation allows for management by exception.

- Process automation paved the way for more services in self-service kiosks. This helped to reduce costs and risks.

- Bank was able to sunset some legacy applications.

---

[14] http://www.computerworlduk.com/news/it-business/20310/deutsche-bank-bpm-initiative-was-wise-to-get-early-management-buy-in/
http://www.processexcellencenetwork.com/lean-six-sigma-business-transformation/articles/deutsche-bank-takes-the-customer-experience-to-the/

CHAPTER 3   USING HYPERAUTOMATION FOR IMPLEMENTING TIME-DRIVEN ABC

- Banks was able to improve business growth.
- Better customer experience.

• Toronto Dominion Bank – BPMS

Case Introduction[15]

The bank understood the need to focus on processes to improve customer experience.

Statement of work

The card center operating model and processes were standardized and automated.

Key Benefits

- Significant improvement in time
- TD Banknorth – BPMS

Case Introduction[16]

TD Banknorth, United States, decided to improve its operating model and its integration competency unit took responsibility for change management.

Statement of Work

Process automation for better alignment of technology with banking processes.

---

[15] http://www.pega.com/de/about-us/news-room/press-releases/td-bank-selects-pegasystems-for-cross-enterprise-business-process-#sthash.ylqbHEWP.dpuf

[16] http://www.softwareag.com/br/Images/Case%20Study-TD%20Banknorth%20Creates%20A%20BPM%20Center%20Of%20Excellence_tcm77-39792.pdf

Key Benefits

- Achievement of higher process maturity
- Better customer relationship management

- Development Bank of Singapore – BPMS

Case Introduction[17]

The bank had continuously improved its operating model to grow from a domestic bank to a regional bank.

Statement of Work

Bank planned to integrate about 20 host applications. Further, the bank planned to provide different customer facing services in different countries from a shared library of back-end services.

Key Benefits

- BPM provided reusable services that DBS could leverage on in deploying the services across countries.
- An integrated architecture allowed the bank to deliver "consistent customer service" in different markets.

---

[17] http://www.tibco.com/multimedia/ss-dbs_tcm8-791.pdf

- Sharjah Islamic Bank – BPMS

Case Introduction[18]

The bank embarked on a business process improvement exercise to improve the service quality.

Statement of Work

The bank identified the following areas for process automation: (a) e-channels transaction processing and (b) 24/7 contact center.

Key Benefits

- Customer service improved
- Better integration between e-channels and other applications

---

Services-based enterprise architecture, enterprise data management, process automation (including robotics process automation), and advanced analytics are **mandatory capabilities** required for accomplishing operating leverage objective. The activity-based enterprise noninterest cost management model is a subset of the enterprise risk-adjusted return model.

---

[18] http://www.ultimus.com/results-case-studies/sharjah-islamic-bank/

3.4.9 Enterprise Data Management – Case Study

A bank of the future should have a data-centric enterprise architecture. This improves enterprise data governance. Process flows should be aligned with data flows.

Case Study for Operational Inefficiency
Standard Chartered Bank
Cause – Weak enterprise architecture, enterprise data management
Impact
Quote
For many firms, their regulatory reporting process **involves spreadsheet controls.** Spreadsheets carry an inherent risk of error because of their vulnerability to overwriting and therefore **require appropriate documentation of key processes, risk and control assessments, judgements, and assumptions as well as robust processes and controls.** The reviews found that not all firms had a sufficiently robust control environment in place for the purposes of generating reliable and accurate returns. Unquote[19]

Consequence[20]

Bank paid hefty fines. PRA fined Standard Chartered Bank £46,550,000 for governance failure and the resulting lack of controls.

The media reported it as *"Standard Chartered, is suffering from its spreadsheet blunders."* A multinational bank with high caliber professionals and best of the breed technology failed to manage data efficiently and paid a massive fine.

---

[19] https://www.bankofengland.co.uk/news/2021/december/pra-final-notice-to-standard-chartered-bank-dated-20-december-2021
[20] https://www.bankofengland.co.uk/-/media/boe/files/prudential-regulation/letter/2021/september/thematic-findings-on-the-reliability-of-regulatory-returns.pdf
https://www.bankofengland.co.uk/news/2021/december/pra-final-notice-to-standard-chartered-bank-dated-20-december-2021

CHAPTER 3   USING HYPERAUTOMATION FOR IMPLEMENTING TIME-DRIVEN ABC

Banks do not report risk-adjusted operational efficiency or risk-adjusted operating leverage.

3.5 Process Automation and Time-Driven ABC

Processes are the building blocks of a bank. **Process-aware information systems** use a set of principles that are consistent with activity-based costing and time-driven ABC.

BPMS is about intelligence-based enterprise process automation. The ability to use ABC/TDABC based activity-based enterprise cost management is an added advantage of using BPMS.

3.5.1 Process Mining Based on Event and Process Logs and Simulation

Process mining is the link between model-based and data-oriented analysis. BPMS and advanced analytics provide a bank with the knowledge to improve risk-adjusted returns. It is an essential part of continuous process improvement. Process mining is further explained in Chapter 5, Section 5.5.3.1.

Process mining makes time-driven activity-based costing more accurate and supports decision-making.

3.5.2 Process-Automated, TDABC Examples

In the background of Chapter 2 worked example on cost allocation, this section illustrates the working of the TDABC methodology explained in Chapter 1, in a process-automated environment. **Accurate resource utilization (staff and system) and staff productivity data** are still pain points for the banking industry.

CHAPTER 3 USING HYPERAUTOMATION FOR IMPLEMENTING TIME-DRIVEN ABC

A simple business situation for understanding time-driven ABC is as follows:

A bank's operating cost may be $300,000,000 for a customer base (volume) of 30,000,000, which could translate into 90,000,000 accounts.

When the bank uses *time as a metric* for measuring resource productivity, it realizes that the customer and account base could have been serviced at an operating cost of $250,000,000, i.e., it has unutilized resource capacity and resource productivity is lower than estimated.

Using TDABC, a bank can derive system usage and compare it with the system capacity in terms of hours. Each system's approved project proposal is the source for data on system capacity.

The following 15 tables, Tables 3-8, 3-8a, 3-8b, 3-8c, 3-8d, 3-8e, 3-8f, 3-8g, 3-8h, 3-8i, 3-8j, 3-8k, 3-8l, 3-8m, and 3-8n, demonstrate how a bank can implement time-driven ABC using BPMS, hyperautomation. The next chapter expands the narration to include monitoring and managing operating leverage.

The examples are illustrative and uses the Chapter 2 cost data as the basis. The focus is on benefits of process automation, robotic process automation, and data analytics.

Tables do not include customer, as the assumption is that, in a commercial bank, the process time is not influenced by the customer of a given product. They are illustrative, and some of the products of the three lines of business used in Chapter 2 **are reworked using time taken and unit cost of resources utilized.**

These examples use the product life cycle approach to delve deeper into activities in each phase and measures the time for each process. The operations cost is a summarized number of underlying business activities.

CHAPTER 3   USING HYPERAUTOMATION FOR IMPLEMENTING TIME-DRIVEN ABC

Table 3-8 provides a template for TDABC. The data on the activities are core to a successful implementation of TDABC. BPMS, as a technology, and process mining, as a tool, facilitate the collection of granular data.

Table 3-8. *The template for TDABC using hyperautomation*

LOB	Product	Process, Activities	Volume	Summarised & Illustrative			
				Activity time Min-Rnd	Total Time (Rnd)	Unit Cost	Total Cost (Rnd)
		Time Driven (TD) process cost= the sum of all its TD activity costs. TD activity based cost = Process Volume * Activity time *Unit cost of activity					
Retail or Corporate		Sales	Risk Management				
		On-boarding	Risk Management				
		Operation	Risk Management				
			Content Management				
			Total:				
		Closure					

Product's TD Non-interest Cost, Cost of Resources utilised

LOB	Product	Process, Activities	Volume	Summarised & Illustrative			
				Activity time Min-Rnd	Total Time (Rnd)	Unit Cost	Total Cost (Rnd)
		Time Driven (TD) process cost= the sum of all its TD activity costs. TD activity based cost = Process Volume * Activity time *Unit cost of activity					
Treasury		Pre-Deal	Risk Management				
		Trade	Risk Management				
		Confirmation, Collateral, Reconciliation	Risk Management				
		Settlement & Accounting	Risk Management				

Product's TD Non-interest Cost, Cost of Resources utilised

Senior managers in the lines of business and support departments can provide the unit cost based on the books of account and their observations. The accuracy of the unit costs can be improved using continuous process improvements and process mining techniques.

CHAPTER 3   USING HYPERAUTOMATION FOR IMPLEMENTING TIME-DRIVEN ABC

The unit cost is calculated as total cost/hours of work. The total cost is a blended cost that includes direct and indirect noninterest cost of resources utilized. The denominator is the work-time estimation done by the bank. The volumes are known from logs.

The time-driven cost examples are to be understood in the background of the explanation on and depiction of process modeling and activity configuration in Sections 3.4.5.1, 3.4.5.2, and 3.4.5.3.

The cost data in the examples in Sections 3.5.2.1, 3.5.2.2, and 3.5.2.3 are illustrative and summarized at a high-level process level. Operational risks are inherent in all business activities.

3.5.2.1 TDABC – Retail Banking

Table below is an extract of Table 2-36a from Chapter 2. It shows the retail banking noninterest cost in the as-is environment. Please compare this table against the summarized time-driven cost shown after Table 3-8f.

Retail Banking	Total Cost Allocated	Comment
Total Resources	427,000,000	In the as is environment, banks are unable to accurately calculate unused capacity. The P&L cost is fully charged out. There is a significant negative impact on *risk adjusted operational efficiency and operating leverage*.
Resource Usage	427,000,000	
Unused Capacity	As is: Banks do not have data on unutilised capacity.	

Tables 3-8a, 3-8b, 3-8c, 3-8d, 3-8e, and 3-8f are examples of time-driven ABC for retail banking products. Table 3-8a is for retail savings account.

Table 3-8a is for retail savings; calculations involve rounding.

CHAPTER 3   USING HYPERAUTOMATION FOR IMPLEMENTING TIME-DRIVEN ABC

Table 3-8a. *Time-driven ABC for product RETSAV using Hyperautomation*

Summarised & Illustrative

LOB	Product		Process, Activities	Volume	Activity time Min-Rnd	Total Time (Rnd)	Unit Cost	Total Cost (Rnd)
			Time Driven (TD) process cost= the sum of all its TD activity costs. TD activity based cost = Process Volume * Activity time *Unit cost of activity					
Retail	RETSAV	Sales	Risk Management	49,936	120	5,992,317	3.89	23,310,115
			On-boarding	45,078	40	1,803,128	1.33	23,98,160
		Account Operation	ATM Withdrawal					
			ATM Cash Deposit					
			Inward Cheque Clearing					
			Outward Cheque Clearing					
			Inward, Outward SWIFT					
			Dormant Account activation					
			Total:	1,000,375	50	50,018,766	1.4	70,026,272
		Closure of Accounts		4,996	30	149,885	1.28	191,853
Product's TD Non-interest Cost, Cost of Resources utilised								95,926,400

In Chapter 2, in the as-is environment, the full allocation of costs as per books of account for retail savings A/c is $119,908,000, whereas as per TDABC method using process automation, the cost is $95,926,400.

Table 3-8b is for time deposit for one year; calculations involve rounding.

Table 3-8b. *Time-driven ABC for product RETFD1 using Hyperautomation*

Summarised & Illustrative

LOB	Product		Process, Activities	Volume	Activity time Min-Rnd	Total Time (Rnd)	Unit Cost	Total Cost (Rnd)
			Time Driven (TD) process cost= the sum of all its TD activity costs. TD activity based cost = Process Volume * Activity time *Unit cost of activity					
Retail	RETFD1	Sales	Risk Management	39,991	120	4,798,899	4.56	21,882,978
				30,117	40	1,204,678	1.26	1,517,894
		Operation	Lien on Deposit					
			Breakage of Deposit					
			Total:	1,990,000	20	39,800,009	0.99	39,402,009
		Closure		11,998	30	359,934	1.23	442,719
Product's TD Non-interest Cost, Cost of Resources utilised								63,245,600

255

CHAPTER 3   USING HYPERAUTOMATION FOR IMPLEMENTING TIME-DRIVEN ABC

In Chapter 2, the full allocation of costs as per books of account for retail one-year fixed deposit A/cs is $79,057,000 in the as-is environment, whereas as per the time taken approach for the same volume of business delivery, Table 3-8b shows the costs to be $63,245,600.

Table 3-8c is for home loans offered to salaried individuals; calculations involve rounding.

Table 3-8c. *Time-driven ABC for product RETHLS using Hyperautomation*

Summarised & Illustrative

LOB	Product	Process, Activities		Volume	Activity time Min-Rnd	Total Time (Rnd)	Unit Cost	Total Cost (Rnd)
		Time Driven (TD) process cost= the sum of all its TD activity costs. TD activity based cost = Process Volume * Activity time *Unit cost of activity						
Retail	RETHLS	Sales	Risk Management	59,954	160	9,592,648	2.73	26,187,929
		On Boarding	Document Management	50,198	60	3,011,889	1.25	3,764,861
		Account Operation	Collections					
			Risk Management					
			Total:	748,184	30	22,445,514	1.11	24,914,520
		Closure	Document Management	7,973	50	398,632	1.25	498,290
Product's TD Non-interest Cost, Cost of Resources utilised								55,365,600

In Chapter 2, the full allocation of costs as per books of account for retail home loans for salaried individuals is $69,207,000 in the as-is environment, whereas as per TDABC method using process automation, the cost is $55,365,600.

Table 3-8d is for consumer durable loans; calculations involve rounding.

CHAPTER 3   USING HYPERAUTOMATION FOR IMPLEMENTING TIME-DRIVEN ABC

Table 3-8d. *Time-driven ABC for product RETCOD using Hyperautomation*

LOB	Product	Process, Activities		Volume	Activity time Min-Rnd	Total Time (Rnd)	Unit Cost	Total Cost (Rnd)
				Summarised & Illustrative				
		Time Driven (TD) process cost= the sum of all its TD activity costs. TD activity based cost = Process Volume * Activity time *Unit cost of activity						
Retail	RETCOD	Sales Process	Risk Management	119,478	160	19,116,510	0.88	16,822,529
		On-boarding		100,769	60	6,046,153	0.4	2,418,461
		Account Operation	Loan disbursement					
			Collections (repayment)					
			Total:	1,006,574	30	30,197,208	0.53	16,004,520
		Closure		20,006	50	1,000,281	0.32	320,090
Product's TD Non-interest Cost, Cost of Resources utilised								35,565,600

In Chapter 2, the full allocation of costs as per books of account for consumer durable loans is $44,457,600 in the as-is environment, whereas as per TDABC method using process automation, the cost is $35,565,600.

Table 3-8e is for cards.

Table 3-8e. *Time-driven ABC for product RETCCD using Hyperautomation*

LOB	Product	Process, Activities		Volume	Activity time Min-Rnd	Total Time (Rnd)	Unit Cost	Total Cost (Rnd)
				Summarised & Illustrative				
		Time Driven (TD) process cost= the sum of all its TD activity costs. TD activity based cost = Process Volume * Activity time *Unit cost of activity						
Retail	RETCCD	Sales Process	Risk Management	119,567	120	14,348,000	1.1	15,782,800
		On-boarding		95,653	30	2,869,600	0.11	315,656
		A/c Operation	Risk Management					
			Total:	1,008,861	30	30,265,839	0.51	15,435,578
		Closure		10,522	50	526,100	0.06	31,566
Product's TD Non-interest Cost, Cost of Resources utilised								31,565,600

In Chapter 2, the full allocation of costs as per books of account for consumer durable loans is $39,457,000 in the as-is environment, whereas as per TDABC method using process automation, the cost is 31,565,600.

CHAPTER 3   USING HYPERAUTOMATION FOR IMPLEMENTING TIME-DRIVEN ABC

Table 3-8f is for locker rentals.

Table 3-8f. *Time-driven ABC for product RETLOC using Hyperautomation*

					Summarised & Illustrative			
LOB	Product	Process, Activities		Volume	Activity time Min-Rnd	Total Time (Rnd)	Unit Cost	Total Cost (Rnd)
		Time Driven (TD) process cost= the sum of all its TD activity costs. TD activity based cost = Process Volume * Activity time *Unit cost of activity						
Retail	RETLOC	Sales Process	Risk Management	119,428	120	14,331,374	0.46	6,592,432
		On-boarding		99,885	30	2,996,560	0.2	599,312
		Account Operation	Risk Management	994,910	30	29,847,314	0.76	22,683,959
		Closure		9,989	50	499,428	0.18	89,897
Product's TD Non-interest Cost, Cost of Resources utilised								29,965,600

The full allocation of costs as per books of account for consumer durable loans is 37,457,000 as shown in Chapter 2, whereas as per TDABC method using process automation, the cost is 29,965,600.

Once the data is collated from the process log and other system logs, the cost of resources consumed for each process is calculated. After the resource utilization is known at the process level, the capacity utilization can be calculated.

- Summary of the Above TDABC Tables – Compare the data below with the data in Table 2-36a at the beginning of the retail banking examples.

			Process automated, time driven activity based costing - cost of consumed resources					
Savings Account	1 Year FD	Home Loan	Consumer Loans	Credit Card	RETLOC	Prodt-7	Total	
95,926,400	63,245,600	55,365,600	35,565,600	31,565,600	29,965,600	29,965,600	341,600,000	

The time-driven retail banking cost is 341,600,000 and the accounting cost of retail banking is 427,000,000. **Hence, retail banking has an 80% resource capacity utilization rate.**

3.5.2.2 TDABC – Corporate Banking

Table below is an extract of Table 2-36a from Chapter 2. It shows the corporate banking noninterest cost in the as-is environment. Please compare this table against the summarized time-driven cost shown after Table 3-8j.

Coprorate Banking	Total Cost Allocated	Comment
Total Resources	268,150,000	In the as is environment, banks are unable to accurately calculate unused capacity. The P&L cost is fully charged out. There is a significant negative impact on *risk adjusted operational efficiency and operating leverage*.
Resource Usage	268,150,000	
Unused Capacity	As is: Banks do not have data on unutilised capacity.	

Tables 3-8g, 3-8h, 3-8i, and 3-8j are examples of time-driven ABC for corporate banking products. Table 3-8g is for letters of credit.

Table 3-8g. *Time-driven ABC for product CORLCI using Hyperautomation*

Summarised & Illustrative

LOB	Product	Process, Activities		Volume	Activity time Min-Rnd	Total Time (Rnd)	Unit Cost	Total Cost (Rnd)
		Time Driven (TD) process cost= the sum of all its TD activity costs. TD activity based cost = Process Volume * Activity time *Unit cost of activity						
Corporate Banking	CORLCI	Negotiations		29,985	160	4,797,636	2.01	9,643,249
		LC Issuance	Risk Management	25,077	60	1,504,621	1.41	2,121,515
		Account Operation	Risk Management	498,102	60	29,886,106	1.21	36,162,188
		Closure	Risk Management	3,990	50	199,516	1.45	289,298
Product's TD Non-interest Cost, Cost of Resources utilised								48,216,250

In Chapter 2, the full allocation of costs as per books of account for letter of credit issuance is $56,725,000 in the as-is environment, whereas as per the time taken approach for the same volume of business delivery, Table 3-8g shows the costs to be $48,216,250.

Table 3-8h is for bills coacceptance.

CHAPTER 3   USING HYPERAUTOMATION FOR IMPLEMENTING TIME-DRIVEN ABC

Table 3-8h. *Time-driven ABC for product CORCOA using Hyperautomation*

Summarised & Illustrative

LOB	Product	Process, Activities		Volume	Activity time Min-Rnd	Total Time (Rnd)	Unit Cost	Total Cost (Rnd)
		Time Driven (TD) process cost= the sum of all its TD activity costs. TD activity based cost = Process Volume * Activity time *Unit cost of activity						
Corporate Banking	CORCOA	Sales Process / Negotiations	Risk Management	24,952	180	4,491,383	1.03	4,626,124
		Payment		19,956	120	2,394,700	0.85	2,035,495
		Account Operation	Risk Management	750,421	20	15,008,421	2.62	39,322,063
		Closure		12,016	30	360,478	0.77	277,568
Product's TD Non-interest Cost, Cost of Resources utilised								46,261,250

The full allocation of costs as per books of account for bills coacceptance is 54,425,000, whereas Table 3-8h shows the costs to be $46,261,250.

Table 3-8i is for a ten-year term loan.

Table 3-8i. *Time-driven ABC for product CORL10 using Hyperautomation*

Summarised & Illustrative

LOB	Product	Process, Activities		Volume	Activity time Min-Rnd	Total Time (Rnd)	Unit Cost	Total Cost (Rnd)
		Time Driven (TD) process cost= the sum of all its TD activity costs. TD activity based cost = Process Volume * Activity time *Unit cost of activity						
Corporate Banking	CORL10	Sales Process	Risk Management	1,000	1100	1,100,116	10.05	11,056,162
		On-boarding	Document Mgt	701	800	560,678	3.17	1,777,350
		A/c Operation	Site Visit					
			Internal Rating					
		Risk Management	Collateral Mark to Market					
			Loan: Risk Exposure monitoring					
			Total:	100,144	90	9,012,931	1.45	13,068,750
		Closure		200	400	80,013	2.94	235,238
Product's TD Non-interest Cost, Cost of Resources utilised								26,137,500

260

CHAPTER 3   USING HYPERAUTOMATION FOR IMPLEMENTING TIME-DRIVEN ABC

The full allocation of costs as per books of account for ten-year corporate loans is $30,750,000, whereas Table 3-8i shows the costs to be $26,137,500.

KPI measures quality, productivity, and business returns. Along with KRIs, these metrics are an integral part of continuous process improvement.

Table 3-8j is for a syndicated loan.

Table 3-8j. *Time-driven ABC for product CORSDL using Hyperautomation*

LOB	Product	Process, Activities		Volume	Activity time Min-Rnd	Total Time (Rnd)	Unit Cost	Total Cost (Rnd)
		Summarised & Illustrative						
		Time Driven (TD) process cost= the sum of all its TD activity costs. TD activity based cost = Process Volume * Activity time *Unit cost of activity						
Corporate Banking	CORSDL	Sales Process / Negotiations	Risk Management	100	2,000	200,005	97.28	19,456,500
		On-boarding	Document Management	95	800	76,005	36.57	2,779,500
		Loan Operation	Risk Management					
			Managing the Consortium					
			Total:	400	120	47,999	112.92	5,420,025
		Closure		10	400	4,000	34.74	138,975
Product's TD Non-interest Cost, Cost of Resources utilised								27,795,000

In Chapter 2, the full allocation of costs as per books of account for syndicate loans is 32,700,000 in the as-is environment, whereas as per the time taken approach for the same volume of business delivery, Table 3-8j shows the costs to be $27,795,000.

Summary of the Above TDABC Tables

	Process automated, time driven activity based costing - cost of consumed resources							
CORLCI	CORCOA	CORL10	CORSDL	Prodt-5	Prodt-6	Prodt-7	Total
48,216,250	46,261,250	26,137,500	27,795,000	26,137,500	26,095,000	27,285,000	227,927,500

The time-driven corporate banking cost is 227,927,500, and the accounting cost of corporate banking is 268,150,000. **Hence, corporate banking has an 80% resource capacity utilization rate.**

261

CHAPTER 3   USING HYPERAUTOMATION FOR IMPLEMENTING TIME-DRIVEN ABC

3.5.2.3 TDABC – Treasury

Table below is an extract of Table 2-36a from Chapter 2. It shows the noninterest cost of treasury in the as-is environment. Please compare this table against the summarized time-driven cost shown after Table 3-8n.

Treasury	Total Cost Allocated	Comment
Total Resources	209,850,000	In the as is environment, banks are unable to accurately calculate unused capacity. The P&L cost is fully charged out. There is a significant negative impact on *risk adjusted operational efficiency and operating leverage*.
Resource Usage	209,850,000	
Unused Capacity	As is: Banks do not have data on unutilised capacity.	

Unlike retail and corporate banking, the life cycle of treasury's portfolio of products is different. A few of the money market operations, e.g., placement and borrowing, might have some common elements, but the underlying purpose is different.

Hence, Tables 3-8k, 3-8l, 3-8m, and 3-8n have a different life cycle structure, i.e., predeal, deal booking, confirmation, collateral, settlement, and accounting.

Table 3-8k is for FX forward contracts.

Table 3-8k. *Time-driven ABC for product TRBFXF using Hyperautomation*

LOB	Product	Process, Activities		Volume	Activity time Min-Rnd	Total Time (Rnd)	Unit Cost	Total Cost (Rnd)
		Time Driven (TD) process cost= the sum of all its TD activity costs. TD activity based cost = Process Volume * Activity time *Unit cost of activity						
Treasury	TRBFXF	Pre-Deal	Risk Management	895,400	5	4,477,000	0.63	2,820,510
		Trade	Risk Management	904,010	2	1,808,019	0.52	940,170
		Confirmation, Collateral, Reconciliation	Risk Management	1,199,917	20	23,998,333	1.11	26,638,150
		Settlement & Accounting	Risk Management	1,175,213	5	5,876,063	0.16	940,170
Product's TD Non-interest Cost, Cost of Resources utilised								31,339,000

CHAPTER 3   USING HYPERAUTOMATION FOR IMPLEMENTING TIME-DRIVEN ABC

The full allocation of costs as per books of account for FX forward contracts is $33,880,000 whereas Table 3-8k shows the costs to be $31,339,000.

Table 3-8l is for currency swaps.

Table 3-8l. *Time-driven ABC for product TRBCRS using Hyperautomation*

					Summarised & Illustrative			
LOB	Product	Process, Activities		Volume	Activity time Min-Rnd	Total Time (Rnd)	Unit Cost	Total Cost (Rnd)
		Time Driven (TD) process cost= the sum of all its TD activity costs. TD activity based cost = Process Volume * Activity time *Unit cost of activity						
Treasury	TRBCRS	Pre-Deal	Risk Management	794,316	5.5	4,368,741	0.54	2,359,120
		Trade	Risk Management	797,000	3	2,391,000	0.37	884,670
		Confirmation, Collateral, Reconciliation	Risk Management	997,731	22	21,950,073	1.15	25,242,584
		Settlement & Accounting	Risk Management	835,522	6	5,013,130	0.2	1,002,626
Product's TD Non-interest Cost, Cost of Resources utilised								29,489,000

In Chapter 2, the full allocation of costs as per books of account for currency swaps is $31,800,000 in the as-is environment, whereas as per the time taken approach for the same volume of business delivery, Table 3-8l shows the costs to be $29,489,000.

Table 3-8m is for interest rate swap.

CHAPTER 3   USING HYPERAUTOMATION FOR IMPLEMENTING TIME-DRIVEN ABC

Table 3-8m. *Time-driven ABC for product TRBIRS using Hyperautomation*

						Summarised & Illustrative		
LOB	Product	Process, Activities		Volume	Activity time Min-Rnd	Total Time (Rnd)	Unit Cost	Total Cost (Rnd)
		Time Driven (TD) process cost= the sum of all its TD activity costs. TD activity based cost = Process Volume * Activity time *Unit cost of activity						
Treasury	TRBIRS	Pre-Deal	Risk Management	495,556	4.5	2,230,000	0.37	825,100
		Trade	Risk Management	495,060	4	1,980,240	0.25	495,060
		Position Monitoring	Risk Management	698,119	25	17,452,963	1.77	30,891,744
		Settlement & Accounting	Risk Management	452,626	5	2,263,131	0.35	792,096
Product's TD Non-interest Cost, Cost of Resources utilised								33,004,000

The full allocation of costs as per books of account for interest rate swaps is $35,680,000, whereas Table 3-8m shows the costs to be $33,004,000.

Table 3-8n is for index-linked credit default swap.

Table 3-8n. *Time-driven ABC for product TRICDS using Hyperautomation*

						Summarised & Illustrative		
LOB	Product	Process, Activities		Volume	Activity time Min-Rnd	Total Time (Rnd)	Unit Cost	Total Cost (Rnd)
		Time Driven (TD) process cost= the sum of all its TD activity costs. TD activity based cost = Process Volume * Activity time *Unit cost of activity						
Treasury	TRICDS	Pre-Deal	Risk Management	404,749	4.5	1,821,369	0.42	764,975
		Trade	Risk Management	398,424	4	1,593,698	0.48	764,975
		Position Monitoring	Risk Management	599,804	25	14,995,112	1.91	28,640,664
		Settlement & Accounting	Risk Management	503,984	5	2,519,918	0.17	428,386
Product's TD Non-interest Cost, Cost of Resources utilised								30,599,000

CHAPTER 3   USING HYPERAUTOMATION FOR IMPLEMENTING TIME-DRIVEN ABC

In Chapter 2, the full allocation of costs as per books of account for index-linked credit default swaps is $33,080,000 in the as-is environment, whereas as per the time taken approach for the same volume of business delivery, Table 3-8n shows the costs to be $30,599,000.

TRBFXF FX	TRBCRS FX	TRBIRS MM	TRICDS	Prodt-5 MM	Prodt-6 Commodity	Prodt-7 Equity	Total
	Only these are shown as examples						
31,339,000	29,489,000	33,004,000	30,599,000	28,101,500	20,840,250	20,738,500	194,111,250

The time-driven corporate banking cost is 194,111,250, and the accounting cost of corporate banking is 209,850,000. **Hence, treasury's resource capacity utilization rate is 92.5%.**

The above examples are used in Chapter 4, Section 4.3.3, to explain operating leverage monitoring.

3.6 Operational Efficiency and Operating Leverage

Using BPMS and the time-driven ABC model, a bank can quantity resources that are idle so that senior management can take steps to redeploy these resources or right size the bank. Products and services consume resources at different rates and require different levels of support. A nonvalue-added activity is one that is not a business need and does not deliver incremental value to the customer.

Please compare resource utilization in Table 3-9 with Table 2-36, in Section 2.3 in Chapter 2. An event- and data-driven, services-based enterprise architecture, enterprise process automation, and enterprise data governance improve the competitive position of a bank, enable business (revenue) growth, and provide the ability to reduce operating cost. **This is the essence of operating leverage.**

CHAPTER 3   USING HYPERAUTOMATION FOR IMPLEMENTING TIME-DRIVEN ABC

Table 3-9. *Illustrative – cost of consumed resources by LOBs*

Process Automated, Time Driven Activity Based Costing Cost of consumed resources			
	Corporate	Treasury	Retail
P&L	268,150,000	209,850,000	427,000,000
TDABC - Cost of consumed resources	227,927,500	194,111,250	341,600,000
Cost of Unutilised Resources	40,222,500	15,738,750	85,400,000
Utilisation Rate	85%	92.5%	80%

With hyperautomation, a bank has the ability to understand the process behavior. It can be done by examining the process diagram, model, or the log. The bank has the capability to

- Identify at the granular level, i.e., process/activity level inadequacies and weaknesses
- Measure resource utilization
- Optimize the cost of doing business and the cost of enterprise risk management
- Increase staff productivity
- Improve profitability
- Manage business delivery more efficiently

The time-driven activity-based costing system is easier to build using hyperautomation. The TDABC model provides cost and profitability information, in addition to providing visibility into process efficiency and capacity utilization. The dimensions are (a) line of business (LOB), (b) products/treasury instruments, and (c) counterparty/customer.

CHAPTER 3 USING HYPERAUTOMATION FOR IMPLEMENTING TIME-DRIVEN ABC

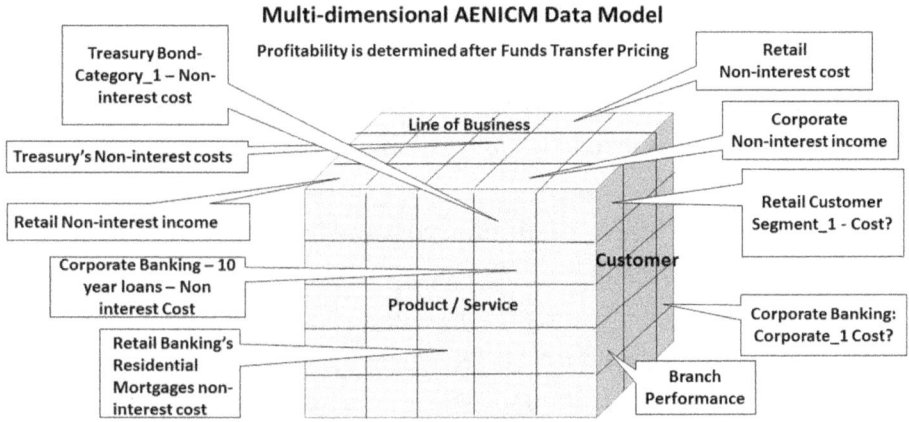

Figure 3-19a. Activity-based ENICM data model

An essential element in the implementation of a customer-centric business model is the balancing of risk, return, and profitability. However, this requires good-quality data. A 360° view of a customer is a critical success factor to build a profitable relationship over time. A bank needs to balance profitability per customer or customer segment and the cost of retaining customers through various programs.

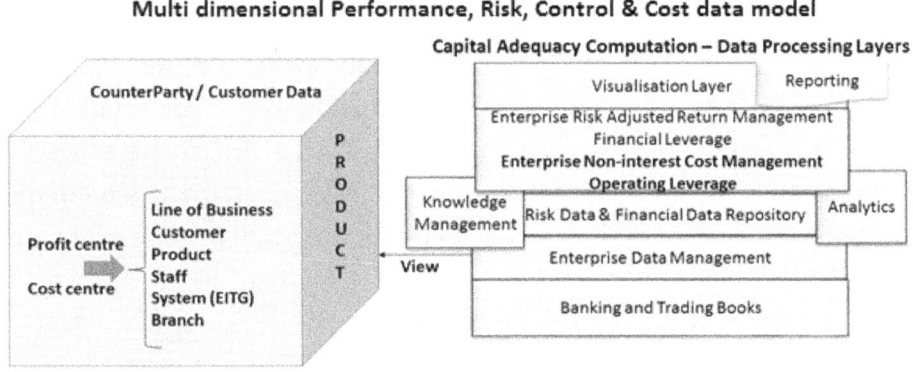

Figure 3-19b. ENICM and ERRM data model

267

CHAPTER 3   USING HYPERAUTOMATION FOR IMPLEMENTING TIME-DRIVEN ABC

Risk-based pricing can align price and costs by increasing the pricing for higher-risk customers. Banks keep one or more products in its portfolio to attract and retain customers even if it is not meeting its profitability criteria. The challenge is to have data for an enterprise risk-adjusted return management.

Retail banking is under continuing cost and earnings pressure. The emergence of new competitors has intensified competition. Other challenges faced by retail banking's pricing policy include regulatory scrutiny over charges and public criticism using social media. Given this situation, pricing policy might need short- and long-term objectives to boost profitability and enhance customer satisfaction. Banks are finding it difficult to acquire new customers for retail banking as they struggle to retain the existing client base. This has increased the focus on the pricing policy and improving customer loyalty.

Banks have to frequently demonstrate a differentiated value proposition and have an effective rationale for their differentiated price.

In corporate and retail lending, advanced analytical models can provide actionable intelligence on customers that will allow banks to lower prices for creditworthy customers with the objective of retaining them and increasing their pool of low-risk customers.

Customer experience and brand recognition for fair and honest dealings are critical success factors for pricing financial service and customer retention.

Figure 3-20 illustrates activity based noninterest cost management that uses time-driven activity-based costing methodology. It provides data for actionable intelligence.

CHAPTER 3   USING HYPERAUTOMATION FOR IMPLEMENTING TIME-DRIVEN ABC

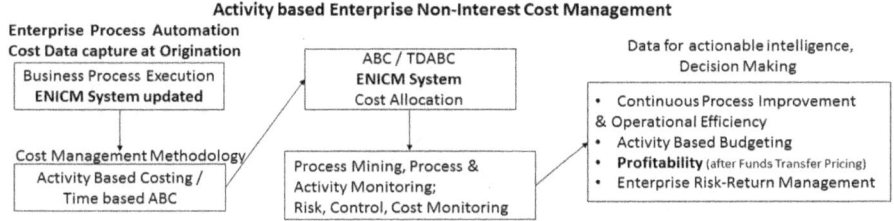

Figure 3-20. *Data for actionable intelligence*

In a speech given at the City & Financial 9th Annual Operational Resilience for Financial Institutions Summit 2022, Bank of England's Mackinnon Duncan emphasized the need for banks to rearchitect or replace legacy systems.[21]

Banks are moving towards an event and data driven, services oriented architecture with process automation.

The next chapter explains the monitoring of performance, risk, control and cost at the process level.

---

[21] https://www.bankofengland.co.uk/speech/2022/may/duncan-mackinnon-speech-at-the-city-and-financial-9th-annual-operational-resilience

CHAPTER 4

Monitoring Operating Leverage

The scope of operating leverage monitoring includes monitoring performance, resource utilization, risk, control, and operating cost.

In the background of the explanation on activity-based costing and time-driven ABC, Section 4.1 guides a bank on the concept of operating leverage. The section covers the limitations of the cost to income ratio, explains operational risk, and analyzes operational risk's causal link with other risk types. There is an imperative need for banks to develop operational metrics that truly reflect operational efficiency and effectiveness.

Section 4.2 explains the key drivers of performance, risk, control, and costs. Section 4.3 takes a deep dive into operating leverage monitoring by analyzing business situations from the perspective of improving revenue, cost of doing business, and operational efficiency. The ability of a bank to have an optimized cost-efficient enterprise operating model depends on the maturity of the banking processes. **The 35 examples highlight the usefulness of the bill of resources and hyperautomation**.

The examples illustrate operating leverage monitoring at the process level.

Section 4.4 uses the examples illustrated in Section 4.3 to explain the actionable intelligence that can be provided for decision-making in key areas. Section 4.5 makes an observation on economy of scale, and Section 4.6 explains the imperative need for banks and its stakeholders to use operating leverage as a performance metric.

CHAPTER 4   MONITORING OPERATING LEVERAGE

4.1 Operating Leverage Concept

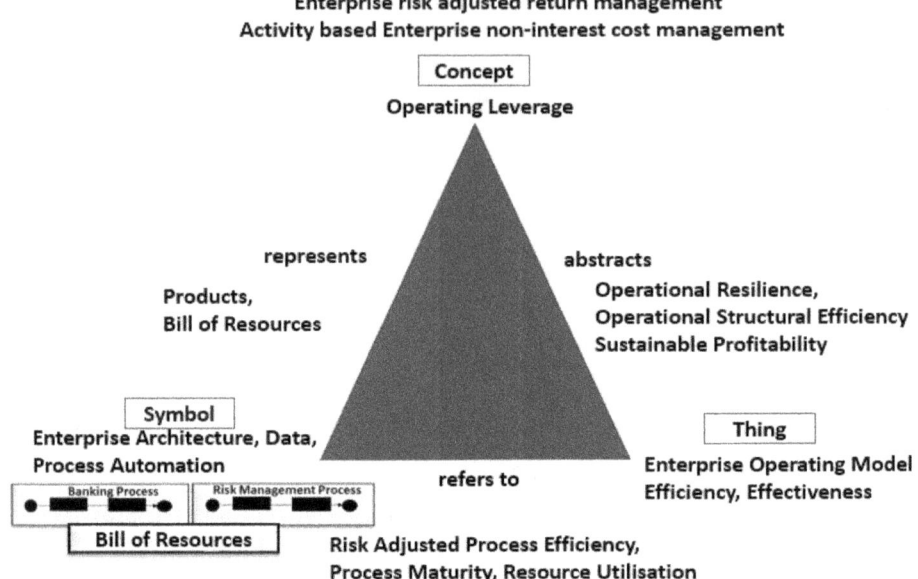

Figure 4-1. *Operating leverage concept*

This book uses operating leverage as a year-on-year ratio, calculated as growth % in revenue – growth % in operating expenses.

Operating leverage refers to the management of a bank's capabilities and capacity to deliver its products and services. The metrics to measure operating leverage are

- Performance
- Risks
- Controls
- Costs (fixed and variable)

The focus of operating leverage is on efficiency and profitability, the core components of the enterprise risk-adjusted return management (ERRM) model.

CHAPTER 4   MONITORING OPERATING LEVERAGE

Operating leverage in banks is about creating and delivering financial value in the form of products and services of a desired quality, efficiently and effectively, to accomplish target risk-adjusted returns.

4.1.1 As-Is Cost-Income Ratio

In the as-is environment, the cost-income ratio is used as a proxy for measuring efficiency.

Table 4-1a is an extract from a SP Global article dated June 2023.

Note FTE in this table stands for fully taxable equivalent. In rest of this book, FTE stands for full-time equivalent.

Table 4-1a. *US banks – efficiency ratio*

Bank	FTE Employees		Efficiency Ratio - FTE		Non-interest expense	
	Actual	QOQ change %	%	QOQ Change pps	$billion	QOQ change %
JP Morgan Chase	292,393	1.1	51.20	-3.5	20.24	5.8
Citigroup	249,522	-0.1	61.5	-9.6	13.25	2.2
Wells Fargo	231,170	-0.2	65.58	-16.1	13.7	-15.0
Bank of America	217,706	0.8	61.45	-1.9	16.51	4.3
Morgan Stanley	82,266	-0.2	71.24	-4.7	10.37	6.8
American Express	78,372	1.4	76.85	-1.2	10.98	-0.8
Bank of New York Mellon	51,600	-0.2	70.71	-2.5	3.09	-3.5
Goldman Sachs	45,400	-6.4	67.3	-7.8	8.23	2.4

Efficiency Ratios - Top U.S. Banks by headcount – Q1 2023

Table 4-1b is an extract from a SAXO research report on financial metrics of European banks.[1]

Relatively, banks with a lower 'efficiency ratio' are deemed more efficient than the ones with higher ratios.

---

[1] https://www.home.saxo/content/articles/equities/financial-metrics-expos-of-european-banks-30092020

273

CHAPTER 4 MONITORING OPERATING LEVERAGE

You may want to take note of the following:

Banco Santander – It has the lowest efficiency ratio, highest NIM, and impressive forward ROE.

Deutsche – It has the lowest forward ROE, the worst efficiency ratio, and weak NIM.

The notes in the two reports indicate that banks compute the cost-to-income ratio also known as 'efficiency ratio', in different ways.

- In calculating the **efficiency ratio, some banks** mention the reduction of income on account of **provisions for credit losses.**

    Noninterest expense / (net interest income + noninterest income – **provision for credit losses**)

- Some banks do not take the provisions into consideration.

    (Noninterest expense) / (net interest income + noninterest income)

Table 4-1b. *Performance metrics of European banks – data of 2019*

European Banks - 2019 Metrics

Bank	Tier 1 Ratio	Efficiency Ratio	NIM	Forward ROE
HSBC	17.6	75.5	1.58	6.17
BNP Paribas	13.5	70.3	1.38	6.07
UBS	20	80.6	0.58	8.19
Banco Santander	13.1	56.6	2.75	5.80
ING	16.7	56.7	1.71	6.56
Deutsche	15.6	108.8	1.45	2.75
Natwest	18.5	66	1.79	5.21
Standard Chartered	16.5	70.9	1.55	4.75

CHAPTER 4   MONITORING OPERATING LEVERAGE

If banks can improve the choice of technology, have a process-based enterprise operating model, and focus on resource utilization, it is possible to have a cost to income ratio of less than 40%.

The inference from the data in Tables 4-1a and 4-1b is that many banks have a cost-to-income ratio (efficiency ratio) that is higher than 60%.

JP Morgan Chase (Table 4-1a), Banco Santander, and ING (Table 4-1b) are the best performers.

Case Study: Banks in Asia[2]

Table 4-1c is an extract from a SP Global report on efficiency of banks in Asia Pacific. The cost-to-income ratio shown in Table 4-1c is computed as: total operating costs (excluding bad and doubtful debt charges) to total income (the sum of net interest and noninterest income).

---

[2] https://www.spglobal.com/marketintelligence/en/news-insights/latest-news-headlines/japanese-banks-efficiency-behind-most-asia-pacific-lenders-chinese-lead-59437330

CHAPTER 4   MONITORING OPERATING LEVERAGE

Table 4-1c. *Cost to income ratio – Asian banks*

Cost to Income ratios of largest banks in Asia Pacific 2019-2020

	H.Q.	Cost-to-income ratio % Lower the Better	
		Q12019	Q12020
Fukuoka Financial Group	Japan	55.24	77.48
Mitsubishi UFJ Financial	Japan	73.61	71.84
Sumitomo Mitsui	Japan	71.93	70.53
NongHyup Financial Group	S.Korea	56.77	64.91
KB Financial group	S.Korea	60.56	64.82
State Bank of India	India	64.47	63.83
Postal Savings Bank of China	China	53.33	52.81
Malayan Banking Bhd	Malaysia	45.42	41.07
DBS Group Holdings Ltd	Singapore	42.19	38.65
Bank of Communications Co Ltd	China	36.58	37.10

Source: S&P Global Market intelligence-data compiled on July10,2020.

In the S&P report, a researcher from the DBS Group mentions that the low cost-to-income ratios of Chinese banks can be attributed to their economy of scale, i.e., large population provides a branch with a larger customer base.

The author of this book opines that economy of scale does not guarantee enterprise operating efficiency and operating leverage.

Smaller banks can have (a) good profitability ratios/profitability trend and (b) high risk-adjusted returns relative to risk appetite by using relevant methodologies and technology.

Ensuring fair competition and protecting consumer rights are priorities for all governments.

CHAPTER 4 MONITORING OPERATING LEVERAGE

4.1.2 Need to Have Metrics for Operational Efficiency, Effectiveness, and Operating Leverage

This section analyzes the data of USA's Signature Bank and UK's HSBC to emphasize the imperative need to have good performance metrics.

Case: US Signature Bank

Table 4-2a provides an overview of FDIC's supervisory recommendations (SR) for a six-year period. Enterprise liquidity management requires operational support in terms of system and staff. The skills for liquidity management include a deep understanding of risk-weighted assets, stable funding, liquidity coverage, and liquidity transfer pricing.

The issues flagged below are NOT reflected in the cost-to-income ratio from an operational perspective.

Table 4-2a. *FDIC report – Signature Bank data*

Scope of Targeted Review	Areas Most Frequently Cited with SRs Remaining Open by Examination Cycle					
	2017	2018	2019	2020	2021	2022
Liquidity Risk Management	3	5	18	15	11	19
Model Risk Management	10	10	10	9	12	
Information Technology	10	9	11	6	4	8
Anti-Money Laundering	6	8	10	6	3	13

In FDIC's report on Signature Bank, page 55 of 63, the supervisor observed that there was an issue with the bank's decision-making structure. Prior to the bank's collapse, FDIC had recommended improvements to setting KPIs and KRIs, improving product implementation processes, risk, and control self-assessments.

The cost-to-income ratio does not reflect these performance, risk, control, and cost issues.

CHAPTER 4   MONITORING OPERATING LEVERAGE

Case: UK HSBC

In 2024, the Prudential Regulation Authority (PRA)[3] fined HSBC £57,417,500 for

- The failure to implement process ownership as required under the Depositor Protection Rules.

- The failure to make senior managers responsible for the performance of the processes and to ensure data integrity as required under the Depositor Protection Rules.

- Marking almost 99% of its eligible beneficiary deposits as "ineligible" for FSCS protection.

- Misleading the PRA by officially confirming that its systems satisfied relevant Depositor Protection Rule requirements.

- The failure to produce finalized versions of annual reports. The directors are required to confirm that the bank has complied with the requirements of the Depositor Protection Rules.

Table 4-3 shows the financial data of the bank for 2022 and 2023. Please note that the cost efficiency ratio

- Shows volatility. This is common in the banking industry. Banks seldom provide an explanatory note for it.

- Does not reflect the risks and weaknesses mentioned in PRA's report.

---

[3] https://www.bankofengland.co.uk/news/2024/january/pra-fines-hsbc-for-failures-in-deposit-protection-identification-and-notifcation

CHAPTER 4   MONITORING OPERATING LEVERAGE

This cost-to-income ratio, which is also be referred to as an efficiency ratio or cost efficiency ratio, provides only limited information about the bank or other money lending institution. It is a plain vanilla ratio from an accountant's perspective. It does not provide information, or only provides limited information, on structural efficiency, fixed and variable cost base, operational risk exposure, non-interest cost management methodology, operational resilience, or how to improve sustainable profitability.

The financial disclosures do not reflect accurately the risk exposure of a bank. In most cases, the risk in the published results of the banks is under stated.

Table 4-3. *HSBC key financial metrics*[4]

	HSBC Key Financial Metrics				
	9 months ended		Quarter Ended		
	30Sep23	30Sep22	30Sep23	30Jun23	30Sep22
Profit After Tax ($M)	24,337	11,588	6,266	7,045	2,657
Cost Efficiency Ratio %	44.2	66.3	49.3	47.1	67.7
Net Interest Margin%	1.70	1.33	1.70	1.72	1.51

In the list of ECB's supervisory priorities for 2023–2025,[5] priority-2 focuses on

- Digital transformation strategies
- Operational resilience framework
- Risk data, availability, and quality

---

[4] 30Oct 2023, HSBC Holdings PLC, 3Q2023: Page 7
https://www.hsbc.com/investors/results-and-announcements/all-reporting/3q-2023-quick-read

[5] https://www.bankingsupervision.europa.eu/banking/priorities/html/ssm.supervisory_priorities202212~3a1e609cf8.en.html

279

CHAPTER 4   MONITORING OPERATING LEVERAGE

Figure 4-2 illustrates a process-based approach to building an enterprise operating model for a 24/7 business delivery.

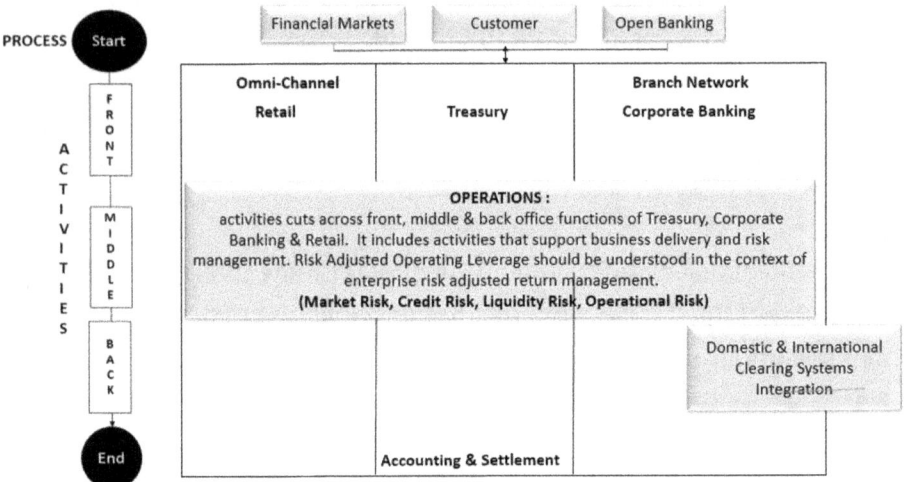

Figure 4-2. Process-based approach to building an enterprise operating model

Banks that adopt a **process-based approach to implementing their enterprise operating model** find it easier to gather granular, internal data and manage their operational risk effectively.

Section 4.6 further explains operational performance metrics.
Sections 4.3, 4.4, and 4.5 explain performance, risk, control, and cost monitoring.

4.2 Performance, Risk, Control, and Costs

4.2.1 Performance

Figure 4-3 illustrates the four business situations that can be used to assess a bank's performance. Quadrant 1 is invariably a long-term strategic play. The bank's ability to go for it depends on the quality of its management.

Quadrant 2 are low cost, high benefits. There are not too many of these opportunities, and the competition to get the business is intense. It is a crowded market, and "the differentiation" factor is a critical success factor. Quadrant 3 is also a crowded market, as most mid-sized and small banks are firmly entrenched in that segment. Quadrant 4 is for high cost, low benefit business situations. This could include non-performing branches, legacy systems that are expensive to maintain or under utilized expensive staff roles.

Investing in human capital and technology in a siloed and complex operating environment will not yield the desired benefits. The objective is to identify the positive and negative consequence(s) (effects) of a decision.

Banks can use prescriptive analytics and discovery analytics for revenue growth. The algorithms can identify strengths (e.g., favorable liquidity ratios) and recommend business opportunities to optimize risk-adjusted return.

CHAPTER 4   MONITORING OPERATING LEVERAGE

Figure 4-3. *Business growth and cost of doing business*

Figure 4-3 is adapted in the following examples:

- In Section 4.3.3.2, Figure 4-18b, Example vii for retail banking

- Section 4.3.3.3, Figure 4-19, Example xii for corporate banking

4.2.2 Enterprise Risk

4.2.2.1 Treasury

Quality of operational support for treasury is reflected in treasury's process efficiency, enterprise operating model efficiency, and operating leverage.

CHAPTER 4   MONITORING OPERATING LEVERAGE

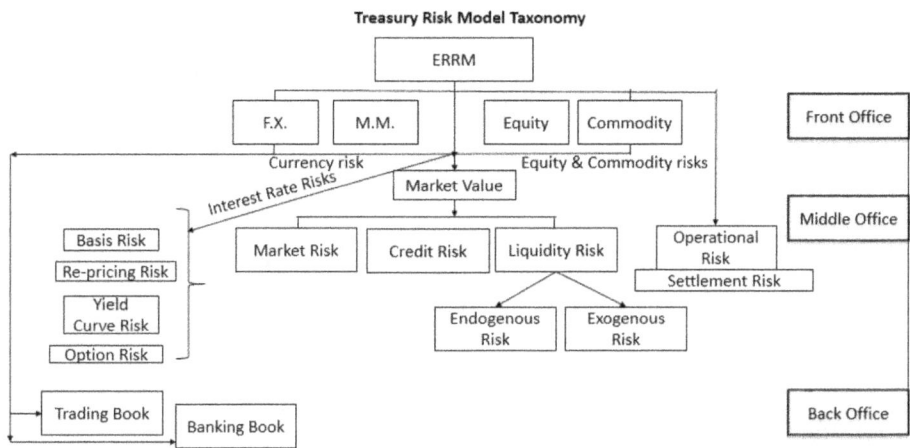

Figure 4-4. *Treasury risk model taxonomy*

Figure 4-4 illustrates the following important aspects of treasury operations:

- The four treasury product portfolio groups: foreign exchange, money market, equity, and commodity.

- The composition of enterprise risk; it comprises market, credit, liquidity, and operational risks.

- Basis, repricing, yield curve, and option are different types of interest rate risks that have an impact on enterprise liquidity management. Basel's BCBS 368 provides the standards for managing the interest rate risk in the banking book.

- Banks are required to segregate their trading and banking books.

All these components have a system and staff dimension. Operating leverage is about efficiently and effectively managing these operational aspects.

Treasury manages enterprise liquidity with the support of the Asset Liability Committee (ALCO). The operational aspects of enterprise liquidity management are explained in Sections 4.2.2.3 and 4.4.1.2.

4.2.2.2 Lending

Relatively, retail lending risks are significantly less than corporate lending risks. However, both have a causation link to liquidity risk. As compared to retail, corporate credit risk management is wider in scope and has more depth.

The information submitted by a borrower includes information on the current and historical audited financial statements including cash flows projections. The following are the categories of credit reports that a bank prepares using the application details: (i) financial analysis, including repayment capacity; (ii) collateral identification and valuation; (iii) peer group comparisons; (iv) guarantor support and related financial information; (v) loan terms, including tenor and repayment structure; (vi) pricing information, including relationship profitability data; (vii) covenants and requirements for future submission of financial data; (viii) exceptions to policy and underwriting guidelines; (ix) risk mitigants; and (x) credit rating. Figure 4-5 illustrates credit risk monitoring.

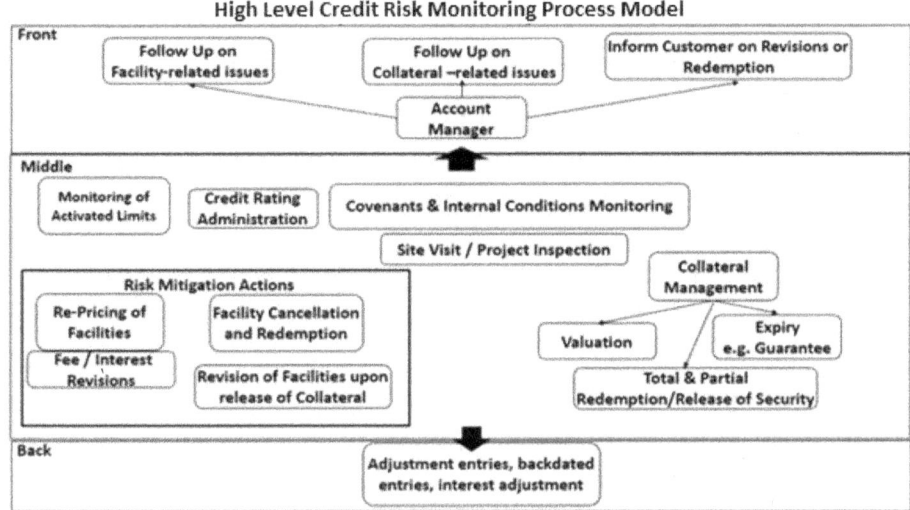

Figure 4-5. *High-level credit risk monitoring process model*

4.2.2.3 Enterprise Liquidity Management

Extending from the narrative on treasury products, the following types of interest rate risks have an impact on enterprise liquidity management:

- Repricing risk refers to the probability that assets and liabilities can reprice at different times or amounts. This can negatively impact a bank's earnings and capital. The known sources of risk are the time difference in the maturity of fixed rate products and the changes to the interest rate for floating rate products.

- Basis risk can arise when there is a change in the relationship between the yield curves of long and short positions with the same maturity, in different financial instruments.

CHAPTER 4   MONITORING OPERATING LEVERAGE

- Yield curve risk reflects exposure to unanticipated changes in the shape or slope of the yield curve.

- Option risk is the risk arising from options embedded in the bank's assets, liabilities, and off-balance sheet items.

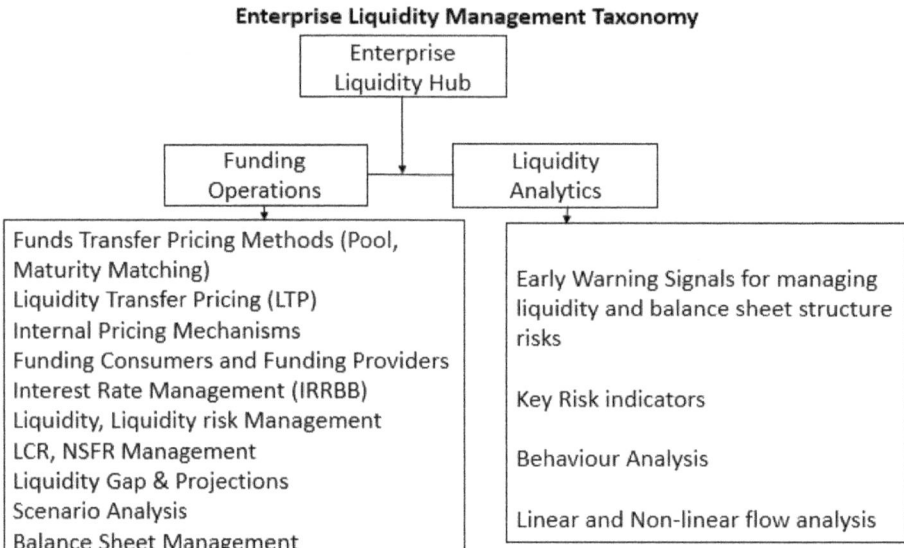

Figure 4-6. *Enterprise liquidity management taxonomy*

The new multicurrency enterprise liquidity paradigm is influenced by the lessons from the 2008 crisis and covers long-term structural funding and short-term liquidity. The two liquidity standards that Basel III provided are the net stable funding ratio (NSFR) and its complementary liquidity coverage ratio (LCR).

Enterprise Liquidity Management is a mission critical function for all banks. It applies to international banks, (case study: Credit Suisse) and domestic banks (case studies: Silicon Valley Bank, Signature Bank, Heartland Tri-State Bank, and First Republic Bank). Enterprise liquidity hub supports enterprise liquidity management and is explained in Section 4.4.1.2 after the examples on performance, risk, control, and cost monitoring.

A bank's enterprise operating model defines the delivery mechanism to accomplish its business goals. It comprises products and services, staff, systems, policies, and procedures. There are risks and costs associated with the implementation of the model for delivering products and services to the markets. The efficiency and maturity of the model determine the bank's ability to create value for its customers.

4.2.2.4 Operational Risk and Operational Resilience[6]

The Basel II accord defines operational risk as "the risk of direct or indirect loss resulting from inadequate or failed internal processes, people and systems or from external events."

The root cause could be any one or more of the following: (a) bank's risk culture, (b) systems, (c) staff conduct or performance, (d) policy and procedure, and (e) external sources.

- Risk culture

    The risk culture manifests itself in the business approach. Examples include the following: a "too big to fail" business approach is characterized by an indifference toward regulatory compliance, unfair business practices, complex product offering, and aggressive selling of products and services.

---

[6] Definition and Application of Operational Risk: https://www.bis.org/bcbs/publ/d508.pdf
https://www.bis.org/basel_framework/chapter/OPE/10.htm?inforce=20191215
https://www.bis.org/fsi/fsisummaries/oprisk_sa.pdf
Review of the Principles for the Sound Management of Operational Risk: https://www.bis.org/publ/bcbs292.pdf

CHAPTER 4 MONITORING OPERATING LEVERAGE

Proactive enterprise risk-adjusted return management is about a data-based, "cost reduction" culture. This is linked to a culture of continuous process improvement and knowledge management.

- Systems (automation)

    The financial industry is one of the largest users of technology. The big banks are early adopters of emerging technology, and some of them collaborate with banking solution vendors to be in the forefront of leveraging technology. Enterprise IT governance minimizes risks associated with automation. The alignment of technical process with business processes is a critical success factor.

- People

    Staff play an important role in building trust and in improving customer experience. They could also be a source of operational risk and create a financial loss for a bank. The cause of the risk event could be traced to a fraudulent intent or linked to inadequate staff skills.

- Policy and procedure

    It might be useful to remember the important differences between process, procedure, and processes. Policies are decision-making guidelines. Process is the transformation of inputs into outputs based on procedures that define the sequence of tasks.

- External sources

    These would include Acts of God and external threats, e.g., hackers.

Basel defines operational resilience as the ability of a bank to deliver critical operations through disruption. This ability enables a bank to identify and protect itself from threats and potential failures, respond and adapt to, as well as recover and learn from disruptive events in order to minimise their impact on the delivery of critical operations through disruption.

Basel's[7] principles for operational resilience mentions the following:

- Corporate Governance, this includes governance structure
- Operational risk management
- Business continuity planning and testing
- Mapping interconnections and interdependencies
- Third-party dependency management
- Incident management and Information and communication technology, including cyber security.

An operational risk management system comprises the following components: (a) risk and control self-assessment, (b) risk monitoring, (c) corrective action, (d) internal loss data collection and external loss data, and (e) economic capital calculation. The following are the main functions of an ORM system:

- Risk identification
  - Activity analysis
  - List of vulnerabilities
  - Root cause analysis

---

[7] https://www.bis.org/bcbs/publ/d516.pdf

- Risk measurement and assessment
  - What has been the frequency of occurrences?
  - What is the probability of a loss? What is the probable loss?
- Control measures
  - Control identification/evaluation
  - Evaluate controls
- Test controls to mitigate risk identified
  - Test cases and test data
  - Testing
  - Residual risk determination
- Review
  - Cost of control vs risk severity
  - Residual risk

Risk and Control Self-assessment (RCSA)

RCSA is a technique that uses staff skills to assess the risk and control in their work units. It is a bottom-up approach to identifying risk exposures and determining corrective action. The risk governance team use interview techniques and customized questionnaires to gather data on the assessment.

Banks can achieve the twin objectives of cost optimization and minimization of residual risks in processes.

This book recommends that a bank builds capabilities that will enable them to use process efficiency and maturity as a metric to implement a risk-based approach to operational risk management.

CHAPTER 4　MONITORING OPERATING LEVERAGE

Internal and external data are required by lines of business and risk events. The following are the two dimensions:

- Business lines[8]

    Corporate finance, trading and sales, retail banking, commercial banking, clearing, agency services, asset management, retail brokerage, private banking, and corporate items

- Event types

    Internal fraud, external fraud, employment practices and workplace safety, clients, products and business practices, disasters and public safety, technology and infrastructure failures, execution, delivery and process management, and malicious damage

Figure 4-7 provides an overview of the operational risk management components.

---

[8] Basel II: The New Basel Capital Accord: https://www.bis.org/bcbs/bcbscp3.htm
Definition and Application of Operational Risk: https://www.bis.org/basel_framework/chapter/OPE/10.htm?inforce=20191215

CHAPTER 4   MONITORING OPERATING LEVERAGE

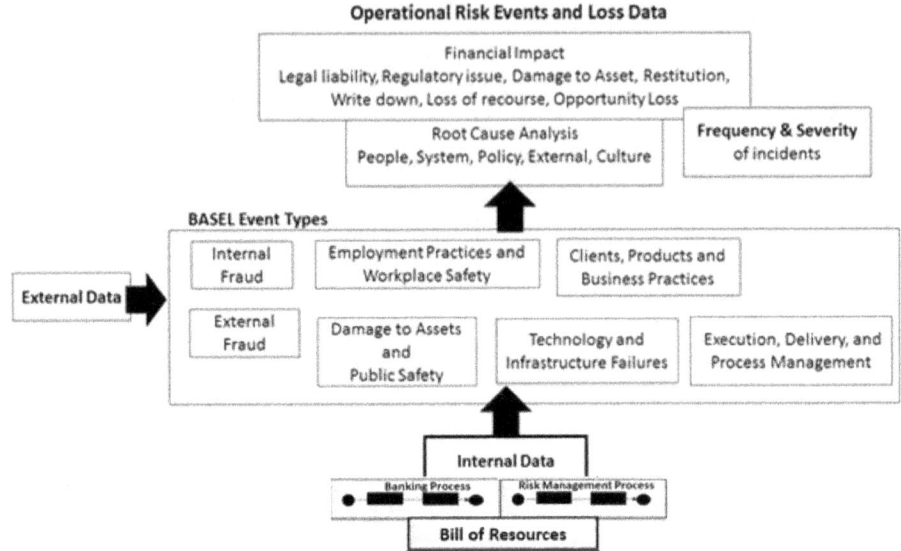

Figure 4-7. *Operational risk events and loss data*

4.2.2.4.1 Operational Risk – Staff Incidents

Many operational risk incidents are caused by the staff. A fundamental requirement for managing the staff is a good Human Capital Management system that is integrated with banking applications.

"Human perimeter" is constantly tested and is a threat in all organizations. Staff recruitment procedures and training are preventive controls and should be part of HR (consistent with Information Security) policy.

Risk Incidents

- Case – In 2016, the media reported that the Hong Kong Monetary Authority expressed their concern over the weakness in staff related controls in a regional Southeast Asian bank in Hong Kong. The police arrested about 20 employees of the bank in Hong Kong for selling customer data.

Enterprise IT governance covers the areas of (I) asset control; (ii) staff access to production, development, testing, and training environments; (iii) source code management; and (iv) staff handover policy and procedures upon resignation. It also brings out the need for a Know Your Employee (KYE) policy. The policy should cover risks that could arise from the behavior of *former employees*. The external factor in operational risk management includes former employees, contractors, and vendors.

Table 4-4a. Human capital system – operational risk incident analysis

Organization	System	Staff	Policy and procedures
Risk culture is always an early warning signal for a risk exposure. This could be at the management level or at the staff level	HR system should include data on recruitment, appraisal, promotion, transfer, training, and termination. Audit and risk management staff should have a 360° view of staff. HR processes should be integrated with mainstream applications for risk management of staff functions		

- Case – In April 2017, a computer engineer in California was arrested for stealing trade secrets from his employer, a global financial services firm. The investigation revealed that the engineer had stolen over three million files of confidential data and computer code. The stolen asset was the source for the company's algorithmic trading models and trading platform.

He was able to gain access to the network's encryption keys, transfer the files to another storage area within the same network, and then shift it to a third-party software development site.

The engineer was also accused of using the login credentials of his colleagues. Under the circumstances, this could be treated as identity theft also.

An investment in technology made by a bank that results in **a "work-unit" output**, flawed or imperfect or virtual or otherwise, is still an asset of the bank. If it is unfinished, it would still be a semifinished or a work-in-progress asset. A person or company cannot use it later and claim that is not the bank's asset.

Table 4-4b. Human capital system – operational risk incident analysis

Risk characterization	Loss of confidentiality, integrity, and availability	Weakness in control
Bank's proprietary software for trading	The bank's asset was compromised	Enterprise IT governance was weak: (a) control over assets, in this case software, and (b) staff access management. HR system did not provide 360° view of staff. Weakness in recruitment and monitoring processes

Case: Dynamic Layering – Internet Share Trading and Algorithms

A criminal investigation found a trader guilty of making several million dollars by using a technique called dynamic layering. This technique is implemented by executing a software that is programmed to rig prices quoted on exchange. The software places, modifies, and cancels orders placed on the exchange within a split of a second. The size of the orders were such as to move the market and the intent was never to execute the trade. It was to manipulate the buy-sell rates.

Table 4-4c. Human capital system – operational risk incident analysis

Risk characterization	Staff	Weakness in control
Staff: Rogue "trades" – market manipulation, price rigging A **risk culture issue** – *some banks set unrealistic targets for their staff*	Staff monitoring is important. Trading room should have dual control and segregation of duties	**Human capital department** should have **KPIs** for • Staff recruitment processes • Matching of staff skills with roles • 360° view of staff • Staff profile and behavioral analysis • Real-time human capital data integration with banking processes • Staff termination procedures

4.2.2.4.2 EITG Risks

Risk Incidents

Case: In August 2017, a problem with a **telco-owned satellite** knocked out thousands of **ATMs in Indonesia.** *It affected about 6000 ATMs, and it took more than a week for a complete recovery.*

Special audit report on this incident mentioned the following lapses:

- Emergency preparedness (BCP readiness) was found wanting.
- System functions like capacity planning were flawed.
- Information technology risk management was not proactive and effective.
- Limitations in human capital management policy and procedures.

Table 4-5a. EITG – business continuity planning and operational risk incident analysis

Risk characterization	Loss of confidentiality, integrity, and availability	Weakness in control
Hardware and software – there could be a risk exposure to several aspects of data management (i.e., fall back and recovery; data backups)	Business disruptions triggered by external events could make services unavailable to customers BCP should adequately cover the data management aspect in the disaster recovery procedures	BCP should involve functional and technical personnel. It should be tested periodically

Case: In November 2016, Halifax and Bank of Scotland suffered a *power failure in their data center*. Its impact was felt by all its branches, and banking services across all channels were unavailable for a full-working day.

Severe weather conditions interrupted the power supply. However, the incident raised several issues over the **quality of data centers and the effectiveness of the BCP**. HBOS power failure highlights importance of business continuity planning.

CHAPTER 4   MONITORING OPERATING LEVERAGE

Table 4-5b. *EITG – business continuity planning and operational risk incident analysis*

Organization	System	Staff	Policy and procedures	External
BCP is wider in scope than disaster recovery Downtime KPIs should be set and measured during BCP testing BCP requires management's commitment	Should be tested for availability	All employees should be trained on BCP procedures *Customer relations management* is critical. It comes under stress when such events happen	BCP is a shared responsibility of business and technology group	Natural calamities

Case: In 2017, **digital bank** Monzo suffered a severe outage at its service provider premises. Monzo's service was disrupted. The problems started when card processor GPS ran an unexpected large migration that knocked out services for cardholders at Monzo. Within a week, Monzo faced **a** second incident that involved incorrect payment displays with their mobile application. It impacted 120,000 customers. The incidents highlighted weaknesses in the data center infrastructure and BCP execution. Monzo moved its card processing in-house after the risk incident.

CHAPTER 4   MONITORING OPERATING LEVERAGE

Table 4-5c. *EITG – business continuity planning and operational risk incident analysis*

Risk characterization	Loss of confidentiality, integrity, and availability	Weakness in control
Risk culture – bank's indifference to enterprise IT governance BCP is not a static program. Changes in technology and business model have an impact on BCP	(i) Weak data center and infrastructure management; (ii) ineffective BCP, resulted in banking services being unavailable for a full day	BCP for a siloed environment is challenging It is a single plan for the entire bank. The tests should include all known scenarios (system failure, weather, hacking)

Data centers are processing hubs, and operational risk incidents could lead to high severity losses.

ECB has identified enterprise IT governance as a supervisory priority for the period 2022–2024.[9]

High severity operational risk causation include

- Enterprise data management
- Outsourcing
- **Data-centric approach** to enterprise IT risk management

---

[9] https://www.bankingsupervision.europa.eu/banking/srep/2022/html/ssm.srep2022_ITandcyberrisk.en.pdf#:~:text=Deficiencies%20in%20IT%20outsourcing%20and%20cyber%20resilience%20have,a%20concern%20for%20supervisors%20and%20significant%20institutions%20alike.

Banks should take a **data-centric approach** to enterprise IT risk management that is consistent with NIST and ISO standards.

Table 4-5d. Hacking of data

Risk characterization	Loss of confidentiality, integrity, and availability	Weakness in control
Cyberattack with a motive to steal customer data	Confidentiality, integrity, and availability were compromised. As of today, the breach is known to be one of the worst in terms data sensitivity	Nonavailability of enterprise security architecture and layers of control

A bank should **baseline its data-item inventory,** *with a classification code for each item.* The classification level determines the access (create, read, update, and delete) and risk management procedures. An example of data classification levels is as follows.

Table 4-5e. Data classification examples

Classification level	Explanation
Unrestricted	Information already in the public domain or information that would have no measurable negative impact to a bank, its customers, or its business partners could be classified as unrestricted
Critical	Information should be classified as "Critical" if its disclosure (i) to bank staff (who have no business need to have access to the data) or (ii) to outsiders would cause harm to the bank
	It could be a financial or nonfinancial risk to the bank
	Data disclosures are governed by legal and regulatory requirements

(continued)

Table 4-5e. (*continued*)

Classification level	Explanation
Sensitive	Information could be classified as "Sensitive" if its unauthorized disclosure has a serious impact on the bank's business. This would include the impact on a bank's share price/financial loss/loss of competitive advantage or could result in regulatory sanction or legal action against the bank
Legally privileged	In some countries, there is a practice of having another category of information classification called "Legally privileged." The legal department of the bank (part of GRC) should provide the necessary guidance on its classification and usage

Operational Risk Appetite and Management

Management should define operational risk appetite and tolerance. The process-based approach to building the operating model and managing operational risk is explained in Chapter 3, Sections 3.4.1 and 3.4.2.

The performance, risk, control, and cost monitoring explained in Section 4.4 of this chapter illustrates the process-based methodology for managing risk (KRIs) and performance (KPIs).

4.2.3 Risk Appetite

Figures 4-8a and 4-8b illustrate the capacity of a bank in terms of risk taking. Capacity, as explained in Chapter 3, can also refer to level of resources, i.e., FTE of staff and system usage.

CHAPTER 4   MONITORING OPERATING LEVERAGE

Figure 4-8a. Risk appetite framework – risk capacity, tolerance, and appetite

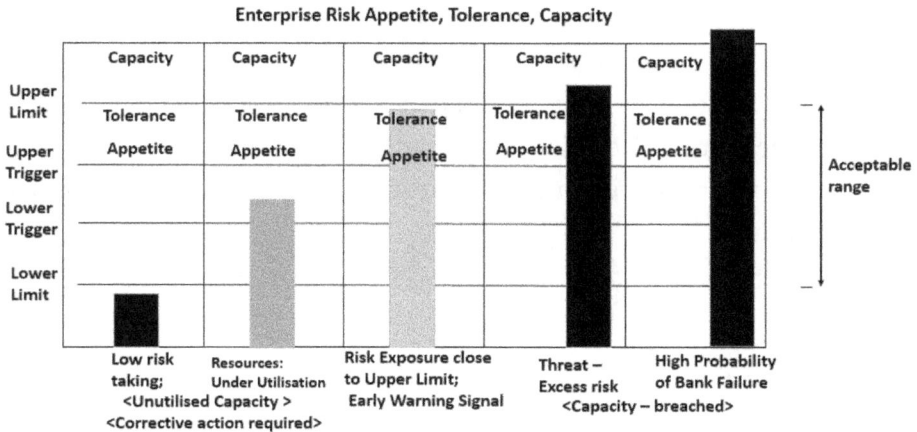

Figure 4-8b. Risk capacity

301

CHAPTER 4   MONITORING OPERATING LEVERAGE

Risk capacity represents a bank's ability to absorb potential losses. This is the risk taking financial strength that is revealed in the balance sheet of the bank. It could have a medium term timeframe.

Risk tolerance policy is defined by the senior management. IT should be consistent with tactical and strategic objectives of the bank and business needs. This provides operational flexibility for the profit centers of the bank.

Risk appetite reveals how much of loss a bank can absorb from market, credit, liquidity, or operational events over a one-year time frame. The risk appetite is operationalized via KRIs.

Activity based enterprise noninterest cost management should be understood in the context of business goals, capital adequacy, risk, controls, and costs.

A Bank's Risk Profile

Risk profile is a snapshot of a bank's overall risk exposure at a specific point in time. It should be consistent with the goals of the bank and the financial strength. The financial health and business activities are assessed using quantitative and qualitative factors. Some banks break down the four risk types into subcategories, and the list could include interest rate risk, price risk, event risk, transaction risk, compliance risk, strategic risk, structural risk, and reputation risk. Transaction risk could include a large wire transfer that remains unreconciled in the nostro account. Structural risks could be there in the balance sheet and can arise from credit concentration risks, movements in interest rates or exposure to variations in currency rates.

4.2.3.1 Penalties Paid by Banks

United States

Over two decades,[10] banks in the United States paid **$200bn** in fines and penalties.

UK[11]

UK banks fined $222 million between June 2022 and June 2023.

Globally,[12] *in 2022*, noncompliance penalties levied by regulators amounted to *$4.17 billion*. AML risk incidents increased by 55% in 2022.

The weaknesses and vulnerabilities in the banks that led to the payment of these fines are not reflected in their existing disclosures.

Banks should report risk-adjusted operational efficiency and operating leverage metrics. Until then, the risk in their financial statements is understated.

Enterprise control frameworks COSO and COBIT are explained in Section 1.4.3.1 under designing the operating model.

SOX and Six Sigma are explained in Chapter 5, Sections 5.3.2. and 5.3.3, under improving operating leverage.

4.2.4 Costs: Fixed and Variable and Reduction and Control

From the perspective of activity-based enterprise noninterest cost management, it is important to understand the difference between cost reduction and cost control.

---

[10] https://www.ft.com/content/989035f3-767a-43c2-b12e-2f6c0be0aa6b
[11] https://finbold.com/uk-banks-fined-222-million-in-the-last-12-months/
[12] https://go.fenergo.com/global-aml-fines-report-2023.html
   https://www.ft.com/content/7a4821e6-96f1-475c-ae55-6401e402061f

Cost reduction is the approach to reducing cost per unit by using new and improved methods and techniques, whereas cost control uses techniques like budgetary control.

The focus of cost reduction is on reducing per unit cost. This can be accomplished by improving operational efficiency and increasing market share. An organic increase in the scale of operation could bring down the unit costs. The same is not necessarily the case with inorganic growth. A merger with another bank increases the scale of operation but may not help in improving profitability. Further, it may not improve the operational efficiency and operating leverage of the merged entity.

4.2.4.1 Cost Reduction and Cost Control

A bank should continuously improve processes by identifying activities that do not add value. These activities should either be eliminated or made productive by improving resource capability and usage.

Table 4-6 illustrates the differences between cost reduction and cost control.

Table 4-6. *Cost reduction and control*

	Cost reduction	**Cost control**
Focus	Unit cost reduction	Control the total cost
Impact on quality	**Retention of quality can be achieved**	Difficult to maintain quality
Time impact	This has a long-term effect and permanent	This has short term effect – maybe a year
Nature of control	A corrective action	Aims to prevent incurring additional costs

4.2.4.2 Scale of Operations: Fixed and Variable Costs

Table 4-7 uses the underlying data that is used in Chapters 2 and 3. The table provides a fixed and variable cost perspective for a bank's P&L. It is just an example and is not based on any banking norm or standard.

Table 4-7. Illustrative fixed and variable cost

Operating Cost - Books of Account	P&L, $ - in millions	ENICM		
		Assumption	Fixed	Variable
Depreciation	20	70% fixed	14	6
Insurance on Assets	5	80% fixed	4	1
Employee cost	300	90% fixed	270	30
Enterprise I.T. Governance cost	200	80% fixed	160	40
Operations: Premises Rent & Utilities	150	80% fixed	120	30
Operations: Office supplies	100	80% fixed	80	20
Sales & Marketing	80	75% fixed	60	20
Director's fees	2	Fixed	2	
Audit fees	3	Fixed	3	
Legal fees	4	Variable		4
Consultant Charges	6	Variable		6
Operations: Repairs & Maintenance (non-I.T.)	25	60% Fixed	15	10
Operations: Travel	10	Variable		10
Total	905		728	177

In most banks, as shown in Table 4-8, the fixed noninterest cost is greater than the variable cost. However, when analyzing financial leverage, it is important to remember that interest expenses have a higher degree of variability. The cost of borrowed funds and the cost of equity funds vary in proportion to market factors, and that includes the "size" of the credit.

CHAPTER 4   MONITORING OPERATING LEVERAGE

Table 4-8. *Illustrative LOB's fixed and variable costs*

Cost Allocation – Enterprise Non-interest Cost Management

(from Chapter-2)	Total Cost	Allocation of Support Department Cost	Total
Retail Banking	383,200,000	43,800,000	427,000,000
Corporate Banking	223,150,000	45,000,000	268,150,000
Treasury	163,500,000	46,350,000	209,850,000
Total	769,850,000	135,150,000	905,000,000

Operating Leverage – Lines of Business: Fixed, Variable Cost

	Fixed Costs	Variable Costs	Total	LOB's (Fixed/Total Cost) %
Retail Banking	352,275,000	74,725,000	427,000,000	82.5%
Corporate Banking	197,352,500	70,797,500	268,150,000	73.6%
Treasury	178,372,500	31,477,500	209,850,000	85%
Total	728,000,000	177,000,000	905,000,000	

The above data is *selectively shown again in the operating leverage examples* in Section 4.4.

Time-driven ABC helps in achieving the objective of operational efficiency by providing an insight into fixed and variable costs. Noninterest costs of retail lending rise less than proportionately with the size of the loan. The causation can be traced to the fixed cost base. There is a link between operating leverage and financial leverage.

Break-even analysis is also referred to as cost-volume-profit analysis. It is a method for examining the relationship between revenue, variable costs, and fixed costs to determine the minimum value of banking business generation necessary to break-even.

CHAPTER 4 MONITORING OPERATING LEVERAGE

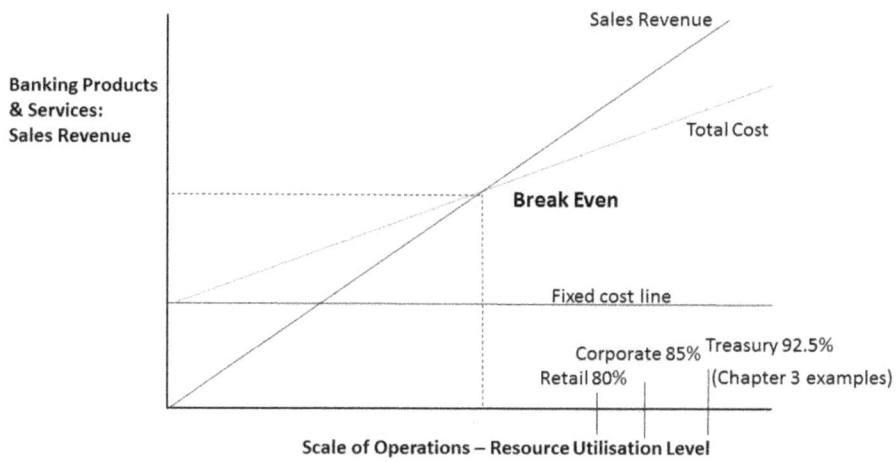

Figure 4-9a. *Cost-volume-profit analysis*

There can be a degree of nonlinear behavior of cost and sales, and this is shown in Figure 4-9b. This would need proactive management to boost revenue and minimize costs and risks.

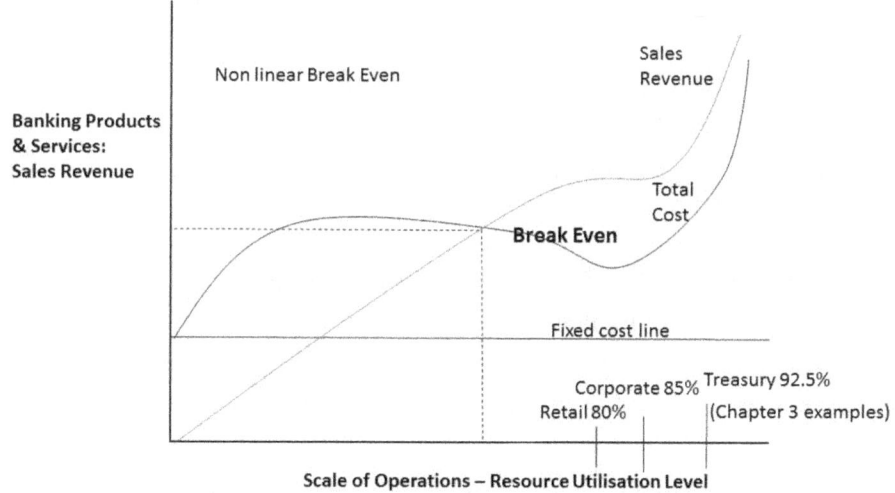

Figure 4-9b. *Nonlinear cost-volume-profit analysis*

307

The following methods can be used for segregating costs into variable and fixed:

i) High-point and low-point methods

ii) Simultaneous equation method

iii) Methods of least square

iv) Scatter diagram method

4.3 Monitor Operating Leverage

4.3.1 Risk-Based Approach

The books recommend that the internal control, risk management, and cost management teams use ***process efficiency score and process maturity score as metrics*** for a risk-based approach to manage banking business.

Further, the teams could focus on

- Twenty percent of the banking products that get 80% of the revenue

- Twenty percent of the high-risk areas that contribute to 80% of the business loss and operational weakness

Data for Maximizing Risk-Adjusted Returns

The effectiveness of operating leverage monitoring depends on the quality and quantity of data analyzed. Figure 4-10 emphasizes the need to have a single view of the truth, i.e., enterprise data presented to data consumers accurately and consistently.

The operating leverage monitoring is effective when internal control, risk managers (both taken as GRC), the lines of business performance monitoring, and cost accountants use a *common template for viewing enterprise data, the single view of the truth.*

CHAPTER 4 MONITORING OPERATING LEVERAGE

Banks should ensure that policy and procedures encourage an exchange of professional opinion. *Members from GRC, internal control, and risk manager and members from finance and the cost accountant should share their notes.*

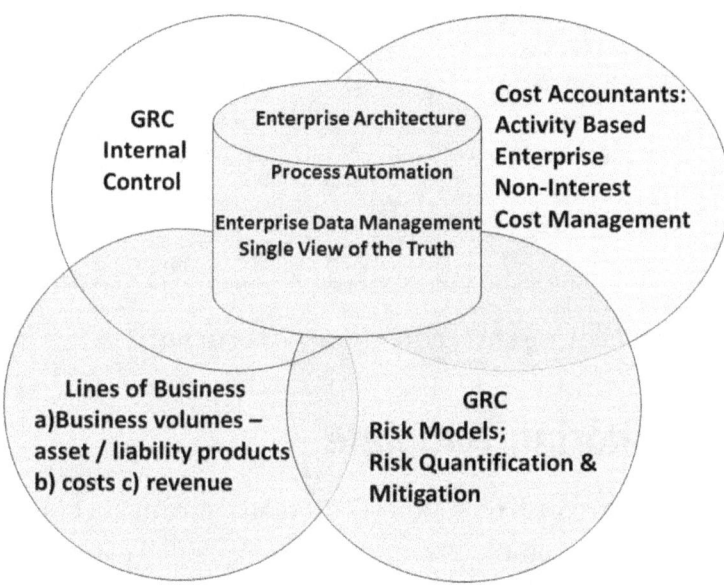

Figure 4-10. *Synergy between teams*

The synergy between the teams is important. For example, the cost accountant or the internal control manager can make recommendations to automate the monitoring process.

Figure 4-11 is a schematic to resolve a recommendation made by the cost accountant to set limits for cost and profit centers. This is not the "as-is account limit," but it is cost center limit that is checked at the time of posting of transaction. The limit excess can be overruled, but it will be tagged as an exception for the immediate action by the cost accountant.

CHAPTER 4 MONITORING OPERATING LEVERAGE

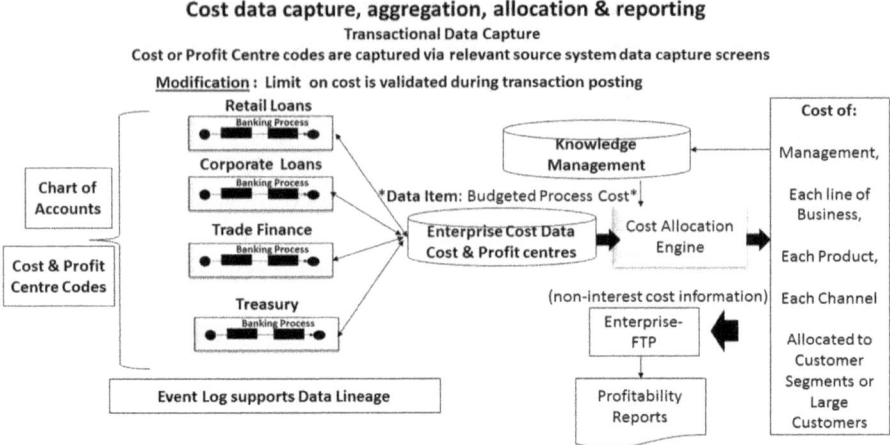

Figure 4-11. Checking cost center limits at origination

4.3.2 Monitoring Template

Activity-based, enterprise noninterest cost management is a bottom-up approach. TDABC-based PRCC monitoring is explained using a template that has five parts, A to E. The templates provided in Tables 4-9a, 4-9b, 4-9c, 4-9d, and 4-9e give an insight into enterprise PRCC monitoring.

The internal control manager and the cost accountant must focus on key performance indicators, and this includes the KPIs related to service level agreements. The team should also review the targeted performance of outsourced functions. Key Performance Indicators should be understood as a measure that helps monitoring the achievement of business goals. This is used from the management level right down to the process level.

Part A: Process – Static Details

Process type: B, banking; T, enterprise IT governance; R, risk management-GRC; H, human capital

CHAPTER 4   MONITORING OPERATING LEVERAGE

All review dates are captured in the system and can be accessed by the internal control, audit, and GRC teams.

Table 4-9a. *Part A: Process header*

\multicolumn{4}{c}{Operating Leverage Monitoring}
Process Id	Process Type	Process Description	
Process Owner	Last Review Date	Reviewed By	Last 5 Reviews: Summary
Product Id or Sub-Function Id:	Process Cost $	Sub-Process Id (if applicable)	Early Warning Signal (Y/N) N

The early warning signal flag could be "system generated." Using advanced analytics, e.g., machine learning, the underlying data can be examined as a background process.

Part B: Bill of Resources and Cost

The cost accountant's focus is on this section.

In all the examples, the Chapter 2 "as-is environment" product costs and the cost of resource consumed in a process-automated, time-driven ABC approach (Chapter 3) are shown.

Table 4-9b. *Part B: Resource costs and utilization*

		Review of the Bill of Resource							
		Activity-1		Activity-2		Activity-3		Activity-4	
		Staff	System	Staff	System	Staff	System	Staff	System
Front, Middle, Back									
						\multicolumn{4}{l}{Summarised & Illustrative}	
LOB	Product	Process, Activities		Volume		Activity time Min-Rnd	Total Time (Rnd)	Unit Cost	Total Cost (Rnd)

Time Driven (TD) process cost= the sum of all its TD activity costs.
TD activity based cost = Process Volume * Activity time *Unit cost of activity

311

CHAPTER 4   MONITORING OPERATING LEVERAGE

Part C: Risk-Adjusted Performance

GRC's focus is on this section. Cost can also be examined by GRC team and the focus could be on cost of risk management.

Table 4-9c. *Part C: Risk, control, and costs*

	Review of the Bill of Resource - Operational efficiency of Outsourced function							
	Activity-1		Activity-2		Activity-3		Activity-4	
	Staff	System	Staff	System	Staff	System	Staff	System
Front, Middle, Back	Sales related risk – mitigation. Refer GRC remarks.							
	Examine KPI,KRI: Performance, Risk, Control, Cost (PRCC)							
PRCC Issue								
Causation								
Risk Appetite breach								
Severity								
Probability of re-occurrence								

Root cause analysis is a best practice for understanding a KPI failure or an early warning signal or a KRI alert. It is necessary to analyze it from several dimensions and perspectives. The analysis should take a deep dive approach to identify the impact on processes, policies, procedures, staff roles, and systems. Root cause analysis is explained further in Section 5.3.5 of the next chapter.

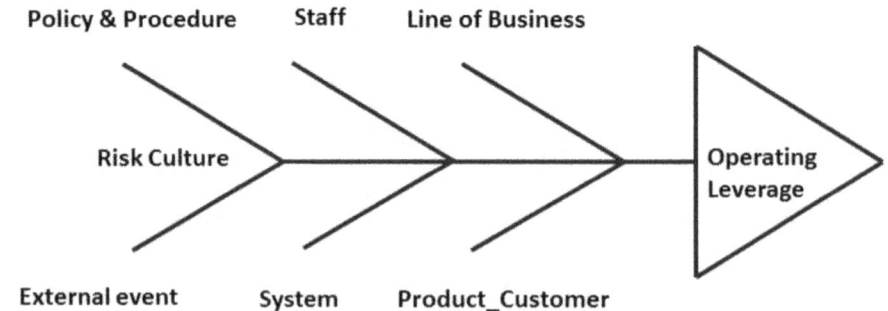

Figure 4-12. *Root cause analysis*

The *three lines of defense model*[13] differentiates the three groups that are involved in enterprise risk-adjusted return management framework, and their functions are

- **Own** and manage (operating management/front office)
- **Oversee** (risk, quality, and compliance functions/middle office)
- Provide independent **assurance** (internal audit/back office)

The book recommends that the first line of defense, i.e., the business, is given clear objectives to manage risk. The first line should not believe that managing risk is the sole responsibility of the second level. This will improve operational efficiency and improve risk-adjusted returns, e.g., predeal analytics in a real-time treasury.

Nature of Controls

Figure 4-13 tweaks the Basel's three-layer recommendation for enterprise controls for business delivery and risk management. Nature of controls in a three lines of defense model is

- First line of defense responsibilities include proactively managing risk profile of the bank, lines of business, and profit centers and monitoring risk appetite and tolerance.
- The second line of defense focuses on **preventive controls and real-time/near real-time** risk management.

---

[13] Review of the Principles for the Sound Management of Operational Risk https://www.bis.org/publ/bcbs292.pdf

CHAPTER 4   MONITORING OPERATING LEVERAGE

- Third line of defense responsibilities is about the independent verification of effectiveness of risk management policies, procedures, and processes.

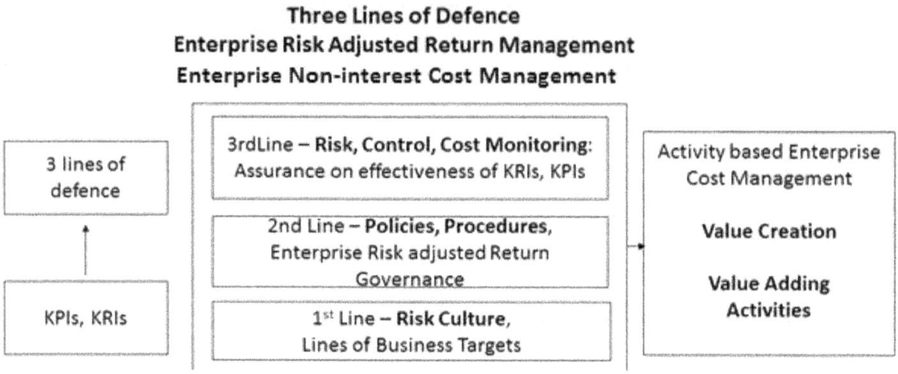

Three Lines of Defence
Enterprise Risk Adjusted Return Management
Enterprise Non-interest Cost Management

3 lines of defence	3rdLine – Risk, Control, Cost Monitoring: Assurance on effectiveness of KRIs, KPIs	Activity based Enterprise Cost Management
↑	2nd Line – Policies, Procedures, Enterprise Risk adjusted Return Governance	Value Creation
KPIs, KRIs	1st Line – Risk Culture, Lines of Business Targets	Value Adding Activities

Figure 4-13. *Three lines of defense*

The enterprise cost model should be designed and monitored within the wider framework of financial budgeting, forecasting, and analysis. These are subcomponents of the enterprise risk-adjusted return model. Activity based enterprise cost management should be "value driven."

Cost of Controls

An important aspect of risk management is to factor the cost of control linked to a quantified risk. The decision to implement a control is based on comparing the quantified risk and the cost of the control.

An accurate and efficient enterprise cost management system improves risk-adjusted return management. The risk appetite framework should provide policy guidance for the periodic evaluation of controls. Enterprise risk monitoring policies should ensure that the quantified risk, the cost of its control, and the effectiveness are periodically evaluated. Figures 4-14a and 4-14b illustrate two different scenarios for risk control trade-off.

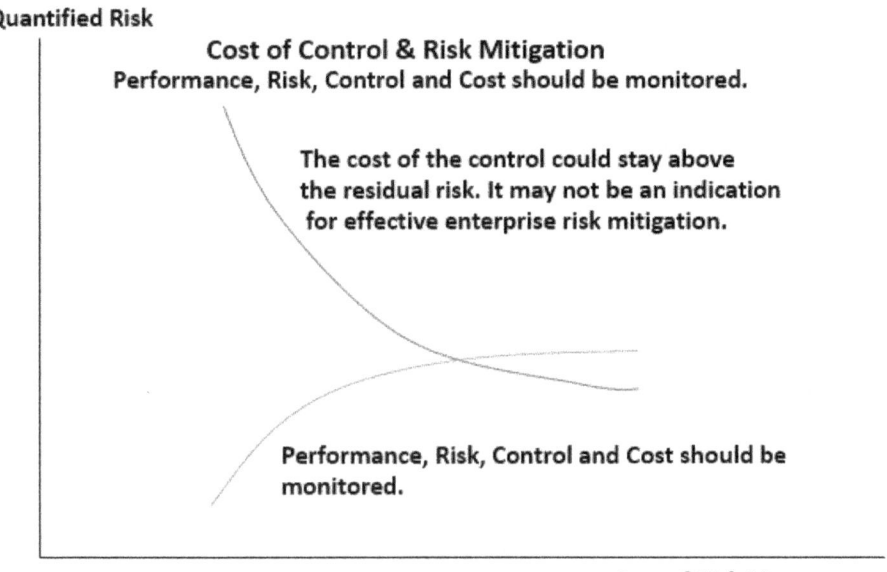

Figure 4-14a. *Cost of control and quantified risk*

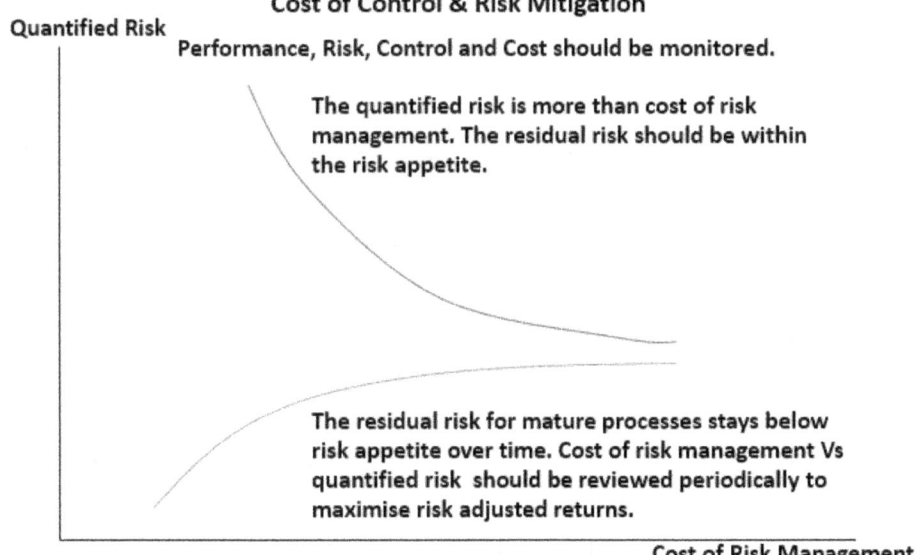

Figure 4-14b. *Cost of control and quantified risk*

CHAPTER 4   MONITORING OPERATING LEVERAGE

Enterprise IT governance requires a tool to collect data, update the ETIG data repository, and transform the data into actionable intelligence. This must be done within a framework that is cost-effective and does not have a major impact upon computing and human resources.

Figure 4-15 emphasizes the importance of (a) human capital and technology and (b) maximizing the usage of resources for accomplishing business objectives.

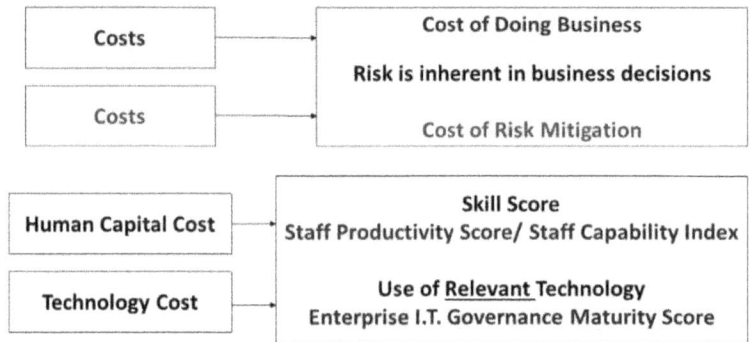

Figure 4-15. *Cost of doing business*

Cost of risk mitigation includes staff, system, and risk model costs. It includes the cost of (i) risk identification and analysis, (ii) corrective action recommendations, (iii) testing and implementing corrections and improvements, and (iv) implementation of the upgrades and corrections.

Staff recruitment is a process that is linked to a bank's ability to attract talent. This process needs to be efficient and rigorous in order to ensure that employees have the right skills and competence to add value to the bank. Like continuous process improvement, periodic skill upgrade is paramount for achieving operational efficiency. Figures 4-16 and 4-17 illustrate the use of bill of resources for improving operating leverage.

CHAPTER 4   MONITORING OPERATING LEVERAGE

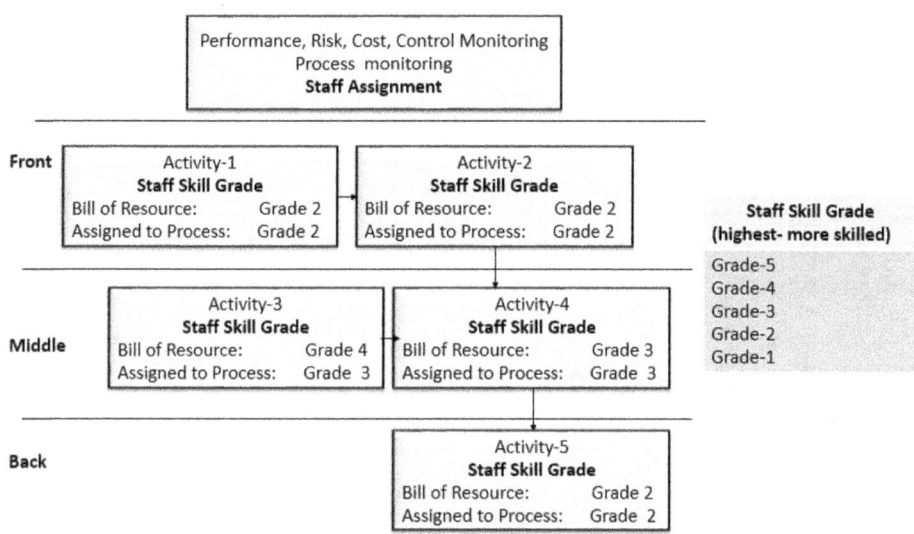

Figure 4-16. *Using bill of resources for monitoring staff performance*

Operating leverage management focuses on activity-based budgeting and activity-based noninterest cost management. Figure 4-17 highlights the importance of monitoring budgeted costs.

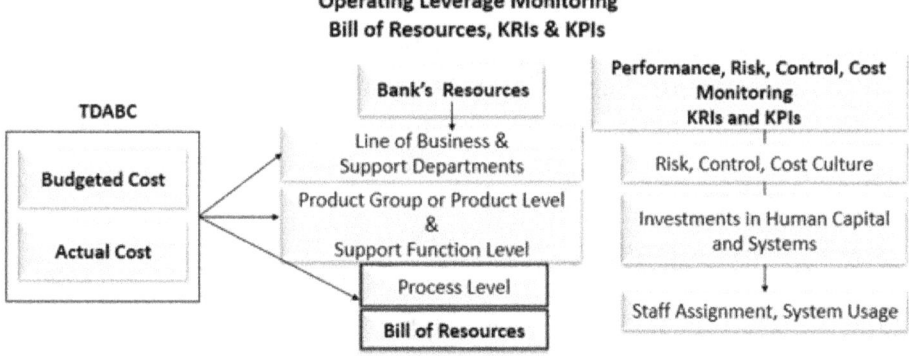

Figure 4-17a. *Operating leverage monitoring*

317

CHAPTER 4   MONITORING OPERATING LEVERAGE

Part D: Corrective Action

Table 4-9d. Part D: Corrective action

Evaluate Process – KPI, KRI Risk Adjusted Return - Corrective Action	
Policy, Procedure	
External - SLAs, other agreements	
Cost / Benefit check	Approval for Change: ■

Part E: Implementation

Table 4-9e. Part E: Implementation

Correction / Improvement
Test Correction & Implement
Measure KPI and Residual Risk

4.3.3 Thirty-Five Examples – Monitoring OL

This section provide 35 examples: **31** are *process-specific* **(Sections 4.3.3.2, 4.3.3.3, 4.3.3.4, 4.3.3.5, 4.3.3.6, 4.3.3.7, and 4.3.3.8) and 4** are recommendations **(Section 4.4) for known business situations** that require actionable intelligence for decision-making at the senior management level.

4.3.3.1 Management

Enterprise risk-adjusted return governance is about how a bank defines and enforces its risk-adjusted return business culture.

The bank's organization structure and quantified goals reflect the risk culture of a bank. The empowerment of risk management functions is critical for accomplishing risk-reward goals at all levels.

Figures 4-17b and 4-17c provide two views of enterprise risk-adjusted return governance with the latter focusing on risk committees.

Figure 4-17b. *Senior management enterprise risk-adjusted return governance*

The BOD's risk oversight responsibilities include monitoring the

- Performance of the risk committees. The enterprise risk-adjusted return model requires a holistic approach to managing performance. Hence, the data provided to the risk committee and the decisions taken by them should (a) be timely, consistent, and accurate and (b) provide a perspective of the implication of an event or perceived threat on all risk types.

- Quality of the enterprise risk control framework. The organization structure should facilitate data flow and decision-making between the three lines of defense.

CHAPTER 4   MONITORING OPERATING LEVERAGE

Figure 4-17c. Risk committees

The enterprise risk committee

- Is distinct from the audit committee
- Should have a chair who avoids conflict of interest
- Includes members who have relevant experience
- Takes a holistic view of enterprise risk management
- Formulates policies and approves risk-adjusted return strategies
- Is required to review, approve, and monitor risk-adjusted returns at desired frequencies
- Monitors risks and risk management effective at frequent intervals

The risk audit committee

- Is a standalone committee
- Evaluates enterprise risk governance
- Reviews the implementation of relevant risk policies
- Reviews the effectiveness of enterprise control framework
- Validates risk models
- Ensures the accuracy of risk-adjusted return processing

The cost of the senior managers mentioned in Figures 4-17b and 4-17c should be taken as management cost. Noninterest cost management policies should provide guidance on the unit cost of management activities and the service level agreement between support departments and lines of business.

Management Quality

The details in Table 4-10 are important from a risk culture perspective. Many banks have "supervisory committees," but these institutions do not have an *independent review of the effectiveness of the management committees*. It is a good practice to have an independent reviews of the meetings. The observations should be made available to the board and the statutory auditor. The goal breakdown and settings of KPIs explained in Chapter 3, Section 3.4.1, should ensure KPIs are set for the management. Good governance should provide transparency over the management meetings.

CHAPTER 4 MONITORING OPERATING LEVERAGE

Table 4-10. *Review of management meetings*

Management Function	Process	Bill of Resources – Quorum & Automation support	TDABC Cost
Enterprise Risk Adjusted Return Management			
Performance, Risk, Control & Cost Monitoring: Bank Management level			
Asset Liability Management	K.P.Is		
Risk Committee meetings	K.P.Is		
Remuneration Committee meetings	K.P.Is	Independent Review of meetings; Agendas / Quorum / Minutes	
Audit Committee meetings	K.P.Is		
Technology Committee meetings	K.P.Is		
Investor Grievance Management meetings	K.P.Is	Implementation & Review of action points	
Staff Grievance Management meetings	K.P.Is		
Whistleblower meetings	K.P.Is		

Retail, Corporate Banking, Treasury, and Pan-Bank

These examples mentioned in Table 4-11 are illustrative. The reader is requested to extend the example into the operating environment in her/his bank and make an assessment of the improvements needed.

Banking is not static. It works 24/7 and the business environment is dynamic. Business volumes have increased and derivatives have increased the complexity of business.

This had made the monitoring of performance, *residual risk, control, and cost,* a "survival" issue.

CHAPTER 4   MONITORING OPERATING LEVERAGE

Table 4-11. Monitoring operating leverage examples

Operating Leverage Monitoring

Process-1 Savings A/c Opening	Process-18 Nostro Reconciliation
Process-2 Fixed Deposit Opening	Process-19 Sub-Process Anti-Money laundering & countering the financing of terrorism check
Process-3 Home Loan - Salaried	
Process-4 Consumer Durable Loan	Process-20 Sub-Process Fraud Prevention & Detection
Process 5 Credit Card	Process-21 Case Management
Process-6 Locker Rental	Process-22 Chart of Accounts, Books of Account; ABCM
Process 7 Omni-Channel Business Delivery	Process-23 Enterprise I.T. Governance tool
Process-8 LC Issuance	Process-24 Incident management
Process-9 Bills Co-acceptance	Process-25 Release Management
Process-10 Term Loan-10 Years	Process-26 Non-production environment - banking
Process-11 Syndicate Loan	Process-27 Human Capital – Staff Recruitment
Process-12 Credit Risk Management	Process-28 Human Capital – Staff Termination
Process-13 Collateral Management	Process-29 Risk Models
Process-14 Internal Credit Rating	Process-30 Stress Testing
Process-15 Currency Swap Input	Process-31 Business Continuity Planning
Process-16 Interest rate Swap Deal Input	
Process-17 Index-linked CDS-Deal Input	**Decisions:** Enterprise Liquidity Management (operations perspective) Rationalisation of Branch Network Outsourcing Reducing Carbon footprint

Operational Resilience is a subset of Enterprise Resilience. The scope of Operating Leverage monitoring will include the assessment of operational resilience at the lines of business level and at the function level. The function level refers to sales, on-boarding, account operation and closure. In the case of treasury, this will map to pre-trade, trade, deal monitoring and settlement.

Resilience monitoring will also include critical end-to-end process such as payments.

4.3.3.2 Retail Banking

4.3.3.2.1 Retail Banking Operations Monitoring Dashboard

PRCC review at line of business level, budget vs actual (revenue and costs)

- **Revenue**

Product Id	Interest	Fees	Charges	Commission
Budgeted				
Actual				

CHAPTER 4   MONITORING OPERATING LEVERAGE

- **Total cost**

Product Id   Cost

Budgeted

Actual

- **Cost breakup**

Fixed costs	Variable costs	Retail – total
352,275,000	74,725,000	**427,000,000**

The table below is from Chapter 2 (Table 2-32b) – retail banking, P&L "fully absorbed" by products.

Cost of Retail Products by Customer

	RETSAV	RETFD1	RETHLS	RETCOD	RETCCD	RETLOC	Prodt-7	Total
Direct Cost	520,00,000	292,50,000	261,50,000	146,50,000	136,50,000	136,50,000	136,50,000	**163,000,000**
Indirect Cost								
Employee	11,000,000	8,500,000	8,500,000	3,000,000	3,000,000	3,000,000	3,000,000	**40,000,000**
Technology	17,800,000	15,200,000	12,200,000	10,700,000	6,700,000	4,700,000	4,700,000	**72,000,000**
Premises	20,000,000	10,000,000	10,000,000	5,000,0000	5,000,000	5,000,000	5,000,000	**60,000,000**
Office Supplies	9,000,000	6,000,000	1,000,000	1,000,000	1,000,000	1,000,000	1,000,000	**20,000,000**
R&M	1,250,000	1,250,000	2,500,000	1,250,000	1,250,000	1,250,000	1,250,000	**10,000,000**
Management	2,600,000	2,600,000	2,600,000	2,600,000	2,600,000	2,600,000	2,600,000	**18,200,000**
Support Functions	6,258,000	6,257,000	6,257,000	6,257,000	6,257,000	6,257,000	6,257,000	**43,800,000**
Total	119,908,000	79,057,000	69,207,000	44,457,000	39,457,000	37,457,000	37,457,000	**427,000,000**

As shown in Chapter 3, Section 3.6, when the time-driven ABC method is used, the retail banking cost is 341,600,000 and the capacity utilization is 80%.

CHAPTER 4   MONITORING OPERATING LEVERAGE

Process Automated Time Driven Activity Based Costing Cost of consumed resources	
P&L (fully absorbed)	427,000,000
TDABC - Cost of consumed resources	341,600,000
Cost of Unutilised Resources	85,400,000
Utilisation Rate	80%

Monitoring of Fixed and Variable Costs

Retail banking relies on its business delivery and product distribution channels. That has a higher than desired fixed cost element. During good times, it is ignored. When revenue targets are difficult to meet, a knee-jerk "cost control" reaction follows.

Fixed costs	Variable costs	Review	Recommendation
352,275,000	74,725,000	Salaries Operations – premises Technology	Continuous process improvement paves the way for quantifying reduction in costs, particularly fixed costs

Costs

LOB	Product	Process, Activities	Volume	Activity time Min-Rnd	Total Time	Unit Cost	Total Cost (Rnd)

Summarised & Illustrative

Time Driven (TD) process cost= the sum of all its TD activity costs.
TD activity based cost = Process Volume * Activity time *Unit cost of activity

The data below is from Chapter 3, Section 3.5.2, process-automated, time-driven activity-based costing of retail banking products.

CHAPTER 4 MONITORING OPERATING LEVERAGE

Process automated, time driven activity based costing - cost of consumed resources

Savings Account	1 Year FD	Home Loan	Consumer Loans	Credit Card	RETLOC	Prodt-7	Total
95,926,400	63,245,600	55,365,600	35,565,600	31,565,600	29,965,600	29,965,600	341,600,000

Cost monitoring focus areas

	Staff	Systems	Branches	E-channels	Support
Fixed	100% FTE	Annual maintenance	Fixed	If fully owned	Focus on (i) EITG cost (ii) operations
Variable	Multiple products/ functions	Usage based	May not apply	If shared – Variable/usage based	

Retail banking is constantly under cost and earnings pressure. The emergence of new competitors has intensified competition. Other challenges faced by retail banking include pricing, regulatory scrutiny over charges collected from customers, and managing social media.

Example of performance monitoring – *sales and onboarding KPIs*:

- True positives in loan application submission and approval 99.5%
- Loan application approval **time** 100% success
- Loan disbursement **time** 99.9% success

*Time-driven ABC

The following are six retail banking PRCC monitoring examples. Omni-channel capability can be used by all lines of business. Retail Banking consumes the bulk of omni-channel transactions.

4.3.3.2.2 (i) Savings A/c

As the sales of many retail products are outsourced, this example *focuses on the sales process.*

CHAPTER 4   MONITORING OPERATING LEVERAGE

Part A

Operating Leverage Monitoring

Process Id	Process 1	Process Type	B ▼	Process Description	Sales – New Savings A/c		
Process Owner		Staff Id	Last Review Date YYMMDD	Reviewed By	Staff Id	Last 5 Reviews:	▼
Product Id	RETSAV	Process Cost Budgeted $ Actual $		Sub-Process id	i. AML ii. KYC	Early Warning Signal (Y/N)	N

Part B

Review of the Bill of Resource - Operational efficiency of Outsourced function

	Activity-1		Activity-2		Activity-3		Activity-4	
	Staff	System	Staff	System	Staff	System	Staff	System
Front, Middle, Back office	Sales related risk – mitigation. Refer GRC remarks.							

GRC remark is in Part C.

Part C

This is an extract from Table 3-8a in Chapter 3, Section 3.5.2. The total cost is $95,926,400.

					Summarised & Illustrative			
LOB	Product		Process, Activities	Volume	Activity time Min-Rnd	Total Time (Rnd)	Unit Cost	Total Cost (Rnd)

Time Driven (TD) process cost = the sum of all its TD activity costs.
TD activity based cost = Process Volume * Activity time * Unit cost of activity

Retail	RETSAV	Sales	Risk Management	49,936	120	5,992,317	3.89	23,310,115

	Examine KPI, KRI : Performance. Risk, Control, Cost,
PRCC Issue	Complaints from the public mention mismatch between Terms & Conditions mentioned by sales persons and the bank's procedures.
Causation	To **save costs**, bank outsourced retail deposit mobilisation sales functions to 3rd party vendors Bank failed to train the external contractor / failed to engage a firm with the correct skills. Bank failed to supervise outsourced work; no effective use of technology.
Risk Appetite breach	Yes
Severity	Reputation risk; Banking Supervisor's strictures and penalty.
Probability of re-occurrence	Medium

CHAPTER 4   MONITORING OPERATING LEVERAGE

Part D

	Evaluate Process – KPI, KRI Risk Adjusted Return - Corrective Action		
Policy, Procedure	Make corrections to policy on vendor / 3rd party evaluation.		
External - SLAs, other agreements	SLAs should ensure Quality of service.		
Cost / Benefit check	Quantified Measure	Approval for Change:	**Y**

Part E

	Correction / Improvement
Test Correction & Implement	Amended Policy and SLA. Vendor evaluation includes a scoring methodology to minimise subjectivity. Reference checks mandatory.
Measure KPI and Residual Risk	The savings from outsourcing the sales function should be measured on a risk adjusted return basis. Residual risk – Low.

4.3.3.2.3 (ii) Fixed Deposit (FD)

This example is for the "Save the Trees" campaign. Banks still consume a lot of paper, and *this example is for a digital deposit receipt.* Many banks have done away with the F.D.R. But there are numerous paper generating activities in the bank that are nonvalue adding and costly.

Part A

				Operating Leverage Monitoring				
Process Id	Process 2	Process Type	B		Process Description	Fixed Deposit Maturity/Termination		
Process Owner	Staff Id	Last Review Date	YYMMDD		Reviewed By	Staff Id	Last 5 Reviews:	
Product Id	RETFD1	Process Cost Budgeted Actual	$ $		Sub-Process id (if applicable)		Early Warning Signal (Y/N)	**N**

Part B

	Review of the Bill of Resource – Cost of Doing Business							
	Activity-1		Activity-2		Activity-3		Activity-4	
	Staff	System	Staff	System	Staff	System	Staff	System
Front, Middle & Back Office	To improve operational efficiency and customer experience, bank has *stopped issuing Fixed Deposit Receipts.* For upliftment, bank introduced a "**Soft Token Based OTP**' based depositor verification.							

Soft tokens are software programs, typically downloadable mobile authenticator applications, such as 'RapidIdentity' Mobile or Google Authenticator, that effectively turn a user's device into an OTP generator.

CHAPTER 4 MONITORING OPERATING LEVERAGE

The cost accountant and the internal control manager can recommend a better usage of technology and staff skills to improve operational efficiency.

This is Table 3-8b from Chapter 3, Section 3.5.2.

					Summarised & Illustrative			
LOB	Product		Process, Activities	Volume	Activity time Min-Rnd	Total Time (Rnd)	Unit Cost	Total Cost (Rnd)
			Time Driven (TD) process cost= the sum of all its TD activity costs. TD activity based cost = Process Volume * Activity time *Unit cost of activity					
Retail	RETFD1	Sales	Risk Management	39,991	120	4,798,899	4.56	21,882,978
				30,117	40	1,204,678	1.26	1,517,894
		Operation	Lien on Deposit					
			Breakage of Deposit					
			Total:	1,990,000	20	39,800,009	0.99	39,402,009
		Closure		11,998	30	359,934	1.23	442,719
Product's TD Non-interest Cost, Cost of Resources utilised								63,245,600

Part C

	Examine KPI, KRI: Performance, Risk, Control, Cost,
PRCC issue	Customer complaints
Causation	Inadequate Usage of technology

Part D

	Evaluate Process– KPI, KRI Risk Adjusted Return - Corrective Action	
Staff	Training in analytics and customer behaviour.	
System	Use relevant technology to automate locker services. It is an "investment", not a cost.	
Cost / Benefit check	Quantified: Benefits > Cost	Approval for Change: **Y**

Part E

	Correction; Improvement
Test Correction & Implement	Eliminating the need for a Fixed Deposit Receipt. A non-value adding set of activities.
Measure KPI and Residual Risk	Customer experience enhanced Residual risk – Low.

Carbon footprint is mentioned in the last section of this chapter.

CHAPTER 4   MONITORING OPERATING LEVERAGE

4.3.3.2.4 (iii) Home Loan – Salaried

This example focuses on outsourcing risk.

Part A

Operating Leverage Monitoring								
Process Id		Process 3	Process Type	B	▼	Process Description	Home Loan - (Sales & On-boarding) for salaried individuals	
Process Owner		Staff Id	Last Review Date	YYMMDD		Reviewed By	Last 5 Reviews: Summary	▼
Product Id		RETHLS	Process Cost Budgeted Actual	$ $		Sub-Process id (if applicable)	Early Warning Signal (Y/N)	Y

Home loans are an important source of revenue for commercial banks. Continuous process improvements will improve operational efficiency ratios. However, banks that outsource the front office functions have limited ability to improve processes of the vendor. Therefore, the selection of the agency, performance, and risk monitoring are critical success factors.

Part B
Sales Process

	Review of the Bill of Resource - Operational efficiency of Outsourced function							
	Activity-1		Activity-2		Activity-3		Activity-4	
	Staff	System	Staff	System	Staff	System	Staff	System
Front, Middle Back Office	To save costs, the bank outsourced home loan sales functions to 3rd parties. Skills of sales persons not known.							

Part C

This is an extract of Table 3-8c from Chapter 3, Section 3.5.2. The total cost is $55,365,600.

LOB	Product		Process, Activities	Volume	Activity time Min-Rnd	Total Time (Rnd)	Unit Cost	Total Cost (Rnd)
			Summarised & Illustrative					
			Time Driven (TD) process cost= the sum of all its TD activity costs. TD activity based cost = Process Volume * Activity time *Unit cost of activity					
Retail	RETHLS	Sales	Risk Management	59,954	160	9,592,648	2.73	26,187,929

CHAPTER 4 MONITORING OPERATING LEVERAGE

	Examine KPI,KRI: Performance, Risk, Control, Cost,
PRCC issue	Many complaints on sales persons – (a) too aggressive (b) unclear / distorted terms and conditions Instances of failure in property title checking
Causation	Effort to cut costs; Poor evaluation of 3rd party vendors for outsourcing sales
Severity	Reputation risk; Loss of new business
Probability of re-occurrence	Medium

Part D

	Evaluate Process – KPI, KRI Risk Adjusted Return - Corrective Action	
Staff		
System	Better supervisory controls required	
Policy, Procedure	Vendor evaluation, Service Level Agreement & SLA Monitoring	
External - SLAs, other agreements	Identify corrective action, as applicable	
Cost / Benefit check	Quantified Measure	Approval for Change: **Y**

Part E

	Correction / Improvement
Test Correction & Implement	Amended Policy and SLA. Vendor evaluation includes a scoring methodology to minimise subjectivity. Reference checks mandatory.
Measure KPI and Residual Risk	Risk appetite not breached. Residual risk – Low.

Enterprise content management refers to the processing of information contained in documents processed by the bank.

The document and content management processes could have a significant portion of non-value adding activities.

CHAPTER 4   MONITORING OPERATING LEVERAGE

4.3.3.2.5 (iv) Consumer Durable Loan

Banks work with reputed retailers to provide loans for consumer durables. This example is applicable to vehicle loans. *This is an example for improving sales and customer onboarding process.*

Part A

			Operating Leverage Monitoring					
Process Id		Process 4	Process Type	B	▼	Process Description	Consumer Durable Loan Application	
Process Owner		Staff Id	Last Review Date	YYMMDD	Reviewed By	Staff Id	Last 5 Reviews: Summary	▼
Product Id		RETCOD	Process Cost Budgeted Actual	$ $	Sub-Process id (if applicable)		Early Warning Signal (Y/N)	N

This example focuses on operational efficiency in the sales and the onboarding processes for retail customers.

Part B

	Activity-1		Activity-2		Activity-3		Activity-4	
	Staff	System	Staff	System	Staff	System	Staff	System
Front, Middle & Back Office	Loan application processing time fails KPI.							

Review of the Bill of Resource – Cost of Doing Business

Part C

This table is an extract of Table 3-8d, from Chapter 3, Section 3.5.2. The total cost is $35,565,600.

LOB	Product	Process, Activities		Volume	Activity time Min-Rnd	Total Time (Rnd)	Unit Cost	Total Cost (Rnd)
							Summarised & Illustrative	
		Time Driven (TD) process cost= the sum of all its TD activity costs. TD activity based cost = Process Volume * Activity time *Unit cost of activity						
Retail	RETCOD	Sales Process	Risk Management	119,478	160	19,116,510	0.88	16,822,529
		On-boarding		100,769	60	6,046,153	0.4	2,418,461
		Examine KPI,KRI: Performance, Risk, Control, Cost,						
PRCC issue		Weak customer experience						
Causation		Weak automation linking bank, retailer and customer						

CHAPTER 4   MONITORING OPERATING LEVERAGE

Part D

	Evaluate Process – KPI, KRI Risk Adjusted Return - Corrective Action		
System	Hyperautomation for integrating bank with retailer and customer. Robotic Process Automation for mature processes.		
Cost / Benefit check	Quantified: Benefits > Cost	Approval for Change:	Y

Part E

	Correction / Improvement
Test Correction & Implement	R.O.I. in Hyperautomation meets target.
Measure KPI	Sustained loan growth

4.3.3.2.6 (v) Credit Card

This is one of the products that sees "aggressive selling" by banks and their agencies. Flawed processes could lead to excess risk taking, and credit card defaults could exceed thresholds.

Part A

			Operating Leverage Monitoring				
Process Id	Process 5	Process Type	B ▼	Process Description	Credit Card		
Process Owner	Staff Id	Last Review Date	YYMMDD	Reviewed By	Staff Id	Last 5 Reviews: Summary	▼
Product Id	RETCCD	Process Cost Budgeted Actual	$ $	Sub-Process id (if applicable)		Early Warning Signal (Y/N)	N

Part B

	Review of the Bill of Resource – Cost of Risk Management							
	Activity-1		Activity-2		Activity-3		Activity-4	
	Staff	System	Staff	System	Staff	System	Staff	System
Front, Middle and Back Office	Skill Mismatch – credit risk staff; Inadequate resourcing for collections.							

333

CHAPTER 4 MONITORING OPERATING LEVERAGE

Part C

This is Table 3-8e from Chapter 3, Section 3.5.2.

						Summarised & Illustrative			
LOB	Product	Process, Activities		Volume	Activity time Min-Rnd	Total Time (Rnd)	Unit Cost	Total Cost (Rnd)	
		Time Driven (TD) process cost = the sum of all its TD activity costs. TD activity based cost = Process Volume * Activity time * Unit cost of activity							
Retail	RETCCD	Sales Process	Risk Management	119,567	120	14,348,000	1.1	15,782,800	
		On-boarding		95,653	30	2,869,600	0.11	315,656	
		A/c Operation	Risk Management						
			Total:	1,008,861	30	30,265,839	0.51	15,435,578	
		Closure		10,522	50	526,100	0.06	31,566	
Product's TD Non-interest Cost, Cost of Resources utilised								31,565,600	

	Examine KPI, KRI : Performance, Risk, Control, Cost,
PRCC issue	Defaults above risk appetite
Causation	'Cost control" culture; Weak credit monitoring & collections
Severity	
Probability of re-occurrence	Medium

Part D

	Evaluate Process – KPI, KRI Risk Adjusted Return - Corrective Action		
Staff			
System	Better retail credit & operational risk management		
Policy, Procedure	Implementation of improvements in Credit Card application appraisal and Credit risk monitoring		
Cost / Benefit check	Cost: Above risk appetite	Approval for Change:	Y

Part E

	Correction / Improvement
Test Correction, Implement	Know Your Employee program enriched and operational.
Residual Risk	Residual risk – Low.

Save the planet – Card processing at merchants should be *paperless.*

CHAPTER 4 MONITORING OPERATING LEVERAGE

With machine learning, self-learning operating leverage algorithms run as background system processes. When there is an indication of a fall in efficiency or an emerging risk, the system can alert the process owner.

4.3.3.2.7 (vi) Locker Rental

Part A

Operating Leverage Monitoring								
Process Id	Process 6	Process Type	B ▼	Process Description		Locker Rental		
Process Owner	Staff Id	Last Review Date	YYMMDD	Reviewed By		Staff Id	Last 5 Reviews: Summary	▼
Product Id	RETLOC	Process Cost Budgeted Actual	$ $	Sub-Process id (if applicable)	i. AML ii. KYC		Early Warning Signal (Y/N)	Y

The locker rental is not a fully automated process in many banks. The focus is again on improving operational efficiency.

(i) Safe custody is a source for feed-based income; (ii) many banks require a time deposit – a boost for deposit mobilization; and (iii) better utilization of premises-fixed cost.

Part B

	Review of the Bill of Resource – Cost of doing business							
	Activity-1		Activity-2		Activity-3		Activity-4	
	Staff	System	Staff	System	Staff	System	Staff	System
Front, Middle, Back Office	Lack of automation – better use of technology can improve operational efficiency and customer experience. Too many manual tasks.							

335

CHAPTER 4 MONITORING OPERATING LEVERAGE

This is Table 3-8f from Chapter 3, Section 3.5.2.

LOB	Product	Process, Activities		Volume	Activity time Min-Rnd	Summarised & Illustrative Total Time (Rnd)	Unit Cost	Total Cost (Rnd)
		Time Driven (TD) process cost= the sum of all its TD activity costs. TD activity based cost = Process Volume * Activity time *Unit cost of activity						
Retail	RETLOC	Sales Process	Risk Management	119,428	120	14,331,374	0.46	6,592,432
		On-boarding		99,885	30	2,996,560	0.2	599,312
		Account Operation	Risk Management	994,910	30	29,847,314	0.76	22,683,959
		Closure		9,989	50	499,428	0.18	89,897
Product's TD Non-interest Cost, Cost of Resources utilised								29,965,600

Part C

	Examine KPI, KRI: Performance, Risk, Control, Cost,
PRCC issue	Too many staff functions and very limited use of technology (e.g. manual registers).
Causation	Enterprise approach needed to improve risk adjusted returns
Risk Appetite Breach	Yes – Bank is unable to achieve budgeted non-interest income.

Part D

	Evaluate Process – KPI, KRI Risk Adjusted Return - Corrective Action	
Staff	Training in analytics and customer behaviour.	
System	Use relevant technology to automate locker services. It is an "investment", not a cost.	
Cost / Benefit check	Quantified: Benefits > Cost	Approval for Change: **Y**

Part E

	Correction / Improvement
Test Correction & Implement	Test new system
Measure KPI	Over the next 5 years – observe Locker Rental Income.

4.3.3.2.8 A Note on Account Closure of Retail Banking Accounts

Account closure activities have been a source of risks and the process is inefficient in many banks. Account closure should be done under dual control and adhere to the principle of segregation of duties. The typical tasks that should be completed prior to account closure are as follows:

Savings

- Determining the reason for closure
- Checking for lien on deposit
- Check for locker facility
- Check for personal guarantees
- Application of accrued interest
- Return of cheque book as applicable
- Destruction of cards associated with account, as applicable
- Cancellation of passbook, as applicable
- Payment of moneys due

Loan accounts

- Checking of loan outstanding and linked accounts; check for GRC comments
- Release of all documents; release of no dues letter

Both asset and liability types

- Checking for any standing orders linked to the account
- Checking for autodebits to the account

CHAPTER 4 MONITORING OPERATING LEVERAGE

If a customer has closed all accounts, then the net banking login Id should be deleted. All payment cards and dongles should be deactivated. If customers are given access cards for meetings in the bank (wealth management lounge), it should be disabled.

The branch staff should be trained in the closure activities, and a process-based approach will ensure compliance with internal procedures.

4.3.3.2.9 (vii) Omnichannel Capability

Cost of Front Office Channel Maintenance and Operational Risks Are Too High

Omnichannel is the capability that allows a bank to provide a customer with the same experience across channels. This includes the ability to initiate the process on one channel, such as a mobile phone and completing the transaction using another channel, such as using the laptop for net banking, without any additional effort. This is facilitated by a services-based enterprise architecture and enterprise data management framework. All lines of business can use this capability. This is analyzed as a capability and not as a process.

Part A

Operating Leverage Monitoring
Process Id	Process 7	Process Type	B	Process Description		Omni-Channel Business Delivery	
Process Owner	Staff Id	Last Review Date	YYMMDD	Reviewed By	Staff Id	Last 5 Reviews: Summary	
Product Id or Sub-Function Id:		Process Cost Budgeted Actual	$ $	Sub-Process id (if applicable)		Early Warning Signal (Y/N)	N

CHAPTER 4   MONITORING OPERATING LEVERAGE

Part B

	Review of Bill of Resources - Cost of Doing Business							
	Activity-1		Activity-2		Activity-3		Activity-4	
	Staff	System	Staff	System	Staff	System	Staff	System
Front office Platform: is integrated with back and middle office functions	As Is: The e-delivery channels include (a) ATM (b) Debit card (c) Credit card (d) Net Banking (e) Mobile Banking (f) Phone Banking. There is a business need for a Omni-channel platform. This will save costs and improve customer experience. The capability can be used by ALL Lines of Business.							

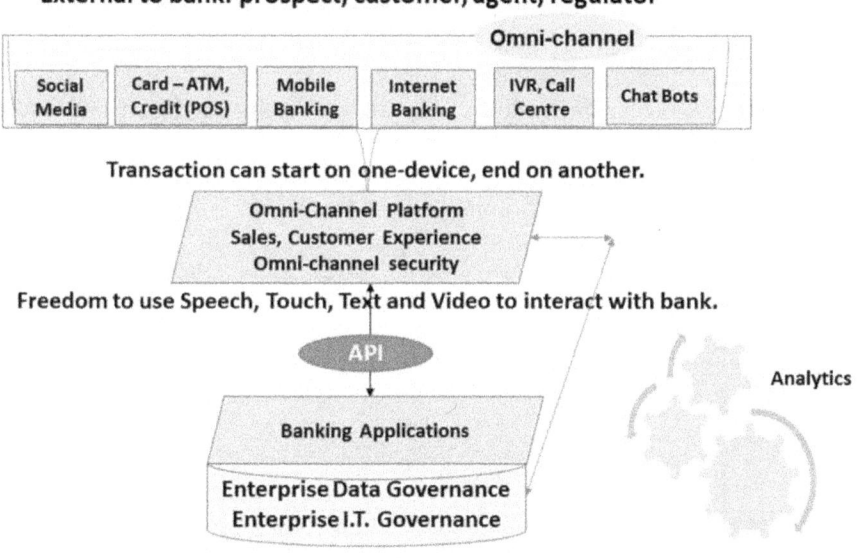

Figure 4-18a. Omnichannel

Part C

	Examine KPI, KRI: Performance, Risk, Control, Cost
PRCC issue	Costs and Operational risk high
Causation	Not adopting relevant technology
Severity	
Probability of re-occurrence	Medium

339

CHAPTER 4   MONITORING OPERATING LEVERAGE

Part D

	Evaluate Process – KPI, KRI Risk Adjusted Return - Corrective Action
Staff	
System	Omni-channel implementation
Policy, Procedure	Amendment to relevant policies and procedures
Cost / Benefit check	Approval for Change: Y

Part E

	Correction; Improvement
Test Correction & Implement	Stable platform
Measure KPI and Residual Risk	Customer experience enhanced Residual risk – Low.

Figure 4-18b is an adaptation of Figure 4-3, business growth and cost of doing business.

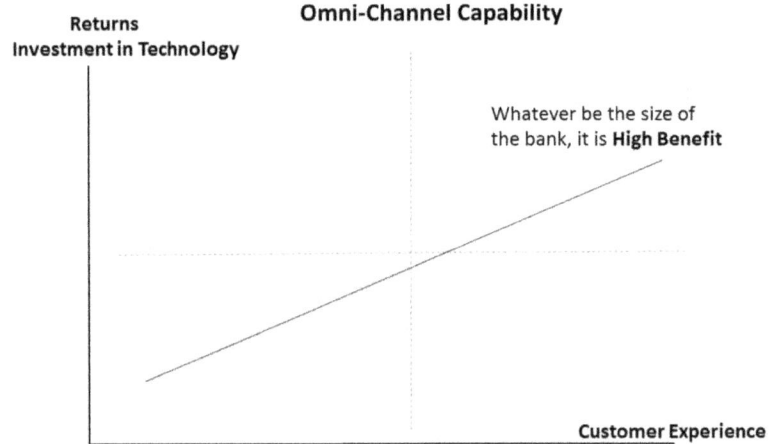

Figure 4-18b. Omnichannel

Omnichannel is a mandatory capability for improving operating leverage.

4.3.3.3 Corporate Banking

4.3.3.3.1 Corporate Banking Operations Monitoring Dashboard

The numbering for the examples will change. It will be from 4.3.3.3.1 to 4.3.3.3.8.

- **Revenue**

Product Id	Interest	Fees	Charges	Commission
Budgeted				
Actual				

- **Total cost**

Product Id	Cost
Budgeted	
Actual	

- **Cost breakup**

Fixed costs	Variable costs	Total
197,352.500	70,797,500	**268,150,000**

From Chapter 2 – P&L "fully absorbed" by products.

CHAPTER 4 MONITORING OPERATING LEVERAGE

Cost of Corporate Banking Products

	CORLCI	CORCOA	CORL10	CORSDL	Prodt-5	Prodt-6	Prodt-7	Total
Direct Cost	10,375,000	10,275,000	11,050,000	13,000,000	11,050,000	11,000,000	13,000,000	79,750,000
Indirect Cost								
Employee	8,000,000	7,000,000	4,000,000	4,000,000	4,000,000	4,000,000	4,000,000	35,000,000
Enterprise I.T. Governance	6,300,000	6,300,000	3,600,000	3,600,000	3,600,000	3,600,000	3,000,000	30,000,000
Premises	7,500,000	7,500,000	3,000,000	3,000,000	3,000,000	3,000,000	3,000,000	30,000,000
Office Supplies	8,000,000	7,000,000	2,000,000	2,000,000	2,000,000	2,000,000	2,000,000	25,000,000
Repairs&Maint.	1,250,000	1,250,000	500,000	500,000	500,000	500,000	500,000	5,000,000
Management	2,800,000	2,600,000	2,600,000	2,600,000	2,600,000	2,600,000	2,600,000	18,400,000
Support Services	12,500,000	12,500,000	4,000,000	4,000,000	4,000,000	4,000,000	4,000,000	45,000,000
Total	56,725,000	54,425,000	30,750,000	32,700,000	30,750,000	30,700,000	32,100,000	268,150,000

As shown in Chapter 3, Section 3.6, when the time-driven ABC method is used, the corporate banking cost is 227,927,500 and the capacity utilization is 85%.

Process Automated Time Driven Activity Based Costing Cost of consumed resources

P&L (fully absorbed)	268,150,000
TDABC - Cost of consumed resources	227,927,500
Cost of Unutilised Resources	40,222,500
Utilisation Rate	85%

The data below is from Chapter 3, Section 3.5.2, process-automated, time-driven activity-based costing of corporate banking products.

Process automated, time driven activity based costing - cost of consumed resources

CORLCI	CORCOA	CORL10	CORSDL	Prodt-5	Prodt-6	Prodt-7	Total
48,216,250	46,261,250	26,137,500	27,795,000	26,137,500	26,095,000	27,285,000	227,927,500

Budget vs Actual – Risk-Based Approach to Monitoring

LOB	Product	Process (Activity Group)	Sub Activity Group	Volume		Time taken		Unit Cost	
				Budget	Actual	Budget	Actual	Budget	Actual

CHAPTER 4   MONITORING OPERATING LEVERAGE

The data below is from Chapter 3, Section 3.5.2, process-automated, time-driven activity-based costing of retail banking products.

Process automated, time driven activity based costing - cost of consumed resources								
CORLCI	CORCOA	CORL10	CORSDL	Prodt-5	Prodt-6	Prodt-7	Total
48,216,250	46,261,250	26,137,500	27,795,000	26,137,500	26,095,000	27,285,000	227,927,500

Corporate Banking: Monitoring of Fixed and Variable Costs.

Fixed costs	Variable costs	Review	Recommendation
		Salaries	Continuous process improvement removes nonvalue-added activities and leads to reduction in costs
		Operations	
		Support: technology	
		GRC, legal	Focus on GRC costs
197,352,500	70,797,500		

	Staff	Systems	Branches	E-channels	Support
Fixed	100% FTE	Annual maintenance	Fixed	If fully owned	GRC and legal expenses could be expensive
Variable	Multiple products/ functions	EITG: usage based	May not apply	If shared – variable/ usage based	

The following are *four product and three risk management examples* for corporate banking PRCC monitoring.

343

CHAPTER 4   MONITORING OPERATING LEVERAGE

4.3.3.3.2 (viii) LC Issuance

Trade finance is a source of fee-based income and an area of business where a bank could use its expertise to be a "differentiator" and stand out from the crowd. In most banks, trade finance process still have a lot of manual activities.

This example is on staff skills for preventing fraud.

Part A

				Operating Leverage Monitoring				
Process Id		Process 8	Process Type	B ▼	Process Description	Letter of Credit Issuance		
Process Owner		Staff Id	Last Review Date	YYMMDD	Reviewed By		Staff Id	Last 5 Reviews: Summary ▼
Product Id or Sub-Function Id:		CORLCI	Process Cost Budgeted $ Actual $		Sub-Process id (if applicable)			Early Warning Signal (Y/N) Y

Part B

	Review of the Bill of Resource – Cost of doing business							
	Activity-1		Activity-2		Activity-3		Activity-4	
	Staff	System	Staff	System	Staff	System	Staff	System
Front, Middle & Back Office.	Staff Skill does not match Role requirement. Banking processes execution should be powered by intelligence to prevent and detect financial crimes.							

Part C

This is Table 3-8g from Chapter 3, Section 3.5.2.

CHAPTER 4 MONITORING OPERATING LEVERAGE

Summarised & Illustrative

LOB	Product	Process, Activities		Volume	Activity time Min-Rnd	Total Time (Rnd)	Unit Cost	Total Cost (Rnd)
		Time Driven (TD) process cost= the sum of all its TD activity costs. TD activity based cost = Process Volume * Activity time *Unit cost of activity						
Corporate Banking	CORLCI	Negotiations		29,985	160	4,797,636	2.01	9,643,249
		LC Issuance	Risk Management	25,077	60	1,504,621	1.41	2,121,515
		Account Operation	Risk Management	498,102	60	29,886,106	1.21	36,162,188
		Closure	Risk Management	3,990	50	199,516	1.45	289,298
Product's TD Non-interest Cost, Cost of Resources utilised								48,216,250

	Examine KPI,KRI: Performance, Risk, Control, Cost
PRCC Issue	1. Cases of LC issuance based on fake documents 2. Cases of LC issuance where customer agrees to pay 'atypical', abnormal flat fee
Causation	Weak supervision over Trade Finance operations; Limited analytics
Risk Appetite Breach	Yes: Credit Risk - Losses
Severity	High
Probability of re-occurrence	High

Part D

	Evaluate Process– KPI, KRI Enterprise Risk Adjusted Return - Corrective Action	
Staff	Staff training - Preventive measures include examining the financial standing of the beneficiary, checking the location, checking the authenticity of bill of lading	
System	Improved system with straight through processing and analytical capabilities; System intelligence should identify atypical and abnormal requests; Implementation of Enterprise Document & Content Management	
Policy, Procedure	Accepting time drafts instead of sight drafts, making it mandatory for the carrier to dispatch the bill of lading to the bank, requiring performance guarantee and use of export credit insurance.	
Cost / Benefit check	Benefits outweigh cost	Approval for Change: Y

Part E

	Correction / Improvement
Test Correction	Staff training by experienced trade finance experts
Implement	Advanced Analytical platform integrated with Trade Financing processes; Straight through processing of Trade financing processes.
Measure KPI and Residual Risk	Fraud prevention; Operational efficiency Low

CHAPTER 4   MONITORING OPERATING LEVERAGE

4.3.3.3.3 (ix) Bills Coacceptance

This example emphasizes the need for *due diligence and enhanced due diligence procedures*. The latter is invoked when there is an atypical activity/behavior.

Part A

			Operating Leverage Monitoring					
Process Id	Process 9	Process Type	B	▼	Process Description	Bills Co-acceptance		
Process Owner	Staff Id	Last Review Date	YYMMDD	Reviewed By		Staff Id	Last 5 Reviews: Summary	▼
Product Id	CORCOA	Process Cost Budgeted $ Actual $		Sub-Process id (if applicable)			Early Warning Signal (Y/N)	Y

Part B

	Review of the Bill of Resource – Cost of doing business							
	Activity-1		Activity-2		Activity-3		Activity-4	
	Staff	System	Staff	System	Staff	System	Staff	System
Front, Middle & Back office	Staff assignment incorrect (skill mismatch) and Lack of Analytics.							

This is Table 3-8h from Chapter 3, Section 3.5.2.

									Summarised & Illustrative
LOB	Product	Process, Activities			Volume	Activity time Min-Rnd	Total Time (Rnd)	Unit Cost	Total Cost (Rnd)	
		Time Driven (TD) process cost= the sum of all its TD activity costs. TD activity based cost = Process Volume * Activity time *Unit cost of activity								
Corporate Banking	CORCOA	Sales Process / Negotiations	Risk Management		24,952	180	4,491,383	1.03	4,626,124	
		Payment			19,956	120	2,394,700	0.85	2,035,495	
		Account Operation	Risk Management		750,421	20	15,008,421	2.62	39,322,063	
		Closure			12,016	30	360,478	0.77	277,568	
Product's TD Non-interest Cost, Cost of Resources utilised									46,261,250	

346

Part C

	Examine KPI, KRI: Performance, Risk, Control, Cost
PRCC Issue	Several risk incidents: Co-acceptance of bills turned out to be **accommodation bills**. In these transactions, there is **no underlying trade** and the counterparty fails to pay.
Causation	Staff Skills; Weak Know Your Employee program to identify internal fraud;
Risk Appetite Breach	Yes: Credit Risk - Losses
Severity	High
Probability of re-occurrence	Medium

Part D

	Evaluate Process – KPI, KRI Enterprise Risk Adjusted Return - Corrective Action	
Staff	Identify corrective action, as applicable	
System	Enterprise data management, data analytics, Know Your Customer, Know Your Employee programs	
Policy, Procedure	Human Capital – Staff Transaction Surveillance	
Cost / Benefit check	Benefits outweigh cost	Approval for Change: **Y**

Part E

	Correction / Improvement
Test Correction	Transformation Plan consistent with management priority – transform from a siloed architecture to a bank of the future
Implement	Enterprise Risk adjusted Return model implemented
Measure KPI and Residual Risk	Fraud prevention; Operational efficiency Low

4.3.3.3.4 (x) Corporate Term Loan 10 Years

Lending is a document processing intensive. Further, the data items have different degrees of criticality for managing the exposure. The skill set for credit appraisal includes knowledge of domestic corporate laws (this example is about *ultra vires borrowing*), banking, and risk management.

CHAPTER 4   MONITORING OPERATING LEVERAGE

Part A

					Operating Leverage Monitoring			
Process Id	Process 10	Process Type	B	▼	Process Description	Corporate 10 Year Loan Application		
Process Owner	Staff Id	Last Review Date	YYMMDD		Reviewed By	Staff Id	Last 5 Reviews: Summary	▼
Product Id or Sub-Function Id:	CORL10	Process Cost Budgeted $ Actual $			Sub-Process id (if applicable)		Early Warning Signal (Y/N)	Y

Part B

	Review of the Bill of Resource – Cost of doing business							
	Activity-1		Activity-2		Activity-3		Activity-4	
	Staff	System	Staff	System	Staff	System	Staff	System
Front, Middle & Back Office	Staff skill mismatch							

Part C

This table is *an extract* of Table 3-8i from Chapter 3, Section 3.5.2. The total cost is 26,137,500.

LOB	Product	Process, Activities		Volume	Summarised & Illustrative			
					Activity time Min-Rnd	Total Time (Rnd)	Unit Cost	Total Cost (Rnd)
		Time Driven (TD) process cost= the sum of all its TD activity costs. TD activity based cost = Process Volume * Activity time *Unit cost of activity						
Corporate Banking	CORL10	Sales Process	Risk Management	1,000	1100	1,100,116	10.05	11,056,162
		On-boarding	Document Mgt	701	800	560,678	3.17	1,777,350
		A/c Operation	Site Visit					
			Internal Rating					
		Risk Management	Collateral Mark to Market					
			Loan: Risk Exposure monitoring					
			Total:	100,144	90	9,012,931	1.45	13,068,750
		Closure		200	400	80,013	2.94	235,238
Product's TD Non-interest Cost, Cost of Resources utilised								26,137,500

CHAPTER 4   MONITORING OPERATING LEVERAGE

	Examine KPI, KRI: Performance, Risk, Control, Cost,
PRCC Issue	Ultra Vires borrowing i.e. borrowing for purposes not allowed in the MOA & AOA. There is no record of resolutions passed by company to authorise borrowing. No Enterprise Document & Content Management.
Causation	Weakness in Staff Assignment / Recruitment
Severity	High
Probability of re-occurrence	Medium

Part D

	Evaluate Process – KPI, KRI Risk Adjusted Return - Corrective Action		
Staff	Role definition and Job description need more attention – Corporate Account Managers responsible for this.		
System	Enterprise Document & Content Management is a mandatory need for the bank.		
Policy, Procedure	Staff recruitment procedures.		
Cost / Benefit check	Quantified Measure	Approval for Change:	Y

Banks can utilize machine learning to extract critical information from documents and use sentiment analysis to identify patterns and assist decision-making.

Case Study – Machine Learning

JP Morgan Chase has developed a proprietary ML algorithm called Contract Intelligence or COiN. It is used to extract and analyze important information from voluminous documentation. The tool enabled the bank to process 12,000 credit agreements in several seconds, instead of 360,000 man-hours.

Triodos Bank uses GNOSS technology to semantically represent the document management system.

CHAPTER 4   MONITORING OPERATING LEVERAGE

Part E

	Correction / Improvement
Test Correction & Implement	Configure system for specific needs of the bank; Test Enterprise Document & Content Management; Staff role & job description enriched.
Measure KPI Residual Risk	Operational lapses cause Credit Risk. There is causation and correlation amongst risk factors. Low

4.3.3.3.5 (xi) Syndicated Loan

This example focuses on staff skills. Loan syndication and project financing require *specialized skills* and relevant experience.

Part A

				Operating Leverage Monitoring				
Process Id	Process 11	Process Type	B	▼	Process Description		Syndicate Loan	
Process Owner	Staff Id	Last Review Date	YYMMDD		Reviewed By	Staff Id	Last 5 Reviews: Summary	▼
Product Id or Sub-Function Id:	CORSDL	Process Cost Budgeted Actual	$ $		Sub-Process id (if applicable)	1. KYC, 2. AML 3. Credit Rating 4. Collateral check	Early Warning Signal (Y/N)	Y

Part B

	Review of the Bill of Resource – Cost of doing business							
	Activity-1		Activity-2		Activity-3		Activity-4	
	Staff	System	Staff	System	Staff	System	Staff	System
Front, Middle, Back Office			•					

---

*Project finance and syndicate loan are sources for **noninterest revenue**.*

Part C
This is Table 3-8j from Chapter 3, Section 3.5.2.

CHAPTER 4   MONITORING OPERATING LEVERAGE

The lead bank's exposure and operational involvement are more than the participant banks. Hence, the term "loan operation" is used in the table below instead of account operation.

LOB	Product	Process, Activities		Volume	Activity time Min-Rnd	Total Time (Rnd)	Unit Cost	Total Cost (Rnd)
					Summarised & Illustrative			
		Time Driven (TD) process cost= the sum of all its TD activity costs. TD activity based cost = Process Volume * Activity time *Unit cost of activity						
Corporate Banking	CORSDL	Sales Process / Negotiations	Risk Management	100	2,000	200,005	97.28	19,456,500
		On-boarding	Document Management	95	800	76,005	36.57	2,779,500
		Loan Operation	Risk Management					
			Managing the Consortium					
			Total:	400	120	47,999	112.92	5,420,025
		Closure		10	400	4,000	34.74	138,975
Product's TD Non-interest Cost, Cost of Resources utilised								27,795,000

	Examine KPI,KRI: Performance, Risk, Control, Cost,
PRCC Issue	Credit Risk losses above risk appetite
Causation	Staff Skill and automation weakness in Syndicate Loan Management processes.
Severity	High
Probability of re-occurrence	High

Part D

	Evaluate Process– KPI, KRI Risk Adjusted Return - Corrective Action	
Staff	Lack of skills in managing syndicated loans	
System	Inadequate automation	
Policy, Procedure		
Cost / Benefit check	Benefits > Cost	Approval for Change: **Y**

Part E

	Correction / Improvement
Test Correction	Syndicated Loan process automation tested with historic data
Implement	Staff assignment (skills) verified
Measure KPI and Residual Risk	Identify and Examine non performing loans over next 2 years Medium

CHAPTER 4   MONITORING OPERATING LEVERAGE

4.3.3.3.6 (xii) Credit Risk Management – Corporate Asset Book[14]

This is an example for enterprise risk-adjusted return management. Market risk and credit risk are usually measured separately. Transactions that are perceived to be driven by market risk tend to ignore credit risk even when market factors increase the possibility of default. Similarly, credit risk is often measured without taking into account the change in the market risk factors.

Part A

Operating Leverage Monitoring							
Process Id	Process 12	Process Type	R ▼	Process Description	Corporate Risk, Enterprise Risk Adjusted Return, Management		
Process Owner	Staff Id	Last Review Date	YYMMDD	Reviewed By	Staff Id	Last 5 Reviews: Summary	▼
Supporting Department	Management	Process Cost Budgeted Actual	$ $	Sub-Process id (if applicable)		Early Warning Signal (Y/N)	Y

Part B

	Review of the Bill of Resource – Cost of Risk Management							
	Activity-1		Activity-2		Activity-3		Activity-4	
	Staff	System	Staff	System	Staff	System	Staff	System
Front, Middle & Back Office	Bank has not invested in Enterprise Risk adjusted Return Management								

Risk analytics is an important aspect of establishing causation. Profiles are maintained at the customer group, customer, account, and transaction level.

---

[14] The Internal Ratings-Based Approach: https://www.bis.org/publ/bcbsca05.pdf
Credit Risk Modeling: https://www.bis.org/publ/bcbs49.pdf

CHAPTER 4 MONITORING OPERATING LEVERAGE

Part C

	Examine KPI, KRI: Performance, Risk, Control, Cost
PRCC Issue	1. Siloed Enterprise Architecture 2. Fragmented data 3. Difficulty with Causation & Correlation
Causation	Risk Culture; Bank is not taking an enterprise approach to automating business
Existing – Risk Appetite	Risk appetite quantification is erroneous
Severity	High
Probability of re-occurrence	Probability of risk events occurring is high

You may want to refer to Processes 5 and 8 in Section 3.4.5 in Chapter 3.

Part D

	Evaluate Process – KPI, KRI Enterprise Risk Adjusted Return - Corrective Action	
Staff		
System	Transform the bank by taking an enterprise approach	
Policy, Procedure	Enterprise Risk model should have the data to assess the combined credit, market and liquidity risk of the bank	
Cost / Benefit check	Benefits outweigh cost	Approval for Change: **Y**

In managing the market risk impact on credit risk, a safety margin is added to the current exposure to reflect future fluctuations of the exposure due to market price volatility. The safety margin could be a function of the product type (e.g., interest rate, FX rate) and the contract's maturity. It is expressed as a percentage of current exposure.

Part E

	Correction / Improvement
Test Correction	Transformation Plan has a strong sponsor, strong project management office, an approved budget and adequate staff
Implement	Skilled team implements (i) transformation and (ii) Enterprise Risk adjusted Return model
Measure KPI and	Significant savings – Higher risk adjusted returns i.e. Higher Risk Adjusted Net Interest Margin;
Residual Risk	Low

CHAPTER 4   MONITORING OPERATING LEVERAGE

Deteriorating market liquidity can force investors to lengthen the horizon over which they can execute their risk management strategies. As this time horizon lengthens, overall risk exposures generally increase, as does the contribution of credit risk relative to market risk. These factors have an impact on risk data distributions.

Figure 4-19 is an adaptation of Figure 4-3, business growth and cost of doing business.

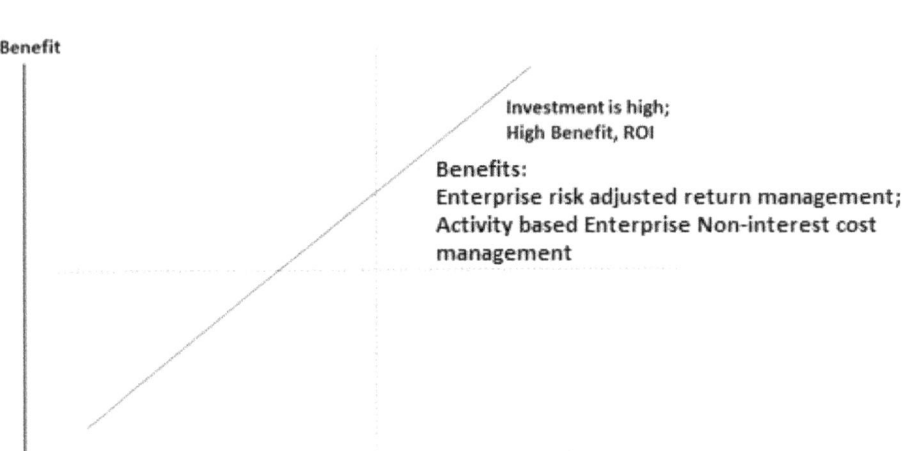

Figure 4-19. Enterprise risk-adjusted return management benefit

4.3.3.3.7 (xiii) Risk Management – Collateral Management

Most banks are weak in the area of enterprise collateral management, a function that has a direct impact on credit and liquidity risks.

CHAPTER 4   MONITORING OPERATING LEVERAGE

Part A

Operating Leverage Monitoring								
Process Id	Process 13	Process Type	R	▼	Process Description	Collateral Checking and Mark to market		
Process Owner	Staff Id	Last Review Date	YYMMDD		Reviewed By	Staff Id	Last 5 Reviews: Summary	▼
Support Department	GRC	Process Cost Budgeted $ Actual $			Sub-Process id (if applicable)		Early Warning Signal (Y/N)	Y

Part B

	Review of the Bill of Resource – Cost of Risk Management							
	Activity-1		Activity-2		Activity-3		Activity-4	
	Staff	System	Staff	System	Staff	System	Staff	System
Front, Middle & Back Office	Automation is insufficient, many manual tasks. GRC to examine.							

Part C

	Examine KPI, KRI: Performance, Risk, Control, Cost,
PRCC Issue	Banks lacks an enterprise collateral management system. Collateral management processes are siloed. Enterprise credit risk, enterprise risk management flawed. Several instances of (a) inadequate collateral (b) missing collateral and c) mark to market has manual overrides.
Causation	Bank is not taking an enterprise approach to managing business
Risk Appetite Breach	Yes
Severity	High
Probability of re-occurrence	High

You may want to recall Processes 5 and 8 in Section 3.4.5 of Chapter 3.

Part D

	Evaluate Process – KPI, KRI Risk Adjusted Return - Corrective Action	
Staff	Staff training on collateral management	
System	New system that is integrated with lending and credit monitoring processes	
Policy, Procedure	Policies for collateral checking at customer site (e.g. hypothecation). Procedures for calling for extra collateral. Margin should factor credit rating of borrower.	
Cost / Benefit check	Benefits outweigh cost	Approval for Change: Y

355

CHAPTER 4   MONITORING OPERATING LEVERAGE

Part E

	Correction / Improvement
Test Correction & Implement	Testing & Approval
Measure KPI and	Monitor the accuracy of Probability of Default, Loss Given Default and Exposure at Default figures for 2 years.
Residual Risk	Medium

4.3.3.3.8 (xiv) Risk Management – Internal Credit Rating

Part A

			Operating Leverage Monitoring				
Process Id	Process 14	Process Type	R	Process Description	Internal Credit Rating		
Process Owner	Staff Id	Last Review Date	YYMMDD	Reviewed By	Staff Id	Last 5 Reviews: Summary	
Support Department	GRC	Process Cost Budgeted Actual	$ $	Sub-Process id (if applicable)		Early Warning Signal (Y/N)	Y

Part B

	Review of the Bill of Resource – Cost of Risk Management							
	Activity-1		Activity-2		Activity-3		Activity-4	
	Staff	System	Staff	System	Staff	System	Staff	System
Front, Middle & Back Office	Post implementation, the cost and efficiency of the internal rating process is reviewed by the Cost Accountant. The cost accountant can mark processes for GRC review as he/she deems fit.							

Part C

	Examine KPI, KRI: Performance, Risk, Control, Cost
PRCC Issue	The bank relies on external credit rating and has a rudimentary process to check credit scores of corporates.
Causation	Credit Risk Management Policy failure
Risk Appetite Breach	Yes
Severity	High
Probability of re-occurrence	High

CHAPTER 4   MONITORING OPERATING LEVERAGE

Part D

	Evaluate Process – KPI, KRI Risk Adjusted Return - Corrective Action	
Staff	Staff training on Rating methodology, Transition Matrix management.	
System	Improvements to Internal Rating system; Data requirement & risk modelling	
Policy, Procedure	Credit Rating methodology should be approved by Risk Committee.	
Cost / Benefit check	Benefits outweigh cost	Approval for Change: **Y**

Part E

	Correction / Improvement
Test Correction & Implement	Testing & Approval
Measure KPI and	Monitor the accuracy of Probability of Default, Loss Given Default and Exposure at Default figures for 2 years.
Residual Risk	Medium

Loan document automation for retail and corporate banking incorporates machine learning algorithms that learns from customer data and compares with standard borrower profiles. The algorithms can be used for risk assessment and performance monitoring.

4.3.3.4 Treasury

4.3.3.4.1 Treasury Operations Monitoring Dashboard

- **Revenue**

Product Id	Profit – deals	Interest	Fees	Charges	Commission
Budgeted					
Actual					

CHAPTER 4   MONITORING OPERATING LEVERAGE

- **Total cost**

Product Id	Cost
Budgeted	
Actual	

- **Cost breakup**

Fixed costs	Variable costs	Total
178,372,500	31,477,500	209,850,000

From Chapter 2, P&L "fully absorbed" by products.

Cost of Treasury Products

	TRBFXF	TRBCRS	TRBIRS	TRICDS	Prodt-5 MM	Prodt-6 Commodity	Prodt-7 Equity	Total
Direct Cost	13,750,000	12,750,000	13,800,000	11,700,000	11,500,000	7,900,000	7,900,000	79,300,000
Indirect Cost								
Employee	2,250,000	2,250,000	3,000,000	2,500,000	2,500,000	1,250,000	1,250,000	15,000,000
Enterprise I.T. Governance	31,50,000	31,50,000	31,50,000	31,50,000	21,50,000	16,50,000	16,00,000	18,000,000
Premises	3,000,000	2,000,000	4,000,000	4,000,000	3,000,000	1,000,000	1,000,000	18,000,000
Office Supplies	2,500,000	2,500,000	2,500,000	2,500,000	2,000,000	1,500,000	1,500,000	15,000,000
Management	2,600,000	2,600,000	2,600,000	2,600,000	2,600,000	2,600,000	2,600,000	18,200,000
Support Departments	6,630,000	6,630,000	6,630,000	6,630,000	6,630,000	6,630,000	6,570,000	46,350,000
Total	33,880,000	31,880,000	35,680,000	33,080,000	30,380,000	22,530,000	22,420,000	209,850,000

Treasury business is more dynamic than retail and corporate banking. This should be taken into for PRCC monitoring.

CHAPTER 4 MONITORING OPERATING LEVERAGE

Product	Process Banking Book separate from Trading Book	Bill of Resources	Process Cost
All	Rate Maintenance	Staff & System:	The process cost should be examined in the context of:
	Reference Data Management		Process Maturity Score;
	Pre-deal	Staff assignment & Usage Indicator;	Process Key Performance Indicator;
	Capture & Verification		Process Key Risk Indicator;
	Confirmation		and Residual Risk in the process.
	Accounting & Settlement	(KPIs)	
	Position Monitoring		
	Enterprise Risk Adjusted Return Management		

Treasury – Resource Utilization

Process Automated Time Driven Activity Based Costing Cost of consumed resources	
P&L (fully absorbed)	209,850,000
TDABC - Cost of consumed resources	194,111,250
Cost of Unutilised Resources	15,738,750
Utilisation Rate	92.5%

LOB	Product	Process (Activity Group)	Sub Activity Group	Volume		Time taken		Unit Cost	
				Budget	Actual	Budget	Actual	Budget	Actual

The data below is from Chapter 3, Section 3.5.2, process-automated, time-driven activity-based costing of treasury products.

Process automated, time driven activity based costing - cost of consumed resources							
TRBFXF	TRBCRS	TRBIRS	TRICDS	Prodt-5 MM	Prodt-6 Commodity	Prodt-7 Equity	Total
31,339,000	29,489,000	33,004,000	30,599,000	28,101,500	20,840,250	20,738,500	194,111,250

CHAPTER 4 MONITORING OPERATING LEVERAGE

Monitoring of Fixed and Variable Costs

	Staff	Systems: real-time treasury management is unavailable in several banks
Fixed	100% FTE	Annual maintenance
Variable	Multiple products/ functions	Usage based

The following are three product and one back-office examples of treasury PRCC monitoring:

4.3.3.4.2 (xv) Current Swap – Contract Input

Reference data management is an important aspect of treasury operations. Many banks lack the ability to have a single view of the truth.

Part A

				Operating Leverage Monitoring			
Process Id	Process 15	Process Type	B	Process Description	Currency Swap		
Process Owner	Staff Id	Last Review Date	YYMMDD	Reviewed By	Staff Id	Last 5 Reviews: Summary	
Product Id	TRBCRS	Process Cost Budgeted Actual	$ $	Sub-Process id (if applicable)		Early Warning Signal (Y/N)	

Part B

	Review of the Bill of Resource – Cost of doing business							
	Activity-1		Activity-2		Activity-3		Activity-4	
	Staff	System	Staff	System	Staff	System	Staff	System
Front, Middle & Back office	Bill of Resources and Assignment mismatch							

CHAPTER 4   MONITORING OPERATING LEVERAGE

Part C

This is Table 3-8l from Chapter 3, Section 3.5.2.

						Summarised & Illustrative		
LOB	Product	Process, Activities		Volume	Activity time Min-Rnd	Total Time (Rnd)	Unit Cost	Total Cost (Rnd)
		Time Driven (TD) process cost= the sum of all its TD activity costs. TD activity based cost = Process Volume * Activity time *Unit cost of activity						
Treasury	TRBCRS	Pre-Deal	Risk Management	794,316	5.5	4,368,741	0.54	2,359,120
		Trade	Risk Management	797,000	3	2,391,000	0.37	884,670
		Confirmation, Collateral, Reconciliation	Risk Management	997,731	22	21,950,073	1.15	25,242,584
		Settlement & Accounting	Risk Management	835,522	6	5,013,130	0.2	1,002,626
Product's TD Non-interest Cost, Cost of Resources utilised								29,489,000

	Examine KPI, KRI: Performance, Risk, Control, Cost
PRCC issue	Inadequate reference data management; Staff KPI failure
Causation	Lack of Enterprise Architecture and Enterprise data management
Risk Appetite Breach	Yes
Severity	Medium
Probability of re-occurrence	Medium

Part D

	Evaluate Process – KPI, KRI Risk Adjusted Return - Corrective Action		
Staff	Improve staff assignment process;		
System	Reference data management		
Policy, Procedure			
Cost / Benefit check	Benefits outweigh cost	Approval for Change:	Y

Figure 4-20 provides an overview of reference data management.

CHAPTER 4   MONITORING OPERATING LEVERAGE

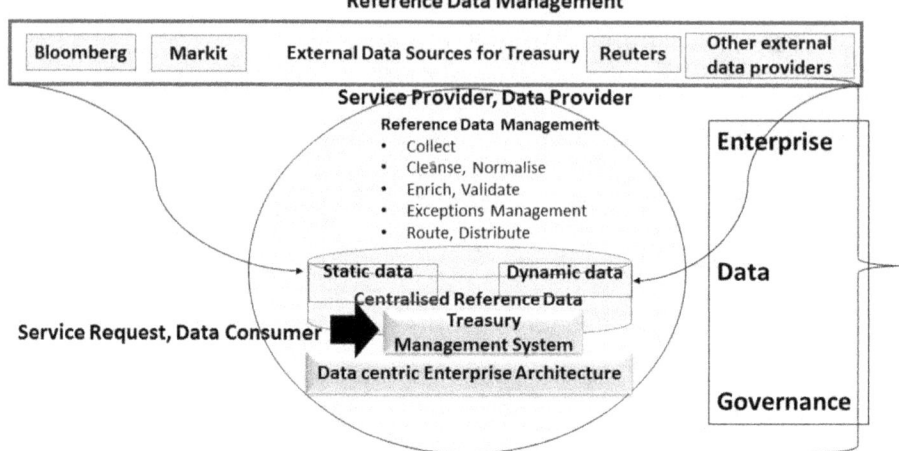

Reference data - relevant information pertaining to financial instruments required to support trading, settlement, accounting, performance, recordkeeping, risk management and regulatory reporting.

Figure 4-20. Overview of reference data management

Part E

	Correction / Improvement
Test Correction & Implement	Reference data management
Measure KPI and Residual Risk	Observe Profitability of Money Market deals over a 12 month period. Low

4.3.3.4.3 (xvi) Interest Rate Swap – Contract Input

In many medium-sized and small banks, straight through processing is a "band-aided," sticky, risky process. Process automation ensures that the flow of activities across front, middle, and back office functions is smooth and data lineage is maintained.

CHAPTER 4   MONITORING OPERATING LEVERAGE

Part A

Operating Leverage Monitoring

Process Id	Process 16	Process Type	B ▼	Process Description	Interest Rate Swap Deal Input		
Process Owner	Staff Id	Last Review Date	YYMMDD	Reviewed By	Staff Id	Last 5 Reviews: Summary	▼
Product Id	TRBIRS	Process Cost Budgeted $ Actual $		Sub-Process id (if applicable)		Early Warning Signal (Y/N)	Y

Part B

Review of the Bill of Resource - Cost of Doing Business & Cost of Risk Management

	Activity-1		Activity-2		Activity-3		Activity-4	
	Staff	System	Staff	System	Staff	System	Staff	System
Front, Middle & Back Office	System does not meet business requirements. Straight Through Processing unavailable. More manual tasks to manage the impact.							
	Annual Maintenance Fee for vendor supplied risk models is high. 3rd party models should be reviewed periodically to determine (a) fit for purpose (b) cost-benefit.							

Part C

This is Table 3-8m from Chapter 3, Section 3.5.2.

					Summarised & Illustrative		
LOB	Product	Process, Activities	Volume	Activity time Min-Rnd	Total Time (Rnd)	Unit Cost	Total Cost (Rnd)
		Time Driven (TD) process cost= the sum of all its TD activity costs. TD activity based cost = Process Volume * Activity time *Unit cost of activity					
Treasury	TRBIRS	Pre-Deal Risk Management	495,556	4.5	2,230,000	0.37	825,100
		Trade Risk Management	495,060	4	1,980,240	0.25	495,060
		Position Monitoring Risk Management	698,119	25	17,452,963	1.77	30,891,744
		Settlement & Accounting Risk Management	452,626	5	2,263,131	0.35	792,096
Product's TD Non-interest Cost, Cost of Resources utilised							33,004,000

363

CHAPTER 4   MONITORING OPERATING LEVERAGE

	Examine KPI, KRI: Performance, Risk, Control, Cost
PRCC Issue	Inadequate reference data management; Inadequate interest rate risk modelling capability.
Causation	Lack of Enterprise Architecture and Enterprise data management
Risk Appetite Breach	Yes
Severity	Medium
Probability of re-occurrence	Medium

Part D

	Evaluate Process – KPI, KRI Risk Adjusted Return - Corrective Action	
System	Straight through Processing is a BPMS feature. Pre-deal Analytics, Verification of deals, VaR limit checks are more effective with better integration of functions	
Policy, Procedure	Banks should invest in proprietary risk models, in addition to, vendor supplied models. This is from a competition perspective, as well as over-dependency on vendors.	
Cost / Benefit check	Benefits outweigh cost	Approval for Change: **Y**

Part E

	Correction / Improvement
Test Correction & Implement	Reference data management; Fit for purpose – Risk Models Straight through processing after architecture transformation.
Measure KPI and Residual Risk	Observe Profitability of Money Market deals over a 12 month period. Low

4.3.3.4.4 (xvii) Index-Linked CDS Input

The focus of this example is on balancing risk, cost, and controls. In many overseas treasury units, the bill of resources, should there be one, will reveal weak assignment of resources. Many frauds have taken place because limited staff strength led to the violation of dual control and segregation of duties.

CHAPTER 4   MONITORING OPERATING LEVERAGE

Part A

Operating Leverage Monitoring

Process Id	Process 17	Process Type	B	Process Description	Index-linked CDS-Deal Input
Process Owner	Staff Id	Last Review Date	YYMMDD	Reviewed By	Staff Id	Last 5 Reviews: Summary
Product Id	TRICDS	Process Cost Budgeted $ Actual $		Sub-Process id (if applicable)	Early Warning Signal (Y/N)

Part B

Review of the Bill of Resource – Cost of doing business

	Activity-1		Activity-2		Activity-3		Activity-4	
	Staff	System	Staff	System	Staff	System	Staff	System
Front, Middle & Back Office	Resources for Dual control and Segregation of Duty unavailable in some overseas locations.							

The table below is an extract from Chapter 3, Section 3.5.2, Table 3-8n. The example uses time-driven activity-based costing. The total resource consumption cost is $30,599,000.

					Summarised & Illustrative			
LOB	Product	Process, Activities		Volume	Activity time Min-Rnd	Total Time (Rnd)	Unit Cost	Total Cost (Rnd)
		Time Driven (TD) process cost= the sum of all its TD activity costs. TD activity based cost = Process Volume * Activity time *Unit cost of activity						
Treasury	TRICDS	Pre-Deal	Risk Management	404,749	4.5	1,821,369	0.42	764,975
		Trade	Risk Management	398,424	4	1,593,698	0.48	764,975
		Position Monitoring	Risk Management	599,804	25	14,995,112	1.91	28,640,664
		Settlement & Accounting	Risk Management	503,984	5	2,519,918	0.17	428,386
Product's TD Non-interest Cost, Cost of Resources utilised								30,599,000

CHAPTER 4 MONITORING OPERATING LEVERAGE

Part C

	Examine KPI, KRI: Performance, Risk, Control, Cost
PRCC Issue	(i) Limited pre-deal analytics available for traders (ii) Rogue Trades (iii) No dual control over Deal Capture i.e. trading and verifications done by same persons in overseas trading desks.
Causation	Risk Culture; **Cost 'control' Culture**
Risk Appetite Breach	Yes
Severity	High
Probability of re-occurrence	High

Part D

	Evaluate Process – KPI, KRI Risk Adjusted Return - Corrective Action	
Policy, Procedure	Implementation of Internal Control Framework should be consistent with policies and procedures.	
Cost / Benefit check	Benefits outweigh cost	Approval for Change: **Y**

Part E

	Correction / Improvement
Test Correction & Implement	Advanced analytics embedded in treasury trading processes; Staff deployed for dual control;
Measure KPI and Residual Risk	Staff strength and FTE should be monitored in overseas Treasury offices. Medium

4.3.3.4.5 (xviii) Nostro Reconciliation

Line of Business	Function	Process	Bill of Resources	Process Cost
Treasury		Nostro Reconciliation		

Part A

			Operating Leverage Monitoring					
Process Id	Process 18	Process Type	B	▼	Process Description	Nostro Reconciliation		
Process Owner	Staff Id	Last Review Date	YYMMDD		Reviewed By	Staff Id	Last 5 Reviews: Summary	▼
Sub-Function Id:	Accounting	Process Cost Budgeted $ Actual $			Sub-Process id (if applicable)		Early Warning Signal (Y/N)	**N**

CHAPTER 4   MONITORING OPERATING LEVERAGE

Part B

	Review of the Bill of Resource – Cost of doing business							
	Activity-1		Activity-2		Activity-3		Activity-4	
	Staff	System	Staff	System	Staff	System	Staff	System
Front, Middle & Back Office	Too many staff in reconciliation activities. There are inherent limitations in existing banking applications. Further, the siloed banking applications are growing in volumes.							

Part C

	Examine KPI, KRI: Performance, Risk, Control, Cost
PRCC Issue	SWIFT Grades not implemented
Causation	Staff Performance
Risk Appetite Breach	Yes
Severity	High
Probability of re-occurrence	High

Part D

	Evaluate Process – KPI, KRI Risk Adjusted Return - Corrective Action		
Policy, Procedure	Better monitoring of software upgrades		
Cost / Benefit check	Benefits outweigh cost	Approval for Change:	Y

Part E

	Correction / Improvement
Operational Efficiency, Risk Mitigation	Nostro Reconciliation SWIFT Upgrades implemented
Measure KPI and Residual Risk	Efficient and Minimal reconciliation Low

4.3.3.5 Subprocesses

The AML and fraud prevention/detection processes are important aspects of operational risk management. Operational risk incident processing can use the case management module of the BPMS suite; this is explained in Example xxii.

CHAPTER 4   MONITORING OPERATING LEVERAGE

4.3.3.5.1 (xix) AML

This is a risk culture issue at the bank level and at the country level. Systemically, corrupt countries do not penalize banks for laundering money. The hefty fines levied by regulators in the United States and Europe have not deterred multinational banks from laundering money for corrupt oligarchs, cronies, and cartels.

Part A

Operating Leverage Monitoring

Process Id	Process	Process Type	R	▼	Process Description	Sub-Process Anti-Money laundering & countering the financing of terrorism check		
	19							
Process Owner	Staff Id	Last Review Date	YYMMDD		Reviewed By		Staff Id	Last 5 Reviews: Summary	▼
Product Id	All	Process Cost Budgeted $ Actual $			Sub-Process Linked to Sub Process	Yes No	Early Warning Signal (Y/N)	Y

Part B

Review of the Bill of Resource – Cost of Risk Management

	Activity-1		Activity-2		Activity-3		Activity-4	
	Staff	System	Staff	System	Staff	System	Staff	System
Front, Middle & Back Office	Weak automation. Non-value adding actitivies.							

Part C

	Examine KPI,KRI: Performance, Risk, Control, Cost
PRCC issue	Money laundering detected in Trade finance transaction.
Causation	Transaction surveillance using a process approach has a higher probability of success to detect AML transactions.
Risk Appetite Breach	Yes
Severity	Yes
Probability of re-occurrence	Yes

CHAPTER 4   MONITORING OPERATING LEVERAGE

All incidents must update the operational risk database as and when the event occurs. This is illustrated in Section 4.4.3.7, Figure 4-21. The next chapter explains the use of analytics for anti-money laundering. The focus should be on preventive controls.

Part D

	Evaluate Process– KPI, KRI Risk Adjusted Return - Corrective Action	
System	Focus should be one Preventive Controls	
Policy, Procedure	Risk Culture issue – Management should be questioned by shareholders	
Cost / Benefit check	Benefits outweigh cost	Approval for Change: **Y**

Part E

	Correction / Improvement
Test Correction	Anti-money laundering system replaced.
Implement	AML policies implemented. Banking processes embedded with preventive and detective controls.
Measure KPI	Observe Regulatory compliance for 3 years
Residual Risk	Medium

4.3.3.5.2   (xx) Fraud Prevention and Detection

Recovery of money is difficult, costly, and time-consuming. **It is mandatory to implement preventive controls that are commensurate with the quantified risk in many "hot spots/critical areas."**

Part A

				Operating Leverage Monitoring				
Process Id	Process 20	Process Type	R ▼		Process Description	Sub-Process Fraud Prevention & Detection (Advanced Analytics)		
Process Owner	Staff Id	Last Review Date	YYMMDD		Reviewed By	Staff Id	Last 5 Reviews: Summary	▼
Products & Support Departments	Pan Bank	Process Cost Budgeted Actual	$ $		Sub-Process	Yes	Early Warning Signal (Y/N)	**Y**

CHAPTER 4   MONITORING OPERATING LEVERAGE

Part B

	Review of the Bill of Resource – Cost of Risk Management							
	Activity-1		Activity-2		Activity-3		Activity-4	
	Staff	System	Staff	System	Staff	System	Staff	System
Front, Middle, Back Office	Bill of Resources does not reflect usage of Fraud Prevention and Detection. GRC to examine.							

Part C

	Examine KPI, KRI: Performance, Risk, Control, Cost
PRCC Issue	Internal fraud, External fraud: In most cases, analysis of staff frauds reveal weakness in the control framework, particularly KYE & KYC polices & procedures.
Causation	"Cost Control" & "Risk indifference" Culture
Risk Appetite Breach	Yes
Severity	High
Probability of re-occurrence	High

All incidents must update the operational risk database as and when the event occurs. This is illustrated in Section 4.4.3.7, Figure 4-21. The next chapter explains the use of analytics for fraud prevention and detection. The focus should be on preventive controls.

Part D

	Evaluate Process – KPI, KRI Risk Adjusted Return - Corrective Action	
System	Advanced Analytics will facilitate detection of internal fraud through intelligent surveillance of transaction, account and customer records. Fictitious entries, Donations, Misappropriations can be minimised with Analytics.	
Policy, Procedure	Implementation of SOX 404 and COBIT (Control Objectives for Information and Related Technology) recommendations could have helped with risk mitigation. Effectiveness Know Your Employee & Customer programs	
Cost / Benefit check	Benefits outweigh cost	Approval for Change: **Y**

Part E

	Correction / Improvement
Test Correction & Implement	Intelligence embedded in Banking Processes; Enterprise Fraud Prevention & Detection analytics
Measure KPI and Residual Risk	Observe Operational Risk incidents over a 2-year period, Medium

CHAPTER 4   MONITORING OPERATING LEVERAGE

4.3.3.5.3 (xxi) Case Management

Hyperautomation comes with a case management capability.

Part A

			Operating Leverage Monitoring					
Process Id		Process 21	Process Type	B	▼	Process Description	Case Management	
Process Owner		Staff Id	Last Review Date	YYMMDD	Reviewed By	Staff Id	Last 5 Reviews:	▼
		Pan-bank	Process Cost Budgeted $ Actual $		Sub-Process id (if applicable)		Early Warning Signal (Y/N)	Y

Part B

Review of the Bill of Resource							
Activity-1		Activity-2		Activity-3		Activity-4	
Staff	System	Staff	System	Staff	System	Staff	System
Too much time spent by staff on search, examination and analysis of risk incidents. This includes reports submitted in the past on weakness and vulnerability in banking processes.							

Part C

Examine KPI, KRI: Performance, Risk, Control, Cost	
PRCC Issue Causation	Enterprise risk adjusted return management is constrained by the absence of case management tools. Cases have a life cycle and a case management tool enables Cost Accountants, Auditors and GRC analysts to create, modify, and monitor cases. These cases are (i) flaws in banking processes (ii) atypical account activities (iii) atypical customer behaviour or (iv) atypical staff conduct. When it process automation is powered by analytics, resolution of cases is faster and improves the quality of outcome.

Part D

Evaluate Process – KPI, KRI Risk Adjusted Return - Corrective Action			
System	The **BPMS suite comes with case management**. This can be integrated with enterprise content management and advanced analytics.		
Policy, Procedure	Policies and procedure for using case management tools should be documented and staff should be		
Cost / Benefit check	Benefits outweigh cost	Approval for Change:	Y

CHAPTER 4   MONITORING OPERATING LEVERAGE

Part E

	Correction / Improvement
Test Correction & Implement	Cast Management and Analytics integrated with Banking Processes
Measure KPI and Residual Risk	Observe Risk incident management over a 2-year period, Low

4.3.3.6 Support Departments

The dashboard data will also apply for the support departments. Budget versus Actual, Resource Utilization and Fixed, Variable cost monitoring are important aspects of managing operating leverage.

4.3.3.6.1 (xxii) Finance Department – Costing and Accounting Chart of Accounts

Support Department	Sub-function	Process	Bill of Resources	Process Cost
Finance	Chart of Accounts P&L, Balance Sheet	Participation in management meetings;		
	Chart of Accounts Activity Based Cost Management	Interactions with Lines of Business;		
	Monthly, Quarterly & Annual Book closure	Interaction with Support Departments;		
	Budgeting			
	Statutory Audit	Interaction with Statutory Auditor;		
		Interaction with Banking Supervisor		

Part A

				Operating Leverage Monitoring			
Process Id	Process 22	Process Type	B ▼	Process Description	Chart of Accounts: (i) Books of Account; (ii) Activity based Cost Management		
Process Owner	Staff Id	Last Review Date	YYMMDD	Reviewed By	Staff Id	Last 5 Reviews: Summary	▼
Product Id & Support Departments	Pan-Bank	Process Cost Budgeted $ Actual $		Sub-Process id (if applicable)		Early Warning Signal (Y/N)	Y

372

CHAPTER 4   MONITORING OPERATING LEVERAGE

Part B

Review of the Bill of Resource – Cost of Doing business

	Activity-1		Activity-2		Activity-3		Activity-4	
	Staff	System	Staff	System	Staff	System	Staff	System
Front, Middle and Back Office	Cost allocation unreconciled with books of account.							

Part C

Underutilization of finance department resources: The **books of account** figures are shown below.

Finance Department's Direct Cost	
Employee cost	5,000,000
Enterprise I.T. Governance cost	500,000
Premises: Rent, Taxes & Lighting	500,000
Office supplies	200,000
Depreciation on own assets	150,000
Repairs & Maintenance (non-I.T.)	100,000
Travel	250,000
Total	6,700,000

Finance Department - Cost allocation to LOBs			
Opening Balance	6,700,000		
Indirect cost Charge In:		Allocation	
Premises	5,000,000	Retail	4,700,000
Enterprise I.T. Governance	5,000,000	Treasury	8,000,000
Office Supplies	5,000,000	Corporate	9,000,000
Total	21,700,000		21,700,000

	Examine KPI, KRI: Performance, Risk, Control, Cost
PRCC Issue	ENICM Chart of Accounts and Book of Account chart needs single ownership; Unauthorised amendments to Chart of Accounts; Errors in Cost allocation traced to weak implementation of ENICM System.
Causation	Roles & Responsibilities need improvement
Risk Appetite Breach	No
Severity	Low
Probability of re-occurrence	Low

Part D

	Evaluate Process – KPI, KRI Risk Adjusted Return - Corrective Action	
Staff		
Policy, Procedure	Organisation structure, roles & responsibilities need review and correction.	
Cost / Benefit check	Benefits outweigh cost	Approval for Change: **Y**

CHAPTER 4   MONITORING OPERATING LEVERAGE

Part E

	Correction / Improvement
Test Correction & Implement	New structure and amended roles & responsibilities
Measure KPI and Residual Risk	Accuracy of Cost allocation & activity based ENICM. Low

4.3.3.6.2 Enterprise IT Governance

Support Department	Sub-function	Process	Bill of Resources	Process Cost
Enterprise I.T. Governance	Enterprise Architecture		Service Level Agreement with Lines of Business & other Support Departments. Cost Budget and KPIs.	The process cost should be examined in the context of: Process Maturity Score; Key Performance Indicator; Key Risk Indicator; and Residual Risk in the process.
	Enterprise Data Governance			
	Enterprise Security Management			
	Capacity Planning			
	Data centre operations			
	Change Management			
	Release Management			
	Project Management			
	Incident Management			

(xxiii) EITG Tool

Part A

			Operating Leverage Monitoring				
Process Id	Process 23	Process Type	T ▼	Process Description	Enterprise I.T. Governance		
Process Owner	Staff Id	Last Review Date	YYMMDD	Reviewed By	Staff Id	Last 5 Reviews: Summary	▼
Sub-Function Id:		Process Cost Budgeted $ Actual $		Sub-Process id (if applicable)		Early Warning Signal (Y/N)	Y

Part B

	Review of the Bill of Resource – Cost of doing business							
	Activity-1		Activity-2		Activity-3		Activity-4	
	Staff	System	Staff	System	Staff	System	Staff	System
Asset control within I.T. Department is weak.								

CHAPTER 4   MONITORING OPERATING LEVERAGE

Part C

Enterprise I.T. Governance Department's Direct Cost	
Employee cost	5,000,000
Enterprise I.T. Governance cost	1,000,000
Premises: Rent, Taxes & Lighting	500,000
Office supplies	2,000,000
Depreciation on own assets	600,000
Repairs & Maintenance (non-I.T.)	1,000,000
Travel	1,500,000
Total	11,600,000

Enterprise I.T. Governance Department - Cost Allocation to LOBs			
Opening Balance	11,600,00		
Indirect cost Charge In:		Allocation	
Premises	10,000,000	Retail	12,000,000
Office Supplies	10,000,000	Treasury	9,600,000
		Corporate	10,000,000
Total	31,600,000		31,600,000

Examine KPI,KRI: Performance, Risk, Control, Cost	
PRCC Issue	User access to non-production systems is weak; Risk incidents in release management.
Causation	Roles & Responsibilities need improvement; Need relevant automation
Risk Appetite Breach	Yes
Severity	Medium
Probability of re-occurrence	Low

Part D

	Evaluate Process – KPI, KRI Risk Adjusted Return - Corrective Action		
System	Enterprise I.T. Governance Tool		
Policy, Procedure	User Access Management		
Cost / Benefit check	Benefits outweigh cost	Approval for Change:	Y

Part E

	Correction / Improvement
Test Correction & Implement	Suitable changes to Roles & Responsibilities; New Enterprise I.T. governance tool
Measure KPI and Residual Risk	Better governance Low

CHAPTER 4 MONITORING OPERATING LEVERAGE

(xxiv) Incident Management

Part A

			Operating Leverage Monitoring					
Process Id		Process 24	Process Type	T	▼	Process Description	Help Desk: Incident management	
Process Owner		Staff Id	Last Review Date	YYMMDD	Reviewed By	Staff Id	Last 5 Reviews: Summary	▼
Sub-Function Id:		EITHIM	Process Cost Budgeted Actual	$ $	Sub-Process id (if applicable)		Early Warning Signal (Y/N)	Y

Part B

	Activity-1		Activity-2		Activity-3		Activity-4	
	Staff	System	Staff	System	Staff	System	Staff	System

Review of the Bill of Resource

1. SLA's could be corrected for improving external customer or internal consumer experience. Incident management for front office activities should be prioritised.

2. Bank could reduce the indirect costs by expanding the scope of the Service Level Agreements. At least 80% of the incident management costs incurred by Technology Department, should be chargeable to Lines of Business directly.

Part C

	Examine KPI,KRI: Performance, Risk, Control, Cost		
PRCC Issue	Data collection for each incident is not updated in the Operational Risk Management database; Data collection should also include Near miss and Vulnerabilities identified; Incident Management escalation procedures need improvement.		
Causation	Roles & Responsibilities need improvement		
Risk Appetite Breach	Yes		
Severity	Medium		
Probability of re-occurrence	Low		

Part D

	Evaluate Process – KPI, KRI Risk Adjusted Return - Corrective Action		
System	Enterprise I.T. Governance Tool; Business Process automation facilitates data lineage and improves data quality.		
Policy, Procedure	Internal loss data collection		
Cost / Benefit check	Benefits outweigh cost	Approval for Change:	Y

CHAPTER 4   MONITORING OPERATING LEVERAGE

Part E

	Correction / Improvement
Test Correction & Implement	SLA's amended, approved and enforced.
Measure KPI and Residual Risk	Better governance Low

(xxv) Release Management

Part A

			Operating Leverage Monitoring					
Process Id	Process 25	Process Type	T	▼	Process Description	Release Management		
Process Owner	Staff Id	Last Review Date	YYMMDD		Reviewed By	Staff Id	Last 5 Reviews:	▼
Product Id or Sub-Function Id:	EITGRM	Process Cost Budgeted Actual	$ $		Sub-Process id (if applicable)		Early Warning Signal (Y/N)	Y

Part B

Review of the Bill of Resource							
Activity-1		Activity-2		Activity-3		Activity-4	
Staff	System	Staff	System	Staff	System	Staff	System
Staff not assigned as per Bill of Resources; No dual control							

Part C

	Examine KPI, KRI: Performance, Risk, Control, Cost
PRCC issue	A weakness in the non-production area could have an impact on the production systems e.g. a wrong software deployment because of a weakness in the release management process.
Causation	Limited automation of Enterprise I.T. Governance
Risk Appetite Breach	Yes
Severity	Medium
Probability of re-occurrence	Low

CHAPTER 4   MONITORING OPERATING LEVERAGE

Part D

	Evaluate Process – KPI, KRI Risk Adjusted Return - Corrective Action		
System	Enterprise I.T. Governance Tool – for banking software solutions and risk models The tool makes Change, Configuration, Release, & Support Management more efficient and effective.		
Policy, Procedure	EITG tool procedural changes		
Cost / Benefit check	Benefits outweigh cost	Approval for Change:	Y

Part E

	Correction / Improvement
Test Correction & Implement	A new Enterprise I.T. Governance tool implemented
Measure KPI and Residual Risk	Better governance Low

Enterprise IT governance tool *is a mandatory requirement and a critical success factor for improving operational efficiency and operating leverage.*

All incidents must update the operational risk database as and when the event occurs. This is illustrated in Section 4.4.3.7, Figure 4-21.

(xxvi) Offices – No Customer Service

Almost all banks have office where they do not offer customer service. It is mentioned here because there could be data collection, quality, and security issues in these locations.

Part A

		Operating Leverage Monitoring					
Process Id	Process 00026	Process Type	B	Process Description	Offices / Branches – No customer service		
Owner	Staff Id	Last Review Date		Reviewed By		Last 5 Reviews: Summary	▼
		Process Cost Budgeted Actual	$ $	Sub-Process id (if applicable)		Early Warning Signal (Y/N)	Y

378

CHAPTER 4 MONITORING OPERATING LEVERAGE

Part B

	Review of the Bill of Resource – Cost of doing business							
	Activity-1		Activity-2		Activity-3		Activity-4	
	Staff	System	Staff	System	Staff	System	Staff	System
This is middle and back office functions.	Asset control in non-service offices weak.							
	Staff deployment and Bill of Resources do not match							

Part C

	Examine KPI, KRI: Performance, Risk, Control, Cost
PRCC issue	**Non-valued added activities** could be high in non-service offices; **Enterprise I.T. (including data) governance** should include all locations.
Causation	Weakness in enterprise risk governance
Risk Appetite Breach	Yes
Severity	Medium
Probability of re-occurrence	Low

Part D

	Evaluate Process – KPI, KRI Risk Adjusted Return - Corrective Action	
Policy, Procedure	Staff assignment and assets need better policies and implementation; Risk monitoring should include non-customer service offices.	
Cost / Benefit check	Benefits outweigh cost	Approval for Change: **Y**

Part E

	Correction / Improvement
Test Correction & Implement	Policy and procedural changes implemented
Measure KPI and Residual Risk	Better governance, lower costs and operational risks Low

CHAPTER 4   MONITORING OPERATING LEVERAGE

4.3.3.6.3 Human Capital

Support Department	Sub-function	Process	Bill of Resources	Process Cost
Human Capital	Recruitment			The cost should be analysed in the context of: Process Maturity Score; Process Key Performance Indicator; Process Key Risk Indicator; and Residual Risk in the process.
	On-boarding			
	Retention			
	Resignation / Termination			

Underutilization of human resources is seen. It is possible that automation is weak or inadequate. The books of account figures are shown below.

Human Capital Department's Direct Cost	
Employee cost	5,000,000
Enterprise I.T. Governance cost	250,000
Premises: Rent, Taxes & Lighting	500,000
Office supplies	150,000
Depreciation on own assets	200,000
Repairs & Maintenance (non-I.T.)	50,000
Travel	1,000,000
Total	7,150,000

Human Capital - Cost allocation to LOBs			
Opening Balance	7,150,000		
Indirect cost Charge In:		Allocation	
Premises	4,000,000	Retail	13,150,000
Enterprise I.T. Governance	8,000,000	Treasury	4,000,000
Office Supplies	5,000,000	Corporate	7,000,000
Total	24,150,000		24,150,000

(xxvii) Recruitment

This is an extremely critical process, and KPI monitoring should be based on staff and role profiles.

Part A

					Operating Leverage Monitoring		
Process Id	Process 27	Process Type	H	▼	Process Description	Human Capital – Staff Recruitment	
Process Owner	Staff Id	Last Review Date	YYMMDD	Reviewed By	Staff Id	Last 5 Reviews: Summary	▼
Function Id:	HCDREC	Process Cost Budgeted Actual	$ $	Sub-Process id (if applicable)	Background Check & References	Early Warning Signal (Y/N)	Y

Part B

Review of the Bill of Resource for the department							
Activity-1		Activity-2		Activity-3		Activity-4	
Staff	System	Staff	System	Staff	System	Staff	System
Recruitment time should be shortened; Recruitment cost (not staff cost) is increasing.							

Part C

	Examine KPI,KRI: Performance, Risk, Control, Cost
PRCC Issue	Rogue trades in treasury and non-performing assets in corporate banking. Risk traced to human factor. Weakness in recruitment processes; e.g.Reference Checks —weak.
Causation	Recruitment procedures and processes need improvement.
Risk Appetite Breach	Y
Severity	H
Probability of re-occurrence	H

Part D

	Evaluate Process – KPI, KRI Risk Adjusted Return - Corrective Action	
Staff	Better team work between Human Capital department and Lines of Business	
Policy, Procedure	Background checks, including references checks, need a more 'role' oriented specification. Should match Role Risk profile and Skill Profile. Policies need to be improved for better engagement procedures with specialised recruitment firms.	
Cost / Benefit check	Benefits outweigh cost	Approval for Change: Y

Part E

	Correction / Improvement
Test Correction & Implement	Policy and Procedural changes approved by Senior Management
Measure KPI and Residual Risk	Monitor staff fraud, staff productivity. Medium

(xxviii) Termination

The exit procedures of employees in many banks do not follow best practices. One of the important risk areas is the disabling of all access to premises and systems.

CHAPTER 4 MONITORING OPERATING LEVERAGE

Part A

Operating Leverage Monitoring								
Process Id	Process 28	Process Type	H	▼	Process Description	Human Capital – Staff Termination		
Process Owner	Staff Id	Last Review Date	YYMMDD		Reviewed By	Staff Id	Last 5 Reviews: Summary	▼
Function Id:	HCDTRM	Process Cost Budgeted $ Actual $			Sub-Process id (if applicable)	I.T. Governance Legal	Early Warning Signal (Y/N)	Y

Part B

Although the focus of this example is on the operational risks linked to termination process, Part B is used to emphasize the need to have accurate data on staff skills, performance, and utilization for taking decisions on right sizing the workforce.

Review of the Bill of Resource							
Activity-1		Activity-2		Activity-3		Activity-4	
Staff	System	Staff	System	Staff	System	Staff	

Cost accountant's remark: Bank's 'right sizing' not based on accurate data. Issue marked to the attention of senior management.

Part C

	Examine KPI, KRI: Performance, Risk, Control, Cost
PRCC Issue	Instances of (a) fraud by terminated employees and (b) access not fully de-activated. Lack of coordination with I.T. Governance; Staff termination by bank needs approval from legal department
Causation	Ineffective policy and procedure
Severity	High
Probability of re-occurrence	Low

Part D

	Evaluate Process – KPI, KRI Risk Adjusted Return - Corrective Action		
Policy, Procedure	Termination policy and procedures amended		
Cost / Benefit check	Benefits outweigh cost	Approval for Change:	Y

CHAPTER 4   MONITORING OPERATING LEVERAGE

Part E

	Correction / Improvement
Test Correction & Implement	Policy and Procedural changes approved by Senior Management
Measure KPI and Residual Risk	Monitor Suspicious and Atypical events and transactions Low

The human capital system should provide data such as

LOB/support department	Resource Id	Skill grade, appraisal, and training	Product or function	Branch

The ENICM system should provide data on resource utilization.

Staff skills by LOB/support and product/function.

For example, how many staff with skill G2 working for corporate syndicate loans?

How many staff with skill G1 work with FX?

4.3.3.6.4 GRC

Support Department: Governance Risk & Compliance	Sub-function Risk Models: Proprietary model (P), ,Vendor model (V)	Process	Bill of Resources	Process Cost
	Business Requirement Document (P&V)			Proprietary Risk Model development methodology is similar to software development methodology.
	Model development (P)			
	Model Release Management (P &V)			
	Monitoring: Model Fit for Purpose Test (P&V)			

Governance Risk & Compliance	Sub-function Risk Management	Process	Bill of Resources	Process Cost
	Enterprise Risk Adjusted Return Model	Pan-bank		
	Market Credit management	Product driven		
	Credit Risk management	Product driven		
	Enterprise Liquidity Management	Pan-bank		
	Operational Risk Management	Includes Support Departments		
	Enterprise Stress Testing	Pan-bank		

CHAPTER 4 MONITORING OPERATING LEVERAGE

Underutilization of GRC is seen. The books of account figures are shown below.

GRC Department's Direct Cost	
Employee cost	10,000,000
Enterprise I.T. Governance cost	1,750,000
Premises: Rent, Taxes & Lighting	500,000
Office supplies	400,000
Depreciation on own assets	250,000
Repairs & Maintenance (non-I.T.)	500,000
Travel	1,000,000
Total	14,400,000

GRC Department - Cost allocation to LOBs			
Opening Balance	14,400,000		
Indirect cost Charge In:		Allocation	
Premises	7,000,000	Retail	7,4000,000
Enterprise I.T. Governance	15,000,000	Treasury	22,000,000
Office Supplies	5,000,000	Corporate	12,000,000
Total	41,400,000		41,400,000

(xxix) Risk Models

Part A

		Operating Leverage Monitoring			
Process Id	Process 29	Process Type	Process Description	Risk Models – proprietary and vendor supplied	
Process Owner		Last Review Date	Reviewed By	Last 5 Reviews: Summary	
		Process Cost Budgeted $ Actual $	Sub-Process id (if applicable)	Early Warning Signal (Y/N)	Y

Part B

The risk models need to be managed using the IT principles recommended for System Development Life Cycle (SDLC).

Review of the Bill of Resource							
Activity-1		Activity-2		Activity-3		Activity-4	
Staff	System	Staff	System	Staff	System	Staff	System
Inadequate skills and staff for risk modelling.							
Mismatch between Business Requirements and Bill of resources-risk modelling.							

Part C

	Examine KPI, KRI: Performance, Risk, Control, Cost
PRCC Issue	Bank is using only vendor supplied models. (i) not configured to specific needs and (ii) losing competitive positioning. All banks use one or more vendor supplied risk management models. Model Governance includes the testing of the model and the periodic review of its 'fit for use' in a changing business and regulatory landscape. Further, this applies to banks that have the capability to develop and use internal models for risk management. Internal models can improve the effectiveness of enterprise risk measurement and capital allocation. Proprietary models could provide a competitive advantage. A 'black box approach' to risk models could create significant additional risk exposure.
Causation	"Cost Control" culture

Part D

	Evaluate Process – KPI, KRI Risk Adjusted Return - Corrective Action	
Staff	Staff with quantitative modelling skills required	
Policy, Procedure	Proprietary models need policy and procedural changes	
Cost / Benefit check	Benefits outweigh cost	Approval for Change: **Y**

Risk models are built for specific business situations, and data is important for testing. GRC's KPIs should include check of **model's fit for purpose check** at least once a year.

Part E

	Correction / Improvement
Test Correction & Implement	Policy and Procedural changes approved by Senior Management
Measure KPI and Residual Risk	Monitor impact on risk adjusted returns, business profitability and growth Medium

4.3.3.6.5 Legal

Support Department	Sub-function	Process	Bill of Resource	Process Cost
Legal	Customer linked	Loan recovery		
	Product linked	Sales		
	Line of Business	Retail Account Maintenance Charges		
	Bank	Whistle-blower: Governance		
	Human Capital	Staff misconduct		
	Technology	Data theft		

CHAPTER 4   MONITORING OPERATING LEVERAGE

Cost accountant's observation: underutilization of resources in the Legal Department.

The books of account figures are shown below.

Legal Department's Direct Cost	
Employee cost	2,500,000
Enterprise I.T. Governance cost	200,000
Premises: Rent, Taxes & Lighting	200,000
Office supplies	50,000
Depreciation on own assets	50,000
Repairs & Maintenance (non-I.T.)	50,000
Travel	500,000
Total	3,550,000

Legal Department Cost - Allocation to LOBs			
Opening Balance	3,550,000		
Indirect cost Charge In:		Allocation	
Premises	1,000,000	Retail	1,550,000
Enterprise I.T. Governance	1,000,000	Treasury	1,000,000
Office Supplies	1,000,000	Corporate	4,000,000
Total	6,550,000		6,550,000

4.3.3.6.6 Operations Department

Support Department	Sub-function	Process	Bill of Resources	Process Cost
Premises	Own - buying			
	Rent new premises			
	Renovation			
	Repairs & Maintenance			

Cost accountant's observation: underutilization of resources owned by the Operations Department.

The books of account figures are shown below.

Operations Department's Direct Cost	
Employee cost	2,500,000
Enterprise I.T. Governance cost	300,000
Premises: Rent, Taxes & Lighting	300,000
Office supplies	200,000
Depreciation on own assets	150,000
Repairs & Maintenance (non-I.T.)	800,000
Travel	500,000
Total	4,750,000

CHAPTER 4 MONITORING OPERATING LEVERAGE

Operations Department Cost - Allocation to LOBs			
Opening Balance	4,750,000		
Indirect cost Charge In:		Allocation	
Enterprise I.T. Governance	1,000,000	Retail	5,000,000
Office Supplies	4,000,000	Treasury	1,750,000
		Corporate	3,000,000
Total	9,750,000		9,750,000

4.3.3.7 Update of Operational Risk Database

As mentioned in Section 4.4.3.5, Examples ix, anti-money laundering; xx, fraud prevention and detection; xxiv, incident management; and xxv, release management, when there is an operational risk incident, the process should be modeled to update the operational risk database.

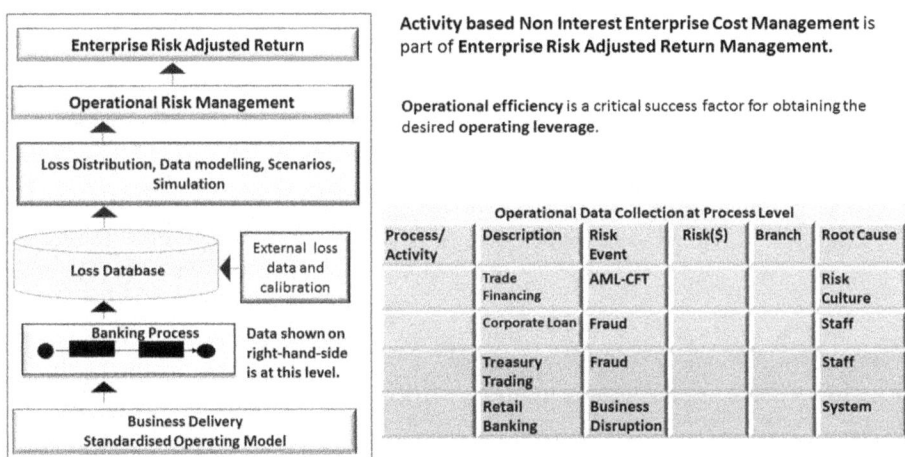

***Figure 4-21.** Operations risk incidents update operational risk database*

CHAPTER 4   MONITORING OPERATING LEVERAGE

4.3.3.8 Enterprise Risk

Enterprise[15] *stress testing* requires the participation of the business heads and support departments heads. The GRC group might have ownership for it.

Similarly BCP is considered an EITG function. However, the ownership lies with the management of the bank, and it requires the participation of the lines of business and IT teams.

4.3.3.8.1 (xxx) Enterprise Stress Testing

Part A

Process Id	Process 30	Process Type	R		Process Description	Stress Testing		
Process Owner	Staff Id	Last Review Date	YYMMDD		Reviewed By	Staff Id	Last 5 Reviews	
Product Id or Sub-Function Id:	Pan Bank	Process Cost Budgeted $ Actual $			Sub-Process id (if applicable)		Early Warning Signal (Y/N)	Y

Operating Leverage Monitoring

Part B

Review of the Bill of Resource

	Activity-1		Activity-2		Activity-3		Activity-4	
	Staff	System	Staff	System	Staff	System	Staff	System
	Staff skill mismatch; Under utilisation of staff.							

---

[15] IMF - WP/20/82 Liquidity at Risk: **Joint Stress Testing of** Solvency and Liquidity, June 2020
https://www.imf.org/en/Publications/WP/Issues/2020/06/05/Liquidity-at-Risk-Joint-Stress-Testing-of-Solvency-and-Liquidity-49325
Working Paper 29, Making **supervisory stress tests** more macroprudential: Considering liquidity and solvency interactions and systemic risk November 2015
https://www.bis.org/bcbs/publ/wp29.pdf
Supervisory and bank stress testing: https://www.bis.org/bcbs/publ/d427.pdf

Part C

	Examine KPI, KRI: Performance, Risk, Control, Cost
PRCC Issue	Bank has not conducted enterprise stress testing of their exposures. As such, risk is under-stated in the balance sheet.
Causation	"Cost Control" culture. Risk Culture is driven by indifference.
Risk Appetite Breach	Yes
Severity	Yes
Probability of re-occurrence	Yes

Part D

	Evaluate Process – KPI, KRI Risk Adjusted Return - Corrective Action	
Staff	Staff training may be required; Risk factor and scenario selections require experiences risk managers.	
System	Good quality enterprise data is important	
Policy, Procedure	The management should issues policy guidelines for stress testing	
Cost / Benefit check	Benefits outweigh cost	Approval for Change: **Y**

Enterprise data management is a prerequisite for stress testing. It is recommended that stress testing includes market, credit, liquidity, and operational risk factors.

Part E

	Correction / Improvement
Test Correction & Implement	Policy and Procedural changes approved by Senior Management
Measure KPI and	Analyse Stress Testing output and take corrective action. Observe enterprise risk adjusted returns over a 3 year period.
Residual Risk	Low

Noninterest cost allocation policy will guide the allocation of the cost to the lines of business.

4.3.3.8.2 (xxxi) Business Continuity Planning

BCP testing is a critical success factor for operational resilience and 24/7 delivery of banking services. Bank management should ensure that system down time is vetted and mentioned in the bank's policy and procedures document. It should be consistent with risk appetite.

Business continuity planning goes beyond disaster recovery. The latter is technical and included in the technical architecture design and infrastructure planning. BCP includes emergency procedures and that includes the safety of the staff and others in the building.

Part A

					Operating Leverage Monitoring			
Process Id		Process 31	Process Type	B	▼	Process Description	Business Continuity Planning	
Function Owner		Staff Id	Last Review Date			Reviewed By	Staff Id	Last 5 Reviews: Summary	▼
Product Id or Sub-Function Id:			Process Cost Budgeted Actual	$ $		Sub-Process id (if applicable)		Early Warning Signal (Y/N)	Y

Part B

	Review of the Bill of Resource						
Activity-1		Activity-2		Activity-3		Activity-4	
Staff	System	Staff	System	Staff	System	Staff	System
Resources for BCP have not been utilised. It reflects (a) "cost control" culture and (b) indifference to enterprise risk.							

Part C

BCP is a risk mitigation for a low frequency, high severity operational risk event.

	Examine KPI,KRI: Performance, Risk, Control, Cost
PRCC Issue	Example: Over the last 12 months there were six incidents when banking services were unavailable to the customers. The downtime (KPI) was breached. Emergency preparedness (BCP readiness) was found wanting; Operational Risk management was not proactive and effective
Causation	Weak Enterprise I.T. Governance; Weak Operational Risk management
Risk Appetite Breach	Yes
Severity	High
Probability of re-occurrence	High

Part D

	Evaluate Process – KPI, KRI Risk Adjusted Return - Corrective Action	
Staff	Staff trained in Fire Drills and Emergency procedures; An important activity is the business-impact analysis assessment, using which the bank defines the priorities for restoration and the execution order. This approach can make BCP more effective.	
System	Preventive Controls should be enforced;	
Policy, Procedure	**BCP Ownership - Management** Physical safety of ALL people in the premises is the top priority. BCP should be tested at least once very year.	
Cost / Benefit	Benefits outweigh cost	Approval for Change: **Y**

Large-scale disruptions are caused by system failures (e.g., system/network crash), power outages, or a natural disaster. Data center management should be a top priority in a bank's IT Governance program.

An effective enterprise IT governance model ensures that services are restored within the acceptable downtime specified in the bank's policy.

BCP takes effect when the production system goes down, thus acting as an effective fallback control.

In many institutions, the focus is primarily on disaster recovery, and less priority is given to the testing of all the other functions of a BCP.

Many banks outsource their data center operations. While this could reduce their operating costs in the short term, vendor evaluation and SLA management are critical success factors.

ISO 22301 governs a bank's service restoration after a disruption, and this book recommends that banks implement the standard by customizing it for their enterprise operating model. The standard helps a bank make a BCP risk assessment and guides the bank on risk mitigation.

The Business Continuity Management System (BCMS) includes planning, testing, change management, and periodic improvements to it. An important elements of a BCMS is the business-impact analysis. The GRC, the IT department, and the heads of the various lines of business are stakeholders.

CHAPTER 4   MONITORING OPERATING LEVERAGE

Part E

	Correction / Improvement
Test Correction & Implement	Policy and Procedural changes approved by Senior Management
Measure KPI and	BCP needs to be routinely tested if the management wishes to maintain a good customer experience track record. Downtime KPIs should be set and measured during disruptions.
Residual Risk	The plan is not static. It requires frequent upgrades. Low

Business continuity planning and testing is one of the focus areas of many banking regulators as it is one of the important factor that influences operational resilience.

4.4 Critical Business Functions – Operational Efficiency and Operating Leverage

*The **five** examples in this section are not granular processes but are critical business functions that require an efficient, mature, and effective enterprise operating model.*

4.4.1 Enterprise Liquidity Management

Operations Support for Enterprise Liquidity Management

Principle 6 of Basel's BCBS 368: Adequacy of **measurement systems** entered **data and governance** to validate applied IRRBB measurement methods. The measures to be applied range from simple and static **models** to more sophisticated and dynamic measurement methods.

4.4.1.1 Funds Transfer Pricing (FTP) and Liquidity Transfer Pricing (LTP)

Section 1.8.3.2 in Chapter 1 provides an introduction into funds transfer pricing. FTP & LTP are "deep dive subjects" and beyond the scope of this book. The narrative below is from the perspective of operating leverage and operational efficiency.

All the three lines of business have sources and application of funds. The Treasury is the hub for enterprise liquidity management, and transfer pricing is a responsibility of the asset liability management committee. The deposits mobilized by retail and corporate banking are placed with treasury. The funding for the loan books of corporate and retail banking is provided by treasury. The asset and liability products of the corporate and retail banking divisions have different interest rate and maturity characteristics. These are the basis for a transfer pricing mechanism.

Principle 4[16] of Basel's Principles for *liquidity risk management* specifies that banks should *incorporate liquidity costs in risk and performance measurement* and that includes product pricing.

The *liquidity transfer pricing*[17] (**LTP**) mechanism charges the users of funds for the cost of liquidity and credits the providers of funds (liabilities/deposits) for the benefit of liquidity. it also replenishes the cost of carrying a liquidity cushion by charging contingent commitments, such as lines of credit, based on their expected use of liquidity.

---

[16] Principles for Sound Liquidity Risk Management and Supervision September 2008
https://www.bis.org/publ/bcbs144.pdf

[17] Liquidity transfer pricing: a guide to better practice https://www.bis.org/fsi/fsipapers10.pdf

CHAPTER 4   MONITORING OPERATING LEVERAGE

Banks are finding it difficult to manage liquidity without an enterprise liquidity hub.

Basel's intraday day liquidity, net stable funding ratio (**NSFR**), liquidity coverage ratio (**LCR**), and LTP requirements **mandate the need for a bank to build the enterprise liquidity hub capability**. The objective can be accomplished only if bank's transform from the "as-is" siloed environment to an interoperable, serviced-based enterprise architecture, with process automation.

Profitability Management

Table 4-12. Loan pricing and profitability template

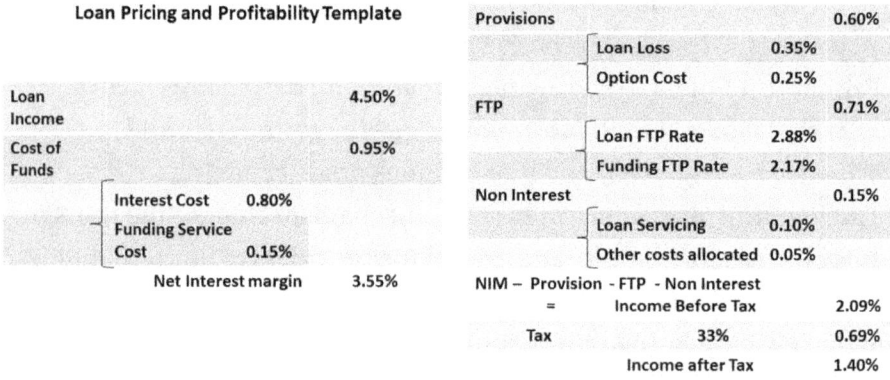

Table 4-12 provides a template for determining product profitability. A bank manages the profitability of its lines of business and products by implementing measures to improve the net interest margin. Banks try to manage the uncertainties of interest-based income by focusing on fee-based products and services.

4.4.1.2 Enterprise Liquidity Hub (ELH)

The ELH is a centralized pool of cash (liquidity) for a bank. The pool is common for all lines of business and support functions. The enterprise architecture and data management can ensure that ELH data is consistent with the books of account at all times. LTP in the figure refers to liquidity transfer pricing.

The system and human capital aspects of ELH come under the scope of enterprise operating model design. As such, operating leverage factors the efficiency of all payment processes.

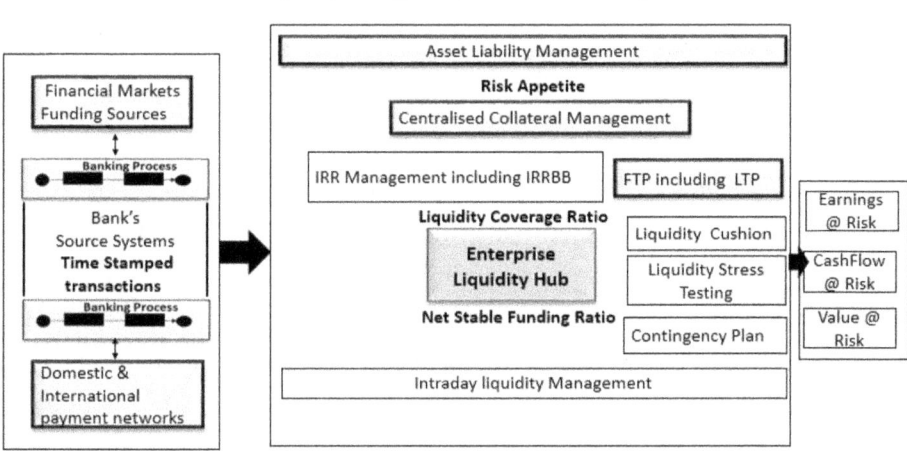

Figure 4-22. Enterprise liquidity hub

Over the years, volatility has increased in the financial markets, customer behavior has changed, and derivatives have added to the complexity of treasury operations. These factors have influenced asset-liability management (ALM) methods, tools, and techniques. ALM has emerged as a science where both sides of the balance sheet have to be holistically and dynamically managed to mitigate interest rate, market, and liquidity risks.

CHAPTER 4   MONITORING OPERATING LEVERAGE

An efficient enterprise risk management framework can provide a capability to manage risks on an intraday basis. Banks may need to restructure their organization so that enterprise liquidity management (**ELM**) becomes a core competency area within treasury.

The intraday liquidity[18] is about managing dynamic transitions in cash positions during the day. It is a core component of enterprise liquidity risk management, and hence, the business and technology architecture of the sub-component must be consistent with the overall framework. The following ratios are important drivers of *liquidity management* and balance sheet management.[19]

Table 4-13. *Liquidity ratios*

Risk Based Capital Ratio	Leverage Ratio	Liquidity Coverage	Net Stable Funding
Common Equity Tier-1	Tier-1 Capital	High Quality Liquid Assets	Available Stable funding over next year
Risk Weighted Assets	Total Exposure	Net Cash Outflows over 30 days	Required stable funding

The manner in which banks respond to central bank interest rates changes is closely linked to their risk profiles. The impact of rate changes on the funding cost of a bank depends on the interest rate sensitivity of their assets and liabilities. The impact is influenced by their balance sheet structure, specifically, their reliance on bank deposits for funding their loan book.

The granularity of the data is an important aspect of ELM, as it enables a bank to isolate the effect of changes in interest rates and track portfolio reallocations, between asset classes across currency.

Enterprise liquidity management is further explained in Section 5.1 under operating leverage.

---

[18] Intraday Liquidity: https://www.bis.org/publ/bcbs248.pdf
[19] Ratios: https://www.bis.org/bcbs/publ/d295.pdf https://www.bis.org/publ/bcbs238.pdf

CHAPTER 4   MONITORING OPERATING LEVERAGE

4.4.2 Branch Network – Right Sizing

During business downturns, the operating costs of retail banking branches and premises occupied by back office functions come under cost management review.

In the current 2023–2024 business slowdown in Hong Kong, Bank of America and Goldman Sachs[20] have reportedly "right sized" their floor space.

Work from Home – Operational Risks vs Benefits

In 2023, Deutsche Bank AG cuts office space by 40% at its Frankfurt base by having some of its employees work from home.[21]

The report did not mention what "actionable intelligence" was used for the decision. Was an impact analysis done? Did the bank assess the criticality of the staff functions? Was it for the short term? How did the information technology department manage the governance aspect of such large number of staff working from home? Was there a technology security audit? These are the differences in a "cost control" approach vis-a-via the cost reduction methodology explained in this book.

The Future of Branches

Historically, banks have closed branches (i) as part of a "strategic profitability improvement plan" or (ii) to manage an internal financial crisis or (iii) to manage a difficult business environment created by an external factor such as a global financial crisis.

Banks are trying to use call centers and website chatbots to interact with customers. In recent years, there has been an increase in the usage of video conferencing for connecting the bank to the customer. A good video conferencing system would work well if there is sufficient bandwidth in the internet connections.

---

[20] https://www.scmp.com/business/banking-finance/article/3256136/bank-america-cuts-back-office-space-hong-kong-amid-impending-new-supply
[21] https://www.bloomberg.com/news/articles/2023-05-17/deutsche-bank-seeks-40-cut-to-frankfurt-offices-on-remote-work

CHAPTER 4   MONITORING OPERATING LEVERAGE

Case: Santander Bank is using video conferencing for connecting its *mortgage advisors* to prospective home loan buyers in the UK. This is to manage the initial mortgage application process.

Many banks are unable to retain their customers in spite of investing in banking technology solutions and a multi-channel business service network.

Many banks are aware that customers prefer to meet a banker for specialized needs or expert guidance. Technology enabled discussions has worked for some products/transactions and with some customer segments.

People with a technical bias continue to write obituaries for branches, ATMs and data centers. However, branches continue to be a relevant part of a holistic **customer value proposition** and is likely to be that way in the foreseeable future.

Optimizing a branch network should not be confused with the relevance of branch banking. Branch networks are a function of the business model (products and services). Some selling and servicing processes have legal ramifications. This involves selling techniques, documentation of customer risk profile, explaining risk factors to prospects, redemption of third-party products, and grievance management.

While the younger generation is comfortable with the changing landscape of technology and may be okay with a virtual bank for retail banking (educational loans and checking accounts), other customer segments with *attractive net worth* would prefer to have the convenience of a home branch. *Several banks are committed to the bricks-and-mortar proposition for face-to-face communications.* They see this as an essential part of building trust and gaining the confidence of the customers.

Specially Designed Branches

Banks are redesigning the branches *for specific customer segments such as small and medium enterprises and high net worth individuals.* The ambience is in keeping with the brand, and the layout facilitates cross-selling of products and services. They are also changing the working hours of some of their staff to match the convenience of their target customer segments.

Case: Media reported that Development Bank of Singapore has implemented a branch design called a *"café and branch" concept.* The target customers cut across ages and net worth. The branch design appeals to people who are comfortable with tech-plus-human interaction. The café-branch infrastructure includes technology and face-to-face interactions. The message to the customer is that the bank understands the changing customer experience needs. The bank has also tied up with several talent-grooming sponsors for reaching out to young artists. The bank's preference for physical social networking rather than reaching out from an office desk to a home desk via "social" media is being well received.

Case: ING bank has completed a branch makeover that offer both digital tools and face-to-face counselling by financial advisors. The bank communicates to their customers that they have technology capabilities and offer true personal service. The objectives are building relationships based on trust and good faith.

Brick and mortar branches will continue to co-exist with "Internet-only" and "mobile-only" banks.

Case: Nationwide, UK[22]

- Nationwide in UK has 605 branches. In 2023, during its rebranding effort, the bank reiterated its commitment for face-to-face service, as it considers it invaluable to its customers.

Some banks have tried "bank on wheels." A mini bus equipped with customer service equipment that connect to the bank's network.

Personal interactions is mandatory for an industry in which fiduciary duty applies for many of its products.

---

[22] https://www.bbc.com/news/uk-england-wiltshire-67054588

CHAPTER 4 MONITORING OPERATING LEVERAGE

Operating Leverage Monitoring

Process Id		Process Type	B	▼	Process Description	Rationalisation of Branch Network	
Process Owner	Staff Id	Last Review Date	YYMMDD		Reviewed By	Staff Id	Last 5 Reviews: Summary ▼
		Process Cost Actual Proposed	$ $		Sub-Process id (if applicable)		Early Warning Signal (Y/N) Y

Review of the Bill of Resource

Activity-1		Activity-2		Activity-3		Activity-4	
Staff	System	Staff	System	Staff	System	Staff	System

Based on Branch profitability reports, the cost accountant submitted her recommendations to Senior Management on merger of branches. The senior management accepted the recommendation to rationalise the branch network.

Branch Productivity: Per Branch Indicators

Customer and account base

Deposits and advances per branch

Total income and total cost

Branch Cost

	Retail Banking	Corporate Banking	Total
Direct Cost	163,000,000	79,750,000	242,750,000
Indirect Cost			
Employee	40,000,000	35,000,000	75,000,000
Enterprise I.T. Governance	72,000,000	30,000,000	102,000,000
Premises	60,000,000	30,000,000	90,000,000
Office Supplies	20,000,000	25,000,000	45,000,000
Repairs & Maint.	10,000,000	5,000,000	15,000,000
Management	18,200,000	18,400,000	36,600,000
Support Services	43,800,000	45,000,000	88,800,000
Total	427,000,000	268,150,000	695,150,000

Process Automated, TDABC Cost of consumed resources

	Corporate	Retail
P&L	268,150,000	427,000,000
TDABC - Cost of consumed resources	227,927,500	341,600,000
Cost of Unutilised Resources	40,222,500	85,400,000
Utilisation Rate	85%	80%

Review of the Bill of Resource

Activity-1		Activity-2		Activity-3		Activity-4	
Staff	System	Staff	System	Staff	System	Staff	System

Based on Branch profitability reports, the cost accountant submitted her recommendations to Senior Management on merger of branches. The senior management accepted the recommendation to rationalise the branch network.

CHAPTER 4   MONITORING OPERATING LEVERAGE

The S&P Global, market intelligence report, mentions that the US banking industry closed 2927 branches, in 2021, as compared to 2126 branches in the previous year.[23]

How many banks in the world have taken decisions on branch rationalization with accurate actionable intelligence on resource utilization, branch profitability, and customer/customer segment profitability?

If banks close branches without actionable intelligence, it may not have a positive impact on their operational efficiency and operating leverage ratios.

Several countries have enacted laws that encourage competition and prevent concentration of economic power in the hands of few large banks.

4.4.3 Outsourcing

This has become the "de facto standard" for cost reduction. The banking industry should weigh the risks, costs, and benefits and take an informed decision.

Operating Leverage Monitoring									
Process Id		Process Type	B	▼	Process Description	Outsourcing			
Process Owner	Staff Id	Last Review Date			Reviewed By	Staff Id		Last 5 Reviews: Summary	▼
Product Id or Sub-Function Id:		Process Cost Actual Proposed	$ $		Sub-Process id (if applicable)			Early Warning Signal (Y/N)	Y
Review of the Bill of Resource									
		Activity-1		Activity-2		Activity-3		Activity-4	
		Staff	System	Staff	System	Staff	System	Staff	System
Based on Cost of Resources, Capacity and Resource Usage, the cost accountant submitted her recommendations to Senior Management on outsourcing of some banking activities.									

---

[23] https://www.spglobal.com/marketintelligence/en/news-insights/latest-news-headlines/us-bank-branch-closures-increase-38-to-new-record-high-in-21-68483121

CHAPTER 4   MONITORING OPERATING LEVERAGE

Process Automated, Time Driven Activity Based Costing
Cost of consumed resources

	Corporate	Treasury	Retail
P&L	268,150,000	209,850,000	427,000,000
TDABC - Cost of consumed resources	227,927,500	194,111,250	341,600,000
Cost of Unutilised Resources	40,222,500	15,738,750	85,400,000
Utilisation Rate	85%	92.5%	80%

Case: Indonesia – Court Judgement on Outsourcing

A panel of judges implicated a manager of Bank Mega Indonesia and other officers in a corruption case that involved the bank and a listed state oil and gas firm. The amount under investigation was Rp 111 billion.

The case had an outsourcing dimension to it, and the learned judge, after getting inputs from subject matter experts, identified certain points in the judgement as follows:

- Commercial banks will not be allowed to outsource *core business work*. This would include due diligence and enhanced due diligence processes, lending processes, and risk management decision-making. It does not include debt collection.

- Banks were instructed to implement *antifraud programs* to minimize business risk.

Prior to taking a decision, banks should consider the following points:

- The outsourcing risk includes vendor risk. Bank is accountable to its customer and other stakeholders, as outsourcing is not a transfer of risk.

CHAPTER 4 MONITORING OPERATING LEVERAGE

- Banks could have a significant operational risk exposure if core business areas, such as payment infrastructure, are outsourced.

	Correction / Improvement
Test Correction & Implement	Outsourcing proposal needs the approval of the Legal department; It is a Senior Management decision. An impact analysis is recommended.
Measure KPI and Residual Risk	Monitor Outsourcing SLA management. Low

How many banks in the world taken a decision on outsourcing after having accurate data on resource utilization and profitability?

- Case Study – Bank in Vietnam – outsourcing risk and SWIFT infrastructure

In 2015, TP Bank in Vietnam intercepted an attempt to make illegal SWIFT transfers and foiled the attempt. The bank could have lost $1.1 million. Staff skills prevented the attack. Later, the bank revealed that it used an outsourced infrastructure. The Vietnamese bank did not reveal the name of the service provider but stated that they had terminated the contract and moved the processing in-house.

- Case Study – ECB, bank losses, and guidance

ECB survey revealed that banks lost €148 million in 2022 due to "unavailability or poor quality of outsourced services." This was a 360 percent increase from 2021. The European Banking Authority released a guidelines on outsourcing arrangements. [24]

---

[24] https://eba.europa.eu/sites/default/files/documents/10180/2551996/38c80601-f5d7-4855-8ba3-702423665479/EBA%20revised%20Guidelines%20on%20outsourcing%20arrangements.pdf

The link provides the EBA guidelines on outsourcing arrangements [25]

- Case Study – Law on outsourcing in the Philippines[26]
- Case Study USA – 2013 FDIC guidance on managing outsourcing risk[27]
- Case Study UK – Outsourcing and operational resilience[28]

There is a consensus on (a) what should not be outsourced, (b) the risks remaining with the bank, and (c) the need to assess and monitor vendor risks.

4.4.4 Central Procurement

In many banks, procurement costs are higher than budgeted costs. It is important for banks to manage procurement as a specialized function and recruit staff who understand the bank's needs, have an understanding of the relevant markets, and have negotiation skills.

4.4.5 Carbon Footprint

4.4.5.1 Minimize Paper Usage

Many banks are improving their processes by significantly reducing paper-based procedures. This includes printed customer statements and passbook. Most banks have completely moved to digital statements and

---

[25] https://www.eba.europa.eu/sites/default/documents/files/documents/10180/2551996/38c80601-f5d7-4855-8ba3-702423665479/EBA%20revised%20Guidelines%20on%20outsourcing%20arrangements.pdf?retry=1
[26] https://elibrary.judiciary.gov.ph/thebookshelf/showdocs/10/41682
[27] https://www.dwt.com/-/media/files/blogs/financial-services-law-advisor/2021/07/fdic--guidance-on-managing-outsourcing-risk.pdf
[28] https://www.fca.org.uk/firms/outsourcing-and-operational-resilience

done away with passbooks. Lending is paper intensive, and retail products like mortgages have internal and external documents.

Digital signatures can be adopted for an efficient execution of agreements. It is important to note that contract finalization is a legal event and an e-signature-based service should be a substitution for (i) signature and stamp, (ii) demonstrate intent to sign, (iii) logically be associated with the rest of the document, and (iv) demonstrate execution and adoption.

This process improvement issue needs the approval of the legal department. The adoption of e-signatures across countries is not standard.

The following are examples of paperless office approach in banks:

- UK's Natwest successfully implemented paperless mortgage several years back. [29]

- 2023: Lloyds Bank introduced its paperless guarantee initiative. [30]

- Trade finance.

Bolero International, a trade finance software solution provider, provides digital trade services. Its Galileo platform connects the trade financing eco-system.

4.4.5.2 Green Data Centers

A green data center is *designed for maximum energy efficiency and minimum environmental impact.* The average age of data centers housing a bank's infrastructure is about 15 years.

---

[29] https://www.natwestgroup.com/news-and-insights/feature-content/our-updates/2011-2020/natwest-launches-uks-first-paperless-mortgage.html
[30] https://fintech.global/2023/10/10/lloyds-bank-launches-paperless-guarantee-initiative-to-boost-trade-efficiency/

CHAPTER 4   MONITORING OPERATING LEVERAGE

The infrastructure equipment is likely to be become inefficient and reach the end of its useful life. The old data centers are inconsistent with the environment protection regulations. Typical data centers use approximately two to three times the amount of power required for the IT equipment.

Reports mention that the cooling and electrical costs represent up to 44% of the total cost of data centers. Some banks cannot deploy more servers because extra electricity is not available easily. In an effort to improve their environment and lower costs of operation, many banks are already working toward reducing electricity and water usage at their data centers.

Several banks have made fundamental changes to the design of data centers with the objective of reducing energy demand. These banks are installing energy-efficient equipment and water-saving cooling devices.

Virtualization and cloud computing can be the biggest drivers for green computing.

At an operational level, the following are some best practices that could be part of EITG:

- Power down PCs after work and enable power management features.
- Upgrade to a newer, more efficient uninterruptible power supply (UPS).
- Prolong notebook battery life.
- Shift to networked laser printers and multifunction printers and copiers.
- Use energy-efficient computers and monitors.
- Consider adopting thin client solutions.
- Consolidate servers, storage and communications networks.

- Reduce travel with video conferencing and unified communications.
- Optimize data center temperature, improve airflow in center, and implement remote power and environment management systems
- Switch to enterprise digital content management.

Climate change is a supervisory priority in many mature countries. ECB's supervisory *priority-3* is managing a climate-related, environment risk.[31]

Enterprise liquidity management, branch network rationalization, outsourcing, central procurement, and carbon footprint are critical business decisions that banks are trying to manage efficiently and effectively.

The system and methodologies explained in this book can help a bank accomplish these strategic objectives.

4.5 Economy of Scale

It is perceived that larger banks are more operationally efficient than smaller ones. The common understanding is that they offer financial products for all needs and are more efficient than smaller banks, as they have better resources.

---

[31] https://www.bankingsupervision.europa.eu/banking/priorities/html/ssm.supervisory_priorities202212~3a1e609cf8.en.html

CHAPTER 4   MONITORING OPERATING LEVERAGE

However, the data in Tables 4-1a, 4-1b, and 4-1c of Section 4.1.1 of this chapter does not fully endorse this view.

The financial dimensions of economy of scale are important to manage. But that does not make smaller banks less profitable or make all large banks profitable.

Small and medium-sized banks can use the recommendations in this book to improve their operational efficiency and operating leverage. Enterprise risk-adjusted return management is not possible without an effective activity based enterprise noninterest cost management model.

In the next chapter, Section 5.2.1 explains efficiency structure theory. Economy of scale is one of the determinants of profits.

Case: New York Community Bancorp and Its Acquisitions[32]

NYCB grew its balance sheet very quickly by buying Signature Bank's loan book in 2023 and rival Flagstar in 2022. After the two acquisitions, NYBC's balance sheet had doubled to $120 billion.

In the last week of February 2024, the management of bank had identified material weakness in loan reviews. Rating agencies raised red flags over the bank's weak earnings, decline in its capitalization, and excessive reliance on wholesale funding. Moody's placed the bank's long-term and short-term ratings and assessments on a review for a downgrade.

Case: A McKinsey report titled "US midcap banking: The shakeout ahead?" dated June 30, 2021, provides data on several bank acquisitions in the United States. The following are important conclusions from an operating leverage perspective: [33]

---

[32] https://www.reuters.com/breakingviews/if-only-banks-were-more-like-chemical-factories-2024-03-01/

[33] https://www.mckinsey.com/industries/financial-services/our-insights/us-midcap-banking-the-shakeout-ahead#/

The midcap mergers are not a success story in recent times. McKinsey uses a proprietary ratio called **combined value creation** that uses the percentage change in companies' combined market cap to determine the success of the merged entity.

The report revealed that the acquiring banks often lose value and/or create little of it.

From the perspective of this book, the author opines that the success of the merged entity depends on the synergy in business model and the successful integration of enterprise operating models.

4.6 Capabilities and Capacity

Capabilities and capacity provide a strong foundation for business growth and for building a strong brand name. This is illustrated in Figure 4-23. Well-governed banks have created centers of excellence (COE) for specific functional and technical areas. A bank's ability to compete is directly related to their ability to attract, develop, motivate, organize, and retain talented people.

Workforce competency includes knowledge, soft skills, and adopting best practices. Competency-based assets include **enterprise architecture design, enterprise data model, knowledge management data model, ERRM and ENICM models, and process inventory.**

Hyperautomation for Enterprise Operating Model efficiency

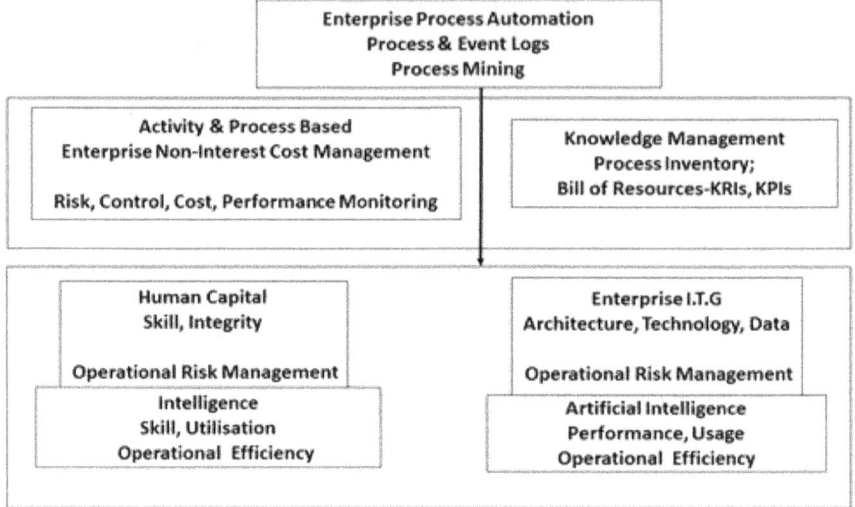

Figure 4-23. Mandatory capabilities

Business models are being re-defined, and banks are attempting to transform into a data-centric enterprise architecture model that drives customer centric business objectives. While automation introduces technology risks, it is the technology that has enabled a 24/7 operating environment and provided the capability to process a very high volume and a variety of banking transactions, without any geographical constraint.

The next chapter explains the methods, tools, and techniques that can be used to improve operating leverage.

CHAPTER 5

Improving Operating Leverage

This chapter is on improving the operating leverage of a bank. Section 5.1 makes a case for a continuous operating leverage improvement program. Section 5.2 introduces relevant theories, and Section 5.3 provides an overview of relevant methodologies. The theories and methods can be used to improve enterprise operating model efficiency and effectiveness.

Section 5.4 explains the tools for improving operational efficiency and operating leverage, and Section 5.5 provides guidance on the implementation of the improvement measures. The standardization of the process-based enterprise operating model, continuous process improvement, advanced analytics, and knowledge management are critical success factors for improving operating leverage. Finally, Section 5.6 provides an approach for quantifying and improving operating leverage.

5.1 Continuous Operating Leverage Improvement Program

It is important that performance ratios are understood in the overall perspective of business growth, competitive position, and business and technology trends. It is not advisable to focus on a few ratios. The ratios should be analyzed in a holistic manner to form an opinion on enterprise risk-adjusted return.

CHAPTER 5   IMPROVING OPERATING LEVERAGE

In this regard, a World Bank paper titled "Measuring Commercial Bank Efficiency: Use and Misuse of Operating Ratios"[1] 1991, is still relevant.

The article submits that a comparison of ratios of banks in different countries should take into consideration the capital structure, product portfolios, accounting standards, and the domestic economy. Even if some ratios are "standard" and can add value for a comparison, good knowledge of local practices is necessary for drawing conclusions.

Even within a country, regulatory requirements could differ depending on asset size and/or capital. For instance, in the United States, banks of a certain size are exempted from publishing their LCR and NSFR.

In its report titled "Beyond Return in Equity – How to Measure Bank Performance," ECB emphasizes the need to maintain consistency of the bank's risk appetite with the business structure and strategy. The institution urged the banking industry to develop sustainable performance indicators that are based on economic models and financial planning frameworks. *The author humbly submits that the operating leverage metric is fit for this purpose.*[2]

When banks are in financial trouble, the first "tactical" step is cost cutting. In most cases, it is a knee-jerk reaction to a self-inflicted adverse business situation. Further, this is done with accounting data rather than accurate cost data on staff, product, customer, and branch profitability.

---

[1] https://documents1.worldbank.org/curated/en/568891468739781885/pdf/multi-page.pdf

[2] https://www.ecb.europa.eu/pub/pdf/other/beyondroehowtomeasurebankperformance201009en.pdf

ENICM and ERRM systems can provide actionable intelligence. Section 4.4 of the previous chapter provides examples on actionable intelligence for decision-making in critical business areas.

This "tactical step" could involve pruning the headcount numbers, hiving off profitable businesses, or closing down some branches. In the short term, the cost control measures will show "results" in the books of account. However, from a long-term strategy perspective, these measures could end up being counterproductive if the underlying data is not accurate and wholesome.

Case: In November 2023, Citigroup announced its first round of layoffs as part of the bank's massive restructuring project, code-named "**Project Bora Bora.**" The objective is to eliminate thousands of positions. [3]

Table 5-1a provides an extract of Citigroup's Quarterly Financial Data Supplement 2023. Please take note of the efficiency ratios. [4]

Table 5-1a. *Citigroup 2023 financial summary*

Citigroup Financial Summary – (amount in $millions)					
Row item description	3Q2022	4Q2022	1Q 2023	2Q 2023	3Q2023
Total revenue, net of interest expense	18,508	18,006	21,447	19,436	20,139
Total Operating expenses	12,749	12,985	13,289	13,570	13,511
Regulatory capital ratios and Performance Metrics					
Return on average assets	0.58%	0.41%	0.76%	0.47%	0.58%
Return on average common equity	7.1%	5.0%	9.5%	5.6%	6.7%
Efficiency Ratio – Total Operating expenses / Total Net revenue	**68.9%**	**72.1%**	**62.0%**	**69.8%**	**67.1%**

---

[3] https://www.reuters.com/business/finance/citigroup-employees-expect-management-reshuffle-layoffs-monday-sources-2023-11-17/

[4] https://www.citigroup.com/rcs/citigpa/storage/public/Earnings/Q32023/3Q23-SUPP-For-WEB.pdf

CHAPTER 5   IMPROVING OPERATING LEVERAGE

Table 5-1b. Citigroup's operating performance metrics

	As-is: 3Q 2023	Points flagged by the author **Bora Bora KPIs – 2024–2026 trend**
Profitability[5] or cost to income		
Revenue/employee	$423,304	**Above 500,000?**
Income/employee	$62,346	**Above 75,000?**
Operational efficiency	Efficiency ratio 67.1%	**Will bank achieve 50% with very limited volatility (2% maximum)?**

If there is NO significant improvement in the operational efficiency trend in subsequent years, we can conclude the Bora Bora initiative was another *cost control exercise* that reflects weak governance.

Case – Barclays[6]

In November 2023, Barclays (BARC.L) announced a plan to cut 2,000 jobs and reduce its operating expenses by about one billion pounds ($1.25 billion) over several years. This headcount reduction is at its Barclays Execution Services, **known internally as "BX."**

---

[5] https://www.wsj.com/market-data/quotes/C/financials
[6] https://www.reuters.com/business/finance/barclays-working-125-bln-cost-plan-could-cut-up-2000-jobs-source-2023-11-23/https://home.barclays/investor-relations/reports-and-events/annual-reports/
https://home.barclays/investor-relations/reports-and-events/financial-results/
Appendix in Barclays Group Annual Report
https://home.barclays/investor-relations/reports-and-events/annual-reports/

CHAPTER 5   IMPROVING OPERATING LEVERAGE

The 1 billion pound cost-saving target represents about 7% of the bank's underlying annual operating expenses of 15 billion pounds in 2022.

Table 5-2a provides an overview of Barclays Group's cost-to-income ratios over 3 years.

Table 5-2a. Barclays Group's cost-to-income ratios over three years[7]

Barclays Group – (amount in £millions)					
Row item description	2021	2022	1Q 2023	2Q 2023	3Q2023
Total Income	21940	24956	7237	6285	6258
Total Operating expenses	14659	16730	4110	3952	3949
Regulatory capital ratios and Performance Metrics					
Return on average tangible shareholders equity	13.1%	10.4%	15%	11.4%	12.5%
Cost to income ratio	67%	67%	57%	63%	61%
Loan loss rate (bps)	(18)	30	52	37	43

Table 5-2b. Barclays's operating performance metrics

	2024–2030 trend
Profitability[8] or cost to income	
Revenue/employee	Not published
Income/employee	Not published
Operational efficiency	Not published
Cost-to-income ratio	**Point raised by author: Will the trend between 2024 and 2030 be 50% with very limited volatility (2% maximum)?**
Operating leverage	Not published

---

[7] https://home.barclays/content/dam/home-barclays/documents/investor-relations/ResultAnnouncements/H12023Results/Barclays-H12023-Results-Announcement.pdf
[8] https://www.wsj.com/market-data/quotes/C/financials

CHAPTER 5 IMPROVING OPERATING LEVERAGE

If the bank fails to significantly improve its operating performance metrics, then we can conclude that the "Operation BX" was a cost control exercise that reflects weak governance.

Tables 5-3a and 5-3b illustrate the imperative need for operational performance metrics that reflect risk, not just operational risk but also the causal link between other risk types and operational risk. The enterprise liquidity hub is one of the operational aspects of enterprise liquidity management.

Case: A comparison of the enterprise liquidity position of Citigroup & Barclays.

Table 5-3a. *The enterprise liquidity position of Barclays and Citigroup for a period of 30 months*[9]

Liquidity Coverage Ratio, Net Stable Funding Ratio

Row item description	CitiGroup			Barclays Group		
	2021	2022	Jun2023	2021	2022	Jun2023
Liquidity Coverage Ratio	115 %	118%		151%	165%	158%
Net Stable Funding Ratio	Not Reported		125%	Not Reported	137%	139%

(i) Citi's average NSFR for the quarter ended June 30, 2023 was **125%**
(ii) Barclays: 2022 figure represents average of the last four spot quarter end positions;
2023 LCR & NSFR is for 6months – as at 30Jun 2023.

This book's recommendations for Enterprise Architecture, Data Management, Operating Model and Process Automation can significantly improve enterprise liquidity management.

From the details, Barclays Group appears to be having higher HQLAs than Citigroup. Similarly, Barclays' NSFR provides more liquidity comfort.

---

[9] https://www.citigroup.com/rcs/citigpa/storage/public/lcr230630.pdf
https://www.citigroup.com/global/investors/annual-reports-and-proxy-statements
https://home.barclays/investor-relations/reports-and-events/annual-reports/

CHAPTER 5   IMPROVING OPERATING LEVERAGE

Case: Credit Suisse

Risk Culture and Enterprise Liquidity Management

Liquidity risk transformed into Solvency risk after a series of scandals[10].

A UBS press release[11] dated June 12, 2023, stated that Credit Suisse Group AG merged into UBS Group AG, and the combined entity is operating as a consolidated banking group.

Table 5-3b provides an extract of the data in the 2022 annual report. The data brings out the **importance of analyzing data holistically.** *Operational efficiency and operating leverage should be understood in the context of the P&L, balance sheet, and off-balance sheet items.*

Table 5-3b. *Credit Suisse ratios*

Annual Report 2022 Credit Suisse Group AG: Extract of relevant data for 3 years

	2022	2021	2020
Net Revenue (**NR**)	14,921	22,696	22,389
Provision for credit losses	16	4205	1,096
Total Operating Expenses (**TOE**)	18,163	19,091	17,826
Cost to Income ratio - %	121.7	84.1	79.6
Return on Equity - %	(16.1)	(3.8)	5.9
Return on Tangible Equity - %	(17.4)	(4.2)	6.6
Operational Efficiency or Cost to Income ratio (**TOE/(NR)**), calculated by author	121.72	84.11	79.6
	Provision for credit losses excluded		

For tangible equity ratio, intangible assets, such as goodwill, are subtracted from the average shareholders' equity balance.

---

[10] Considering liquidity and solvency interactions and systemic risk November 2015 https://www.bis.org/bcbs/publ/wp29.pdf

[11] https://www.ubs.com/global/en/media/display-page-ndp/en-20230612-ubs-credit-suisse-acquisition.html

CHAPTER 5   IMPROVING OPERATING LEVERAGE

It is interesting that Credit Suisse, in its Annual Report for 2022, mentioned "liquidity coverage ratio (LCR) and the net stable funding ratio (NSFR) at the Group level **were maintained at all times."** The NSFR had fallen. [12]

Annual Report 2022 Credit Suisse Group AG: Extract of LCR, NSFR
CHF Million

	2022	2021
Liquidity Coverage Ratio		
High Quality Liquid assets	119,954	227,193
Net cash outflows	83,202	112.156
LCR %	144	203
Net Stable Funding Ratio		
Available Stable Funding	343,158	436,856
Required Stable Funding	292,524	342,870
Net Stable Funding ratio	117	127

Banks do not publish data on (i) profitability and their noninterest cost management methodology, (ii) operational efficiency, and (iii) operating leverage. Banks do not report risk-adjusted net interest margin and the same applies to the cost-to-income ratio. This adversely impacts the performance assessment made by investors, rating agencies, banking supervisor, and other stake holders.

A continuous operating leverage improvement program can enable banks to proactively improve process efficiency and enterprise model effectiveness.

---

[12] https://www.credit-suisse.com/about-us/en/reports-research/annual-reports.html

5.2 Theoretical Base for Operating Leverage

5.2.1 Efficiency Structure Theory

In 1966, Harvey Leibenstein submitted that **efficiency** is the "central determinant of profits" and is the metric that should be used for understanding the differences in profitability amongst firms. According to this theory, a more efficient firm is in a better position to gain more profits than a less efficient firm. This theory uses two metrics, X-efficiency and scale efficiency.

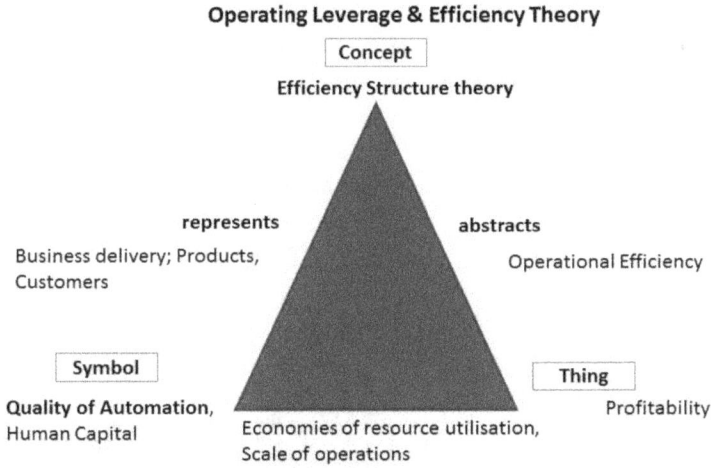

Figure 5-1. *Efficiency Structure theory concept*

The focus of X-efficiency is on technology, and the focus of scale efficiency is on the volume of business, i.e., number of customers, customer account, transactions, and the product portfolio. Please note that volume of business is more relevant for commercial banks that have a large retail base.

CHAPTER 5   IMPROVING OPERATING LEVERAGE

The efficiency theory is consistent with hyperautomation and activity-based enterprise noninterest cost management model explained in this book. Continuous process improvement ensures that the bill of resources is constantly reviewed and the corrective action is taken during the monitoring of operating leverage. This paves the way for better utilization of resources.

5.2.2 Resource-Based Theory

From a banking perspective, the resource-based theory is interesting as it obliquely touches upon capital adequacy and intangibles such as goodwill. Goodwill is linked to the more tangible "brand value." Therefore, the theory can be understood as one with a long-term focus.

Figure 5-2 submits that operational efficiency = "f (financial capital, human capital, technology)."

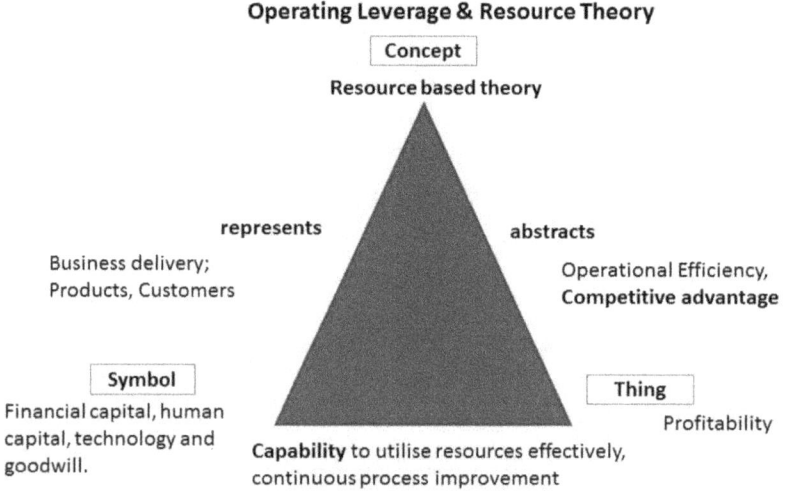

Figure 5-2. *Resource-based theory concept*

Effective utilization of available resources is a critical success factor for improving operating leverage.

CHAPTER 5   IMPROVING OPERATING LEVERAGE

A data-centric, services-based, process-automated enterprise noninterest cost management system, driven by analytics and powered by knowledge management, offers the best of both the above theories.

Performance ratios are not static numbers, and it varies by business cycles and situations. Operating leverage is positive when revenue growth is higher than expense growth. An interesting aspect of revenue growth is that wide spreads could boost revenue and overstate operating *leverage*, and on the flip side, a flat yield curve can understate it.

It is recommended that banks identify and *remove atypical movements in data* from the calculations and provide an explanatory note, rather than avoid publishing the operating leverage.

Managing operational efficiency and leverage are critical success factors for obtaining the desired rating. Figure 5-3 should be understood in the context of the efficient structure and resource theories.

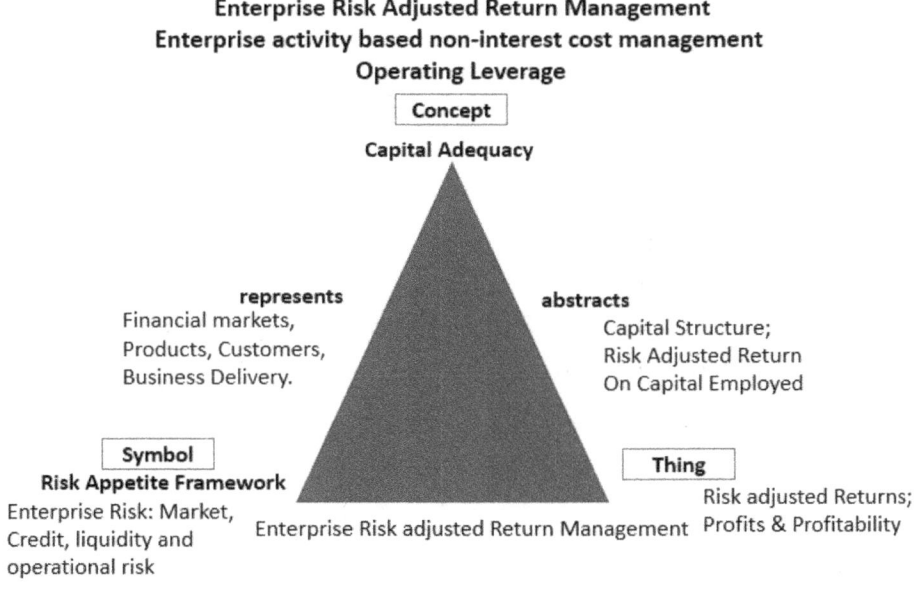

Figure 5-3. *Capital adequacy concept*

Bank Rating

The four pillars of a bank's rating are

i. Capital Adequacy – As determined using risk-weighted assets, stressed liquidity, and leveraged ratios

ii. Stable and easy access to funding and maintaining liquidity, as evaluated under stressed periods by (a) cost of funding and (b) leverage ratio

iii. Stable earnings growth

iv. Stakeholder confidence as reflected in (a) category/peer rating and (b) reputation

---

Risk-adjusted operating leverage provides an insight into points iii and iv above.

5.3 Methods: Improving Operating Leverage

Enterprise noninterest cost management comprises activities that can be grouped under cost of delivering business and another set of activities that fall under cost of risk management. An ERRM model is a capability that harmoniously blends these two distinct, yet intertwined, set of business and risk management activities.

5.3.1 Total Quality Management (TQM)

TQM is a customer-oriented culture that is committed to designing, building, and delivering products and services of the highest quality. TQM's three dimensions are quality control (the past), quality assurance (present), and the *forward-looking quality management.*

The important aspects of the method are

- The ability to identify the market and customer segments

- The ability to understand customer behavior and identify customer expectations

- Defining a mechanism to incorporate market feedback into decision-making

- Selecting a relevant quality benchmark and compare the bank's performance with competitors

- The implementation of quality improvement measures

All the above can be achieved with an effective enterprise data and knowledge management programs, explained in Sections 5.4.1 and 5.4.2.

5.3.2 Sarbanes–Oxley Act (SOX) – Sec 404 and Sec 302

SOX recommends a risk-based approach using the 80-20 principle. This approach can be customized for *performance, risk, control, and cost* (PRCC) monitoring in a bank.

CHAPTER 5   IMPROVING OPERATING LEVERAGE

Sec 302 of Sarbanes–Oxley Act defines the corporate responsibility for financial reports, and Sec 404 defines the management's assessment of internal controls. The quality of financial reporting is dependent on the quality of data. Figure 5-4 provides a flavor of a customized SOX approach for accomplishing operational efficiency objective.

SEC's 2003 White Paper Proposing Practical, Cost Effective Compliance Strategies is a useful read even from an operational efficiency perspective.[13]

SOX could be used to identify the value of business delivered by lines of business, products, and profit centers. For example, for treasury, derivative business could be an activity group for leverage monitoring and improvement.

The 80-20 principle can be interpreted in the following manner:

Risk

Twenty percent of the processes that contribute to 80% of the operational risk incidents

Twenty percent of threats and vulnerabilities that contribute to 80% of the operational risk exposure

Revenue and Returns

Twenty percent of staff that contribute to 80% of the revenue

Twenty percent of the products that contribute to 80% of the revenue

---

[13] https://www.sec.gov/files/rules/proposed/s74002/card941503.pdf

CHAPTER 5   IMPROVING OPERATING LEVERAGE

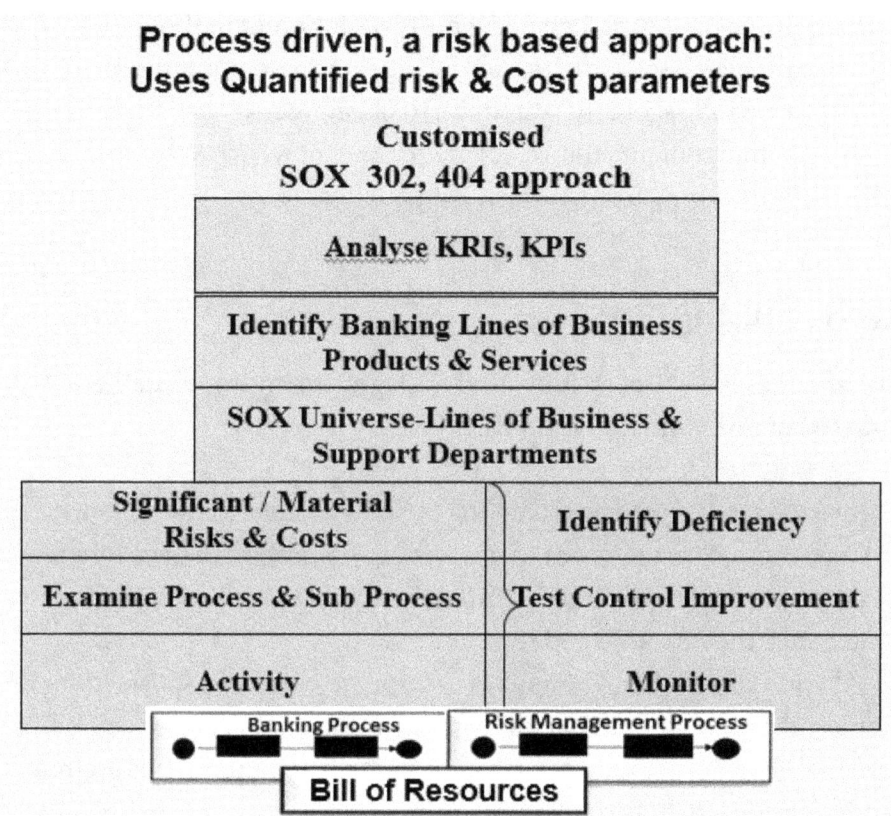

Figure 5-4. *SOX approach to operational efficiency*

Please note 80-20 is not a thumb rule. For instance, in the case of human capital, the bank wants to identify 60% of the staff that bring in 90% of the revenue or 40% of the products that bring in 90% of the revenue.

This could be understood from the following perspectives:

- Accounting Perspective – In this, the financial statements of the institution's data are analyzed to identify the *value of business delivered* by lines of business, products, and relationship managers/profit centers.

425

CHAPTER 5   IMPROVING OPERATING LEVERAGE

- Nonaccounting Perspective – Risks inherent in the process because of (a) lack of an enterprise noninterest cost management system, (b) lack of process improvement culture, (c) inadequate enterprise control framework, and (d) weak data quality.

5.3.3 Six Sigma[14]

Several banks have successfully used Six Sigma to improve **business growth and risk-adjusted returns**. [15]

The rationale for the approach is as follows:

Everything is a process (banking business delivery components/activities can be broken down to processes). All processes have inherent risks, and enterprise data management is critical to understand, identify, and manage the risk-adjusted returns.

The primary goal of Six Sigma is to improve customer satisfaction. By reducing defects (operational incidents), profitability is increased. While there have been other quality programs with good content, this approach stands apart for the following reasons:

- It focuses on business delivery.
- Approach is feasible as it *does not have a zero defect bias*.

Figure 5-5 illustrates the focus of the processes by emphasizing on front-, middle-, and back-office functions.

---

[14] https://asq.org/quality-resources/six-sigma
[15] https://www.isixsigma.com/financial-services/bank-america-hoshin-kanri-and-six-sigma/

CHAPTER 5 IMPROVING OPERATING LEVERAGE

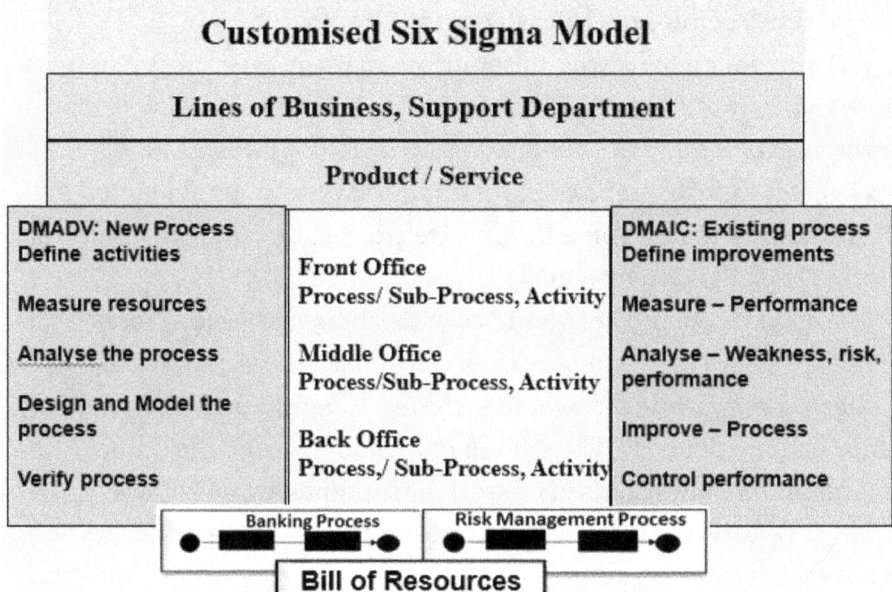

Figure 5-5. Customized Six Sigma for improving operational efficiency

The Six Sigma is a data-driven approach and methodology for eliminating defects. A process *must not produce more than 3.4 defects in a million opportunities.*

The two methodologies for a Six Sigma approach are the following:

The **DMADV** process (define, measure, analyze, design, verify) is an approach for developing new processes or products.

The **DMAIC** process (define, measure, analyze, improve, control) is an approach to define existing processes and improving process inefficiencies.

427

CHAPTER 5   IMPROVING OPERATING LEVERAGE

5.3.4 ITIL and ITSM

Information Technology Infrastructure Library

ITIL provides a bank with the ability to manage their processes in a cost-effective way and is a good source of best practices. *ITIL is neither a standard nor a set of rules or regulations. ITIL is a framework, not a solution.* It is industry agnostic, and some banks have implemented the ITIL framework to build an efficient enterprise IT governance framework (referred to as **EITG** in this book).

ITIL focuses on and enables IT services to be managed across their lifecycle by creating and using a centralized *service knowledge management database* that would include configuration items, changes, events, and incidents. ITIL has seven core modules, and the scope, contents, and relationships of the various modules are as follows:

```
https://www.axelos.com/certifications/itil-service-
management/
```

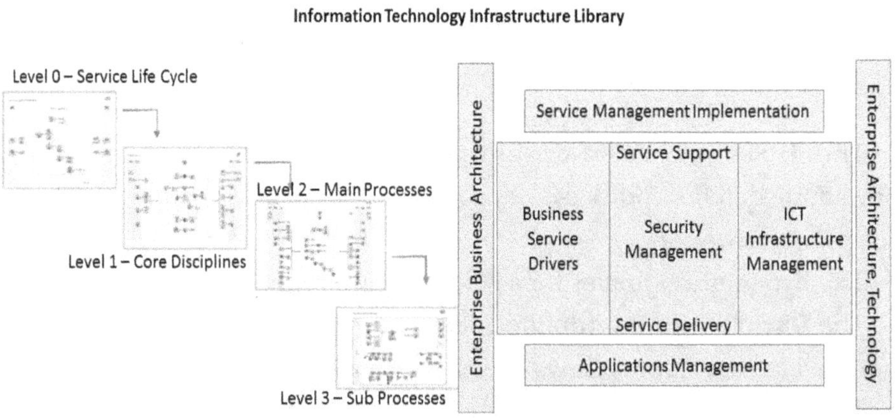

Figure 5-6. ITIL governance process framework

i. The **business perspective** provides guidance on the alignment of EITG functions with business needs and requirements.

ii. **Service delivery** covers the processes required for the planning and delivery of quality IT services and looks at the longer term processes associated with improving the quality of IT services delivered.

iii. **Service support** describes the processes associated with the day-to-day support and maintenance activities associated with the provision of IT services.

iv. **ICT infrastructure management** covers the identification of business requirements, the tendering process, testing, installation, deployment, and ongoing operation optimization of the ICT components and IT services.

v. **Application management (risk model development falls under this)** covers all stages in the application lifecycle. It places emphasis on ensuring that IT projects and strategies are tightly aligned with business requirements, to ensure that the business obtains best value from its investment.

vi. **Security management** details the process of planning, baselining, and managing the residual risks. It also includes the assessment and management of risks and vulnerabilities and the implementation of countermeasures that are consistent with the *risk appetite statement.*

The Sarbanes–Oxley Act mandates that organizations benchmark their internal control systems against best practices frameworks such as COSO (Committee of Sponsoring Organizations) and COBIT (Control Objectives for Information and Related Technology).

CHAPTER 5   IMPROVING OPERATING LEVERAGE

The identification of the risk, improving the controls and testing of the same, **is an iterative process.** The residual risk at the process level should be monitored and kept below the risk appetite of the bank.

Case Studies – Six Sigma, ITIL ISIM

Case: An international bank with its headquarters in the United States successfully implemented a **lean Six Sigma project**.[16]

Benefits:

- Missing items on customer statements were reduced by 70%.
- Defects in electronic channels decreased by 88%.
- Mortgage applications reduced average cycle time by 15 days.
- Noncredit losses, including fraud, were driven down by 28% on a per-account basis.
- Same-day payments improved by 22%.
- Deposit processing by 35%.
- The cumulative financial benefits exceeded $2 billion.
- The **customer delight metric** has increased by 25% across the bank.

IT Services Management (ITSM) Case: Saudi Hollandi Bank – The bank's challenge was to manage a complex IT environment in a scenario where the go-to market was slow and support for lines of business was inefficient.

---

[16] https://www.lasaterinstitute.com/casestudy/Financial%20Services/Bank%20of%20America(Lean%20Six%20Sigma).pdf

Statement of Work

The bank wanted to streamline the IT support function and gain visibility of the data in their applications. They had no tool in the IT department to manage key functions. After considerable information gathering, an assessment was made to use a best of the breed tool and focus on processes. They chose ITIL's service management.

Key Benefits

- Incident resolution time improved
- Better go-to market time for business
- Cost reduction

ITIL Case: Arab Bank wanted a tool to govern technology. The focus was on (a) preventive and detective controls, (b) productivity, (c) process ownership, and (d) alignment of functional and technical goals.

Statement of Work

The bank preferred to use ITIL and chose a vendor for assisting with ITIL implementation.

Key Benefits

- Asset control improved
- Bank standardized several service functions and was able to reduce costs through economies of scale

ITIL Case: GH Bank chose ITIL for improving efficiency.

Statement of Work

Management approved a project that was overseen by a group of experts belonging to business, IT, quality improvement, audit, and risk management.

The disciples implemented were (i) service strategy, (ii) design, (iii) transition, (iv) operations, and (v) continuous service improvement.

CHAPTER 5   IMPROVING OPERATING LEVERAGE

Key Benefits

Improvements in

- Staff productivity
- Service Quality – Able to deliver standardized services
- IT Capability – For creating value
- Competitive Advantage – Quicker go-to market, better business deliver

Total quality management (TQM), benchmarking, and business process reengineering (BPR) are examples of *horizontal management improvement initiatives*.

5.3.5   Causal Analysis of Enterprise Risk

This is an improved version of Figure 4-12 in Section 4.3.2, Part C, Root Cause Analysis in Chapter 4. The improvement highlights the need to factor market, credit, and liquidity risks that can be traced to operational weakness in measuring and managing operating leverage.

Operational risk is inherent in all business activities, as all business activities are influenced by one or more of the following: (i) staff, (ii) system, (iii) policy, (iv) procedure, (v) external threat, or (vi) risk culture. Therefore, operational risk can have a causal link to liquidity, market, and credit risks. Figure 5-7 highlights operating leverage metric's relationship with risks by placing it as the 'fish head'.

The fishbone diagram illustrates a methodology for causal analysis. The risk, weakness, and threat are identified and analyzed in the context of causation factors and other risk types.

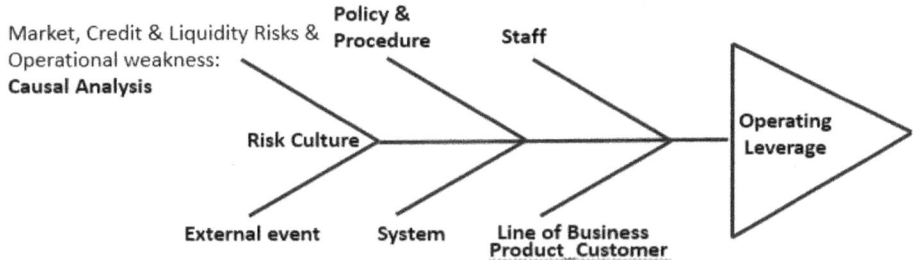

Figure 5-7. Operating Leverage is a component of ERRM

5.3.5.1 Causal Analysis – Operational and Market Risk Factors

Rogue Trade

A derivative dealer's unauthorized trades led to losses of $2.3billion for its exchange traded funds business in a mature financial market. He was convicted for fraud and was sentenced to a seven-year jail term.

Risk preventive methodology is to have a process-based risk-adjusted, enterprise operating model that is compliant with SOX302 and 404 provisions. The causation could be one or more of the following:

- A Know Your Employee program failure.

- The recruitment, employee's performance, and behavior monitoring processes could be weak.

- Bonus package is not based on long-term performance.

- The segregation of duties, dual control, and exceptions management procedures could be weak.

5.3.5.2 Causal Analysis – Operational and Credit Risk Factors

Staff Skills

In trade financing, coacceptance of a bill is an undertaking by the bank to make payment to the drawer of the bill (exporter) on the due date even if the importer fails to make the payment on the due date. If the bank officer fails to conduct a proper due diligence, the transaction could turn out to be an *"accommodation bill" between two related firms*. This is a fraudulent financing technique to obtain a loan with no underlying trade. In almost all such situations, banks fail to recover the loan.

Operational weaknesses include staff skill or an internal fraud. Human capital management system is weak in many banks. In fact, small- and medium-sized banks have only a payroll system.

System

Corporate Loans and Collateral Management

Banks should have good collateral management system that facilitates document management, mark to market valuations and dynamic checking of loan to collateral value ratio.

Operational weakness could be in collateral:

- Valuation
- Expiry checking
- Redemption or
- Release processes

5.3.5.3 Causal Analysis – Operational and Liquidity Risk Factors

Treasury-Centralized Real-Time Collateral Management[17]
Real-Time Centralized Collateral Management

Collateral management has transitioned from a "support function" to a **center of excellence.** The function cut across lines of business, asset classes, and front-, middle-, and back-office functions. Business and regulatory requirements are forcing banks to centralize their treasury's collateral management system. A wrong choice or improper use of collateral can negatively affect business returns. To avoid these risks, a bank will need a single view of the full inventory of collaterals.

Managing collaterals and exposures with the objective of improving the risk-adjusted return on capital (RAROC) is not an easy task. The assignment of collateral from a collateral pool is a dynamic activity in intraday liquidity management. The pool requires dynamic adjustments for market and counterparty changes. Banks have to avoid an excess collateral situation, as this could impair portfolio return.

Posted collateral is evaluated for its funding and opportunity cost. A bank might be forced to post cash as collateral, if no other eligible asset is available. As this could adversely affect the business return, banks need real-time data to evaluate the impact of posting cash instead of offering instruments as collateral.

Real-time centralized collateral management system helps to

- Achieve visibility into the collateral inventory across functions
- Ensure all collateral schedules and legal agreements are easily accessible

---

[17] Developments in collateral management services September 2014
https://www.bis.org/cpmi/publ/d119.pdf

- Take a centralized view of different types of obligations and requirements

- Efficiently use collateral in a manner that reduces the loss given default and help avoid overcollateralization, as it freezes capital without generating any return

Weak treasury collateral management processes adversely impact risk-adjusted operating leverage.

Enterprise Liquidity Hub (ELH)
Operational Support for Enterprise Liquidity Management
The **enterprise liquidity hub (ELH)** is a centralized pool of cash for a bank. The pool is common for all lines of business and support functions. A data- and event-driven, services-based, process-automated enterprise architecture can ensure that ELH data is at all times consistent with the books of account. The following are core features of the ELH:

- Maturing time periods of assets and liabilities.

- Scheduled cash inflows and outflows include those arising contractual obligations.

- Projected outflows from liabilities that can reprice overnight (such as savings deposits).

- Estimated drawdowns of undrawn commitments.

- Contingent liquidity risks in derivative transactions.

- Real-time processing needs, i.e., volumes of cash flows.

- Internal integration needs with accounting and collateral management systems.

- External integration needs with clearing and settlement systems.

An efficient enterprise risk management framework can provide a capability to manage risks on an intraday basis. Banks may need to restructure their organization so that enterprise liquidity management (ELM) becomes a center of excellence. The intraday liquidity is about managing dynamic transitions in cash positions during the day and is driven by a configurable time factor. It is a core component of enterprise liquidity risk management, which, in turn, is at the core of the enterprise risk-adjusted return (ERRM) model.

ALM has emerged as a science where both sides of the balance sheet have to be holistically and dynamically managed to mitigate interest rate, market, and liquidity risks. The ELH is a mandatory capability for enterprise liquidity management. The lack of an ELH will adversely impact risk-adjusted operating leverage.

> Risk-adjusted operating leverage is an important measure of enterprise risk-adjusted return management.

5.3.5.4 Supervisory Reports on US Bank Failures

The following three cases are examples for causal analysis that trace the causation of other risks to operational risk. Operating leverage goes beyond operational risk and also includes the operational activities that support business functions that can trigger market, credit, and liquidity risks.

Abbreviations

  i. MRBA – Matters Requiring Board Attention

  ii. SR – Supervisory Recommendation

CHAPTER 5   IMPROVING OPERATING LEVERAGE

Case: Signature Bank, FDIC Press Release 2023[18]

Signature Bank	2021	2020	2019
Net interest income A	1880	1519	1312
Non-interest income-B	121	75	62
Non-interest expense-C	704	614	529
Operational efficiency ratio- Calculated by author from available data (C/(A+B))	35.18	38.52	38.5

With reference to FDIC's report, the following are relevant:

- Page 9 mentions that the bank failed to implement preventive controls and have a case management that supports proactive risk management.

- Page 10 mentions that failure of the bank to conduct stress tests. As explained in Section 4.3.3.8, Example xxx, the operational aspects of stress testing includes enterprise data and a risk model that is fit for purpose.

- Page 19 mentions model risk management and anti-money laundering (Model) are the responsibility of governance, risk, and compliance.

- Page 55 mentions numerous issues related to enterprise IT governance. It includes vulnerability identification and management, risk assessment, asset inventory, and business continuity management.

FDIC's statement on the failure of Signature Bank mentions governance, balance sheet structure, and failure to manage enterprise liquidity.

---

[18] https://www.fdic.gov/news/press-releases/2023/pr23033a.pdf

CHAPTER 5   IMPROVING OPERATING LEVERAGE

Case: Silicon Valley Bank[19]

Silicon Valley Bank	2022	2021
Net interest income	4485	3179
Provisions for credit losses	420	123
Non-interest income	1728	2738
Non-interest expense	3621	3070
Operational efficiency ratio	3621/(4485+1728)= 58.28%	51.88%

Page 4 of FDIC's reports mentions that the bank's risk management capacity failed to keep up with rapid asset growth. This implies that the operational support for enterprise risk-adjusted return management was weak.

Case: First Republic Bank[20]

2022: First Republic Bank
Revenues: $5.9 billion
Net Interest Income: $4.8 billion
Efficiency Ratio: 61.7%

Page 2 of FDIC's report mentions weaknesses in risk management processes and controls. Page 59 of 62 again mentions weakness in risk management processes.

---

[19] https://www.federalreserve.gov/publications/files/svb-review-20230428.pdf

[20] https://www.fdic.gov/news/press-releases/2023/pr23073a.pdf

CHAPTER 5   IMPROVING OPERATING LEVERAGE

Page 23

- Dodd-Frank Act Stress Test – Model risk management (MRM)
- Operations Risk – Business process controls and information security program

---

The three banks failed because of governance and structural balance sheet problems. But the performance ratios in their quarterly results and annual reports **did not provide an early warning signal of an impending** crisis.

There is an imperative need to have risk-adjusted performance metrics. This includes operating leverage that reflects performance, risk, control, and cost.

5.3.5.5 FDIC Chairman

Martin J. Gruenberg, Chairman, FDIC – Statement Before Committee on Financial Services, US House of Representatives – November 15, 2023[21]

Page 12 of 26 mentions weakness of operational capabilities in banks. This is related to payment, clearing, and settlement activities; collateral; management information systems; and shared and outsourced services.

The case studies on the three banks that collapsed in the United States in 2023 emphasize the need for banks to have enterprise risk-adjusted return (ERRM) capability. Risk-adjusted operating leverage is linked to ERRM.

---

[21] https://docs.house.gov/meetings/BA/BA00/20231115/116578/HHRG-118-BA00-Wstate-GruenbergM-20231115.pdf

5.3.6 Improved Operational Risk Management

This is a continuation of the narration on enterprise risk-adjusted return management in Sections 4.2 and 4.3 of Chapter 4.

The following granular data items are needed at the activity or activity group level for operational risk management:

- The system components used by the activity or activity group
- Staff identifier
- Policy and procedure that applies to execution of the business activities
- Relevant control Id for the activity
- Cost of the activity
- The key risk and performance indicators

As explained earlier, process automation can provide the above data at the activity/process level for managing operational risks.

Table 5-4 provides an overview of the tools that can be used for an effective operational risk management. The success of improvement measures depends on a standardized enterprise operating model, human capital, processes, the usage of an EITG tool, and advanced analytics.

CHAPTER 5   IMPROVING OPERATING LEVERAGE

Table 5-4. Tools for managing operational risks

Operational Risk Management Requirement ⬇ Tool ➡	Standardised Process based Operating model	BPMS	EITG tool	Human Capital Capability	Advanced Analytics
Operational Risk Appetite: Define, Monitor, Mitigate	Supports – from lines of business to process	Supports	Process-based EITG		Supports
Threats & Vulnerabilities	All support - Identification, Measurement & Mitigation				
Internal Operational Risk Loss data			Yes – granular wholesome data		Machine learning
External Operational Risk Loss data	Supports calibration of external data				
Operational Risk Scenarios	Supports		Risk process modelling; BCP, I.T. Capacity planning	Subject matter experts	Forward Looking
Business Environment and Internal Control Factors (BEICF)	Supports – configure and monitor				Preventive controls
Activity based Enterprise non-interest cost management	Essential for Activity based enterprise non-interest cost management				
Enterprise risk adjusted return management	Essential for Enterprise risk adjusted return management				

The implementation aspects of standardizing the enterprise operating model and analytics are explained in Section 5.5.2.

5.3.7 Different Types of Cost Reduction Techniques

Recap: The cost of doing business has two dimensions, the cost of business delivery and the cost of risk management. The following are some of the techniques that a bank could use to accomplish their cost reduction objectives.

5.3.7.1 Target Costing

Target costing determines what customers are willing to pay for a financial product. The profit margins and allowable costs are calculated using the price that the market is willing to pay. Retail banking is a very competitive business. The key drivers are competition, acquiring and retaining customers, product's market share, and bank's competitive position.

CHAPTER 5   IMPROVING OPERATING LEVERAGE

This is an important aspect of activity-based enterprise noninterest cost budgeting and *setting limits for cost centers*. The latter is different from accounting book-based P&L limit for operating costs.

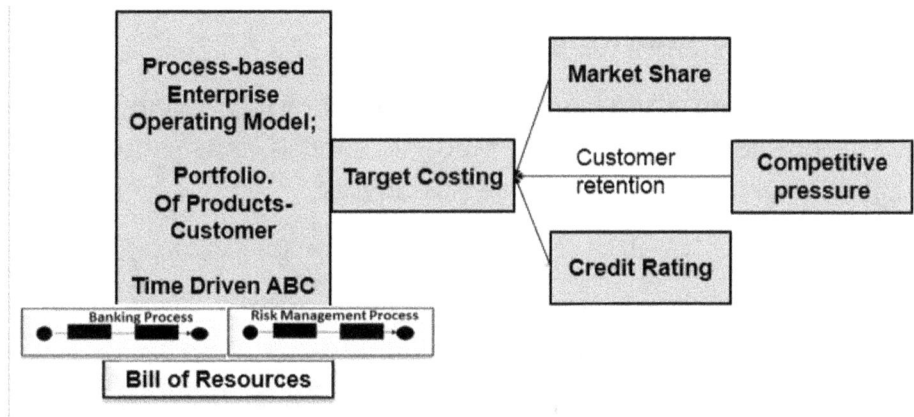

Figure 5-8. Target costing

5.3.7.2 Product Life Cycle Costing

Product life cycle costing involves tracing of costs and revenues of each product over several calendar periods through the entire life cycle. The identifiable phases of a financial product life cycle are shown in Table 5-5.

Table 5-5. Product life cycle costing

Financial Product	Introduction	Growth	Maturity	Decline
Sales Volume	High	Higher	Plateau	Fall
Product Promotion cost	High	Medium	Not Material	Stopped
Non-interest Cost Base	High	Medium	Flat	Relatively High
Competition – new in the market	Medium	Medium	Medium (advantage of being early)	Fall
Competition – existing in the market	High	Medium	High	Fall
Risk Adjusted Return	Above Target	Meets Target	Challenge	Probably Negative

443

CHAPTER 5   IMPROVING OPERATING LEVERAGE

The entry of non-banks in the retail banking space has made it necessary for banks to review product profitability trend and take an informed decision on sun setting nonprofitable products.

5.3.7.3 Benchmarking

Benchmarking provides a bank the ability to make a logical comparisons, with the objective of improving its processes, models, and methodologies.

Benchmarking exercises may be classified as

- Results-based, which compares performance metrics
- Process-based, which looks behind the metrics to analyze banking process

The following are common benchmarking approaches:

- Internal benchmarking compares one activity group with another.
- External benchmarking compare internal data with peer group.
- In functional benchmarking, internal processes are compared with external processes.

5.3.8 Pricing

- Dynamic Pricing could be relevant for some treasury instruments.
- Loyalty pricing is an important aspect of retail customer retention and has worked well for products like credit cards.
- Behavioral pricing is based on "rewarding" a good customer. This is a risk-based approach.

The activity-based enterprise noninterest cost management explained in this book fully supports all noninterest cost management and pricing methods. A data-centric enterprise architecture makes it possible to have a knowledge management capability that can support the accurate pricing of products.

5.4 Tools: Improving OL

5.4.1 Ontology-Driven Knowledge Management (KM) [22]

When data usage is democratized, a bank's ability to transform into a **"knowledge-driven bank"** gets better. This is the foundation for the examples on operating leverage (PRCC – performance, risk, control, and cost) monitoring in Chapter 4.

Figure 5-9 provides a summarized view of an *ontology*-based, data-centric ERRM that includes an activity-based ENICM. [23]

---

[22] https://www.isda.org/2019/09/04/isda-taxonomy-2-0-finalized/
https://spec.edmcouncil.org/fibo/data-dictionary
https://spec.edmcouncil.org/fibo/ontology_tools.html

[23] https://www.edmcouncil.org/dcam https://spec.edmcouncil.org/fibo/

CHAPTER 5   IMPROVING OPERATING LEVERAGE

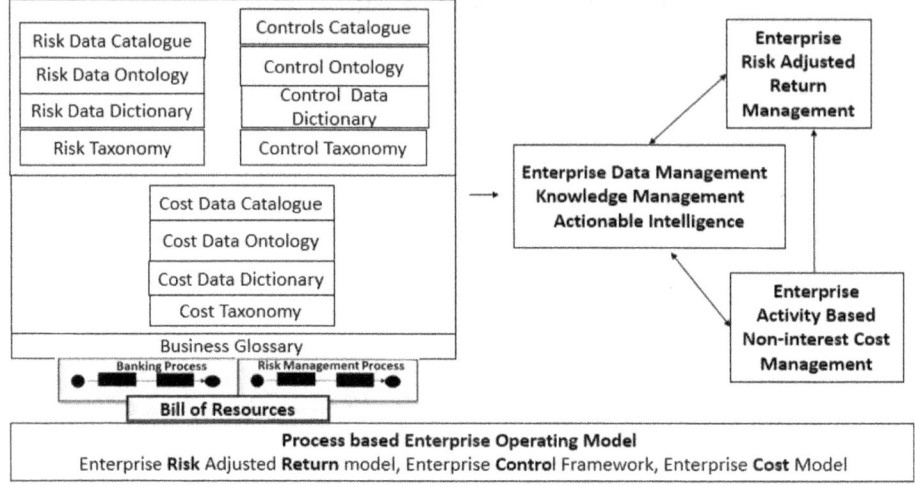

Figure 5-9. Ontology-driven knowledge management

Knowledge management[24] cuts across the lines of business, front-, middle-, and back-office functions. With a single view of the truth capability, KM can make a qualitative impact on ERRM. In treasury for example, risk managers have limited influence over front-office trading behavior. Checks and balances are effective when the different levels of the organization hierarchy have a single view of truth. Table 5-6 provides the different components and dimensions of knowledge management.

---

[24] Knowledge Management
http://www.apo-tokyo.org/publications/wp-content/uploads/sites/5/ind-43-km_tt-2010.pdf
https://www.apqc.org/expertise/knowledge-management/interactive-km-framework

Table 5-6. *Knowledge types*

KNOWLEDGE TYPES								
		Resides in		< KNOW >				
Tacit	Explicit	Person	Social	< Declarative	Procedural	Causal	Conditional	Relational >
Experience Belief, Value	Articulated, Demonstrated	Self	Team	About	How	Why	When	With
Executive Team	Domain Knowledge	Initiative and Project;	Team Work;	Goals; What is ERRM? What is the Risk Appetite?	How to accomplish ERR objectives?	Interest rate FX rate Prices: Equity Commodity	Risk Events, Economy	Causation & Risk Types.
Staff Skill Grade 1st, 2nd and 3rd levels of defence	Risk-Return Management	Risk Types: Market Credit ALM Liquidity O.R.	Risk Types: Market Credit ALM Liquidity O.R.	What Capabilities are required? What is the cost of doing business?	How to implement EA? How to implement EDM? How to use Analytics?	Defaults Liquidity Customer Product Policy System Staff	Counterparty / Customer rating, Funding Cost, Enterprise Overheads	Risk, Control and Costs – the equation.
	Enterprise Non-Interest Cost Management	Enterprise Non-Interest Cost Management						

EA- Enterprise Architecture; EDM-Enterprise Data Management; ERR-Enterprise risk adjusted return, O.R. Operational risk

An institution has a "knowledge culture" when the work environment enables and motivates employees to *create, share, and apply knowledge* for the **enduring success** of the institution. A KM framework, as illustrated in Figure 5-10, is an important component of the enterprise architecture and enterprise data management. The framework guides the CTO, CDO, and GRC teams to build and disseminate knowledge for improved decision-making.

CHAPTER 5   IMPROVING OPERATING LEVERAGE

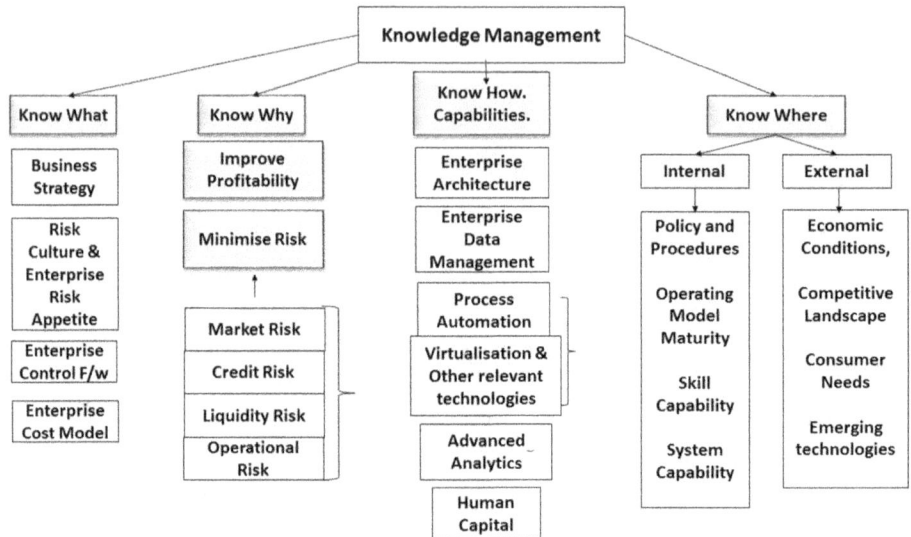

Figure 5-10. *Knowledge management*

KM is a specialized domain that can significantly improve decision-making by strengthening the quality of actionable intelligence provided to line bankers and support functions. The KM framework includes the following phases: identifying, acquiring, creating, storing, sharing, and using knowledge. This is illustrated in Figure 5-11.

KM is a continuous process, and it starts with the formation of a knowledge base, i.e., a database of related information items. The method has the following main phases:

   i. Identify, acquire, and create

   ii. Harness – Store and share

   iii. Harvest – Apply and use

CHAPTER 5   IMPROVING OPERATING LEVERAGE

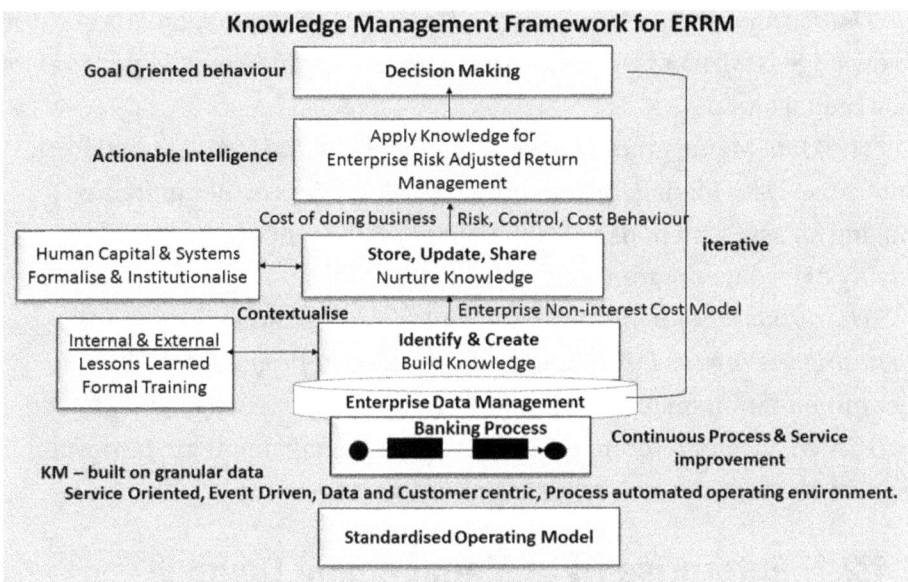

Figure 5-11. *Knowledge management framework*

KM improves staff productivity, system usage, and quality of decisions. Hence, it is a tool to accomplish operational efficiency and operating leverage targets.

It is important for banks to (i) know their resource utilization levels, (ii) scale of operations, and (iii) understand the fixed and variable costs at defined levels of operations.

5.4.2 Enterprise Data Management

The following frameworks that have found acceptance from the banking industry.

Data Management Association's (DAMA)[25] Data Management Body of Knowledge (**DMBOK**) is a collection of processes and knowledge areas for data management.

The Data Management Capability Model (**DCAM**) was created by the Enterprise Data Management Council (EDMC). It provides guidance for making an assessment of a bank's data management maturity and the quality of its data program.

The author opines that the DCAM model is best suited for improving operating leverage as it uses an ontology-based approach. DMBOK's recommendation on interoperability, data virtualization (now endorsed by DCAM), master reference, and metadata management are important aspects of enterprise risk-adjusted return management.

5.4.2.1 Enterprise Data Management Council (EDMC) Framework

The EDMC's framework[26] is explained with the objective of providing guidance on managing the data in the sources systems, to create and maintain a pan-bank data model for meeting the information/knowledge requirements of the bank.

The EDMC provides a standard-based infrastructure, identification of financial instruments and business entities, legally language for financial contracts, and a data classification scheme for aggregation and analysis. FIBO is an Open Financial Industry Data Standard that provides business conceptual and operational ontologies. It is a collaborative initiative to describe financial data standards using semantics. Many financial institutions are contributing to the FIBO standard.

---

[25] DAMA-DMBOK https://dama.org/
[26] DCAM https://www.edmcouncil.org/dcam

FIBO

- Provides standard definitions of financial contracts, concepts, and business rules
- Ensures better compliance with data standards
- Maximizes commonality and reuse by integrating with other global data standards
- Provides semantic mapping for creating a common business data standard for integration
- Supports the identification of risk exposures across legal entity ownership hierarchies and their counterparties

Case Studies
Adoption of EDMC's DCAM

An international bank with its headquarters in Germany leveraged FIBO to standardize content and meaning across the enterprise.

The as-is environment was a fragmented data architecture. The bank started with treasury data. The bank *abstracted the market data that it buys from* vendors into a common language, converted it into a triple-store format (RDF), designed a market data portal using FIBO terms, and enabled their business users to search through the portal without predetermined source knowledge.

The bank used linked data, semantic triple stores, and RDF and was able to improve the quality of its data model (including entities, attributes, and relationships):

- Redundant market data feeds were removed. Each feed was mapped against FIBO data concepts.
- Eliminate duplicates.

- Minimize vendor feeds and storage system requirements.
- Move from business rules to intelligent processing.
- The taxonomy (classifications and hierarchies). This led to an improvement in data quality.

After a period of manual intervention, the bank automated the mapping of incoming market data onto FIBO so that the **content is tagged as it is received**. It is now realizing the benefits of FIBO operational ontologies and EDM Council's data management framework.

Case: A **Nordic bank** set the following objectives and implemented a data governance model to accomplish the same:

- Implement EDM principles so that business data owners are able to accomplish their EITG KPIs.
- Create and support maintenance and management of a **knowledge base** that facilitates EITG activities.
- Ensure that metadata complies with the principles set out in BCBS-239 for effective risk data aggregation and risk reporting.

5.4.3 Machine Learning and Operating Leverage

Using machine learning, a bank can improve its activity-based ENICM. The system can learn the relationships between cost drivers and cost resources. Extending from it, *machine learning can identify business opportunities, improve predeal analytics, increase profitability, and support long-term business growth.*

Machine learning methods construct predictive models from representative samples extracted from large datasets. These models provide data-driven algorithms that are easier to construct. Their performance is better than traditional modeling techniques.

Supervised, Unsupervised, and Reinforced Learning

The three models are illustrated on Table 5-7. The two broad categories of machine learning are supervised and unsupervised. In supervised learning, data is labeled, i.e., input and output data are available. This is equivalent to testing a range of independent variables for determining relationship with the dependent variable in traditional statistics. In unsupervised learning, only input data is available and the model discovers the details of the structure of the data.

Table 5-7. *Machine learning models*

	Supervised Learning	Unsupervised Learning	Reinforced Learning
Framework to balance Risk, Control, & Costs. Minimise Risk & Maximise Return	Algorithm based and uses labelled data. Forward and Backward data processes are checked and a target function created. **Cost of Control vis-à-vis quantified risk.**	Group and interpret input data; Inputs are used to create a model of the data. Unlabelled data is analysed, information gathered and inferences made without supervision. **Used for identifying non-value adding activities.**	Develop predictive **non-interest cost management model** based on both input and output data.
Math & Statistical methods	Classification Discriminant Analysis, Random Forest, K-Nearest, Support Vector Machine, Naïve Bayes. Regression Linear Regression, Ensemble method	Clustering K-Means, Hierarchical Clustering, Gaussian mixture Dimensionality Reduction Linear Factor analysis, Principal component analysis,	Dynamic programming Q learning Temporal-difference State–action–reward–state–action Policy gradient Evolutionary programming Genetic programming
	<	Decision Trees and Markov model	>
	<	Neural Network	>

The following are examples of algorithms:

- K-nearest neighbors (**KNN**)

    KNN is a supervised machine learning algorithm that can be used to solve both classification and regression problems. A core assumption is that similar things exist in close proximity.

CHAPTER 5   IMPROVING OPERATING LEVERAGE

- Support vector machines **(SVM)**

    SVM is a supervised learning algorithm that separates available data using hyperplane. Support vector classification **(SVC)** can be used for classification and support vector regression **(SVR)** for solving regression problems.

Both algorithms are widely used in credit risk management.
Reinforcement Learning (RL)
RL is based on a feedback mechanism, and the model takes actions based on a defined policy. *The parameters driving the policy can be adjusted to increase the reward function.*

Key features of RL are as follows:

- The agent acts in identified processes, and the reactions are defined in the model.

- The model has two major parts, transition probability and a reward function.

- There are transition probabilities between states. After an action is taken, the environment delivers a reward as a feedback.

The model defines the reward function and transition probabilities. The following are usage scenarios:

a) User is not familiar with the model and invokes learning with incomplete information: in this situation, the user can use model-free RL or choose learning the model explicitly.

b) When information is not a constraint, use a model-based RL. When the environment is known, optimal solution can be found using dynamic programming.

CHAPTER 5 IMPROVING OPERATING LEVERAGE

Figure 5-12 provides an overview of model selection for supervised and unsupervised machine learning applications. PCA stands for principal component analysis.

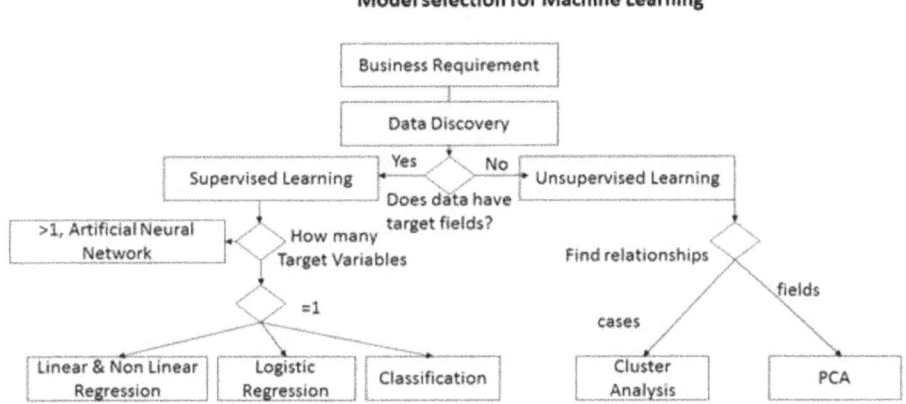

Figure 5-12. *Model selection for machine learning.*

Machine Learning: Model Creation and Usage

Figure 5-13 provides an overview of a machine learning model creation and usage processes. It starts with defining the hypothesis and identifying the data and moves to creating algorithms and training the model. The process moves into self-learning mode, and the model will refine its outputs over time. The user can stop the iterative process when the output has met the user's objective.

Machine Learning for Operating Leverage

Banks may wish to include a continuous learning mechanism for implementing their enterprise risk-adjusted return model. This would involve defining forward-looking business scenarios and defining external threats and opportunities. The configuration parameters will include KPIs and KRIs at the process level.

455

CHAPTER 5   IMPROVING OPERATING LEVERAGE

For activity-based, enterprise noninterest cost management, a bank can stress test its fixed cost base and use its knowledge of variable costs to estimate profitability of forward-looking business scenarios.

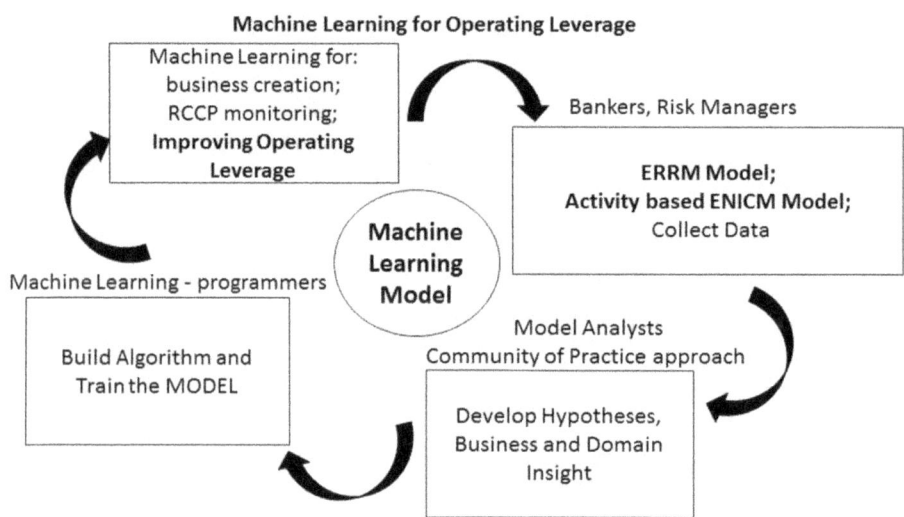

Figure 5-13. *Machine learning model creation and usage*

In a way, the knowledge management capability is a pan-bank intelligence system that includes the bank's goals, its risk profile, customer risk profiles, staff skill profile, and behavioral analytics data. Figures 5-13, 5-14, and 5-15 provide a high-level guidance on using advanced analytics for business growth, ERRM, and operating leverage.

CHAPTER 5   IMPROVING OPERATING LEVERAGE

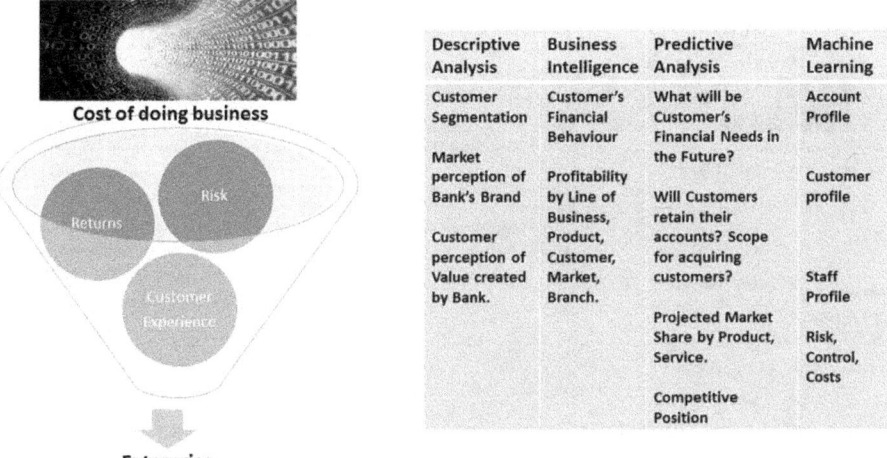

Figure 5-14. Analytics for operational efficiency and operating leverage

Advanced analytics is a tool for

- Identifying opportunities, improving resource utilization, and increasing growth
- Risk identification, mitigation, and monitoring of residual risk

CHAPTER 5   IMPROVING OPERATING LEVERAGE

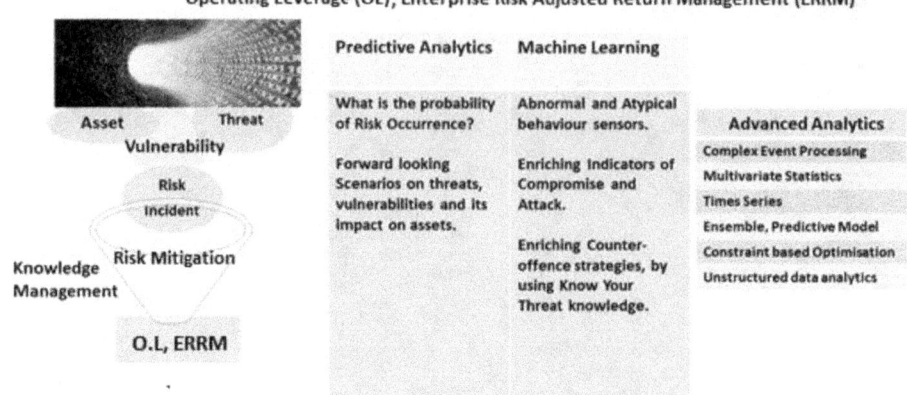

Figure 5-15. Analytics for operating leverage and ERRM

Neural Network System for Fraud Prevention

Neural networks can be used in predictive, prescriptive, and descriptive analytics. The inherent nature of neural networks is the ability to learn and represent complex relationships. The motivation for using NN technology is to embed intelligence into banking processes. They add a layer of intelligence in processing by

- Acquiring knowledge through learning
- Representing linear and nonlinear relationships

Most networks consist of three layers. The input layer comprises raw information and is connected to a layer of "hidden" units, which is connected to the output layer. The weights on the connections between the input and the hidden units determine the flow of activity. The behavior of the output units depends on the activity of the hidden units and the weights between the hidden and output units.

CHAPTER 5   IMPROVING OPERATING LEVERAGE

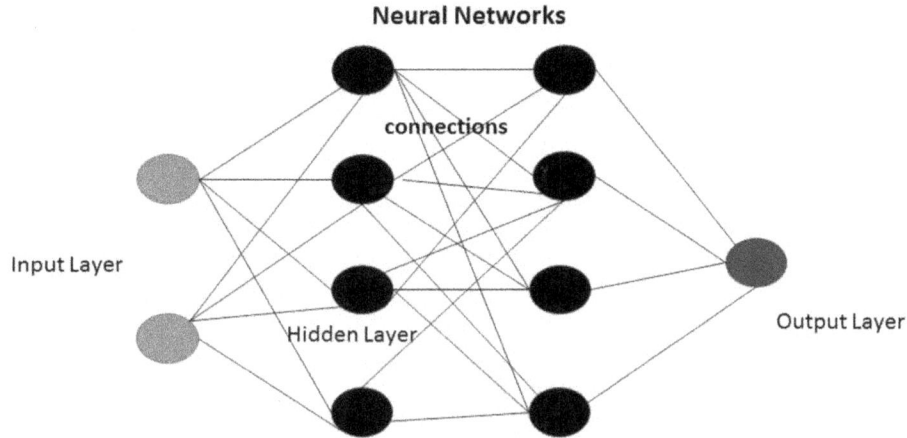

Figure 5-16. *Artificial neural networks*

Weak enterprise security, encompassing functional and technical controls, has significantly increased the number of "white collar" crimes. New fraud topologies emerge frequently. Many banks find it difficult to fight fraud as they still use primitive rule-based systems for detecting risk incidents.

Most banks are at least a decade behind in using relevant technology for preventing fraud and proactively managing risks. *The rule-based system does not have the depth of statistical modeling-based intelligence capability.* Supervised clustering combines traditional clustering and multidimensional histogram analysis. The automatic modeling system (AMS) creates neural network models. The fraud detection engine can apply the AMS-generated model on the input data stream and significantly reduce fraud through real-time prevention and decision-making.

CHAPTER 5   IMPROVING OPERATING LEVERAGE

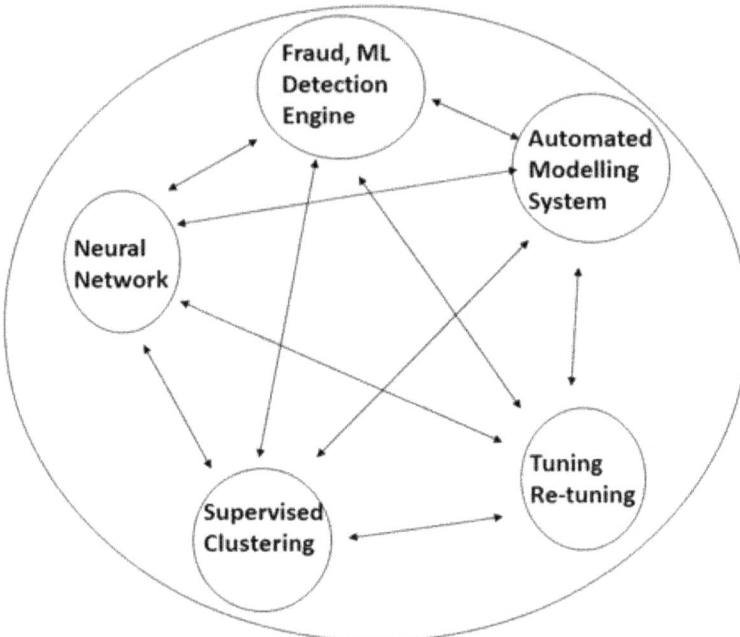

Figure 5-17. Neural network for anti-money laundering and fraud prevention

Anti-money Laundering and Countering the Financing of Terrorism (AML-CFT)

From a system perspective, AML-CFT can be configured as a different set of fraud scenarios, within the operational risk management domain. The AML-CFT laws and regulations require some material changes to the configuration. However, using event-driven architecture and process automation, these types of changes can easily be done.

The core analytical dimensions of AML-CFT risk monitoring are transaction, account, customer, customer group, and country. These components are driven by *behavior monitoring algorithms*. The profile captures expected behavior on several key dimensions, such as type of deposit or withdrawal, frequency, and volumes. If the actual activity or behavior deviates from the standard profile, an alert is generated. In AML and fraud management systems, atypical behavior will generate alerts to risk managers.

Within the operational risk management domain, AML-CFT solutions have introduced supervised machine learning algorithms, including decision tree (**DT**), random forest (**RF**), support vector machine (SVM), and artificial neural network (ANN) for surveillance. The traditional approach to surveillance uses a maximum likelihood logistic regression (**MLLR**) model. To address the impact of rare event data on MLLR fitting, a machine learning algorithm, Bayes logistic regression (**BLR**), has been introduced in solutions that use sophisticated analytics.

Advanced Analytics for Operating Risk Management

Banks may wish to include a continuous learning mechanism within their enterprise operational risk management system processes. The analytical engine can use the knowledge management database for pattern matching and self-learning algorithms. Financial messages and transactions are checked by active models, and alerts are generated. The performance is optimized by using in-memory technology. A services-based architecture in a process-automated environment with in-memory computing is the recommended approach for preventing fraud. Machine learning can generate early warning signals when abnormalities and atypical behavior are detected.

Preventive controls are effective in this environment and minimize operational risks.

Enterprise fraud management is a pan-bank intelligence system that includes investigations into the following: (a) financial messages, (b) financial transactions, (c) contracts/deals/trades, (d) customer accounts, (e) internal accounts, and (f) corporate customer intragroup transactions.

A powerful, advanced analytical engine is required for risk prevention/risk detection and intelligence (risk)-based surveillance.

CHAPTER 5   IMPROVING OPERATING LEVERAGE

Case Study – UK [27]

A UK-based bank used AI to improve

- Operational risk management
- Processing accuracy
- Quality of controls

This book recommends that banks focus on preventive controls. Detective controls are important as a security layer.

5.4.4 Timed Colored Petri Net Model

Petri net is mentioned in the context of enterprise process automation, robotic process automation, and complex event processing. There is a behavioral relation between Petri nets and BPMN models. The relationship can be used for conformance checking and performance analysis techniques.

Colored Petri net (CPN) is a simulation technique that has a high capability for modeling and evaluation of a system's performance. CPNs extend the classical Petri net formalism with **data, time, and hierarchy**. These additional attributes make it possible to model complex processes. When time concepts are introduced, the model is called timed colored Petri net model, and when hierarchy is also introduced, it is called a hierarchical timed colored Petri net.

Scheduling requires a decision that uses execution start time of banking, and this is an input to a data-centric, services-based, process-automated enterprise architecture. Colored Petri net is an extension of

---

[27] https://www.gov.uk/government/case-studies/how-a-uk-based-bank-used-ai-to-increase-operational-efficiency

traditional Petri net and is useful for monitoring performance evaluation of process-based information systems. A two-level hierarchical model could be used a bank's transaction processing system enterprise architecture.

These models can be used to measure and predict performance, e.g., payment processes and enterprise liquidity management. Machine learning can improve the benefits provided by TCPN models.

5.5 Implementing Improvements to OE and OL

This section focuses on the implementation of improvements.

5.5.1 Standardized Enterprise Operating Model

Nonstandardized, Siloed Enterprise Operating Model

A bank's enterprise operating model defines the conceptual, logical, and physical delivery mechanism to accomplish its business goals. It comprises products and services, delivery channels, staff, systems, policies, and procedures. In executing the model, the bank is able to deliver business to its customers and integrate with the financial markets. There is an associated cost and risk. The efficiency and maturity of the model determine the bank's ability to create value for its customers at a competitive cost and minimal risk.

This is a continuation of the explanation on business architecture under gap analysis in Chapter 2, Section 2.4. The focus of business architecture is on the delivery of products and services. While the lines of business define the human capital requirements, the CTO, CDO, and EA determine the architecture and technology for internal use and delivering products. Delivery capability should consider the anticipated growth in business.

CHAPTER 5 IMPROVING OPERATING LEVERAGE

A standardized enterprise operating model is consistent with the **laws of simplicity** and facilitates enterprise data ontology documentation. It facilitates data standardization, lineage, and democratization.

Business variations in the enterprise operating model can happen for a number of reasons, and the differences could be in

- Customer's eligibility criteria
- Rate of interest, fees, and charges
- Computation of interest, fee, and charges
- Tenor of the product
- Margin requirement
- Minimum amount
- Maximum exposure
- Linking to other banking product and facilities
- Documentation for opening, operating, and closure
- Approval process for opening
- Limits management
- Drawdowns
- Limit excess
- Account closure formalities

Examples of variations across branches:

Know Your Customer Procedure (e.g., Documents Collected)

Tables 5-8a, 5-8b, and 5-8c are examples of templates that can be used for standardizing the enterprise operating model. The information gathering will also include subprocesses such as KYC, to ensure that there are no deviations in critical processes.

Treasury products offer less of a challenge as compared to others business. Retail products are those with maximum variations.

Table 5-8a. KYC

KYC			
	Proof 1	Proof 2	Proof 3
Branch 1			
Branch N			

Table 5-8b. Account opening – eligibility

Product Id: eligibility	Age	Income	Borrowings
Branch 1			
Branch N			

Table 5-8c. Product characteristics

Product Id:	Interest	Fees	Tenor	Margin	Limit	Min-$	Collateral	Others
Branch 1								
Branch N								

In retail banking, home loans could have the largest number of products. The definition of the standard product (for each product category) is an input for the compilation of the "Standard List of Product & Services" and the documentation of the "tweaked" products.

Standardized Enterprise Operating Model

CHAPTER 5   IMPROVING OPERATING LEVERAGE

The variation risk benefit (impact) assessment must quantify the risk return and the rationale for the variation. If the approval for the variation has an expiry date, the plan of action post that date should also be monitored and implemented. It is important to assign ownership for approved variations and enforce accountability.

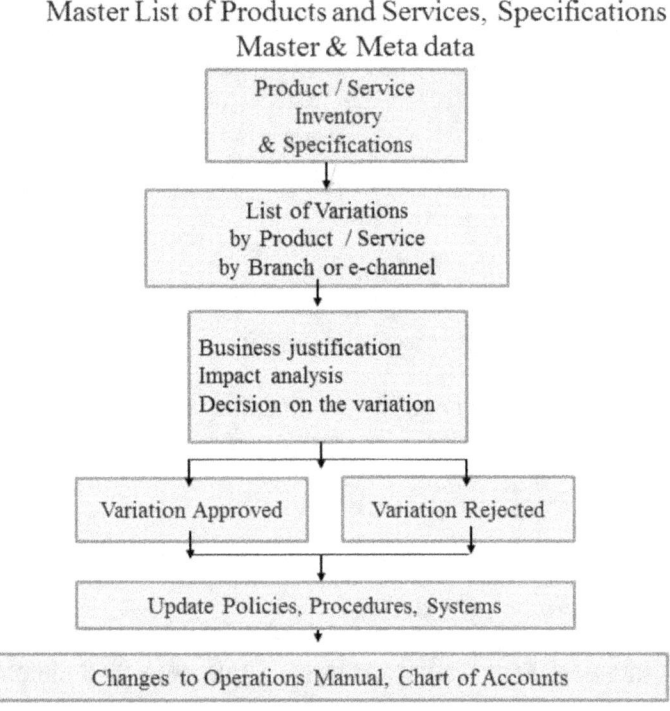

Figure 5-18a. Master and metadata of products

Enterprise IT Governance – The reason for variations include different operating systems (including mobile), database, messaging protocols, and manufacturers. The enterprise IT control framework and standards incorporated in the policies will influence the decision.

CHAPTER 5   IMPROVING OPERATING LEVERAGE

A sample list of variations/deviations in technology deployment is provided below:

- More than one ATM manufacturer
- More than one mobile operating system
- Multiple operating systems
- Multiple database systems
- Multiple messaging protocols

Figure 5-18b provides a schematic of the approach to creating and maintaining a SOM. The approach to standardization can vary by bank. For each variation, the risk appetite and business benefit assessment will influence the approval for a variation.

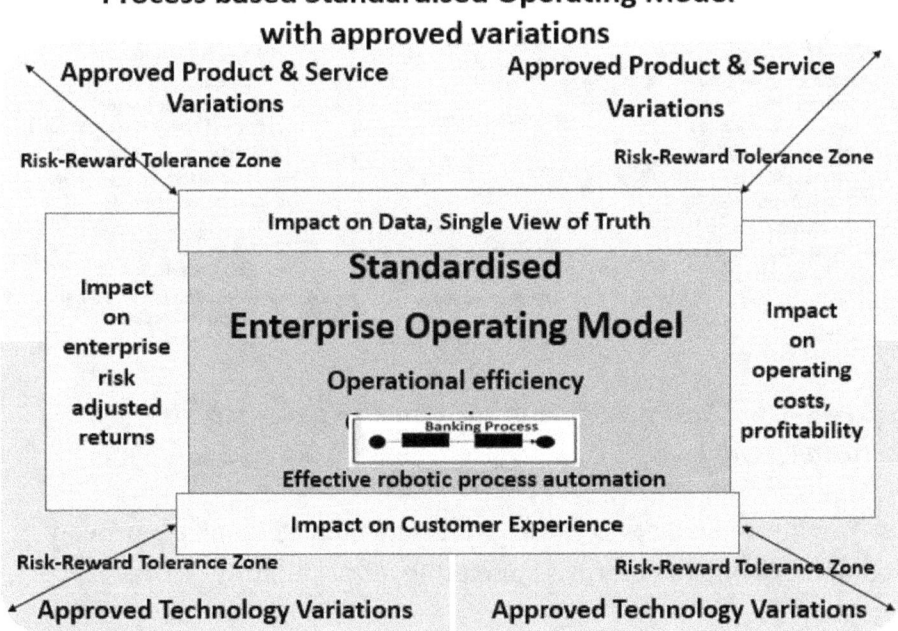

Figure 5-18b. Standardized enterprise operating model

CHAPTER 5   IMPROVING OPERATING LEVERAGE

This makes it challenging to implement and monitor policies and procedures across the delivery network. Banks with a governance model ensure that operating model variation gets the approval of the *change control board*. An impact analysis is a standard operating procedure for "material" or "significant" changes. These issues are guided by the bank's enterprise risk appetite framework and enterprise risk-adjusted return governance policies and procedures.

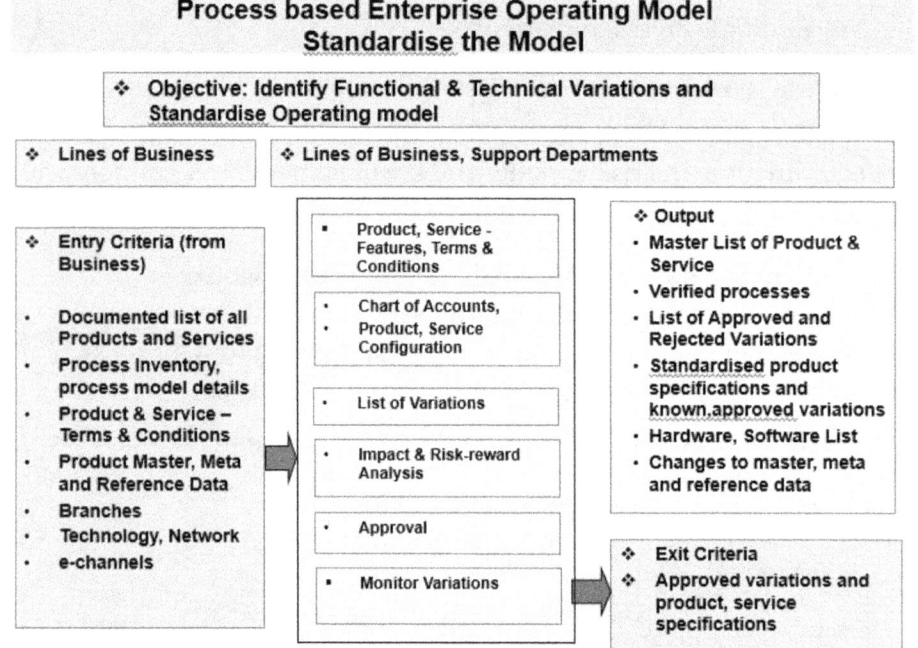

Figure 5-18c. *Rationalize and standardize the enterprise operating model*

With improvements to process and data management, a bank can accomplish a higher enterprise operating model maturity score.

The following can improve the quality of the model and pave the way for improved operational efficiency and leverage:

i. Creating a Baseline for a Standardized Enterprise Operating Model (SOM) – This should be consistent with the master and metadata, process inventory, and risk and control registers.

ii. The baselined SOM should be aligned with enterprise process taxonomy, enterprise data inventory, and enterprise risk register.

iii. The SOM should be consistent with the risk appetite framework and statement.

iv. Simplify business processes by increasing automation of tasks.

v. Building/improving centers of excellence in key areas to increase operational efficiency.

vi. Developing a culture of continuous improvement of capabilities to minimize risks, decrease costs, and maximize returns.

vii. Operationalize knowledge management and analytics.

5.5.2 Risk-Adjusted Return Analytics
5.5.2.1 Behavioral Analytics, Customer, and Staff

Deep Learning with Keras Library to Predict Customer Churn

Keras and R algorithms can be used to predict customer churn with a degree of accuracy. It can be used for customer acquisition and retention. Deep learning algorithms are superior to linear and logistic regression because of the ability to model interactions between features that would otherwise go undetected.

CHAPTER 5   IMPROVING OPERATING LEVERAGE

5.5.2.2 Human Capital

Table 5-9 provides a staff capability and measurement model. A bank's policies and procedures should be driven by the twin objectives of minimizing staff risks and maximizing business returns. Strong brands are adept at attracting, developing, and retaining individuals with the right skills and experience. Human capital management includes the measurement of the return from human capital. The return has some very important nontangible factors. **Trust is the fundamental element for maintaining a fiduciary relationship with the customer.**

Table 5-9. *Staff capability measurement model*

Bank Staff Capability and Risk measurement model				
Initial	Managed	Defined	Predictable	Optimised
Insufficient Management attention to HR Policy and Procedures	Management provides basic HR framework.	Management believes in investing in Human Capital	Organisation Structure reflects changing business landscape and competitive positioning.	Management committed to continuous improvement and building capabilities.
	Focus on Staff	Focus on Competency	Focus on Centres of Excellence (e.g. Analytics)	
		Staff Accountability established	Risk Culture defined and permeates all levels	Focus on Change Skilled Workforce
Weak HR Policies	Non-standardised Operating Model	KRI, KPI set for staff	Empowered Workforce	Risk-adjusted Performance evaluation.
		Training imparted as required	Enterprise Knowledge Management	
	Reactive Customer Management	360° view of staff	Analytics to support decision making	
		Weakness in Automation	Customer-centric culture; Data centric Enterprise Architecture	

Like other maturity models, the people maturity model is process based. The model assumes that standardized workforce practices are implemented and subject to continuous improvement. The following principles influence the evaluation of the workforce maturity:

- Staff skills are linked to a bank's business goals.
- An efficient goal breakdown is necessary for accurate KPI definition for each staff member.

- Motivated staff improve customer retention and competitive advantage.
- Customer and quality orientation should be reflected in all functions.
- Staff capability is measured against risk-adjusted business performance.
- Soft skills are important personal attributes. This includes the ability to be a team member. Teamwork evaluation is an important aspect of maturity evaluation.
- Bank's investment in improving the capability of its workforce is an important evaluation criteria.
- Bank management must be committed to a continuous improvement culture and develop new workforce competencies.
- Knowledge management is effective when a bank uses a staff competency model.

360° View of Human Capital (Employee)

Figure 5-19 provides an overview of a knowledge-driven, Know Your Employee program.

CHAPTER 5 IMPROVING OPERATING LEVERAGE

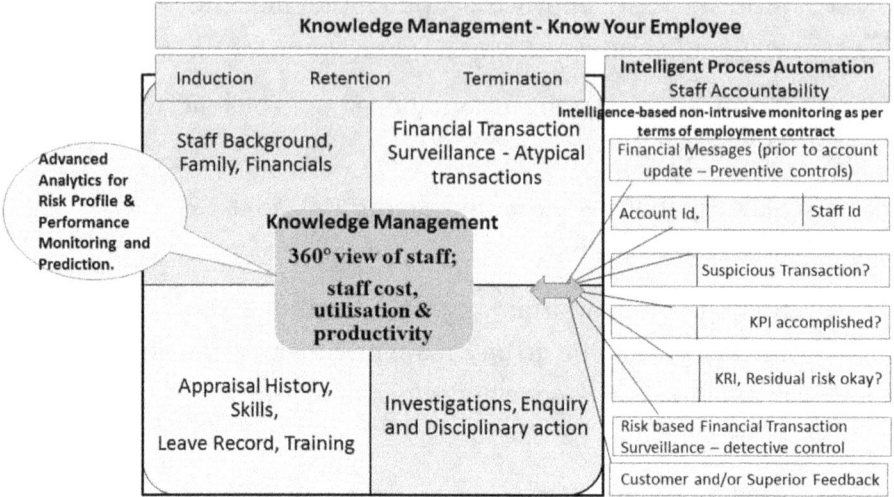

Figure 5-19. *360° view of human capital*

Employee and/or contract staff behavior is the root cause for a significant number of frauds. Frauds are operational risks and can cause market, credit or liquidity risks. An operational weakness can be one of the causes for a liquidity risk. The liquidity risk could evolve into a solvency risk and threaten the bank's existence.

Banks apply different methods to manage human capital. This includes aligning bonus to long-term performance, process improvements, team building, employee training, grievance management, job rotation, team-based work objective, and flexible work arrangements. Staff skills can be improved by providing training or by improving recruitment specifications.

Early warning signal for atypical staff behavior can be inferred from employee attrition, sick leave, overtime hours, and mandatory leave compliance failure. However, banks have not yet built a capability to manage their human capital and its associated risks. They still have elementary "HR systems."

Machine learning, e.g., recursive learning, will help in constructing profiles for the unknown area using behavioral analysis algorithms.

Enterprise human capital management should have the following KPIs:

- Improve staff recruitment policies
- Work with business to ensure staff assignment is based on updated staff profile
- Elimination or minimizing manual processes
- Work with IT on 360° view of staff and enterprise data protection
- Provide comprehensive staff data for management decision-making
- Secure the HR application

5.5.2.3 Customer/Counterparty

360° View of Customer

Figure 5-20 provides an overview of data collection from customer accounts and transactions using process automation and providing a 360° view of customer for analytics and knowledge management.

As illustrated in Figure 5-20, there are four phases in the process of getting actionable intelligence on customers.

CHAPTER 5   IMPROVING OPERATING LEVERAGE

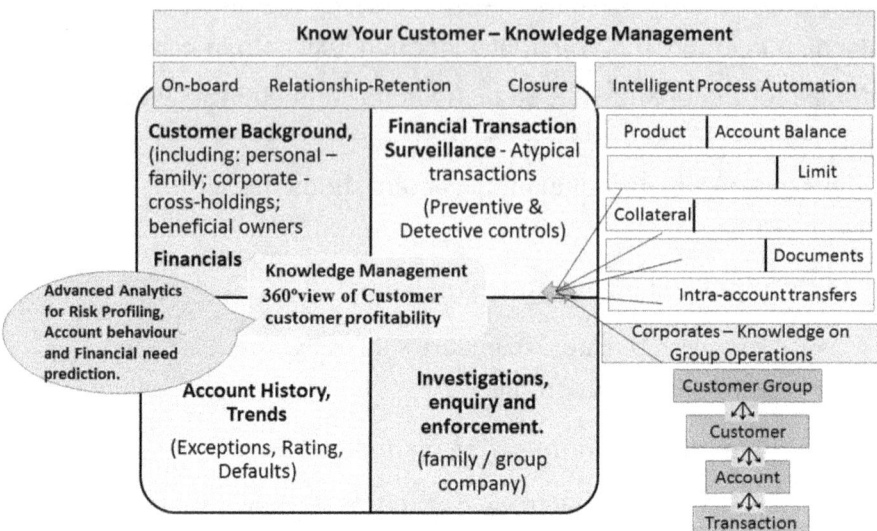

Figure 5-20. 360° view of customer

Table 5-10 provides an overview of Customer Experience ranking of some banks in the USA.

Table 5-10. *Advise satisfaction index ranking*[28]

Bank	Advise Satisfaction Index Ranking
BOA	**839**
PNC	833
Well Fargo	828
Citibank	826
Chase	819
INDUSTRY AVERAGE	819
BB&T	815
Capital One	815
Fifth Third	810
Keybank	807

Figure 5-21a illustrates end-to-end customer experience management. This is applicable across the product life cycle. The technologies and methodologies make this feasible and efficient.

---

[28] https://thefinancialbrand.com/news/customer-experience-banking/banking-consumer-feedback-bofa-customer-experience-84792/

CHAPTER 5   IMPROVING OPERATING LEVERAGE

Figure 5-21a. Customer experience management

In this age of empowering technology, customers can shift loyalties with a click of a mouse. Gaining competitive advantage is a strategy that can be implemented successfully only when a bank's management gets a senior team with requisite skills and experience to use relevant technologies to accomplish business objectives.

Figure 5-21b illustrates a different stages in customer experience management cycle. The banks needs to

(a) Use the right balance of technology and face-to-face interaction to gain and retain customers.

(b) Be innovative and implement a continuous service improvement culture.

(c) Use a data-centric enterprise approach to create the single version of the truth data model. Advanced analytics should use data of good quality for creating actionable intelligence.

CHAPTER 5   IMPROVING OPERATING LEVERAGE

(d) *Customer-centric business does not refer to a department but a staff attitude.*

Criteria	Initial	Managed	Defined	Knowledge Management	Optimised
Management commitment for Customer-centric culture	No	No	Yes	Continuous Service improvement	
Omni-channel capability	Unavailable			Yes	Yes
Single View of Truth	Unavailable			Continuous Process Improvement	
Customer Need Profile; Financial behaviour, Risk Profile	No	No	Yes but inaccurate (false positives)	Behavioural analysis	Forward Looking
Customer experience metrics	Unavailable			Yes	Yes
Customer experience data collection			Yes but fragmented	Yes	Yes
Loyalty program	Unavailable		Available	Yes	High Retention
Relationship and Accountability	Limited focus		Available	Yes	Goodwill Management

Figure 5-21b. *Phases in customer experience management*

5.5.2.4 Corporate Governance[29]

Basel provides 13 principles for corporate governance, and it is important to understand them from a pan-bank perspective in trying to assess the approach to enterprise architecture (EA), enterprise data management, and enterprise risk-adjusted return management. The key Basel principles are explained below from the perspective of this book.

---

[29] Corporate governance principles for banks- https://www.bis.org/bcbs/publ/d328.pdf

CHAPTER 5   IMPROVING OPERATING LEVERAGE

- Principle 1 – Board's overall responsibilities include setting the strategic objectives, defining the **culture**, and setting up a governance framework. The main take way for the chief risk officer and the head of operations and technology from this principle is that the *risk appetite statement (RAS) is the board's responsibility,* and these roles have an important role in providing the necessary inputs on technology vis-à-vis bank's business objectives and a risk assessment on the IT infrastructure to the management. *Like the goals, risk appetite should be rolled down to the process level.*

- Principle 2 – Board qualifications and composition: the *board should possess the ability to assess the relevance of technology,* for delivering business and improving customer experience.

- Principle 3 – Board's own structure and practices: *the integrity and intellect of the board are valuable assets. They are important for building the bank's brand value.*

- Principle 4 – Senior management should be responsible for the composition, scope, and usage of an *enterprise control framework and enterprise IT risk management.*

- Principle 5 covers governance of group structures.

Principles 6, 7, 8, 9, and 10 cover various aspects of data-centric enterprise risk-adjusted return management:

- Principle 6 is on risk management. This book recommends that a bank's enterprise risk committee should include the roles of chief EA, chief data officer (CDO), chief technology officer, and chief information security officer.

- Principle 7 covers risk identification, monitoring, and controlling, and this has been explained in Chapter 4.
- Principle 8 stresses the importance of risk communication within an effective risk governance framework.
- Principle 9 is on compliance, and it recommends that a bank's policy, procedure, and processes should be designed and implemented in a manner that it supports the identification, assessment, monitoring, and reporting of risks in ensuring compliance.
- *Principle 10 is on internal audit*, and an emphasis is placed on the independent assurance to the management on the governance of the bank.
- Principle 11 is on compensation, Principle 12 is on *disclosure and transparency*, and Principle 13 is on supervision.

5.5.2.5 EITG

In the past, EA experts have pointed out certain differences between EA and enterprise IT governance. *EA governance is about planning and execution, whereas enterprise IT governance model focuses on* performance and resource utilization. As banks are attempting to resolve siloed structures and improve accountability, this book treats EA as a component of EITG.

Objectives of enterprise IT governance are predictability, transparency, risk minimization, cost optimization (reduction), and improving capabilities and competencies.

CHAPTER 5   IMPROVING OPERATING LEVERAGE

The financial market changes include *globalization, merger and acquisition, regulatory changes, and emergence of new competitors.* The changes to business objectives include *financial and technology innovation, customer expectations, business growth, profitability, and compliance.*

Best practices in providing IT services and support include the following:

- Policies and procedures should be customer, data, event, and service centric.

- The EITG framework is based on an understanding that business drives technology.

- Business architecture should be consistent with business goals and management's risk appetite.

- IT processes should be aligned with business processes, and the technical architecture is aligned with business architecture.

- IT governance is driven by the goals of the bank's management and their risk appetite statement.

- KPIs are set for all components of enterprise IT governance. IT security (KRIs) are managed to keep technology risk within acceptable threshold. Service level agreement (SLA) between IT and the users (lines of business and support departments) should specify the relevant KPIs.

- EITG should ensure that IT resources are effectively and efficiently utilized.

- The top level IT team should obtain management's commitment to *continuous process improvement.*

CHAPTER 5   IMPROVING OPERATING LEVERAGE

- EITG should manage change efficiently and effectively.
- Independent audit of EITG processes and procedures.

5.5.3 Continuous Process Improvement (CPI)

CPI is an enterprise-wide program that constantly examines processes, products, and resources with the objective of increasing productivity, raising quality, reducing costs, and facilitating change. Process mining provides granular data for CPI, and banks that have a process-based enterprise operating model and process automation are able to fully leverage the benefits of an enterprise CPI program.

CPI, when used with knowledge management, is very effective. Table 5-11 provides a perspective of a knowledge management work down structure for improving operating leverage.

Table 5-11. *Knowledge management work breakdown structure*

Knowledge Management – Work Breakdown Structure		
Strategic – work units **Management** *Governance*	**Tactical – work units** **Executive Team** *Event & Functions*	**Operational – work units** **Banking Process-Business Delivery** *Behaviour*
Business Goals Enterprise Risk Appetite Statement	Standardised Operating Model Services-based, Event driven Architecture; Banking & Risk Management Processes Single View of Truth	Staff & Process Objectives, Key Performance & Risk Indicators Continuous Process & Service Improvements Bill of Resources, Resource Utilisation Time Driven Activity based costing
Enterprise Data Management Strategy; Data is an Asset – Knowledge is the lever.	Data as a Service, Virtualisation Graph Database In-memory management	Data Lineage, Data Quality, Risk-Return Models. 360° view of Customer and Staff. Enterprise Liquidity Hub for intraday liquidity and NSFR & LCR.
Enterprise Risk adjusted Return Measurement	Enterprise Registers: Risk & Controls Enterprise costs, cost model. Enterprise Risks, Enterprise Liquidity Management, Enterprise Stress Testing Framework.	Early Warning Signals Risk Limits, other Preventive and Detective Controls. 3-levels of risk management defence. Expected Shortfall, VaR. Liquidity Adjusted Market Risk, Liquidity Adjusted Credit Risk, Stressed VaR.
Enterprise activity based non-interest cost management.	Resource Cost, Unit cost of resources, Activity Costs.	Enterprise activity based non-interest cost budgeting, allocation and monitoring.

CHAPTER 5   IMPROVING OPERATING LEVERAGE

One of the many advantages of using SOA and hyperautomation is the ability to eliminate or significantly reduce the need for reconciliations. The following are common reconciliation work in the "as-is" siloed environment:

- Reconciliation of teller cash
- Reconciliation of ATM cash management
- Drafts and pay order reconciliation
- Interest accrual
- Interest taken to suspense
- Suspense accounts
- Branch transfers – reconciliation
- Nostro reconciliation
- FX revaluation
- Off-balance sheet items
- Funds transfer pricing
- Fixed asset register and depreciation

Almost 90% of the above reconciliation tasks are **nonvalue adding activities**. Process automation, with analytics, knowledge management, and continuous process improvement, can improve the operational efficiency and operating leverage.

5.5.3.1 Process Mining

Process mining is a concept that helps bank discover, monitor, and improve banking processes. It is the link between model-based process analysis and data-oriented analysis techniques. It is an essential part of continuous process improvement.

CHAPTER 5   IMPROVING OPERATING LEVERAGE

The event and process logs (BPMS) have the data on the processing of transactions. They can provide the contextual information for operating leveraging monitoring and management. For instance, the log can reveal atypical flow of the processes.

Process mining can leverage enterprise data science and machine learning.

Tables 5-12a, 5-12b, 5-12c and 5-12d are process mining examples.

Table 5-12a. *Treasury process mining – event log*

	Treasury – extract of event log			
Process Id.	Process, Activity	Date & Time Stamp	Staff	System
Over the Counter derivatives	Process Start			
	Pre-deal analytics - Start			
	Pre-deal analytics - End			
	Collateral Management-Start			
	Collateral Management-End			
	Process End			

It is based on event data, and it includes the time stamp, an important data point for modeling causality in liquidity and market risk management.

Table 5-12b. *Corporate banking – process mining – event log*

	Corporate Banking – extract of event log			
Process Id.	Activity / Activity Group	Date & Time Stamp	Staff	System
Term Loan – 10 Year	Process Start			
	Application checking & approval - Start			
	Application checking & approval - End			
	Process End			

483

CHAPTER 5 IMPROVING OPERATING LEVERAGE

There are three types of discovery processes: [30]

- The discovery process has no knowledge of the informative content of the event log.

- In the second, the event log is used with an existing process to identify risks and vulnerabilities.

- The third, the enhancement approach, uses an a priori model.

Table 5-12c. *Retail banking process mining – event log*

Process Id.		Activity / Activity Group		Date & Time Stamp	Staff	System
Retail Banking – extract of event log						
New Customer, Savings A/c	Process Start					
		Customer on-boarding	- Start			
		Customer on-boarding	- End			
	Process End					

Banking processes could have a high degree of interrelated activities. Further, in many banks, planned activities may occur out of order or skipped. Process mining gives a bank the ability to resolve the challenges that arise from these issues. It can

- Support process analysis and provide granular data on what staff and systems are doing and when

- Help investigate where and why processes deviated from the expected flow

---

[30] https://www.ibm.com/topics/process-mining

Process mining supports the identification and visualization of inefficient activities in the banking processes based on data from event logs. The bank can also perform root cause analysis to resolve issues related to performance, risk, control, and cost. The bank can use it as a tool for process performance optimization.

Table 5-12d. *Human capital process mining – event log*

Process Id.	Activity / Activity Group	Date & Time Stamp	Staff	System
	Human Capital – Extract of event log			
Recruitment	Process Start			
	Approval to recruit received - Start			
	Staff selected			
	On-boarding	End		
	Process End			

Continuous improvement – Process mining is a core component of the process management lifecycle that can be used to

- Align processes to goals
- Identify improvements
- Implement or change activities to improve quality
- Improve process maturity

5.5.3.2 BPR (Business Process Reengineering)

The performance, risk, control, and cost monitoring examples in Chapter 4, Section 4.3.3, provide an insight into the need for business process reengineering. BPR is a program that banks implement periodically based on the feedback from internal control, audit, and GRC teams.

The input for a BPR program is data on performance, risk, control, and cost examined in Chapter 4.

CHAPTER 5   IMPROVING OPERATING LEVERAGE

BPR Example – Syndicated Loan

This is a BPR explanation for Process 11, Chapter-4, Section 4.3.3.3.4.

BPR – Corrective Action – Statement of Work

- Human Capital – Skills upgraded.
- Corrective Action – Loan origination data capture, due diligence on customer, and loan requirements.
- Process automation to include GRC and legal activities.
- Risk Management – Valuation is integrated with loan exposure, collateral expiry/calling in for additional collateral, and substitution – part of improvements to collateral management.
- External process automation as in Figures 5-22a and 5-22b.

Figure 5-22 provides a high-level process flow of the loan that takes into consideration all the activities, of all participants. The syndicate loan process model includes origination, appraisal, disbursement, monitoring, and closure phases. As all the participant banks have a common objective, i.e., a successful project closure, the model should ensure transparency. This will lead to better credit monitoring and bring synergy into the credit monitoring and loan operations.

CHAPTER 5 IMPROVING OPERATING LEVERAGE

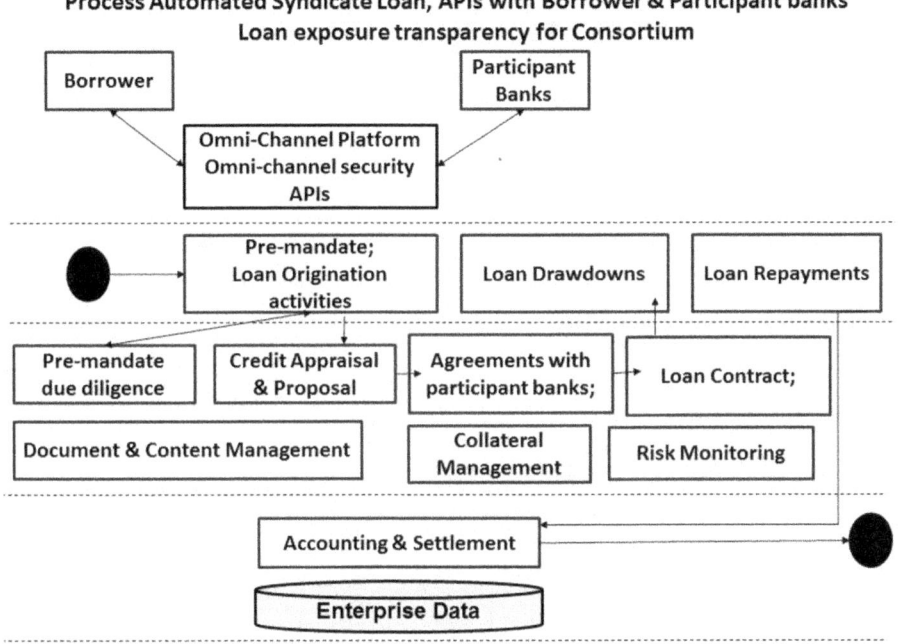

Figure 5-22. *BPR – syndicate loan*

Figure 5-23 provides the components of 360° view of the borrower. The view is common for all members of the consortium. They share a single view of the loan details, i.e., credit exposure at a consolidated level and at the level of each participant.

Credit risk modeling uses data on probability of default, expected, and unexpected loss.

CHAPTER 5   IMPROVING OPERATING LEVERAGE

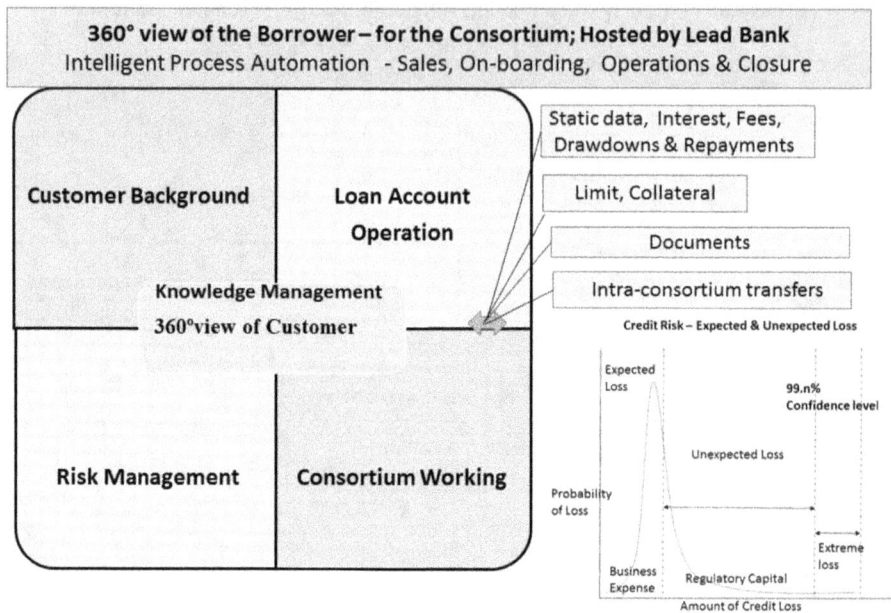

Figure 5-23. *BPR – syndicate loan*

Using process documentation and modeling, significant improvements can be made to a process-based enterprise operating model. The quality of operational risk management will get better as more data is collected at the most granular level and process maturity will be driver for operational efficiency.

Continuous process improvement will include risk management processes. Hence, process automation improves the working of the enterprise risk-adjusted return model.

CHAPTER 5   IMPROVING OPERATING LEVERAGE

BPR Example –Collateral Management Processes[31]

- Retail and corporate
- Treasury

Figure 5-24a is a generic (retail, corporate, and treasury) *collateral management schematic* for improving operating leverage. Please note that in the

- Collateral cycle, the settlement activity could apply only to treasury
- Pretrade process are applicable only to treasury

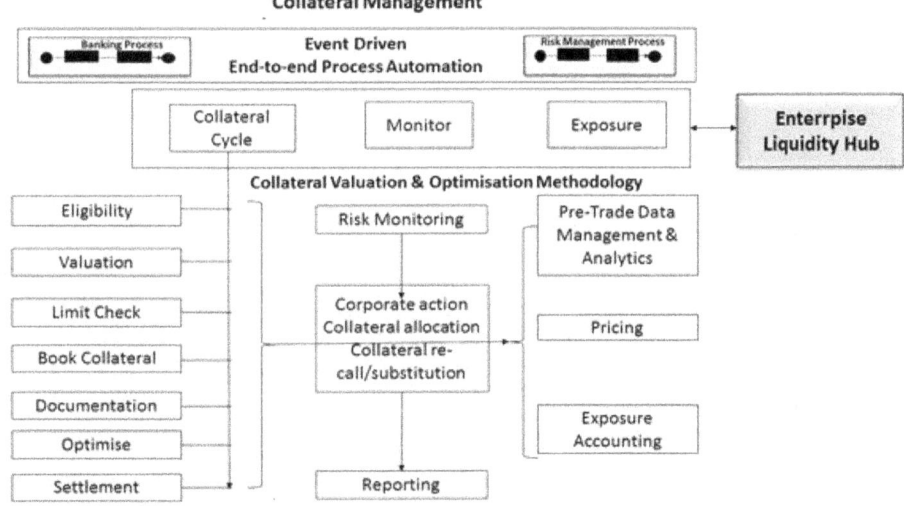

Figure 5-24a. BPR – *collateral management processes*

---

[31] Developments in treasury collateral management services September 2014
https://www.bis.org/cpmi/publ/d119.pdf

489

CHAPTER 5   IMPROVING OPERATING LEVERAGE

Enterprise process automation will ensure that all payment processes update the enterprise liquidity hub.

Figure 5-24b illustrates a high-level real-time treasury management process flow. This is a capability that many banks do not have. A real-time treasury's centralized collateral management significantly improves operating and financial leverage.

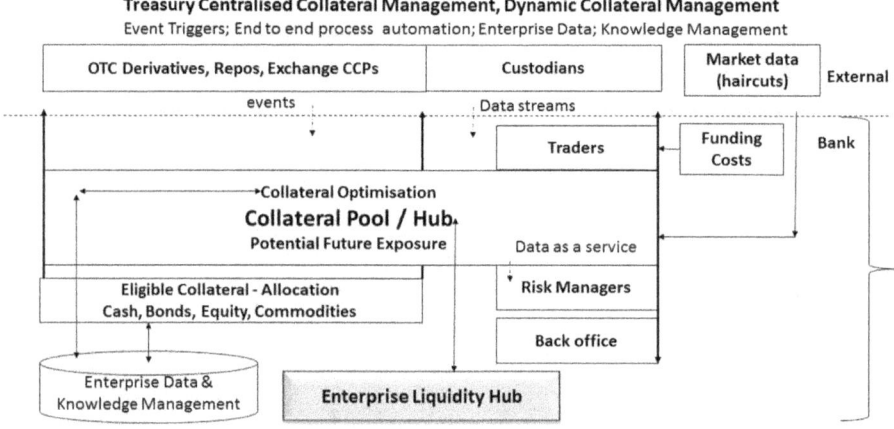

Figure 5-24b. BPR – treasury collateral management processes

BPR Example – Document/Asset Movement Tracking

Barcoding and RFID technology can be used enterprise-wide for asset/document tracking. It can be interfaced with the back-end application. The GR&C functions (including internal control/audit) can have a dashboard view of all assets with their movement history.

Paperless office has been a "mere slogan" for more than 20 years now. Asset, document, and tracking technologies can help to resolve the following vulnerabilities/weakness:

- Inability to access documents and track assets
- Loss of documents and asset pilferage
- Unproductive staff time and poor customer service

CHAPTER 5   IMPROVING OPERATING LEVERAGE

Banks are often penalized by the Banking Ombudsman or a Court for negligence in handling documents. However, many banks **do not initiate any correction action** for improving weak *document management processes*.

Figure 5-25a illustrates the following features of asset movement control. Whenever the assets are taken "in" or "out" of the zone, the RFID portal gateway at the zone automatically captures the RFID asset tag data as well as the staff who is carrying the asset. The RFID system checks for authorized movement of the asset and/or personnel and alerts the administrator on atypical activity.

The RFID tag data is master data of the asset.

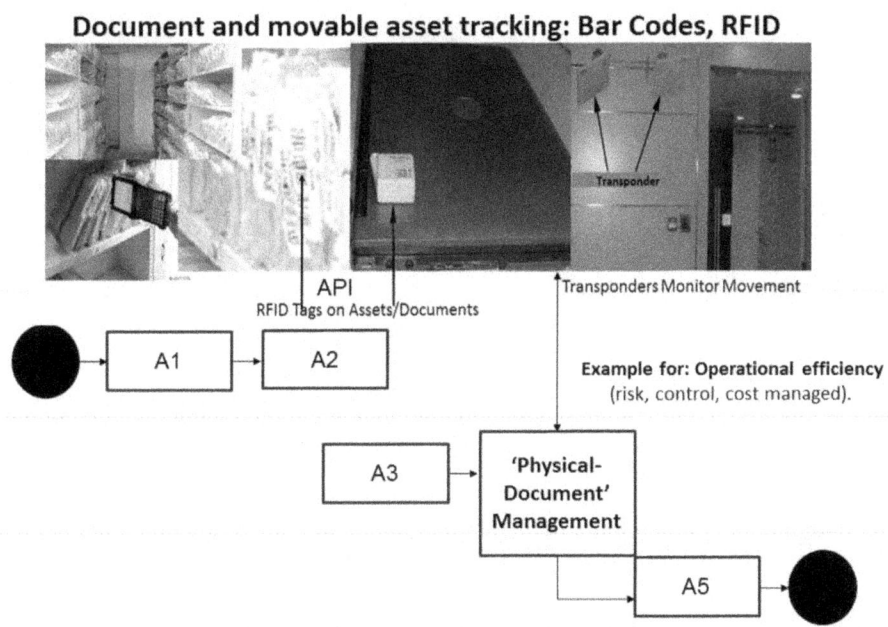

Figure 5-25a. APIs and RFID-based asset/document tracking

CHAPTER 5   IMPROVING OPERATING LEVERAGE

The movement of the assets is automatically captured in the back-end database without any manual supervision. At any point of time, an administrator can get the details of a particular asset including its location. Automated asset inventory can be done at the click of a button. BPMS can seamlessly integrate front-, middle-, and back-office activities.

The document or asset movement data is transactional data.

Figure 5-25b illustrates how the sales process for new retail customers can be made more efficient. Some of the components will also apply for account closure.

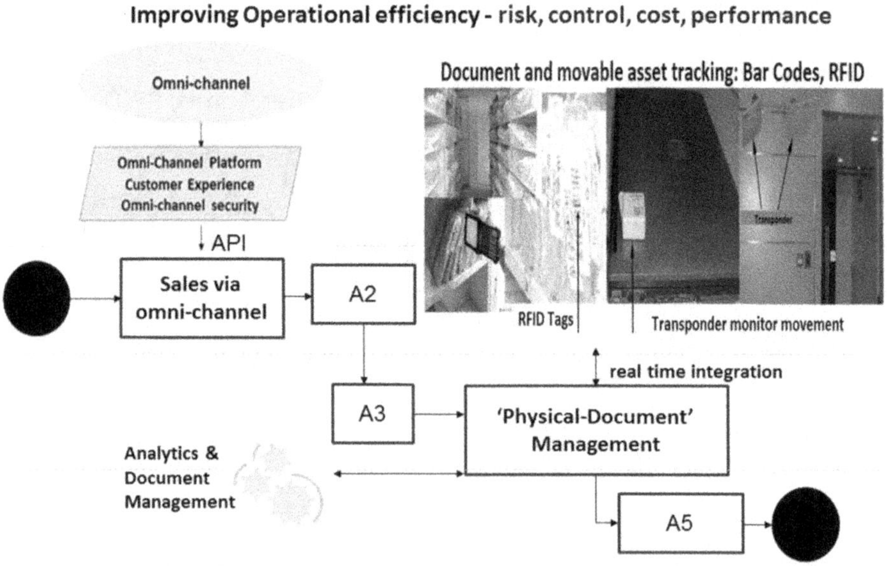

Figure 5-25b. Retail sales and omnichannel platform API

Figure 5-26 illustrates enterprise document and content management. Banking is a document intensive activity. This would include bank letters, external communications, application forms, onboarding document set, loan agreements, and computerized reports.

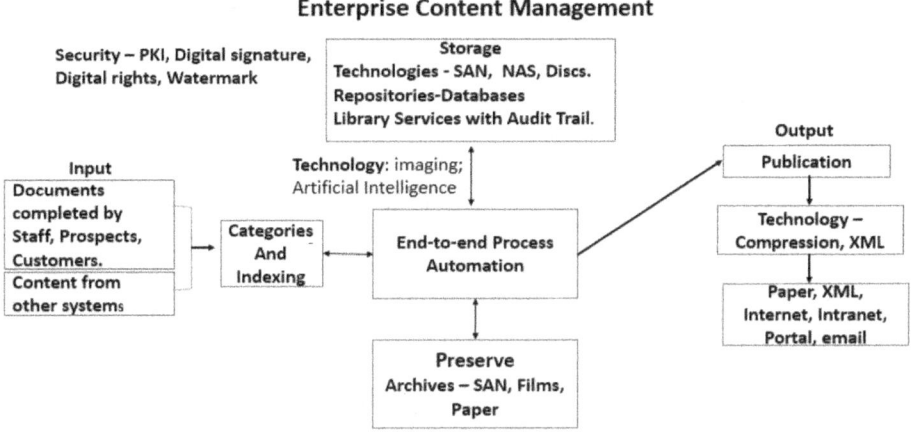

Figure 5-26. BPR – enterprise content management

Risk incidents suggest that several vulnerabilities exist in a bank's document management functions. A lack of an enterprise approach could increase operational risks and costs.

In the as-is environment, several million square feet of office space is locked for storing different types of preprinted and blank stationery, customer, and internal documents. An effective digitalization program using relevant technology can reduce office supply and premises costs.

5.5.3.3 Robotic Process Automation (RPA)

Top end BPMS vendors provide RPA. It supports the automation of repetitive, structured business activities. It can be used for banking and risk management processes. The method used for selecting the processes determines the efficiency and effectiveness of the enterprise operating model. The following points have to be considered prior to implementing RPA:

CHAPTER 5   IMPROVING OPERATING LEVERAGE

- Banks that do not have a **standardized enterprise operating model** (Section 5.4.1) would do well to complete a standardization project.

- Banks that do not have a process and service improvement culture would need to implement relevant enterprise frameworks.

- Banks should evaluate their enterprise operating model efficiency and maturity.

- RPA is not recommended for a "band-aided" complex environment.

- Processes must not have a history of changes.

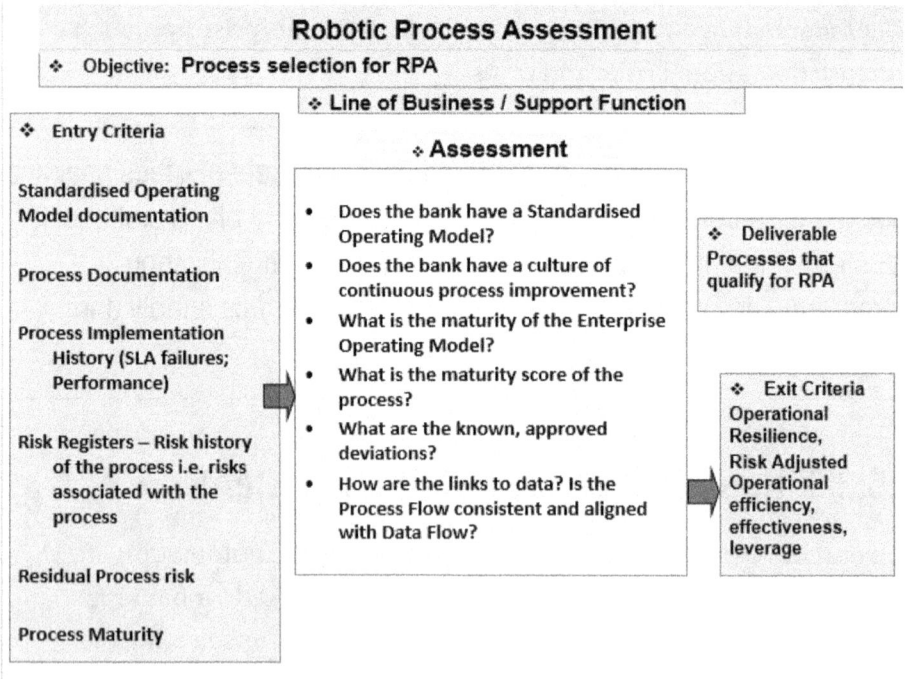

Figure 5-27. Process selection for robotic process automation

The following are key benefits of RPA:

- Decreased processing time
- Improved service levels, i.e., SLAs are met
- Improved accuracy
- Operational efficiency at minimum cost

Risk Management and Robotic Process Automation

Several risk management processes can be brought under robotic process automation, e.g., certain types of hedging, retail credit scoring, and collateral valuation.

5.5.4 Budgeting

5.5.4.1 Target Resource Utilization

Banks need to accurately estimate their resource capacity. This includes staff and systems. Sections 5.5.4.1.1 and 5.5.4.1.2 provide an overview of the parameters.

5.5.4.1.1 Staff

The US Bureau of Labor Statistics department calculates labor productivity for commercial banking by measuring the change in the relation between the output of the banking industry and the time spent by employees to produce that output.

Banking business areas included in the output are as follows:

- Demand deposit transactions
- Commercial, consumer, and real estate loans
- Administration of trusts and estates and the purchase and sale of securities

CHAPTER 5   IMPROVING OPERATING LEVERAGE

Commercial banking output is added on the basis of weights which reflect labor requirements per unit of service. The output index is then divided by an index of employee hours for commercial banking, so as to obtain an index of **output per employee hour**, i.e., United States' measure of labor productivity.

It also measures the **change over time** in the ratio of the weighted output to employee hours.

5.5.4.1.2 System

Examples for system capacity:
Core Banking System

- The Finacle core banking solution **processed interest accruals** for more than one billion term deposit accounts in less than 87 minutes, or an average of 213,000 records per second. [32]

- **Interest payments to more than 79 million savings accounts** were processed in 32 minutes, at around 41,000 transactions per second.

The 2023 Temenos Highwater Benchmark[33]

It was a benchmark using 50 million retail customers and 50 million embedded customers with 100 million accounts and 200 million loans with 150,080 transactions.

The findings included (ms, millisecond):

- Funds reservation response time is 30 ms and achieved 76 tps pre core.

- Query response time is 11 ms.

---

[32] https://www.oracle.com/docs/tech/infosys-finacle-wr-osc.pdf
[33] https://www.temenos.com/wp-content/uploads/2023/08/Highwater-Benchmark-Report-2023_Whitepaper_V09.pdf

CHAPTER 5   IMPROVING OPERATING LEVERAGE

The finance department and the enterprise IT governance teams of every bank should have a template for documenting the total cost of ownership and capacity of every system at the time of purchase. It may have some technical details, but the information should be clear to the financial accountant and cost accountant. It should be specific to the bank's business model and level of operations. *The document will be the basis for cost and performance monitoring of the system.*

Time-driven activity-based budgeting should assess the target resource utilization for the year under consideration. In the production model, the cost budget is based on the target resource utilization level.

Table 5-13a. *Time-driven activity-based cost budget*

	Bill of Resources and Resource Capacity Utilisation					
	Retail Banking		Treasury		Corporate Banking	
	Available	Utilised	Available	Utilised	Available	Utilised
Staff						
Systems						
Premises						

Cost variances can arise from the utilization level achieved. The variances will be positive, if the bank achieves or exceeds its target resource utilization level.

Premises have been included here to highlight the need for better asset utilization and fixed cost management. Several banks have back office functions occupying precious real estate space. Banks with a *process-based enterprise operating model* will be able to effectively manage the relocation of back office functions to less expensive premises.

5.5.4.2 Activity-Based Budgeting

Activity-based budgeting (ABB) is intertwined with activity-based costing (ABC) as it focuses on the business processes. It uses the process data explained in Chapter 4 and the process mining concept explained in Section 5.5.3.1 of this chapter.

ABB determines the cost of performing certain processes as opposed to the traditional function based budgeting categories. ABB is a quality enabler as it helps identify opportunities for cost reduction and for the elimination of nonvalue adding activities. ABB improves operating leverage by identifying cost-to-performance relationships. The following are the phases in ABB:

- Estimate business volume by individual products and customers
- Ascertain the resources requirements using the *bill of resources*
- Estimate and align capacity utilization with resource assignment for delivery of estimated business

Time-driven ABB is a core component of activity based enterprise noninterest cost management. The following template provides guidance on the specifics of a time-driven ABC budgeting approach.

CHAPTER 5   IMPROVING OPERATING LEVERAGE

Table 5-13b. *Time-driven activity-based cost budget for product RETSAV*

LOB	Product	Process, Activities		Volume	Activity time Min-Rnd	Total Time (Rnd)	Unit Cost	Total Cost (Rnd)
					Budgeted: Summarised & Illustrative			
		Time Driven (TD) process cost= the sum of all its TD activity costs. TD activity based cost = Process Volume * Activity time *Unit cost of activity						
Retail	RETSAV	Sales	Risk Management					
		On-boarding						
		Account Operation	ATM Withdrawal					
			ATM Cash Deposit					
			Inward Cheque Clearing					
			Outward Cheque Clearing					
			Inward, Outward SWIFT					
			Dormant Account activation					
			Total:					
		Closure of Accounts						
Product's TD Non-interest Cost, Cost of Resources utilised								

Table 5-13c. *Time-driven activity-based cost budget for product RETCCD*

LOB	Product	Process, Activities		Volume	Activity time Min-Rnd	Total Time (Rnd)	Unit Cost	Total Cost (Rnd)
					Budget: Summarised & Illustrative			
		Time Driven (TD) process cost= the sum of all its TD activity costs. TD activity based cost = Process Volume * Activity time *Unit cost of activity						
Retail	RETCCD	Sales Process	Risk Management					
		On-boarding						
		A/c Operation	Risk Management					
		Closure						
Product's TD Non-interest Cost, Cost of Resources utilised								

CHAPTER 5   IMPROVING OPERATING LEVERAGE

Table 5-13d. *Time-driven activity-based cost budget for product CORLCI*

					Budget: Summarised & Illustrative			
LOB	Product	Process, Activities		Volume	Activity time Min-Rnd	Total Time (Rnd)	Unit Cost	Total Cost (Rnd)
		Time Driven (TD) process cost= the sum of all its TD activity costs. TD activity based cost = Process Volume * Activity time *Unit cost of activity						
Corporate Banking	CORLCI	Negotiations						
		LC Issuance	Risk Management					
		Account Operation	Risk Management					
		Closure	Risk Management					
Product's TD Non-interest Cost, Cost of Resources utilised								

Table 5-13e. *Time-driven activity-based cost budget for product CORL10*

					Budget: Summarised & Illustrative			
LOB	Product	Process, Activities		Volume	Activity time Min-Rnd	Total Time (Rnd)	Unit Cost	Total Cost (Rnd)
		Time Driven (TD) process cost= the sum of all its TD activity costs. TD activity based cost = Process Volume * Activity time *Unit cost of activity						
Corporate Banking	CORL10	Sales Process	Risk Management					
		On-boarding	Document Mgt					
		A/c Operation	Site Visit					
			Internal Rating					
		Risk Management	Collateral Mark to Market					
			Loan: Risk Exposure monitoring					
			Total:					
		Closure						
Product's TD Non-interest Cost, Cost of Resources utilised								

500

Table 5-13f. Time-driven activity-based cost budget for product TRBCRS

LOB	Product	Process, Activities		Volume	Activity time Min-Rnd	Total Time (Rnd)	Unit Cost	Total Cost (Rnd)
		Budget: Summarised & Illustrative						
		Time Driven (TD) process cost= the sum of all its TD activity costs. TD activity based cost = Process Volume * Activity time *Unit cost of activity						
Treasury	TRBCRS	Pre-Deal	Risk Management					
		Trade	Risk Management					
		Confirmation, Collateral, Reconciliation	Risk Management					
		Settlement & Accounting	Risk Management					
Product's TD Non-interest Cost, Cost of Resources utilised								

5.5.4.3 Zero-Based Budgeting (ZBB)

Extending the definition of ABB, in ZBB, the costs of processes and activities that compose it are re-set and revalued each time the exercise is done. ZBB is a decision-oriented approach that enables efficient resource allocation. Knowledge management and advanced analytics make it easier to implement ZBB and is another tool for improving operating leverage.

Improving Operating Leverage

Improvements identified in Section 5 are critical for improving ERRM. The need to increasing fee-based income is back in focus.[34] The recommendations for improving operational efficiency and operating leverage in this book are relevant for increasing noninterest revenue. The following products and services are sources for fees, commission, and service charge:

---

[34] Fee-Based Income
https://www.bloomberg.com/news/articles/2023-11-09/eu-banks-pour-money-into-fee-businesses-as-end-to-boom-from-rate-hikes-looms

- Selling third-party insurance policies
- Selling government's investment schemes
- Credit cards
- Trade finance

Some of the less leveraged areas for fee-based income are

- Loan syndication
- Arranging foreign collaboration
- Advising on acquisition or mergers
- Project counselling
- Advising on balance sheet management

5.6 Process and Enterprise Operating Model Efficiency and Maturity

Knowledge management is a culture, and the enterprise knowledge repository is created using enterprise data management and advanced analytics.

This capability can be used for building and monitoring process maturity and, from it, the enterprise operating model maturity. Extending from Chapter 4, Section 4.3.3, process maturity can be quantified using a scoring system that uses performance, risk, control, and cost factors.

The lines of business and support departments are the process owners. The maturity of the processes owned by them determined the quality of operating leverage in each LOB/support department.

Figures 5-28a, 5-28b, and 5-28c illustrate the approach toward measuring the enterprise operating model efficiency and maturity.

Lines of Business
Retail Banking – Process maturity

Product Processes	Process Maturity Scores				
	1	2	3	4	5
Savings Account			✓		
Fixed Deposit			✓		
Home Loan – Salaried Group		✓			
Loan for Consumer Durables		✓			
Credit Card		✓			
Locker Rental		✓			

Figure 5-28a. *Enterprise operating model efficiency and maturity – product and line of business*

EITG Process Maturity

EITG Processes	Processes by Maturity score					Score
	1	2	3	4	5	
Incident Management			✓			
Problem Management			✓			
Change Management		✓				
Release Management			✓			
Enterprise Security		✓				
EITG Maturity						3

Figure 5-28b. *Enterprise operating model efficiency and maturity – support department and product*

CHAPTER 5   IMPROVING OPERATING LEVERAGE

Best Practices for Improving Maturity

Banks should

- Use the bill of resources
- Make an effort to standardize their enterprise operating model
- Have a culture of continuous process and service improvement
- Ensure that enterprise process automation should be aligned with enterprise data management

It is a bottom-up from the process to the products and support department functions, to the lines of business and support departments, and then to the bank.

Process based Operating Model Maturity

	Process Maturity by Lines of Business, Support Department					Score
	1	2	3	4	5	
Retail Banking		35	30			
Corporate Banking		20	25			
Treasury		20	10			
EITG		6	24			
Human Capital		6	4			
Finance		5	5			
						2.5

Figure 5-28c. Bank's enterprise operating model efficiency and maturity

Banks are implementing services & event-based enterprise architecture, enterprise data model and hyperautomation to improve their operating leverage.

Operating Leverage case study:

Treasury's Mission Critical Platform Following a proof of concept, ABN AMRO, Microsoft, and Murex moved on to migrate the MX.3 platform in 2022. The system is now entirely operational on the Azure cloud. "The key focus for us was always to make sure that we could **automate most processes** while preserving its **operational excellence** and key features," says Kees van Duin.[35]

---

[35] https://customers.microsoft.com/en-us/story/1521795340874612568-abnamrobanking-capital-markets-azure-en-netherlands

CHAPTER 6

Conclusion

A bank's ability to compete is directly linked to its ability to utilize human capital and technology effectively. Workforce competency includes knowledge, soft skills, and accumulated assets such as best practices, reusable cases, reusable work templates, empirical evidence, and historic data.

The assessment of a bank should be done holistically, using analyzing risk-adjusted performance metrics.

6.1 Bank of the Future Business Delivery

Figure 6-1 provides a schematic of a bank of the future. The capabilities and capacities mentioned therein are critical success factors for gaining competitive advantage. A continuous process and service improvement culture will support the improvement of operational efficiency and operating leverage on a sustained basis.

CHAPTER 6 CONCLUSION

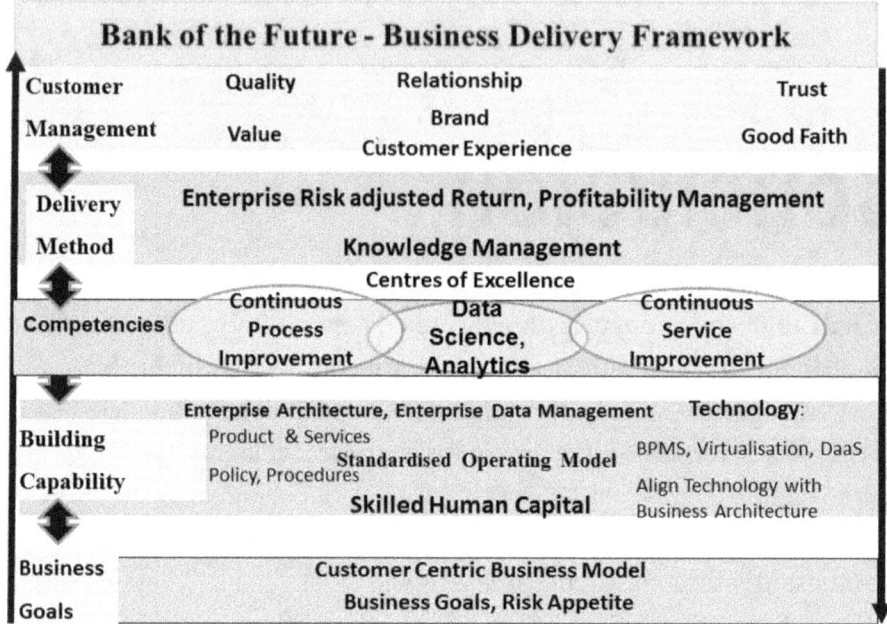

Figure 6-1. *Bank of the future – business delivery framework*

- Human capital of a bank of the future.

The following roles are emerging as an important aspect of a bank-of-the-future transformation and governance.

- A data scientist uses technical skills to create value from data by using mathematical and statistical tools and converting it into actionable intelligence. Their output is dependent on the inputs from business translators.

- Business translators are able to describe what the data reveals, place it into a useful context, and work with the data scientists in creating knowledge management databases. Business translators are skilled at linking data with business practices and requirements.

- Data steward's main responsibility is to ensure effective control and use of data assets.

CHAPTER 6 CONCLUSION

- Continuous process and service improvement.

  Business and technology governance require a deep knowledge of a bank's processes, both functional and technical. Banks that have implemented Lean Six Sigma initiatives have improved operational efficiency and attained their ROI targets.

- Chief enterprise architect.

  An enterprise architect aligns the business architecture with enterprise information technology. She / he is responsible for building a technology blueprint for the lines of business and support functions such as HR and facilities management. The output of it should provide an environment for risk-reward optimization and a more seamless customer (or end user) experience. It is a forward-looking function as the architecture should be scalable.

  The chief enterprise architect works closely with the chief data officer, chief technology officer, and chief information security officer.

- Chief customer experience.

  The role of a chief customer experience officer is getting a lot of attention in the background of the focus on data quality and management. They should be empowered to provide inputs to the technology department and lines of business.

Return on Investment in Technology

It is important for banks to evaluate technologies in terms of total cost of ownership, quantified returns, and its impact on their operational efficiency and operating leverage. Banking industry does not have a reference

CHAPTER 6   CONCLUSION

model for computing the return on investment in technology. There is no consensus as yet on the concepts, methods, and models for measuring investments in IT. Financial models used in calculating ROI in technology are an accountant's perspective of returns, and there are challenges related to *quantifying of intangibles such as data quality, service quality, and customer experience.*

A bank's management might believe that it has invested in computerized systems and yet find itself losing ground to competitors. The accountant's calculation will not reveal the threats and weaknesses in the operating environment. It is the *Enterprise IT governance process maturity scores* that provide a clear idea on the technology risks and the business return potential.

The EDM Council's framework for data management practices, with its shared ontology, and **BIAN**'s[1] SOA-based enterprise architecture, with its semantic service domains, are leading the industry's effort to collaborate and create an operating environment for a bank of the future.

Figure 6-2 illustrates an Enterprise Data Model for improving operating leverage and managing enterprise risk adjusted return effectively.

The four main risk types, market/credit/liquidity/operational, can be associated with one or more of the dimensions. The LOBs are treasury, corporate, and retail. The products and instruments are the product portfolios of each LOB (asset and liability). In this regard,

- Treasury counterparty exposures are contract specific and centered around OTC contracts.
- Depositors are creditors and borrowers are debtors.
- The traders and relationship/account managers are the risk takers.

---

[1] Banking Industry Architecture Network – www.bian.org
The Open Group Architecture Forum – http://www.togaf.org

CHAPTER 6   CONCLUSION

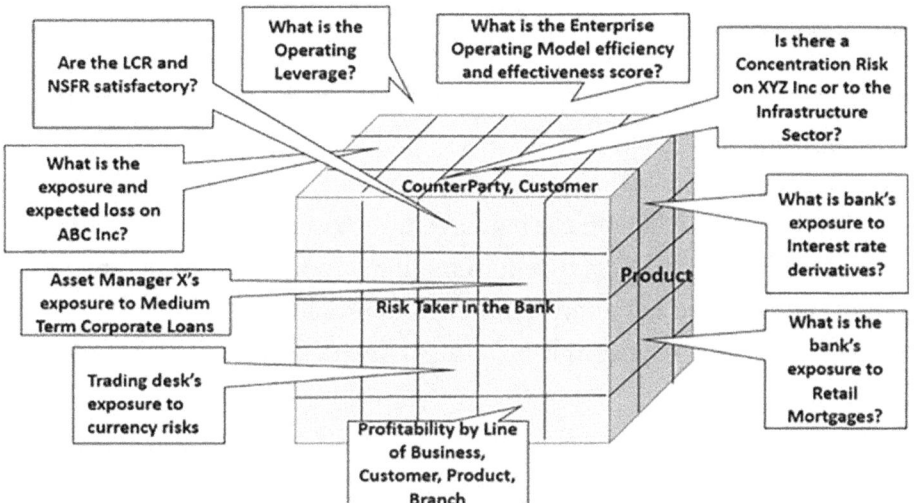

Figure 6-2. *Multi-dimensional Enterprise Data Model: Improving Operating Leverage and ERRM*

The pan-bank transformation is driven by functional and technical factors. It will improve the return on capital employed and ROI in technology. A bank's strategic initiatives should focus on operational efficiency, maximizing risk-adjusted return and improving customer experience. To accomplish this and maintain healthy growth, they would need to understand the business needs, leverage technology to minimize risks and maximize business returns. Banks must take the effort to standardize their operations and build capabilities and competencies. This is the best approach for keeping their operating environment simple and efficient.

The transformed bank has a customer-oriented business model that is powered by knowledge and managed on an exception basis, by a skilled workforce.

CHAPTER 6   CONCLUSION

6.2 Risk-Adjusted Operating Leverage

Presently, performance metrics are not risk adjusted. Further, enterprise operating model, operational efficiency, operating effectiveness and operating leverage have not been defined by Basel or by any other regulator. A formal definition will help the banking industry in managing risk adjusted returns. There is no regulatory requirement to report risk adjusted metrics such as risk adjusted net interest margin and risk adjusted operating leverage. This should be a priority for the banking industry and its stake holders.

6.3 Bank of the Future – ERRM Knowledge Management

Many banks do not have an enterprise risk governance framework, a holistic risk policy making mechanism, and an effective risk appetite statement.

Risk governance framework and risk appetite framework and statement are excellent techniques for optimizing risk-adjusted returns in managing customers, trades, and transactions. These policy documents must be adaptable to changes in the business and regulatory environment.

By having activity and time-driven activity metrics at the process level, the bottom-up phase of goal-business activity alignment gets easier. Key performance metrics can include operational efficiency drivers such as time, risk-adjusted returns, customer retention, and market share.

Knowledge management (Figure 6-3) future-proofs the banks by delivering competitive advantage.

Figure 6-3 summarizes the knowledge management explanation in Chapter 5 section 5.4.1.

Figure 6-4 illustrates the importance of enterprise data governance for providing actionable intelligence.

CHAPTER 6   CONCLUSION

These are inter-dependent mandatory capabilities for a bank of the future.

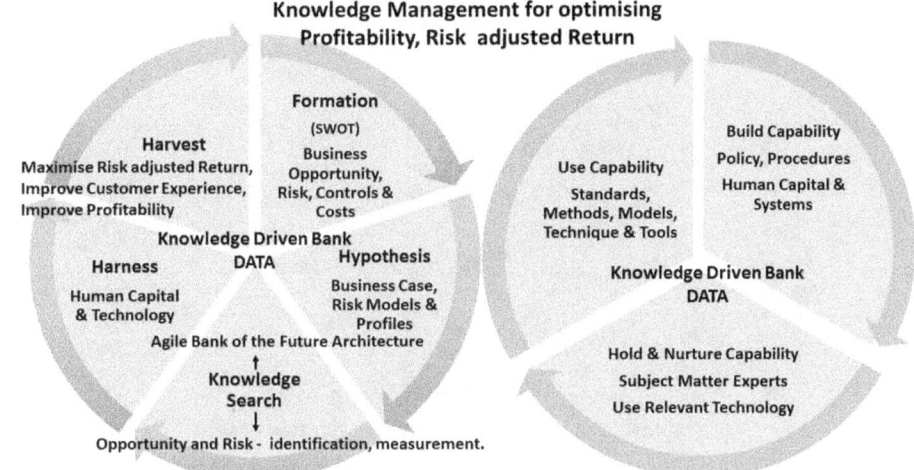

Figure 6-3. *Bank of the future – knowledge management*

Customers expect a cohesive digital experience across all channels. Banks should connect to their customers through a seamless, personalized experience in delivering products. This should be quicker than competitors and at a lower cost.

Non-bank competitors are technically more agile and in a position to meet retail customer expectations for payment transactions and retail loans. Cost to the customer and service time are key factors. The non-bank entrants are ushering in an *"unbundling of retail services."* The top end of this nontraditional source of competition is also moving toward meeting the financing needs of small and medium enterprises.

CHAPTER 6   CONCLUSION

Data Centric Enterprise Architecture supports Customer Centric Business Model
Customer Service is not a department. It an attitude enabled by actionable intelligence

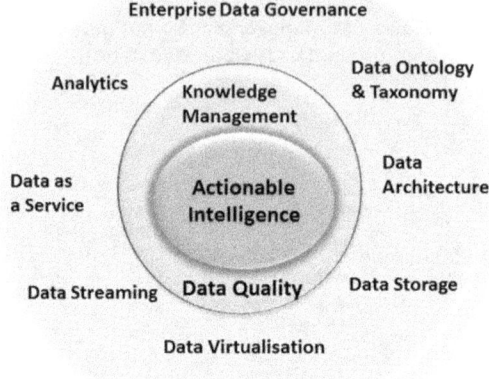

Figure 6-4. Bank of the future – actionable intelligence

An end-to-end automation of a bank using *relevant technologies* is a challenge for most banks. This requires a multidisciplinary team to take an enterprise approach to implement a large business transformation change management program. New banks would need to ensure that their approach and methodologies are in alignment with international best practices and implement frameworks that give them the capabilities and competencies to scale-up over time and compete with established banks.

The impact of a transformation is felt the most in the banking shop floor.

Customer Experience Management

The main determinants of customer experience are as follows:

- Seamless delivery of business across delivery channels
- Focus on customer-oriented KPIs that are consistent with business goals
- Actionable information for decision-makers

- Relationship pricing
- Building trust and enduring relationships

EITG helps achieve customer fulfilment in the following ways:

- Identifies sales opportunities
- Increases the probability of success in marketing efforts
- Enhances bank's capability to know their customers
- Expands customer relationships, increases customer loyalty, and supports new customer acquisition
- Improves customer acquisition and retention rates
- Allows a bank to map products and services to customer and customer segments
- Facilitates the assignment of skilled staff to financial advisory (front office) roles

---

Two decades have gone by since Mr. Bill Gates said that "Banking is necessary, banks are not." Several technology experts from Bengaluru and elsewhere have made similar noises.

Trade within domestic borders and international trade will continue to thrive as they breathe life into global economies. Banks will continue to be in existence to fund the global growth. The banks of the future will use relevant technologies, including some emerging ones, to maximize their business returns and play the important role of financial intermediary with greater efficiency.

CHAPTER 6   CONCLUSION

In 2020,[2] the International Business Council (IBC) of the World Economic Forum and the Sustainability Accounting Standards Board published the Stakeholder Capitalism Metrics.

It is a set of 21 core and 34 expanded metrics and disclosures that can be categorized under the four themes: People, Planet, Prosperity and Principles of Governance.

Self-regulation through good governance is key to managing the risk exposure of financial institutions. This was very eloquently stated by Mr. Preet Bharara, United States Attorney for the Southern District of New York, when he said "History has shown that one cannot legislate a culture of integrity. And yet, one of the paramount responsibilities and challenges of corporate leadership is to ensure such a culture. Without it, a troubling phenomenon that should be anathema to any company emerges: The penchant to test the legal and ethical line."

The book has provided an insight into a process-based approach to managing profitability, operational efficiency, and operating leverage. Mr. Jon Cunliffe, the Bank of England's deputy governor for financial stability, said: "Disorderly bank failures can imperil financial stability, including interrupting the most important services banks provide to their customers."[3]

---

[2] https://www.weforum.org/stakeholdercapitalism/our-metrics/
[3] https://www.bankofengland.co.uk/news/2018/december/boe-pra-consultations-on-resolvability-assessment-framework

Abbreviations

ABB	Activity-based budgeting
ABC	Activity-based costing
AENICM	Activity-based enterprise non-interest cost management
ALM	Asset liability management
As-is	The present operating environment in banks
Basel	www.basel.org
BCP	Business continuity planning
BPMS	Business process management suite
COBIT	Control Objectives for Information and Related Technology
Comm	Commodity
COSO	Committee of Sponsoring Organizations of the Treadway Commission
CR	Credit risk
DRS	Disaster recovery system
EDM	Enterprise data management
EIT	Enterprise information technology
EITG	Enterprise information technology governance

(*continued*)

ABBREVIATIONS

ELM	Enterprise liquidity management
ENICM	Enterprise non-interest cost management
EQ	Equity
ERR	Enterprise risk-adjusted return
ERRM	Enterprise risk-adjusted return management
FTP	Funds transfer pricing
FX	Foreign exchange (currency)
GRC	Governance, risk, and compliance
ISDA	International Swaps and Derivatives Association
LCR	Liquidity coverage ratio
LTP	Liquidity transfer pricing
MM	Money market
MR	Market risk
NSFR	Net stable funding ratio
OPS	Operations
OR	Operational risk
ORM	Operational risk management
RAS	Risk appetite statement
RCCP	Risk, control, cost, and performance

(*continued*)

SOA	Services-oriented architecture
SOX	Sarbanes–Oxley Act
TBB	Treasury banking book
To be	The target operating environment
TTB	Treasury trading book
ZBB	Zero-based budgeting

Index

A

ABB, *see* Activity-based budgeting (ABB)
ABC, *see* Activity-based costing (ABC)
Actionable intelligence, 63, 137, 268, 269, 514
Activity-based budgeting (ABB), 63, 317, 498–500
Activity-based costing (ABC)
    business activities, 35
        FX forward, 36, 38
    consume activities
        direct cost, 34
        indirect cost, 34
    ENICM, 39
    objective/concept, 33, 34
Activity-based enterprise noninterest cost management (AENICM), 138, 145, 155, 157, 183, 267
    classifications, 48
    concept/objectives, 49
    definition, 47
    direct and indirect, 47
    disclosure, 48
    fixed, 48
    function, 48
    measure, 47
    noninterest costs, 47
    payment transactions, 49, 51, 52
Advise satisfaction index ranking, 475
AENICM model, *see* Activity-based enterprise noninterest cost management (AENICM)
ALCO, *see* Asset Liability Committee (ALCO)
ALM, *see* Asset-liability management (ALM)
AML-CFT laws and regulations, 460
AML-CFT risk monitoring, 460
AMS, *see* Automatic modeling system (AMS)
Artificial neural networks, 459, 461
As-is environment, 133
    cost data capture, 86
    ENICMS, 86
    fragmented datasets, 144
    processing components, 133
    total resource supplied/total used, 134

INDEX

Asset Liability Committee (ALCO), 64, 284
Asset liability management (ALM), 5, 51, 80, 393, 395
Automatic modeling system (AMS), 459
Automation, 53, 60, 147, 184, 288, 380, 410

B

BAM, *see* Business activity monitoring (BAM)
Banking business, 1, 141, 183, 306, 308
Banking industry, 401
    core banking system, 53, 54
    customer relationship management, 56
    general ledger, 54
    lending software, 55
    support functions, 57
    trade finance, 55
    treasury management system, 55, 56
Banking process, 14, 24, 139, 145, 176, 271, 484
Bank managements, 63, 88, 138, 390, 471
Bank of the future
    actionable intelligence, 514
    business delivery framework, 508, 509
    customer experience management, 514
    EITG, 515
    ERRM, 510
    knowledge management, 513
    LOB, 510
    multidimensional enterprise data model, 511
    risk adjusted, 512
    risk governance framework, 512
    risk types, 510
    ROI, 509
Banks
    business situations, 281, 282
    call centers/website chatbots, 397
    choice of technology, 275
    close branches, 401
    closed branches, 397
    customers, 398
    data-centric approach, 299
    data-item inventory, 299
    fines and penalties, 303
    internet-only/mobile-only, 399
    ML, 349
    objectives, 290
    operating leverage, 273
    paper-based procedures, 404
    paperless office approach, 405
    policy and procedures, 309
    prescriptive analytics/discovery analytics, 281
    process-based approach, 280
    procurement costs, 404

INDEX

profitability ratios/
  profitability, 276
reports, 303
retailers, 332
risk profile, 302
risk types, 302
UK HSBC, 278, 279
US Signature Bank, 277
Bank's enterprise operating model
  maturity, 504
Bank's rating, 422
Basel principles, 477
BCMS, *see* Business Continuity
  Management
  System (BCMS)
BCP, *see* Business continuity
  planning (BCP)
Behavioral pricing, 444
Benchmarking, 432, 444
Bill of materials (BOM), 92,
  186, 187
Bill of resources (BOR), 187–190,
  192, 203, 216
  activity-based enterprise cost
    management, 188
  cost allocation, 187
  operational efficiency and
    operating leverage, 187
  process-automated
    environment, 188
  product life cycle, 188
Bills discounting, 7, 55
Blockchain technology, 144
BOM, *see* Bill of materials (BOM)

Bond futures, 5
Bonds, 4, 55
Books of account, 67, 97, 113, 190,
  242, 255–261, 386, 413
BOR, *see* Bill of resources (BOR)
BPEL, *see* Business Process
  Execution Language (BPEL)
BPMS, *see* Business process
  management suite (BPMS)
BPR, *see* Business process
  reengineering (BPR)
Branch network
  branch productivity, 400
  café and branch concept, 399
  closed branches, 397
  designed branches, 398
  face-to-face service, 399
  financial advisors, 399
  landscape of technology, 398
  mortgage advisors, 398
  operational risks *vs* benefits, 397
  technical bias, 398
Brand name, capabilities and
  capacity, 409
Break-even analysis, 306
Budgeting
  ABB, 498–500
  target resource utilization
    core banking system, 496
    staff, 495, 496
    system capacity, 496
    2023 Temenos Highwater
      Benchmark, 496
  ZBB, 501

523

INDEX

Business activity monitoring (BAM), 183, 244
Business Continuity Management System (BCMS), 391
Business continuity planning (BCP), 29, 79, 289, 390–392
Business growth, capabilities and capacity, 409
Business metadata, 164
Business models, 1, 69, 167, 267, 398, 410
Business Process Execution Language (BPEL), 179
Business process management suite (BPMS), 61, 147
  BAM, 183
  BPEL, 179
  BPM engine, 181
  BPMN, 180
  called/invoked process, 181
  case management, 183
  case studies, operational efficiency improvement
    BNY Mellon Wealth Management, 244
    Deutsche Bank, 246
    Development Bank of Singapore, 248
    INDUS Ind Bank, 246
    Sharjah Islamic Bank, 249
    TD Banknorth, 247
    Wells Fargo, 245
  CIP/KYC process, 181
  components, 178, 182
  EAI, 183
  enterprise document/content management, 183
  hyperautomation, 184, 185
  intelligence and rules engine, 182
  process orchestration, 181
  RPA, 184
  SOA-BPMS convergence, 185, 186
  subprocesses, 180
Business process modeling, 179
  BPEL, 179
  BPMN, 180
  called/invoked process, 181
  CIP/KYC process, 181, 182
  subprocesses, 180
Business process reengineering (BPR), 485, 486
  document/asset movement tracking, 490–493
  operational risk data update, 489, 490
  syndicated loan, 486, 487

C

Café and branch concept, 399
Called/invoked process, 181
CBOE, *see* Complex banking operating environment (CBOE)
CDS, *see* Credit default swaps (CDS)

INDEX

Centers of excellence (COE), 409, 469
Central Bank, 50, 396
Certificate of Deposits (CDs), 5
Chart of accounts
    accounting books, 68
        account number, 68
        features, 69
        fixed account code, 69
        fixed deposit account, 69
        ENICM (*see* Enterprise non-interest cost management system (ENICM))
    structure, 70
    treasury, 70
Choice of technology, 275
Climate change, 407
Cloud computing, 406
COBIT, *see* Control Objectives for Information and Related Technology (COBIT)
COE, *see* Centers of excellence (COE)
Colored Petri net (CPN), 462
Commercial bank, 2, 25, 91, 155, 187, 252
Commercial Papers, 5
Committee of Sponsoring Organizations (COSO), 18, 429
Committee on Payment and Settlement Systems (CPSS), 50
Commodity futures, 6

Commodity swap, 6
Competency-based assets, 507
Complex banking operating environment (CBOE)
    causes, 58
    characteristics, 59, 60
    constraint, 62
    David Levy's treatment, 58
    environmental scenarios, 60, 61
    Moses, J., 58
    Siloed, 60
    Sussman, J., 58
Conceptual analysis, 14
Continuous operating leverage improvement program
    Barclays Group's cost-to-income ratios, 415–417
    Citigroup 2023 financial summary, 413
    Citigroup's operating performance metrics, 414
    Credit Suisse ratios, 417
    ENICM and ERRM systems, 413
    enterprise liquidity position, Citigroup & Barclays, 416
    Project Bora Bora, 413
    regulatory requirements, 412
    sustainable performance indicators, 412
Continuous process improvement (CPI), 420, 480
    BPR (*see* Business process reengineering (BPR))
    enterprise-wide program, 481

INDEX

Continuous process improvement (CPI) (*cont.*)
  knowledge management work breakdown structure, 481
  nonvalue adding activities, 482
  process mining, 481–485
  RPA (*see* Robotic process automation (RPA))
  SOA and hyperautomation, 482
Contract Intelligence (COiN), 349
Control Objectives for Information and Related Technology (COBIT), 20
  design phase, 22
  functional control frameworks, 22
  IT framework, 21
  success factors, 20
Corporate banking, 55, 91
  bills coacceptance, 346, 347
  collateral management, 354, 356
  corporate term loan, 347–349
  cost breakup, 341
  credit risk management, 352, 354
  fixed and variable costs, 343
  internal credit rating, 356, 357
  LC issuance, 344–346
  ML, 357
  process-automated, time-driven activity-based costing, 342
  products, 7–10, 128
  revenue, 341
  syndicate loan, 350, 351
  time-driven ABC method, 342
  total cost, 341
Corporate governance, 138, 141, 289, 477–479
Corporate Loans
  overdraft/current accounts, 9, 10
  retail banking, 10, 12
  syndicated loans, 10
  term loans, 9
  working capital loans, 10
COSO, *see* Committee of Sponsoring Organizations (COSO)
Cost accountant, 308–311, 329, 386
Cost allocation approach
  financial and costing books, 126
  support department costs, 124, 125
Cost data catalog, 165
Cost management verification procedures, 97
Cost reduction, 63, 288, 304, 401, 431, 442
Cost reduction techniques
  benchmarking, 444
  product life cycle costing, 443, 444
  target costing, 442, 443
Coupon bonds, 4, 55
CPI, *see* Continuous process improvement (CPI)
CPN, *see* Colored Petri net (CPN)

INDEX

CPSS, *see* Committee on Payment and Settlement Systems (CPSS)
Credit default swaps (CDS), 217, 264, 265
Credit risk, 6, 80, 174, 201, 352, 434
Credit risk modeling, 352, 487
Customer-account level taxonomy, 158
Customer-centric business model, 167, 267
Customer experience management, 475–477, 514
Customer relationship management, 56, 248
Cyberattack, 299

D

DAMA, *see* Data Management Association's (DAMA)
Data centers, 296, 298, 398, 405, 406
Data-centric, process-automated operations, 150
Data Management Associations (DAMA), 450
Data Management Body of Knowledge (DMBOK), 450
Data Management Capability Model (DCAM), 450
DCAM, *see* Data Management Capability Model (DCAM)
Deposit mobilization, 91

Digital signatures, 405
Direct costs, 94, 98
    allocation, 99
    corporate banking products, 111
    cost objects, 86, 95
    depreciation, 99, 100
    director/auditor fees, 106
    direct staff cost, 100
    EITG and premises costs, 100
    enterprise IT governance, 101
    external professional services, 106
    factors, 98
    human capital, 99
    insurance, 103, 104
    line of business, 108–110
    LOB's cost, 107, 110
    management cost, 108
    office supplies, 102
    premises, 101, 102
    repairs and maintenance, 105
    retail product, 110
    sales and marketing, 103
    support departments, 99, 111–113
    travel, 105
    treasury products, 110
DMBOK, *see* Data Management Body of Knowledge (DMBOK)
Document and content management processes, 331
Domestic banks, 24, 158, 286

INDEX

Dynamic layering, 294
Dynamic Pricing, 444

E

EAI, *see* Enterprise application integration (EAI)
ECR, *see* Export Credit Refinancing (ECR)
EDMC's framework, 450–452
Efficiency structure theory, 408, 419, 420
Efficiency theory, 420
EITG, best practices, 406, 407
ELH, *see* Enterprise liquidity hub (ELH)
ELM, *see* Enterprise liquidity management (ELM)
End-to-end automation, 151, 514
Enterprise activity-based noninterest cost management, 156
Enterprise application integration (EAI), 179, 183
Enterprise architecture, 144, 153–156, 171
Enterprise content management, 331, 493
Enterprise cost management system, 137
Enterprise data management, 389, 447
  core principles, 159, 160
  cost data owners, 158
  customer-account level taxonomy, 158
  customer master data, noninterest cost, 161–163
  data architecture and management, 159
  data structure, ENICM system, 160
  DCAM, 450
  DMBOK, 450
  EDMC's framework, 450–452
  ERRM and activity-based ENICM models, 157
  metadata, cost, 164, 165
  NIM, 158
  noninterest cost allocation taxonomy, 156, 157
  ontology, 155
  reference data, treasury operations, 166, 167
  Standard Chartered Bank, case study, 250
  taxonomy, 154–156
  transaction data, 167
Enterprise event ontology, 153
Enterprise fraud management, 461
Enterprise human capital management, 473
Enterprise liquidity hub (ELH), 395, 436, 437
Enterprise liquidity management (ELM), 52, 285, 286, 392
  data granularity, 396
  ELH, 395

INDEX

FTP, 393
funding cost, rate changes, 396
intraday liquidity, 396
LTP, 393
profitability management, 394
ratios, 396
treasury, 393
Enterprise Noninterest Cost Accounting
financial and costing books, 64
FTP, 65, 66
profitability, 64
Enterprise noninterest cost allocation, phases, 85
Enterprise non-interest cost management system (ENICM), 1, 12, 13, 310
banking, 91
banks, 87, 91
branch cost, 130, 131
components, 147
cost allocation, 89, 91, 146
direct costs (*see* Direct costs)
lines of business, 97
operations department, 96
P&L account, 94, 95
products/branch, 98
result, 97
cost drivers, 93, 94
customers and customer groups/segments
corporate customer cost, 130
noninterest costs to customers, 128
retail customer cost, 129
data items, 71
elements of costs, 92
environments, 87, 88
lines of business, 91
mapping, 71
noninterest cost of products
corporate banking products, 128
retail products, 127
treasury products, 127
objectives, 146
ownership of costs, 92
product noninterest revenue, 132, 133
structure, 71, 72
treasury
business delivery environment, 89, 90
cost of risk management, 90
Enterprise operating model
ABC/TDABC cost model, 139, 140
banking process, 145
building
as-is business view, 25, 26
Basel operational risk incident, 26
BASEL operational risk incident, 27
complete, 23
departments service, 25

529

INDEX

Enterprise operating model (*cont.*)
    inputs, 22, 23
    organization structure, 24
    policy and procedures, 25
    risk management, 24
    standards, 27, 28
    support function, 24
  capabilities, 410
  COBIT, 20–22
  concept, 15
  controls and
    standards, 18, 19
  corporate goals, 16
  COSO application, 20
  cost management, 145
  data challenges, 142
  delivery mechanism, 287
  design and
    implementation, 15, 16
  dimensions, 20
  enterprise risk-adjusted returns, 142, 143
  ERRM and AENICM
    models, 143
  gaps, 138
  maturity, 503
  noninterest cost
    management, 142
  operations phase
    case studies, 30–32
    inputs, 28, 29
  organization structure/human
    capital, 141
  policies, 140
  process-based, 139, 144, 280
  RAS, 141
  risk culture, 138
  services-and process-based, 151, 152
  technologies, 17
Enterprise process
  automation, 184, *See also*
    Process automation
  BOM, 186, 187
  BOR (*see* Bill of
    resources (BOR))
  BPMS, 150
  capture of cost data at
    source, 239–243
  financial update and costing
    books, 242, 243
  goal breakdown, 167–170
  granular data collection, 243, 244
  process-based operating model
    (*see* Process-based
    enterprise
    operating model)
Enterprise process taxonomy, 174, 177, 469
Enterprise risk-adjusted return
  management (ERRM), 1, 52, 138, 272, 288, 422, 437
Enterprise risk, causal
  analysis, 432
FDIC Chairman, 440
First Republic Bank, 439
fishbone diagram, 432

operational
and credit risk factors, 434
and liquidity risk factors, 435–437
and market risk factors, 433
and other risk factors, 433
Signature Bank, FDIC Press Release 2023, 438
Silicon Valley Bank, 439
Equity options, 6
Equity swap, 6
ERRM, *see* Enterprise risk-adjusted return management (ERRM)
ERRM data model, 155, 157, 267
Eurodollar short-term deposit, 5
Event-driven architecture, 153, 177, 181
Export Credit Refinancing (ECR), 8, 55

F

Financial and costing books, 64, 126, 137, 242, 243
Financial Market Infrastructure (FMI), 50
Fixed expenses, 48
FlexiPay home loan, 163
FMI, *see* Financial Market Infrastructure (FMI)
Forward rate agreement, 4, 55
FTP, *see* Funds transfer pricing (FTP)
Funds transfer pricing (FTP), 63–66, 158, 161, 393–394

G

General ledger (GL), 54, 79, 97, 145
GL, *see* General ledger (GL)
GNOSS technology, 349
Golden Source, 162
Goodwill, 417, 420
Governance, risk, and compliance (GRC), 2, 71, 112, 438
Granularity, 20, 146, 396
GRC, *see* Governance, risk, and compliance (GRC)
Green data center, 405–407

H

Hierarchical timed colored Petri net, 462
Home loan, 11, 107, 163, 201–203, 256, 330
Human capital, 470, 472
Human capital management, 142, 232, 292, 470, 473
Human capital system, 57, 116, 239, 293–295, 383
Human perimeter, 292
Hyperautomation, 184, 252
BPMS, 185
robotic process automation, 185
SOA, 185

531

I, J

IBC, *see* International Business Council (IBC)
ICC, *see* International Chamber of Commerce (ICC)
Index-linked credit default swap, 264, 265
Indirect costs, 94, 114
    allocation, 114, 115
    cost pools, 86, 95
    EITG, 117–119
    indirect employee cost, 115, 116
    office supplies, 121
    premises, rent/utilities, 119
    repairs and maintenance costs, 122, 123
    summarization, 123, 124
Information security management system (ISMS), 28
Information Technology Infrastructure Library (ITIL), 428
    application management, 429
    business perspective, 428
    governance framework, 428
    ICT infrastructure management, 429
    ITIL governance process framework, 428
    security management, 429
    service delivery, 429
    service management, 431
    service support, 429
Interest rate option, 5
Interest rate swap (IRS), 5, 37, 38, 44, 220, 263, 264, 362–364
Internal control manager, 309, 310, 329
International Business Council (IBC), 516
International Chamber of Commerce (ICC), 18
International Organization of Securities Commissions (IOSCO), 50
International Swaps and Derivatives Association (ISDA), 18, 19
Intraday liquidity, 51, 52, 396, 437
IOSCO, *see* International Organization of Securities Commissions (IOSCO)
ISDA, *see* International Swaps and Derivatives Association (ISDA)
ISMS, *see* Information security management system (ISMS)
ITIL, *see* Information Technology Infrastructure Library (ITIL)
IT Services Management (ITSM) Case Saudi Hollandi Bank, 430

INDEX

K

Keras and R algorithms, 469
KM, *see* Knowledge management (KM)
Knee-jerk "cost control" reaction, 325
Knowledge management (KM), 63, 144, 224, 445–449, 502
Know Your Employee (KYE), 25, 235, 237, 238, 293, 433

L

LC, *see* Letter of Credit (LC)
LCR, *see* Liquidity coverage ratio (LCR)
Lean Six Sigma project, 430
Lending software, 55
Letter of Credit (LC), 8, 9, 55, 259
Lines of business (LOB), 2
    bank staff costs, 134, 135
    branch cost, 132
    commodity options/futures, 6
    commodity swap, 6
    corporate banking
        LC, 8, 9
        loans, 9
        nonfunded, 8
        trade finance, 7, 8
    cost allocation, 97
    cost data, 116
    and departments, 121, 123
    direct costs, 99, 108, 109
    equity options, 6
    equity swap, 6
    foreign exchange
        currency futures, 3
        currency option, 3
        currency swap, 3
        FX forward, 3
        FX spot, 2
    indirect costs, 114
    money market
        bonds, 4
        interest rate caps and floors, 4
        interest rate collar, 4
    staff cost, 135
    treasury, 2
Liquidity coverage ratio (LCR), 286, 394, 412, 418
Liquidity risk, 50, 80, 222, 284, 393, 417, 432, 436, 437, 472
Liquidity transfer pricing (LTP), 66, 277, 393–395
Loan document automation, 357
LOB, *see* Lines of business (LOB)
Loyalty pricing, 444
LTP, *see* Liquidity transfer pricing (LTP)

M

Machine learning (ML), 349, 452
    broad categories, 453
    methods, 452

INDEX

Machine learning (ML) (*cont.*)
    model creation and usage processes, 455
    neural network system, 458, 459
    for operating leverage, 455–457
    RL, 454
    supervised learning, 453
    unsupervised learning, 453
Market liquidity, 354
Market risk, 66, 80, 352–354, 433
Master customer data, 161
Master data, 71, 131, 161–163
Master data management, 162
Maximum likelihood logistic regression (MLLR) model, 461
Meshing of actions, 14
Microservice architecture, 134, 153
ML, *see* Machine learning (ML)
Monitoring, operating leverage
    BCP, 388, 390–392
    bill of resource and cost, 311, 316, 317
    BOD's risk, 319
    corporate banking (*see* Corporate banking)
    corrective action, 318
    effectiveness, 308
    enterprise IT governance
        customer service, 378, 379
        EITG tool, 374–376
        incident management, 376, 377
        release management, 377, 378
    enterprise risk, 388
    enterprise risk-adjusted return governance, 318, 319
    enterprise risk committee, 320
    enterprise stress testing, 388, 389
    examples, 323
    financial department, 373, 374
    GRC
        risk models, 384, 385
        underutilization, 384
    human capital, 380
        data, 383
        recruitment, 380, 381
        termination, 381–383
    implementation, 318
    importance, 317
    legal department, 386
    management
        meetings, 321, 322
        quality, 321
    operational risk database, 387
    operations department, 386
    process, static details, 310
    retail banking (*see* Retail banking)
    risk adjusted performance, 312
        cost of controls, 314, 315
        cost of doing business, 316
        enterprise IT governance, 316
        nature of controls, 313, 314

risk mitigation, 316
root cause analysis, 312
staff recruitment, 316
three lines of defense model, 313, 314
risk audit committee, 321
risk-based
approach, 308–310
risk committees, 319, 320
subprocesses
AML, 367–369
case management, 371, 372
fraud prevention/detection, 369–371
treasury
cost breakup, 358
current swap, contract input, 360–362
fixed and variable costs, 360
index-linked CDS input, 364, 366
interest rate swap, contract input, 362–364
Nostro reconciliation, 367
PRCC monitoring, 358
process-automated, time-driven activity-based costing, 359
resource utilization, 359
revenue, 357
total cost, 358
Mortgage advisors, 398
Multinational banks, 24, 250, 368

N

Net interest margin (NIM), 158, 394
Net stable funding ratio (NSFR), 286, 394, 412, 416, 418
NIM, *see* Net interest margin (NIM)
Non-bank competitors, 513
NSFR, *see* Net stable funding ratio (NSFR)

O

Omnichannel, 42, 91, 338–340, 492
Ontology, 81, 155, 157, 445, 510
Ontology-driven knowledge management, 446
KM, 446, 448, 449
knowledge culture, 447
knowledge types, 447
ontology-based, data-centric ERRM, 445
PRCC, 445
Ontology-driven system design, 155
Operating leverage, 169, 187, 244, 252, 266
banks, 273
concept, 272
cost-income ratio deviation, 274
efficiency ratio, 273
performance metrics of European banks, 274
uses, 273

INDEX

Operating leverage (*cont.*)
  cost reduction and cost control, 304
  data classification levels, 299, 300
  economy of scale, 407, 408
  EITG risks
    business continuity planning, 296–298
    data centers, 298
    Monzo's service, 297
    power failure, 296
    telco-owned satellite incident, 295, 296
  enterprise risk
    ELM, 285–287
    retail lending risks, 284, 285
    treasury risk model taxonomy, 282, 283
  fixed and variable costs, 305
    cost-volume-profit analysis, 306, 307
    funds, 305
    interest expenses, 305
    LOB, 305, 306
    methods, 308
    nonlinear cost-volume-profit analysis, 307
    time-driven ABC, 306
  hacking data, 299
  metrics, 272
  monitoring (*see* Monitoring, operating leverage)

operational resilience, 289
operational risk
  causation, 298
  components, 289, 290, 292
  data, 291
  external source, 288
  human capital system, 293–295
  people, 288
  policy and procedure, 288
  RCSA, 290
  risk culture, 287
  staff incidents, 292–294
  systems, 288
performance, 282
risk appetite, 300–302
risk capacity, 301, 302
risk culture, 293
risk tolerance, 300, 302
S&P report, 276
UK HSBC
  ECB's supervisory priorities, 279
  financial data, 278
  financial metrics, 279
  PRA, 278
US Signature Bank, 277
year-on-year ratio, 272
Operational efficiency, 169, 184, 185, 187, 188, 244, 265–269, 393, 414
Operational risk (OR), 80, 195, 254, 292, 432

INDEX

Operational risk management (ORM), 27, 229, 234, 289, 291, 441, 442
ORM, *see* Operational risk management (ORM)
Outsourcing
    court judgement, 402
    decision, 402
    EBA guidelines, 404
    ECB survey, 403
    SWIFT infrastructure, 403
Overdrafts, 9–11

P, Q

Packing credit, 7, 55
Pan-bank transformation, 511
Participant banks, 10, 351, 486
Performance ratios, 411, 421, 440
Performance, risk, control, and cost (PRCC), 19, 62, 139–141, 281, 310, 323, 423, 445
Petri nets, 462, 463
P&L, *see* Profit and loss (P&L)
Postshipment Finance, 7
PRA, *see* Prudential Regulation Authority (PRA)
Process automation, 190
    corporate
        corporate customer onboarding, 209, 210
        corporate loan credit risk monitoring, 212–217
        corporate loan disbursement, 211, 212
        corporate term loan application, 204–206
        credit risk appraisal, corporate loan application, 207, 208
    and data lineage, 190
    EITG
        incident management, 231–233
    examples, 191
    existing customer's new term deposit, 196–198
    GRC
        anti-money laundering and countering terrorism financing, 227–230
    home loan application, salaried individuals, 199–203
    human capital
        recruitment, 233, 235, 236
        retention, 236, 237
        termination, 238, 239
    new term deposit opening, new customer, 193–196
    process mining, 251
    process modeling dimensions, 192
    tasks for implement activity-based ENICM, 189
    template for TDABC, 253
    time-driven ABC (TDABC), 252

INDEX

Process automation (*cont.*)
    corporate, 259–261
    retail, 255–259
    treasury, 262–265
    treasury
        index-linked CDS deal input, 217–220
        interest rate swap deal input, 221–223
        OTC derivative, 224–226
Process-aware information systems, 251
Process-based enterprise operating model, 169
    banking process definition, 176–178
    bank's process inventory, 171
    customized process-based enterprise control framework, 176
    front, middle, and back-office functions, 175
    high-level credit risk management process, 174
    process inventory, 171, 173
    process level, 174
    product/service delivery process, 171, 172
Process mining, 251, 253, 482–485, 498
Product hierarchy, 162
Production model, 1, 12–13, 497
Profiles, 7, 204, 352, 380, 456
Profit and loss (P&L), 67, 70, 87, 94

Project Bora Bora, 413
Prudential Regulation Authority (PRA), 278
Pull cost modeling, 40
Push cost modeling, 32, 33

R

RAROC, *see* Risk-adjusted return on capital (RAROC)
RAS, *see* Risk appetite statement (RAS)
Real-time centralized collateral management system, 435–436
Real-time gross settlement (RTGS), 50, 51, 172
Reference data, 160, 166–167, 360, 362
Reinforcement learning (RL), 454
Repos, 5, 55
Resource-based theory, 420
    bank's rating, pillars, 422
    capital adequacy concept, 421
    goodwill, 420
    operational efficiency, 420
    revenue growth, 421
    theory concept, 420
Retail banking, 91, 181, 193, 254, 268
    account closure, 337
    budget *vs.* actual, 323, 324
    business delivery/product distribution channels, 325

INDEX

consumer durable loan, 332, 333
cost, 324
cost and earnings pressure, 326
cost breakup, 324
cost monitoring focus areas, 326
credit card, 333, 334
customers, 338
fixed deposit (FD), 328, 329
home loan, salaried, 330, 331
knee-jerk cost control reaction, 325
locker rental, 335, 336
omnichannel, 338–340
performance monitoring, 326
process-automated, time-driven activity-based costing, 325, 343
retail products cost, by customer, 324
revenue, 323
savings account, 326, 328
total cost, 324
Retail products, 110, 118, 127, 326, 405, 465
Risk-adjusted return analytics
behavioral analytics, customer and staff, 469
corporate governance, 477–479
customer/counterparty, 473–477
EITG, 479–481
human capital, 470, 472
Risk-adjusted return management, 11, 314
Risk-adjusted return on capital (RAROC), 435
Risk analytics, 352
Risk appetite statement (RAS), 140, 174, 429, 478, 512
Risk management, 185, 296, 299, 312, 314, 318, 354–357
Risk management experts, 57
Risk management process, 140, 141, 174, 190, 439, 488
Risk mitigation, 29, 141, 181, 316, 390, 391
RL, *see* Reinforcement learning (RL)
Robotic process automation (RPA), 184, 185, 252, 462, 493–495
Root cause analysis, 289, 312, 313, 432, 485
RPA, *see* Robotic process automation (RPA)
RTGS, *see* Real-time gross settlement (RTGS)

S

Sarbanes–Oxley Act (SOX), 18, 176
accounting perspective, 425
80-20 principle interpretation, 424
nonaccounting perspective, 426
operational efficiency, 425
revenue and returns, 424

INDEX

Sarbanes–Oxley Act (SOX) (*cont.*)
  risk, 424
  risk-based approach, 423
  Sec 302, 424
  Sec 404, 424
Scale efficiency, 419
Semivariable expenses, 48
Senior managers, 63, 136, 253, 278, 321
Service level agreements (SLA), 24, 62, 78, 169, 310, 480
Service-oriented architecture (SOA), 134, 152, 153, 185
Short-term interest rate futures, 5
Siloed and complex operations, 12
Siloed consequences, 133–137
Siloed environment, 63, 87, 133, 183, 298, 394
Six Sigma, 426, 427
  DMADV process, 427
  DMAIC process, 427
SLA, *see* Service level agreements (SLA)
SOA, *see* Service-oriented architecture (SOA)
SOA-BPMS convergence, 185, 186
Society for Worldwide Interbank Financial Telecommunications (SWIFT), 51, 53, 55, 172, 403
Solvency risk, 417, 472
SOX, *see* Sarbanes–Oxley Act (SOX)

SR, *see* Supervisory recommendations (SR)
Staff capability measurement model, 470
Staff recruitment, 292, 316, 473
Standardized enterprise operating model, 464, 467
  enterprise IT governance, 466
  KYC procedure, 465
  master and metadata of products, 466
  nonstandardized, siloed enterprise operating model, 463–465
  standardization, 467
  technology deployment, 467
  variation risk benefit (impact) assessment, 466
STP, *see* Straight through processing (STP)
Straight through processing (STP), 59, 61–63, 150, 362
Supervisory recommendations (SR), 277, 437
SWIFT, *see* Society for Worldwide Interbank Financial Telecommunications (SWIFT)
Swiss National Bank (SIC), 51
Syndicated Loans, 10, 261, 350–351, 486
Syndicate loan process model, 486

INDEX

T

Target costing, 442, 443
Taxonomy, 140, 154–158, 174, 283, 452, 469
TDABC, *see* Time-driven activity-based costing (TDABC)
Term loans, 9
Three lines of defense model, 313, 314
Timed colored Petri net model, 462–463
Time-driven ABB, 498
Time-driven ABC, 1, 41, 134, 150, 254–256, 306, 326, 342
Time-driven activity-based costing (TDABC), 149, 244, 252, 253, 256–258, 261, 266
   benefits, 46
   concept, 41
   measure, 45
   methodology, 42, 44
   objective, 41
   pull cost modeling, 40
Time-driven corporate banking cost, 261, 262, 265
Total quality management (TQM), 188, 423, 432
TQM, *see* Total quality management (TQM)
Trade finance, 7–9, 55, 344, 405, 502
Transactions, 18, 49, 54, 128, 229, 352, 496, 512
Transformed bank, 152, 511
Treasury bills, 5
Treasury management system, 55, 56, 69, 219
Treasury products, 2–3, 118, 127, 285, 359, 465

U

Ullman triangle, 1, 13–15
Uninterruptible power supply (UPS), 406
UPS, *see* Uninterruptible power supply (UPS)
US midcap banking report, 408

V

Variable expenses, 48
Virtualization, 406, 450

W

Workforce competency, 409
Working capital loans, 10, 450

X, Y

X-efficiency, 419

Z

ZBB, *see* Zero-based budgeting (ZBB)
Zero-based budgeting (ZBB), 501–502
Zero coupon bonds, 4

GPSR Compliance

The European Union's (EU) General Product Safety Regulation (GPSR) is a set of rules that requires consumer products to be safe and our obligations to ensure this.

If you have any concerns about our products, you can contact us on

ProductSafety@springernature.com

In case Publisher is established outside the EU, the EU authorized representative is:

Springer Nature Customer Service Center GmbH
Europaplatz 3
69115 Heidelberg, Germany

www.ingramcontent.com/pod-product-compliance
Lightning Source LLC
LaVergne TN
LVHW010332260326
834688LV00036B/669